CLARENCE DARROW

CLARENCE DARROW

A Sentimental Rebel

Arthur and Lila Weinberg

G. P. Putnam's Sons
New York

Library of Congress Cataloging in Publication Data

Weinberg, Arthur, date.
  Clarence Darrow: a sentimental rebel.

  Bibliography: p.
  Includes index.
  1. Darrow, Clarence Seward, 1857–1938. 2. Lawyers
—United States—Biography. I. Weinberg, Lila Shaffer,
joint author. II. Title.
KF373.D35W44   345.73′0092′4 [B]   79-29697
ISBN 0-399-11936-1

For our parents
Sam and Blanche Hyman Shaffer
Abe M. and Anna Avedon Weinberg

Contents

Introduction

Clarence Darrow was born in 1857, the year president-elect James Buchanan in his inaugural address condemned slavery agitation, and the United States Supreme Court decreed in its Dred Scott decision that Congress had no power under the Constitution to prohibit slavery. He died in 1938, the year Germany annexed Austria; British Prime Minister Neville Chamberlain met with Hitler in Munich and proclaimed "peace in our time"; and Winston Churchill, who became Britain's wartime prime minister, inveighed against Chamberlain's promise and declared the choice for Britain and France was war or dishonor.

During Darrow's lifetime America suffered convulsions and dislocations generated by the country's shift from an agrarian-commercial to an urban-industrial focus, from weak craft-oriented trade unions to strong industrial unions. The nation, with its policy of isolationism, rejected the League of Nations, a move with which Clarence agreed, but for different reasons: "Compelling nations not to fight would mean the establishing of a central organization strong enough to destroy any two or three countries indicating opposition, and such an organization would be a menace to the freedom of the world."[1] Three years after Darrow died, the United States entered World War II as a superpower. It would become one of the founders of the United Nations.

Domestically, there had been no daring innovations on the political, social, and economic scene until Franklin D. Roosevelt ascended to the presidency in 1932. Though Roosevelt did not break either with the capitalist culture and the traditional ideas of free enterprise or with big business and the rights of property, his administration offered to patch up the abuses. It introduced the Agricultural Adjustment Act (AAA) for the farmer, the National Recovery Administration (NRA) for big business, and the famous Section 7(a) of the NRA which provided employees with the right to organize and bargain collectively for labor.

Clarence Darrow became the best known, the most controversial lawyer of his era; the most fearless defender of men and women charged with crime, whether the crime be against property, against life, or a crime of dissent. He became the interpreter of labor and of the radical movement.

Max Eastman called Darrow and his friends—Lincoln Steffens, Fremont Older, Hutchins Hapgood—"Sentimental Rebels" because "they had no historical tradition and they had no international connections. They were as purely American a phenomenon as the red Indian," and "came into sympathy with the labor struggle, not by the road of theory or plan of action, but by the road of Christian sentiment bereft of Deity yet carried to a bellicose extreme." He characterized them as having "a Christlike fondness for the society of publicans and sinners."[2]

United States Supreme Court Justice Hugo Black in his dissent in the Anastaplo case pointed out that men like Clarence Darrow, Lord Erskine, James Otis, and many others "dared to speak in defense of causes and clients without regard to personal danger to themselves."[3]

Clarence Darrow, says William Kunstler, attorney for dissidents, was "invaluable in creating the vision of the courageous attorney who was not afraid to take on the system, who possessed limitless literary skills and utilized them very well in this pursuit and who brought humanity and compassion into the courtroom on a national scene." Kunstler believes that Darrow's life paved the way for his own acceptance "more readily by the general public, judges and adversaries. This is because he established the ideal of the fighting brave lawyer who will go to the limits of his endurance, skill and courage for a client."[4]

Charles Morgan, Jr., civil rights lawyer and an attorney for the American Civil Liberties Union, calls Darrow "the soul of American law."[5]

To the poet Carl Sandburg, Darrow was "somewhat to Chicago what Diogenes was to Athens."[6]

Darrow is a rarity among lawyers for his wide range of interests. Like Alexander Pope, his study was man. There may be greater criminal lawyers, more effective defenders of civil liberties, civil rights, of dissenters. There may be more forceful speakers and better writers. But none has the combination that went into making Clarence Darrow the man.

Over six feet tall, broad-shouldered, slightly stooped, he gave the impression of being even larger than he was. And his face—a craggy island reflecting the pain and suffering of the damned. He preached love and mercy, and in a deep, clear voice, not above using seduction, he fought always for what he believed was justice.

He had enormous vitality and curiosity. Though he posed as a pessimist, his actions belied his evident hedonism. Too much of a doubter to be awed by anyone, he held to his convictions with strength and stubbornness, independent of what others thought. Burdened with a sense of responsibility toward society's victims, his life was committed to those who needed his help. He mocked the absurdities of life, was bitter over its inequities; not to himself—he had no quarrel there—but to the oppressed and underprivileged.

An aura of freedom, of ability, of compassion, of a vast pleasure in living hung over him. In reality, he was also cynical, lonely, melancholy. He craved companionship and fed on good talk and debate. He loved people—and mixing with them and exchanging ideas, his wit honed to rapierlike sharpness with each encounter. The delighted and shocked reactions of the audiences at his lectures left him exuberant and exhilarated.

His characteristic mood was pity for all humankind. There is a fine line between this and maudlin sentimentalism, and Darrow was as guilty of the latter as he was representative of the former. He was a sensitive pragmatist who knew confidently how to manipulate his audience—the judge, the jury, the reader, those who attended his lectures and listened as he challenged his opponents' arguments.

To have been associated with Darrow has become a badge of honor. The obituary of Judge C. N. Hollerich, Spring Valley, Illinois, dead at the age of ninety-six, notes that, during his term as Bureau County state's attorney from 1912 to 1916, "he won a case against the renowned Clarence Darrow in the trial of a suspected murderer from Cherry."

Elmer Gertz, a Chicago attorney who obtained parole for Nathan Leopold, Darrow's former client, proudly calls himself "a footnote to Darrow."[7]

In the courtroom of Judge Robert S. Whitehead, Howard County, Kokomo, Indiana, hang two photographs—one of Darrow as he addressed the judge at the Leopold and Loeb trial, the other of Justice Oliver Wendell Holmes, Jr. To Judge Whitehead, Holmes and Darrow are "the two all encompassing personalities in American law."[8]

There have been two biographies of Darrow.* Charles Yale Harrison's *Clarence Darrow* (1931) had the cooperation of both Clarence and Ruby Darrow. Irving Stone's excellent book, *Clarence Darrow for the Defense* (1941), published three years after the attorney's death, is by far the more important of the two. It was the beneficiary of Stone's perceptions and the "firsthand

---

*Since this book was completed, a third Darrow biography has been published (*Darrow, A Biography*, by Kevin Tiereny).

knowledge" of many of Darrow's contemporaries as well as of his widow. The price paid for these advantages is the perspective of time. In addition, Professor Abe C. Ravitz, in his book *Clarence Darrow and the American Literary Tradition* (1962), presents a valuable critical analysis of Darrow's writings.

There are few personal Darrow files. He seems not to have had a sense of history about himself. He kept no journals, saved few letters.

We have been fortunate to locate more than forty letters Clarence wrote to Mary Field, and we have relied heavily on these as well as on Mary's diary entries to give a new dimension of Darrow. From the Field papers, and from Darrow letters to Henry Demarest Lloyd and to Fremont Older, among others—portions from all of which are published here for the first time—the portrait of this hauntingly lonely man, who has been a hero to generations, is more clearly etched.

During Darrow's own trial for jury bribery in Los Angeles, the exchange of letters between him and Eugene Victor Debs, also published for the first time, reveals a man desperately in need of friendship and unable to understand why many of his former friends have deserted him.

The major focus of this volume, however, is on Darrow's own trial in Los Angeles in which he was charged with jury bribery. Fifteen volumes of Darrow trial transcripts, ten thousand pages in all, aided us in this study. Never before has this case been so detailed and so analyzed.

We have had help from many during our research and writing of *Clarence Darrow: A Sentimental Rebel*—from encouragement, criticism, and constructive ideas to assistance with research. Howard Sulkin of DePaul University, Chicago, read the entire manuscript and made valuable suggestions. We owe much to his encouragement and to his belief in this book. Stanley Chyet, Hebrew Union College, Los Angeles, also read the entire manuscript. We are grateful for his historical and literary suggestions and his editorial insight.

The chapters on the two Darrow trials in Los Angeles were read for legal and technical accuracy by Elmer Gertz and Leon Despres, prominent Chicago attorneys. Gertz opened to us his personal collection of Darrow memorabilia.

Constance Sulkin and Drs. Alex and Klara Tulsky read parts of the manuscript. They, as well as Harry Barnard, author of *Eagle Forgotten,* and Ruth Barnard, spent many evenings with us discussing Darrow and his times and offered sage advice and insights. Harry Barnard shared his own research with us as it touched on Darrow.

Our thanks to Margaret Parton who shared her Darrow memories with us and made available to us the letters from Darrow to her mother, her mother's diaries and notebooks, and her own unpublished biography of her mother; and to the Darrow heirs—Clarence's granddaughters, Blanche Chase and Mary

Simonson—who gave us carte blanche permission to use Darrow writings and were most cooperative and encouraging.

We want to thank the late Ned A. Bush, Sr., executive vice-president, Debs Foundation, and Marguerite Debs Cooper who gave us permission to reprint Debs's letter to Darrow as it related to Darrow's indictment and trial in Los Angeles.

During the almost ten years we worked on this book we traveled to or corresponded with many libraries, including New York Public; Columbia University; University of California, Los Angeles; University of California, Berkeley; University of Michigan, Ann Arbor; University of Illinois, Champaign-Urbana; Library of Congress; Kinsman Free Public Library; Idaho State University, Pocatello; University of Chicago; and the Chicago Public. The staffs in these libraries have been most cooperative.

Our major research was done at the Newberry Library, Chicago, and we must express our gratitude to Dr. Lawrence Towner and his staff who provided us with the facilities in the Newberry that made our task infinitely easier.

Others who have helped us on this volume include Morris Star, emeritus, University of Illinois, Circle Campus, who first indicated to us that Margaret Field Parton had in her possession Darrow letters written to her mother; Albert W. Alschuler, University of Colorado; Neil Basen; Howard Browne; Fanny Butcher; Melvyn Douglas; Ash and Gloria Gerecht; Judge Lynn B. Griffith, Sr., Warren, Ohio; Milton Heumann, University of Michigan; Herman Kogan; Robert Krasnow; David Lowe; Lowell Mason; Durham Monsma; Roy H. Pollack; Ilene Schatz; Herbert Shapiro, University of Cincinnati; Gladys E. Trosper of the Kinsman Free Public Library; and Floyd Waters of Kinsman, Ohio.

Finally, to our daughters—Hedy, Anita, and Wendy—who encouraged us, helped with research, had constructive suggestions—and lived this book with us.

Darrow used the law to promote social justice as he saw it. Yet the law and the lawyers were to him reactionary forces. Their faces were usually turned backward. Great reforms came not from within the law but from without. It was not the judges and barristers who made the significant advances toward social justice. They were made in conventions of the people and in legislative halls. Yet Darrow, working through the law, brought prestige and honor to it during a long era of intolerance.

—Supreme Court Justice William O. Douglas
Foreword to *Attorney for the Damned*

I

"Who Is This Man Darrow?"

1

EARLY on the morning of October 1, 1910, a bomb destroyed the *Los Angeles Times* building, leaving twenty dead and scores wounded. The *Los Angeles Times* promptly published a special edition from its recently completed auxiliary plant and charged in large black headlines:

UNIONISTS' BOMBS WRECK THE TIMES

The American Federation of Labor categorically denied knowledge of the dynamiting and countercharged. It blamed the explosion on a faulty gas fixture and held Harrison Gray Otis, antiunion publisher of the newspaper, responsible because he had ignored employees' complaints about gas leakages.

Immediately after the *Times* bombing, James N. Gillett, governor of California, ignoring constitutional guarantees that a man is presumed innocent until proven guilty, asserted, "Whether guilty or not, the labor movement will have to be blamed for the crime, until shown they are not guilty, as everything points to a desire to wipe out property and lives of those who have been fighting against labor for years."[1]

On the other hand, the independent Hiram Johnson, who would soon

succeed Gillett, refrained from passing judgment although he believed that
"no punishment is great enough for the criminal who planned it or for the
loathsome miscreant who carried it into execution."[2]

Samuel Gompers, president of the American Federation of Labor, summed
up the official attitude of unions toward violence: "Labor does not stand for
such outrages, nor contemplate such a crime. I can not believe that a union
man has done it, and I deeply hope no one who was connected with the labor
movement will be found to have done it." He added that if a labor man had
indeed planted the bomb, the union could not be held responsible "for the deed
of a man devoid of any human feeling, as the perpetrator of this horrible
catastrophe must have been."[3]

A few days later, speaking at a public meeting in Battle Creek, Michigan,
Gompers said, "The greatest enemies of our movement could not administer a
blow so hurtful to our cause as would be such a stigma if the men of organized
labor were responsible for it." He promised that union men would "immediately turn the dynamiters over to the proper authorities if we could lay hands
on them."[4]

Almost seven months later, on April 23, 1911, the *Los Angeles Times* carried
a banner headline:

DYNAMITERS OF THE TIMES BUILDING CAUGHT CRIME TRACED DIRECTLY TO HIGH UNION OFFICIALS

Red-Handed Union Chiefs Implicated in Conspiracy

Arrested were John J. McNamara, secretary-treasurer of the Structural
Iron Workers Union, his brother James B., a union activist, and Ortie
McManigal who had confessed to the bombings and implicated the McNamara
brothers.

Labor officials immediately turned to Clarence Darrow.

2

Who was this man Darrow?

Almost four years earlier, in 1907, when he had defended William ("Big
Bill") Haywood, militant secretary-treasurer of the Western Federation of
Miners, the magazine *Current Literature*[5] posed the same question to a
nationwide audience. Chicago had asked that same question back in 1888 after
Darrow spoke on "Labor and Taxation" at a Single Tax convention at the
Central Music Hall.

"A smooth face deeply furrowed with lines that he will never permit a photographer to eradicate because 'it cost too much to get them there'"; the article in *Current Literature* described him, "long dark hair with an unruly lock that drops effectively over his right eye; somewhat after the Webster, Clay or John Brown mold."

Then the writer focused on Darrow's philosophical makeup when he commented that, as the Haywood and Moyer trials proceeded, it became "evident that Darrow is more than a hired attorney in this case. He is pleading for a cause as well as arguing for a client, and the cause is one very near to his heart. Yet it is one of the paradoxes of the day that this man who is defending so ardently labor leaders accused of having carried on for years a terrorist campaign in America is himself committed to the doctrine of non-resistance."

To Darrow, of course, it was no paradox. He believed that labor struggles "take on the psychology of warfare, and all parties in interest must be judged from that standpoint."[6] He further believed that the ideal labor leader "is a man who is practical, who has his mind fixed upon what can be done today and tomorrow and next week, who is willing to examine all questions fairly in the light of the world, as the world is today, who is always faithful to the men he represents, and who still has a vision large enough to work for some better condition of society than the one he is living in now."[7]

3

Given a choice, Clarence Darrow would not have selected the sleepy village of Farmdale, Ohio, for his birthplace, nor would he have chosen to grow up in Kinsman, a hamlet several miles away. As he said in his autobiography, he would have preferred a "noisy city where the crowds surged back and forth as if they knew where they were going, and why."[8]

About his family background, however, he had no complaint. His parents were freethinkers and skeptics, often in rebellion against the religious and political creeds of their narrow, puritanical community. They were better educated than most of their neighbors, and their ambitions for their children went beyond the boundaries of the obscure community in which they lived. "I came of a very old family. A considerable number of people say that it runs back to Adam and Eve," said Darrow, though he added whimsically that he could not "guarantee the title."[9]

The first Darrow in America arrived with fifteen other Englishmen a century before the Revolution, recipients of a royal land grant for the town of New London, Connecticut. He continued in New London to practice his profession as an undertaker—which prompted his iconoclastic descendant to observe, "My ancestor chose a profession where the demand for his services would be fairly steady."[10]

In 1795, in a search for better opportunities, the Ammiras Darrow family moved from Connecticut to Boonville, in Oneida County, New York. As the cost of land in the East climbed, however, the acreage available in the Western states attracted pioneers willing to suffer the hardships of frontier settlement for a future that held hope and prosperity. After Great-grandfather Ammiras's death in 1824, the Darrows left Boonville, driving horse and wagon for months across the hundreds of miles separating Oneida County from the still wild Ohio country. They settled in Trumbull County, Ohio, where Clarence's grandfather, Jedediah, plied his trade of chairmaker to provide a precarious livelihood for his three young sons.[11]

Clarence's maternal ancestors, the Eddys, were farmers, also from Connecticut. They, too, were attracted by the promise of the West and traveled to what would become Windsor, Ohio. The land was good to Grandfather Eddy, and he became a "fairly prosperous farmer."[12]

Emily Eddy and Amirus[13] Darrow, Clarence's parents, met at the Ellsworth Academy in Amboy, in northern Ohio. The love of books and study that drew them together remained an integral part of their lives, and they nurtured their sons and daughters in this tradition.

Soon after their marriage in 1845, they moved to Meadville, Pennsylvania, where Amirus attended first the Methodist-sponsored Allegheny College and then the Unitarian seminary. This was the golden age of Unitarianism. Its theologians emphasized learning, literature, and rational religion. Its leaders promoted peace societies, headed movements for prison reform and helping the poor. Amirus studied the philosophies of such thinkers as William Ellery Channing, Ralph Waldo Emerson, and Theodore Parker. The Unitarian abolitionist, Edward Everett—who traveled throughout the North speaking for the Union cause and was billed as the principal orator at Gettysburg when President Lincoln delivered his famous address—so impressed the young couple that they named their firstborn son Everett.

Even the mild tenets of Unitarianism, however, could not hold Amirus. Long before Clarence, the fifth Darrow child, was born on April 18, 1857, Amirus began the questioning and doubting which would be his legacy to his son. Soon Amirus rejected the church completely and resigned from the ministry to follow in ancestral footsteps and become a furniture maker and the town undertaker. But he was a dreamer, and the orders for his handcrafted furniture often piled up while he escaped into the pages of a book—English, Latin, Greek, Hebrew. Amirus was always involved in one or another unpopular cause. If one came to a successful conclusion, he was already too far into another to do any celebrating. Had his father "lost his idealism with his religion," said Clarence, "he would no doubt have had greater worldly prosperity."[14]

Emily, both by nature and of necessity, was more practical. Her children were raised in accordance with a rigid New England sense of duty. Unlike her husband, she believed that a show of affection indicated weakness. Kindly, yet stern and reserved, she managed her home efficiently, raised her children, and helped in the small furniture business. She also played an active role in the suffragette movement and as a woman's rights advocate. She was well read and aware of what was happening in the world outside their small community, and her sympathies, like those of Amirus, lay with the world's oppressed and unfortunate.[15]

4

Despite the lack of money which always plagued the family, Amirus managed to acquire books, and the children were exposed not only to the classics in literature and history but to the most advanced thinking on scientific issues. Their Kinsman home—like Clarence's own in Chicago many years later—overflowed with books: in bookcases, on tables, chairs, the floor. Amirus, an early disciple of Charles Darwin, introduced his son to the evolutionist's writings at a young age. Clarence not only read and assimilated *The Descent of Man* and *On the Origin of Species* but also studied the writings of other contemporary Britons, the biologist and educator Thomas H. Huxley, the physicist Tyndall, and Herbert Spencer, the philosopher of evolution. From these, and from Voltaire and Thomas Paine whom Amirus also admired, Clarence received his initial concepts of natural selection, free thought, and the relation of science to society. Their influence set the pattern of his philosophy.

Clarence was devoted to his father, who lived to be eighty-six. He credited Amirus with shaping his ideas, and he took as his own Amirus's outlook on life. "I am sure," Clarence wrote, "that more than anything else my father influenced the course of my life and its thought and activities. Above all things else his deep convictions and his devotion to ideals as he conceived them did the most to keep alive a certain sense of duty to what seemed to me the good and the true."[16]

Just as strongly, the complexities of his intellect were shaped by the opposing forces prevalent during the last half of the nineteenth century. The social, intellectual, political, and theological upheavals in America during this time opened him to divergent viewpoints—slavery versus freedom, good versus evil, materialism versus idealism, orthodoxy versus agnosticism. He had to think his own way through or blindly accept the conservative premises of his neighbors. Taking up the challenge, he became the aroused gadfly and outraged activist against injustice. He was shadow and color, burdened with a sense of responsibility toward society's victims while at the same time, though not often admitting it, finding life zestful and rewarding. He was the consummate humanitarian, with a deft irreverence for pomposity. Imbued with a sense of society's flaws, he would dramatize in the courtroom, on lecture platforms, and in his writings the social dilemmas of mankind.

The world into which Clarence was born and the values he learned as a child served him throughout his lifetime. Essentially, even though it had become highly industrialized, the nation still lived by a basically Jeffersonian-agrarian orientation. It remained domestic oriented, its foreign policy reasonably isolationist. Nineteenth-century virtues were still plausible. Rationalism and sentimentalism constituted the basic world view of America up to the beginnings of World War II. From then on it was no longer possible to hold reasonable assumptions, it was no longer possible to hold on to the certainties. Notwithstanding Darrow's pessimism, the world to him was not a mysterious place; one could still account for what was taking place. Life was simple, most problems solvable. With the advent of World War II, the atomic bomb, and America's entry as a superpower, the world lost part of its humanism. It was a world Clarence Darrow never knew.

Religiously the Darrow family stood alone in the community. Their friends were the few "queer" people who espoused the same infidel convictions they did. Religious prejudice penetrated Clarence's awareness at a young age when "the ignorant neighbors looked askance" at Amirus and hurled the word "atheist" at him as if it were a foul epithet. Instead of warping Clarence's mind and embittering his youth, the experience helped teach him "to be independent of the opinions of those with whom my life was cast." [17]

Though Amirus and Emily were no longer churchgoers, they nevertheless believed their children should have an understanding of religion. The younger Darrows regularly attended Sunday school where they learned hymns and biblical verses. Captured by enthusiasm, young Clarence and his friends sang fervently, "I want to be an angel!—and with the angels stand; a crown upon my forehead, a harp within my hand."

At the age of seventy-five, Darrow noted the paradox: he was "still fighting to stay on earth" despite the passion and joy which those words had excited in the child Clarence. About the sermons, however, he was bitter: "I can never forget the horror and torture of listening to an endless sermon when I was a child. Of course I never understood a word of it, any more than did the preacher who harangued to his afflicted audiences." [18]

The Darrows, rebels and outcasts in religion, were one with their neighbors on the subjects of slavery and abolition. Amirus and Emily listened avidly to Senator William H. Seward of New York, later to become President Lincoln's secretary of state. Seward spoke on the extreme left of the abolition question and prophesied, "Emancipation is inevitable and is near." He saw the coming clash between the North and the South as an inevitable conflict and contended that any attempts at compromise were "vain and ephemeral."

Filled with admiration for the abolitionist, Amirus insisted on giving a newborn son the name Seward, which was added to Clarence, Emily's choice. "The boys never could think up any nickname half so inane as the real one my parents adorned me with," Darrow blithely wrote.[19]

John Brown and many of the abolitionists who fought at Harpers Ferry frequently met at the Darrow home, an underground station serving runaway slaves in flight to freedom. Lying in his bed at night, Clarence could hear the whispered voices, the dangerous plans for escape. Moved by the drama and the sense of doom, he promised himself with childlike determination to help the black man. His father talked to him about the fighters for black freedom—Frederick Douglass, Parker Pillsbury, Sojourner Truth, Wendell Phillips.[20] Clarence never forgot. He was an early protagonist in the fight for black equality, and the cause of the blacks would occupy much of his attention.

The meadows behind the white-frame, one-and-a-half-story house in Farmdale where Darrow spent his early years held many joys for a young growing boy. There were hickory nuts and chestnuts to pick, rabbits to chase, trees to climb, skating, and sledding down the hill in the wintertime into the nearby creek. In the summer a bronzed Clarence went fishing there. His short, straight blond hair sunbleached almost white, the boy sat at the water's edge happily dangling his line of twisted thread with a bent pin holding the bait, an improvisation of Emily's.[21]

5

When Clarence was seven, Amirus moved his family from Farmdale to neighboring Kinsman where he bought one of the few octagonal houses in the county. The very oddity of the construction of the two-story stucco house made it an appropriate setting for the lone freethinker residing in the midst of his conservative churchgoing neighbors. Built in 1838 on the main road just north of the town square, the house—with its many bedrooms, nooks, and crannies, and a veranda around all but one of its eight sides—was large enough for the seven Darrow children.[22] In a shop on the edge of his land Amirus made the coffins and furniture with which he supplied the townspeople.

McGuffey's Reader was a virtually universal presence in late nineteenth-century America and dominated Clarence's school hours. In addition to reading, writing, and arithmetic, the textbook provided instruction in religion and ethics, conduct and morals; it attacked the decadence of tobacco and liquor and emphasized the profits of virtue. The girls, too, threatened the boys:

> The lips that touch liquor
> Shall never touch mine.

Clarence, however, seems not to have been intimidated. During the intensified battle for prohibition which years later became part of the American scene, he chafed at the restrictions prohibition threatened to impose on individual liberty. His antagonism drove him up and down the country to lecture against the "dry" movement. After the prohibition amendment to the United States Constitution was passed in 1920, unleashing a fury of bootlegging, he observed wryly, "From what I see and hear of the present generation I should guess that Doctor McGuffey and his ilk lived in vain."[23]

An America still loyal to the puritan tradition decreed that work is good for the soul and, more, builds strong character. Young Clarence, hired to clean up Farmer Brown's potato fields, "killed bug after bug all that long morning, and then I threw the kerosene can in the general direction of that army of bugs and ran home, declaring through tears that I would never do a lick of work again in my life. And I never have."[24] For Darrow, the Protestant work ethic was early laid to rest.

He defined work simply as something one did not like to do. Baseball, for example, or golf, would be hard, arduous work, he reasoned, if the player did not like the game. "The law is work for some law clerks who ought not to be in it. It isn't work for me; just one fascinating moment after another."[25]

6

Not only the law, baseball, too, provided such moments. Before the Civil War the game was relatively unknown and played mostly in the Northeastern states. During the war it became popular with the Union soldiers. The first rulebook for baseball was written a year after Clarence's birth. By the time he was old enough to play, it had become a national sport. Like most of the Kinsman boys, Clarence became an addict.

Darrow, whose brilliant courtroom summations brought him worldwide honor and fame, proudly remembered the most minute details of his triumphs on the baseball field: the score tied in the last half of the last inning in a game against the town's "oldest and most hated rivals." Two men out, two men on base! Like the legendary Casey, Clarence comes up to bat. After two strikes he swings and, unlike Casey, "the ball went flying over the roof of the store, and rolled down to the river-bank on the other side. I had gone quite around the ring before anyone could get near the ball. I can never forget the wild ovation in which I ran around the ring, and the mad enthusiasm when the home-plate was reached and the game was won." Clarence Darrow, a pacifist almost all his life, could only describe his triumph that day in terms of the military "Caesar's return to Rome."[26]

He and his young friends were appalled at the professional players who "cared nothing whatever for patriotism but only for money," with rival towns hiring one another's players. "No Kinsman boy would any more give aid and comfort to a rival town than would a loyal soldier open a gate in the wall to let an enemy march in." [27] He described the professionals as "no more players than mercenary troops are patriots." [28]

This love affair lasted all his life. "Never has life held for me anything quite so entrancing as baseball," he would reminisce. Into his later years he still read the baseball scores before any other part of the paper and remained an avid fan of the Chicago Cubs. [29]

Each year Amirus brought his family to the Fourth of July picnics held near the river just outside Kinsman. Clarence thrilled to the excitement of rural America's Independence Day celebrations with its brass bands, firecrackers, lemonade, and the crowds of people who came to take part in the festivities. A visiting attorney, elegantly dressed, always delivered the main speech, pounding his fist into the palm of his open hand as he harangued on patriotism and love of country. As the crowd cheered and applauded, the local lawyers beamed at the glory and grandeur of their colleague.

The schoolboy Clarence was captivated by the flowery oratory and the adoration bestowed upon the speaker. He decided he "would rather be a lawyer than anything else in the world." [30] He started to visit the tinshop across the road from his home where the justice of the peace held court. He listened to the pettifoggers argue and pretended he was already one of them. Next door to the tinsmith was the blacksmith, also a lawyer, who opened his law library to the sixteen-year-old.

From the Kinsman Academy, Clarence, like Amirus, went to Allegheny College at Meadville where he continued to study Latin and Greek—and to play baseball. He could not understand why Amirus so insistently imposed language requirements. Not until many years later did he realize that Amirus's only escape from the narrow confines of village life into which fate had thrust him would be for his children to fulfill his dreams: Everett, Channing, Mary, Herbert, Clarence, Hubert, Herman, Jenny. All but one reached adulthood. All but one loved books and learning.

"John Stuart Mill began studying Greek when he was only three years old," Amirus would urge as a reluctant Clarence shuffled in from play to do lessons with his father. [31]

"The other day I found the first opportunity in my life to use Latin," Darrow recalled at age sixty-eight. "The hours I spent trying to master the declination of the Latin word 'mensa,' meaning table, were repaid when I came across the word in a cross-word puzzle." [32]

The overworked and overburdened Emily, long ailing, died about the time Clarence started at the academy. She was buried in the churchyard at Kinsman next to Herbert, who had died at age two shortly after Clarence's birth.

Gauging Emily Darrow's influence on Clarence—who was fourteen at her death—is difficult. Darrow himself confessed in later years that his memory of her was "blurred and faded." He spoke little of her and only in general ways. He was uncritical and praised her devotion, yet gave her little credit for his development beyond the general and characteristically Victorian statement that "her infinite kindness and sympathy have done much to shape my life."

Perhaps it was a subconscious rebellion against his mother's death that his "remembrance of her is not very clear." [33] A hidden resentment at having been abandoned at an early age may account for the fact that Darrow stood aloof from the woman's rights movement and that both of his marriages were with women who built their lives entirely around him to the exclusion of other interests. Moreover, the women he created in his fiction were always beaten down by life's hardships. Even so, the female companions he sought outside of his home were aggressive and independent personalities. Perhaps Darrow, the man, saw his mother in contrasting roles—his two wives and fictional heroines emulated Emily the homemaker; those women eager for intimacies with him, those his second wife called "ladies-in-waiting," [34] were more reminiscent of Emily the activist.

One can only conjecture. No diaries, no letters, no family stories have been handed down. Only the few brief mentions in the autobiography offer insights into the relationship between mother and son.

7

The Panic of 1873 ended Clarence's Allegheny College education after one year. That summer he worked in Amirus's shop and helped build furniture. In the winter he taught in a district school for $30 a month plus board and lodging offered each night at a different home, though he would return to his own for the weekend. The "board" meant he was "company," and the housewives competed in the "elegance" of the meals they put before him. He relished the steady diet of pie and cake and gleefully noted, "We had it three times a day." [35]

His first night as a teacher brought the son of the village infidel to the home of a pillar of the local church. After supper they began to argue religion. "My host was a good talker," Darrow conceded, "utterly impregnable to my youthful onslaughts, so I finally terminated the argument as politely as I knew how—by dropping off to sleep in a comfortable rocking chair." [36]

Clarence was a picturesque sight as he traveled to school driving an old sleigh mounted on buggy wheels. Wrapped in a fancy bed quilt and wearing a black plug hat befitting his status as a schoolteacher, he would drive down the middle of the mud road, a lawbook on the seat at his side. He had by now seriously begun the study of law.

His teaching career in the district school spanned three winters, with "50 scholars" ranging in age from seven to one or two years older than their teacher. As a pedagogue, he continued the family tradition of dissent. Although corporal punishment was the conventional method of discipline, the young schoolmaster rejected this approach and vowed it would never be used in his classroom. He remembered all too clearly how the teacher had boxed his ear when he fidgeted during school hours. Now Clarence joined his students in their games, lengthened the recess and lunch periods, widened the breadth of subjects and discussions, and tried to make the school day stimulating and pleasurable for his young charges. Whether they learned more is open to question, but that they were a happy group was obvious.

These were happy days for Darrow, too. He loved teaching, he was fulfilled in his law studies, and he had a steady girlfriend, Jessie Ohl, whom he would soon marry.

Perhaps something of these early idyllic years came to life again in the courtroom. He did seem to have a gift for teaching which showed up not only in the schoolroom but later in the courtroom and on the lecture platform. For a brief time he lectured at the Illinois College of Law, now Kent College, Chicago. The "schoolmaster of the courtroom," he would be called fittingly enough.

On weekends, Clarence participated in Kinsman's Saturday night debates. He had learned early that he could mesmerize his listeners, and he enjoyed expressing his ideas to an audience. In 1878, at a reunion of former students of the Kinsman Academy, the twenty-one-year-old Clarence delivered the main oration. Yellowing newspaper clippings at the Kinsman Free Public Library describe it as "strong and eloquent. The speaker pleasantly recalled many scenes of the past and seemed disposed to trace a connection from them to the experiences of the present and the probabilities of the future. He closed with a high eulogy of schools and their influences and earnestly recommended that they be more carefully fostered and cherished hereafter in Kinsman. He was heartily applauded." The past, the present, the future—and how they interrelate; Darrow used this theme constantly in courtrooms and on lecture platforms; it was his basic strategy.

Clarence's ego and his sense of the dramatic delighted in shocking or awing a crowd. In the beginning, like many a young contemporary, he tried to emulate the popular oratorical style of Robert G. Ingersoll—a style rhythmic and poetic, each sentence a carefully analyzed and measured cadence. He soon decided that, while a formal style, structure, and delivery worked well for the great agnostic orator, they were artificial for him. "The best I could do was to be myself." [37] He became an informal lecturer with an instinctive sense of timing and emphasis. His drawling baritone, with its slightly raspy quality, poured forth in full volume or strained to a whisper as he slowly and deliberately articulated his thoughts. He never changed his style. As the years passed he became more convinced of the absence of eternal truths, the impossibility of absolutes. Always sure of his argument, he was certain, too, that he had something worthwhile to say. He made no efforts at subtlety, interspersed his thoughts with pungent witticisms, and almost always took the negative side of a question.

Long after he had become an internationally known lecturer and debater, Darrow continued to argue the negative. Norman Thomas, veteran Socialist leader in the United States and six-time candidate for U.S. president on the Socialist ticket, recalled a debate in the mid-1920s on American membership in the World Court on the basis of a protocol approved by Charles Evans Hughes.

As the debaters moved to the platform, Darrow whispered to Thomas, "Norman, do you have a copy of the protocol of the court?"

"No, not with me," responded Thomas. "I am only the chairman. Does this mean you haven't read it?"

"Yes," was the whispered confession.

"Then how will you debate it?"

"Trust me. I can debate any question in the negative." [38]

Another time, after he had debated the negative on the question "Is Life Worth Living?" a circle of admirers surrounded Darrow. A young man wondered how Darrow could say that life is not worth living after he had devoted most of his own to the struggle for improved social conditions.

"Because my emotions haven't caught up with my intellect," was the lawyer's quick response. [39]

8

Once Clarence decided to become a lawyer, the family insisted that he attend the University of Michigan Law School at Ann Arbor. Everett and Mary, both schoolteachers now, and Amirus helped to pay his tuition of $25 as an out-of-state student plus the annual fee of $25. [40]

No records of his class standing are available for the 1877–78 academic year he spent at Ann Arbor, but indications are that he was an average student, studied hard, made few friends, found few inspiring or stimulating instructors, and received few accolades. The only time he received any public attention was in an exchange of letters in the local newspaper regarding a rent quarrel with his landlady. Clarence denied cheating her as she alleged, explained how the misunderstanding had occurred, and ended his letter to the editor by asserting, "Although poor, I value my reputation too highly to dispose of it for the small sum in controversy." [41]

After his year at Ann Arbor, Darrow read law in a lawyer's office in Youngstown, Ohio, then appeared at the Tod House Bar in Youngstown. "The examiners" were at the bar and "along towards dawn they told me I was admitted. That probably accounts for my love of the bar room," Darrow would tell a reporter in 1932.[42] He lamented the absence of that spirit in later years. Taking one of his famous jabs at the Establishment, he said, "The Lawyers' Union is about as anxious to encourage competition as the Plumbers' Union is, or the United States Steel Co., or the American Medical Association."[43]

When the Illinois Bar Association in 1922 debated whether admission to the bar should be confined to law school graduates, Darrow spoke out against formal educational requirements. He called them an unnecessary "handicap" for the poor. "The doors ought to be open," he said, "as wide as we can open them, and we ought to trust to the examination that he must pass to know whether he is qualified." He urged the bar to let "nature and life weed out the unfit. Whether a lawyer has been to college or whether he has not been to college, he is gradually weeded out, and those best fitted and qualified, just as everywhere in life, are the ones who succeed."[44]

Darrow could have started his practice in Youngstown, but he was diffident about life there. The city of fifteen thousand appeared very large to one nurtured in the comforting simplicity of a small village. For a brief time he considered locating in McPherson, Kansas. He rented office space there but never moved in.[45] Since Kinsman already had a lawyer, the first Darrow law shingle went up ten miles from Kinsman, in Andover, Ohio, a farming center of five hundred, where he shared an office with the mayor of the town.

His early practice consisted mainly of cases involving bad debts and actions of replevin, as well as defending clients accused of selling liquor and watering the milk. There was nothing to suggest that within a decade this legal novice would direct the law department of the City of Chicago and a few years later head the defense in a major labor case. No one in Andover would have predicted that the centennial of his birth would be publicly celebrated and that Richard J. Daley, mayor of Chicago, would say of him, "I hope the future of the Bar of our community and our nation will produce advocates who have the principles and the courage and the determination and the judgment of Clarence Darrow."[46] Nothing in the Andover experience prefigured the career which would lead one of the top trial lawyers in the country, Melvin Belli, to describe Darrow forty years after his death as "not only a hell of a great lawyer, cross-examiner and arguer, but lecturer and idealist as well."[47]

9

On May 15, 1880, Clarence married Jessie Ohl in the sunlit parlor of the Ohl home in Sharon, Pennsylvania. The Ohls had been neighbors of the Darrows, and Jessie had regularly attended the Saturday night entertainments in Kinsman when Clarence debated. Afterward there would be square dancing, and she was always his partner. She was pretty, relaxed, and

considerate of the young student who courted her. They were easily attracted
to each other and seemed well-suited. Clarence conducted his law practice
from the small apartment which they rented in Andover. Jessie kept house and
attended to her young husband's needs. In December 1883 their only child,
Paul, was born.

Before long Andover became too confining for Clarence. The town offered
too little opportunity and too little diversification for an interesting law
practice. The couple moved to Ashtabula, on the shores of Lake Erie, a
thriving industrial city of five thousand, where Clarence opened a law office.
With the greater opportunity of the city, he moved into politics. He
successfully campaigned for the office of city solicitor using the public-
speaking tactics he had developed in his debate days in Kinsman, and to his
law income was added the municipal salary of $75 a month.

Clarence's practice thrived. Law had been a good choice. Extraordinarily
verbal, he enjoyed matching wits with his opponents and with witnesses
during cross-examination. Jessie made few demands on his time and gave him
freedom to go his own way. He enjoyed his talk-filled evenings with friends,
the poker games, the debates.

His horizons began to expand when Amos Hubbard, an Ashtabula banker,
introduced him to Henry George's *Progress and Poverty,* giving him his initial
perceptions into radical political doctrines. The book argued that land and its
wealth belonged to all and that a single tax on land earnings—with no other
taxes—would lead to economic and social justice. It opened a new political
gospel to Clarence that promised social equality and opportunity. His first
"sane" ideas of crime and criminals came from John Peter Altgeld's *Our Penal
Machinery and Its Victims,* given to him by Judge Richards, an Ashtabula police
magistrate. The unsophisticated country lawyer responded enthusiastically to
Altgeld's theories, and for the rest of his life he remained convinced that
poverty and slums and lack of opportunity were major causes of crime, that the
poor made up the majority of the vast prison population, and that punishment
without rehabilitation was an exercise in futility. Both the book and its
author, who became Darrow's close friend and later, for a brief period, his law
partner, markedly influenced his life. Seminal to his intellectual and political
development, both books shifted the direction and perspectives of his thinking.

In 1886, Clarence and Jessie decided to buy a house. Their $500 bank
account was enough to cover the down payment on the $3500 house which
they chose. They liked the house and were pleased to be putting down roots.
The next day, however, the owner apologetically confessed that his wife,
whose name was also on the deed, refused to sign the bill of sale: "She doesn't
believe you'll be able to keep up the payments, so I can't sell you the house."

A humiliated and very angry Clarence retorted, "All right, I don't want your
house anyway. I'm going to move to Chicago."

It was a sudden decision, but a sound one. Chicago was not too far away. Everett and Mary were there to give moral support, and Clarence feared he would need a lot of that. This was, after all, the same Clarence who had not started his law practice in Youngstown because the city was too large for him. Although two years passed before the final break, eventually the Ashtabula office was closed and Clarence left for Everett's home in Chicago. Before long Jessie and their young son joined him in the modest apartment he had rented on South Vincennes Avenue. At 94 LaSalle Street in downtown Chicago, he opened his first law office in the city.

Darrow, who always insisted that man has no control over his own destiny, contended that the refusal in Ashtabula reshaped his life. "If I had stayed I might have been in the graveyard or jail. I don't know where I would have been, but it would not have been the same life."[48]

The chances are, however, that before too long he would have begun to balk at the limited horizons of a small-town legal practice. House or no house, he would have moved on.

II

In Search of Intellectual Stimuli

1

CHICAGO during the late 1880s was a frightened city in turmoil, facing strikes and boycotts, riots and violence. It was a center of radicalism as labor struggled for an eight-hour day and fought to narrow the economic extremes between the haves and the have-nots, between the despoilers and the despoiled, between George Pullman and Cyrus McCormick and Potter Palmer and the myriads of unknown families who worked in the stockyards and factories and lived in the squalor of slums and poverty.

Mother Jones, the militant organizer of the conservative United Mine Workers, described the state of the city: "Foreign agitators who had suffered under European despots preached economic salvation to the workers. The workers asked only for bread and a shortening of the long hours of toil. The agitators gave them visions. The police gave them clubs."[1] The newspapers referred to these "foreign agitators" as "anarchists" and described them as "bomb-throwers."

Into this maelstrom of discontent came the thirty-year-old Clarence Darrow. Photographs of him at the time of his arrival in Chicago show a serious young man with a broad, sensitive face and deep-set searching eyes. His hair, parted on the left side and combed back, exposes a full forehead with a receding hairline. He is dressed conventionally in a three-piece suit, a stiff, white-winged collar with a large bow tie, its ends tucked under the collar. There is no hint of the disheveled suit and the lock of falling hair, affectations of a later date.

2

All his life Darrow regretted that he had not been able to participate in the defense of the Haymarket anarchists in Chicago. The trial was held in an atmosphere fraught with fear and prejudice and in a city determined to wipe out anarchism. It grew out of a protest meeting called by labor organizations at Haymarket Square on May 4, 1886, "to denounce the latest atrocious act of the police" at the strikebound McCormick Reaper Works on the South Side of Chicago. A fight between strikers and scabs brought police, who added to the chaos by clubbing and shooting the strikers, killing several and injuring many more.

The Chicago newspapers had demanded suppression of the Haymarket meeting, but Mayor Carter Harrison, Sr., a stubborn champion of individual liberty, refused to intervene. He believed that freedom of speech controlled the disaffected masses more effectively than repression and insisted, "I have no right to interfere with any peaceful meeting of the people. So long as they are orderly, I will not interfere."[2] Harrison attended the meeting. Standing at the fringes of the crowd, he listened to the speakers and studied the audience, then left, stopping at police headquarters to advise Inspector John Bonfield that all was well and to suggest that the large force of police on call be sent home.

At Haymarket Square, Samuel Fielden, an active anarchist, was concluding his talk from the speakers' platform, a horseless wagon, when Inspector Bonfield marched his police into the dwindling crowd. Bonfield's antagonism to radical political activists was so intense that it would not allow him to honor the mayor's recommendation.

"I command you, in the name of the people of the State of Illinois, to immediately and peacefully disperse!" ordered Bonfield.[3]

"But we are peaceable—" Fielden protested.

His words were cut off by the explosion of a bomb thrown into the police ranks, whose immediate reaction was to fire into the crowd and lash out with clubs. The riot, over in a few minutes, left seven policemen and one civilian dead, seventy officers and twelve civilians wounded.

For days afterward bombs continued to be found all over the city; a police dragnet arrested "suspicious" persons: anarchists, Socialists, and labor men. Many of the activists in the eight-hour-day movement were German anarchists, and the city, engulfed in a wave of antiforeign sentiment, made no distinction between aliens who believed in anarchism and those who opposed it. On June 21, 1886, almost seven months after the Haymarket bombing, eight men were put on trial charged with throwing the bomb. No specific evidence linked them with the act—and, in fact, it has never been proved who actually threw the bomb—but the reasoning of the authorities was simple: since some anarchists urged the use of bombs, the arrested anarchists had to be guilty.

Judge Joseph E. Gary, in his instructions to the jury, agreed with the prosecution's claim that a person not present at the scene of a crime can still be held for murder if he has had a relationship with the actual criminal, even where the perpetrator is not produced or identified. According to this theory, the defendants were accessories to the act, part of a conspiracy.

The trial of the accused anarchists attracted worldwide attention. While newspapers called for conviction, the prosecutor shouted, "Anarchy is on trial." "The jury was shamelessly packed to procure conviction," Darrow would recall.[4]

The jury, as expected, brought in a verdict of "guilty"; seven of the eight defendants were sentenced to death by hanging and the eighth, Oscar Neebe, to a fifteen-year prison term. Higher courts refused to reverse the verdict. The day before the execution Governor Richard Oglesby commuted the death sentences of two of the defendants—Samuel Fielden and Michael Schwab—to life imprisonment. That night Louis Lingg, another defendant, committed suicide in his cell. The others—Albert Parsons, August Spies, Adolph Fischer, George Engel—died on the gallows November 11, 1887.[5]

But the Haymarket case did not end with the executions. Darrow, now in Chicago, would play an active role in the nationwide movement to secure pardons for the imprisoned and exonerations for the dead.

3

German-born John Peter Altgeld moved to the United States with his parents at the age of three months. The Altgelds barely eked out a livelihood on their farm near Mansfield, Ohio. Unlike Darrow's father who encouraged his children to study, the elder Altgeld was a stern disciplinarian who distrusted education and placed obstacles in his son's path to learning. In rebellion, John Peter left home at an early age to work as an itinerant laborer and field hand. The self-educated young man taught school, then read law and began his law practice in Savannah, Missouri, where he was elected prosecutor. Soon enough, however, he decided that the system of which he had become a part was "a grist mill which, in one way or another, supplies its own grist." He resigned, opened a law office in Chicago, and prospered both in his law practice and in his real-estate investments. In 1886 Altgeld was elected a judge of the Superior Court in Chicago. By 1892 he had all the requisites necessary to obtain the Democratic nomination for governor of Illinois: The Democratic machine needed the German vote, and he was of German extraction. The party wanted a candidate who was a friend of labor, and he had long shown his sympathy to labor. Furthermore, he was wealthy and could make a substantial contribution to the campaign fund.

With this background he easily won both the nomination and the election.

From the very start of his spectacular career, Altgeld was known as a friend of the poor. He never forgot his impoverished youth nor the doubts about criminal justice awakened during his career as a prosecutor. In 1884 he published *Our Penal Machinery and Its Victims,* which condemned the entire penal system, claiming it made "criminals out of many that are not naturally so," made it difficult "for those convicted ever to be anything else than criminals," and failed "to repress those that do not want to be anything but criminals."

Darrow, already influenced by Altgeld's thinking, was eager to meet him and sought him out soon after coming to Chicago. They became colleagues in social protest and dissent.

When Altgeld was elected governor, his friends, Darrow among them, expected him to pardon the Haymarket martyrs and were disappointed that he did not do so immediately. Darrow reported to him that his supporters were impatient. "Go tell your friends," was the governor's curt response, "that when I am ready I will act. I don't know how I will act, but I will do what I think is right."[6]

Within six weeks, on Monday, June 26, 1893, Altgeld issued his pardon message: he not only freed the three imprisoned men but also exonerated the dead. In a vitriolic criticism of the judge, the usually restrained Altgeld declared that Gary's rulings had been unfair and biased and condemned him for the miscarriage of justice.

An outraged public and press reacted immediately, labeling the governor "John 'Pardon' Altgeld." It is a tragedy of Altgeld's life that he allowed his courageous pardon of the Haymarket accused to be tarnished by a personal attack on Judge Gary.

Although jubilant over the pardons, Darrow was dismayed at the governor's bitter outpouring: "To severely blame Judge Gary meant blaming a judge for not being one in ten thousand, and few men can be that and live," Darrow believed.[7]

4

The early years in Chicago were lonely for Clarence. He had few friends and acquaintances. Jessie felt insecure and alienated. She found it difficult to adapt to the impersonal big-city life and preferred to insulate herself at home, while Clarence was excited by the vitality of the city, its vast stretches humming with the sounds of life. He sensed endless possibilities.

An era of expansiveness had begun in Chicago, scarcely more than a half century after its founding and less than a decade after the devastating fire which had almost wiped it out—and Darrow desired to be part of the new growth. Chicago—big and hard and successful; crude and shallow, yet straining with ideals. It was a brutal city and a romantic city, a polyglot of more than 1.2 million people. Dreams flourished in the mire of the muddy streets, and many reached fruition.

In a poignant attempt to feel part of his new surroundings, Clarence would stand on the corner of State and Madison streets, the city's busiest corner, looking in vain for a familiar face.[8] He longed for intellectual stimulation, the challenge of debate; he craved companionship. Ever an insatiable reader, he absorbed the current political and social theories, steeping himself in Socialism, anarchism, biology, art, geology, literature, and the concepts of free trade and the single tax.

For a while he became a disciple of the political economist Henry George. George's single tax theory was "so simple, so fundamental, so easy to carry into effect" that Darrow had "no doubt it will be about the last reform the world will ever get."[9] What finally moved Darrow away from the single tax philosophy was precisely its "simplicity," its "cocksuredness," and the "small value" that George placed on the selfish motives of men. Darrow, moreover, did not believe in the private ownership of land nor that there could be any radical social progress so long as anyone owned any part of the earth.

Socialism appeared to him more "logical and profound" because it recognized that men themselves must make the world better through mutual effort. In 1903 he wrote to Henry Demarest Lloyd, one of his early friends in Chicago, suggesting that it was time they joined the Socialist party. "I think we must all come to it," Darrow told Lloyd, "but I think both of us should not come out the same year. You do it now and if the weather is not to [sic] cold I will jump in next."[10] Lloyd, a millionaire lawyer and journalist, had written the muckraking volume *Wealth Against Commonwealth,* in which he excoriated the Standard Oil Company for its growth through graft, treachery, and corruption. Lloyd and Darrow often discussed radical political doctrines; both had been active in the "free trade" movement and had associated with radicals.

Yet Darrow never did "jump in." He would go to the brink, but ultimately he found membership in any political party too confining. None provided enough freedom for personal judgments. Characteristically, his excuse for not joining was flippant: "I'd be too lonely, and I don't like being lonely."[11] In a more serious mood, Darrow explained that he could "never find myself agreeing" with the method of the Socialists. "I had too little faith in men to want to place myself entirely in the hands of the mass." He did not believe that "Socialism so far elaborated was consistent with individual liberty."[12]

What impressed him more as a political and social philosophy was the anarchism taught by Peter Kropotkin, Jean Jacques Reclus, and Leo Tolstoy. Darrow saw in this philosophy an ideal where people would live in harmony and mutual aid, without submission to man-made law. While he remained a philosophical anarchist all his life, he looked upon the ideal as a distant dream unrelated to the reality of the world.

5

Searching for intellectual stimulation, he joined both the Single Tax Club and the Sunset Club where the important political, social, and literary leaders of the city gathered.

The object of the Sunset Club was "to foster rational good fellowship and tolerant discussion among business and professional men of all classes." The club met informally every other Thursday evening. Dinner over, cigars lit, members listened to a speaker who presented his arguments in twenty minutes, with each discussant limited to eight minutes.[13]

Sunset Club meetings "have a wonderfully humanizing effect," reported the *Chicago Herald*. "When men of pronounced anarchistic and socialistic views, whose personality is unknown outside their immediate following, but whose names are familiar to every newspaper reader, are seen at the Sunset Club gatherings, and their more conservative brethren are thus brought in direct contact with them and see that, like themselves, these leaders are real human beings, faulty in judgment, mayhap, but terribly in earnest, it engenders a certain respect in their hearts that in no other way could have been attained."[14] At the dinner table clergymen sat with atheists and anarchists, a railroad magnate with a labor agitator, a financier with a clerk.

In a newspaper critique of the club, it was noted that the ladies found no objection to their husbands attending club meetings because they adjourn "at an hour that permits the members to return home in time for family prayers."[15]

At the Sunset Club, Darrow met such prominent men as S. S. Gregory, with whom he would be associated in the Prendergast and Debs cases, and Henry Demarest Lloyd, who was to work with him in the 1902 anthracite miners arbitration. He listened intently as his friend Altgeld discussed "What Shall We Do with Our Criminals?" a reaffirmation of the thoughts he had expressed earlier in his book.

Before long Darrow assumed an active role at the meetings and impressed the membership both as a speaker and a discussion participant. It is ironic that for one who deliberately removed himself from the woman's rights struggle, Darrow in one of his first speeches at the Sunset Club, in 1891, challenged the male's right to arrogate to himself not only the determination of his own sphere but that of women, too. The future, he proclaimed, would regard "woman as an individual and leave her to work out her destiny for herself." [16]

Darrow himself seems always to have preferred the individual woman to women en masse whom he found took themselves much too seriously. In an *Esquire* article on jury selection, he referred to this tendency and asserted, "Luckily, as I feel, my services were almost over when women invaded the jury box." [17]

In a tongue-in-cheek piece for *Vanity Fair,* he mentioned dislike of certain innovations: prohibition, for one; for another, the invasion of women "soon after they begin to bob their hair into what was once man's domain—the barbershop." [18]

Writing to a friend on the results of the 1920 presidential election, he said sarcastically that it showed evidence of "the wonderful intellect of man" and that it confirmed his prophecy of the effect of woman suffrage. "In Chicago," he pointed out, "where they take the votes of men and women and put them in separate boxes (no doubt for moral purposes) I figured out that 48% of the prohibition vote was women, 39% of the Republican vote was women, 30% of the Democratic vote was women, 25% of the socialistic vote was women, about 20% of the farmer labor vote was women. Those who thought that the woman's vote would help radicalism or progressive ideas ought to know this, but probably never will." [19]

Since he believed that those with ability would surface while the inept fell away, he saw no need for a woman's movement. He did not consider women a downtrodden segment of the population, as he did the Negro. He held no sexist prejudice, and welcomed ability wherever he found it. In an age before the "token woman" and the "token black" became a relatively common business practice to forestall cries of "prejudice," Nellie Carlin, one of the earliest female attorneys in Chicago, was a practicing member of his law firm from 1895 to 1910.

Clarence enjoyed both the Sunset Club and the Single Tax Club. The Single Tax, in particular, furnished a forum for ambitious young lawyers, and his activities there resulted in his being invited to campaign on behalf of the Democratic party in the 1888 election.

Despite his sympathies for the Socialist aims and his professed allegiance to the concepts of philosophical anarchism, despite his conflict with what he considered "the injustice of the present system," he generally voted Democratic. He explained, "I believed in keeping society flexible and mobile, and embracing what seemed like opportunity to bring about a fairer distribution of this world's goods. Living in the North, and holding these views, I have always

been driven to the support of the Democratic party, with few illusions as to
what it meant."[20]

In the Democratic political meetings in which he intially participated, he
was generally one of the last on the roster; the hall was usually already half
empty by the time he was called to the podium. If by chance he caught the
attention of the audience, his speech was continually interrupted by candidates entering the hall.

Darrow desperately desired recognition, the notice of the press. He was
ambitious and increasingly impatient to make a name for himself. "Through
the first half of my life I was anxious to get into the papers," he wrote in his
autobiography; "in the last half I have often been eager to keep out. In neither
case have I had much success."[21] He recalled the words of the author Bret
Harte, who had catapulted from obscurity to fame, that the only sure thing
about luck was that it would change. And Darrow wondered when his would
change.

The young attorney spoke at a Free Trade convention where Henry George
led the roster of speakers. George held the audience spellbound, and they
responded with a standing ovation when he finished. As the applause
subsided, people rushed to the exits. Darrow tugged at the chairman to
introduce him without delay: "For goodness sake get busy before every one
leaves the house!" he pleaded. As he stood at the lectern and began speaking,
he pulled from his "harried worried brain" all the "striking phrases he could
think of, and the audience reacted almost immediatcly. They paused, sat
down, listened. The reporters were soon "plying their pencils, recording my
words." The next morning the newspapers carried accounts of his speech.
Chicago "did not look so big, nor feel so cold now."[22]

The applause at this meeting not only brought him new clients, it also
opened the door to political advancement. He joined DeWitt C. Creiger's
campaign for mayor on the Democratic ticket and, the day after Creiger's
election, the eloquent young campaigner was invited to become special
assessment attorney for the city. An exultant Darrow, however, hesitated.
Well aware of his inexperience, he needed time to think about the offer.
When Judge Altgeld advised him to take the $3000-a-year position and
promised to "see that you get the proper instruction," Darrow accepted.

Destiny, fate, luck again played a part in Darrow's advancement in the city's
law department. Within three months the assistant corporation counsel
resigned and Darrow was promoted to the position, with an increase in salary
to $5000 per year. When the corporation counsel left less than a year later,
Darrow became acting corporation counsel of the City of Chicago. As the
attorney for every city official who needed a legal opinion, he dispensed advice
freely, "often simply making the best guess" he could and "almost invariably
finding that my advice settled the whole controversy." An old attorney had

once told him that if anybody ever came to him for an opinion on law to "tell them, even if you don't know. That's the best advice I ever received."[23]

Holding a position where he was in contact with most of Chicago's politicians, Darrow decided that, although "they are generally kindly and genial, and often very intelligent," they lacked "real courage." Although he enjoyed "political questions," he disliked "politicians"; he "never wanted political office," he insisted, although twice he would run for office, once unsuccessfully for the U.S. Congress, and once for the state legislature where he served one term.

6

Darrow's potential flowered as his world widened. The years spent with the city's law offices were enjoyable if not altogether stimulating, but, most important, they extended his horizons. After several years, the Chicago & Northwestern Railway Company offered him the job of corporation counsel at a much higher salary. He realized that his economic and social opinions and general views of life were not compatible with those of a corporation lawyer, but after a great deal of hesitation and soul-searching he accepted the offer.

To his surprise he discovered that he enjoyed corporate law. Broad and varied, the practice led him into new fields; his opinions were sought on matters of liability, personal injuries, lost freight claims, statutes, ordinances—whatever touched the railroad's operations—though most often his sympathies were with those injured by the railroad.

His employer recognized his bias; his views on labor, the Haymarket tragedy, and the eight-hour day were not unknown to the executives who ran the railway, and they were also well aware of his remarks at the Sunset Club that "the average working day at the present time is a little over six and a half hours, and the reason that some must toil 10 or more hours is that other men who come to the Sunset Club and boast of how long 'we' labor may live without any labor, or practically none."[24]

Still, they trusted his fairness and allowed him to work out his own decisions. With the aid of the company's general claims agent, Ralph C. Richards, he believed he helped many people without hurting the company financially.

During this period, an acquaintance meeting Darrow on LaSalle Street, then as now the "Wall Street of Chicago," was struck by his prosperous air.

"Clarence, how are you?" the acquaintance asked. "But I don't need to ask how you are. You're looking unusually well." With a sidelong glance at the well-tailored suit: "Business must be looking up."

Darrow smiled in his most disarming manner. Shyly he offered a handsome engraved card which read:

Clarence Seward Darrow
Attorney
Chicago & Northwestern Railway Company

"Why, Clarence, what does this mean?"

"It means, my child, the difference between theory and practice." His inflection on the word "practice" was unmistakable and held the unexpected promise of financial success.[25]

As time passed, however, Darrow became dissatisfied. The fine technicalities of corporation law began to irk him, and he found it more and more difficult to act for the railroad when his sympathies lay elsewhere.

He documented his dissatisfaction with corporate law in a series of essays which would be published in the Hearst *Chicago Evening American* in 1902. Using actual cases, he addressed himself to two points of law: the Doctrine of Assumed Risk, and the Doctrine of Fellow Servants. His first group of examples was based on the legal concept that in "dangers normally and necessarily incident to the occupation" the employer cannot be held responsible. James Clark, a construction laborer working on a sixteen-story building, loses his balance and plunges to his death while walking across a six-inch wide girder. The judge instructs the jury to return a verdict in favor of the company on the ground of assumed risk: that Clark should have known better than to work on such a dangerous job. In another case, Tony Salvador's leg is severed by a train as he cleans railroad switches. The judge decrees that Tony should have known better than "to work in such a dangerous place." The verdict favors the railroad.

In his comments on the Doctrine of Fellow Servants, Darrow again used the railroads to show the inhumanity of corporations and the courts, and how the "principles of justice have been warped and twisted by our commercial life." Two men are killed during a railroad accident caused by the negligence of the conductor. The widow of the wealthy passenger is awarded $5000 in an out-of-court settlement. The widow of the brakeman fights her case in the courtroom only to hear the judge pronounce that, unfortunately, her husband was a fellow servant and his death was due "to negligence of the conductor," a fellow servant. Darrow moralizes: The widow of the passenger goes to France "to soothe her sorrow"; the brakeman's widow "is now doing washing for the neighbors."

Darrow's sharply delineated characters, his compassion and sensitivity for the despoiled, and his concern over the impersonality of business and the inequities of the legal machinery make these essays an effective exposition of the suffering the workingman endured.

The promise of wealth which beckoned to Clarence only five years away from Ashtabula did not keep him from becoming restless. Soon he took time off from his duties at the railroad to defend Eugene P. Prendergast, the assassin of Mayor Harrison.

III

"I Can't Stand to Have a Client Executed"

1

LONG before the Columbian Exposition opened in Chicago in 1893 to celebrate the four-hundredth anniversary of the discovery of America, discussion raged over whether the fair should be open or closed on Sundays. No conflict of church versus state obscured the issue for those in favor of the Sunday closing laws. As one proponent argued, "The Sunday question is an important one, for there is a large element that is at war with our established American Sunday, an element containing many respectable men, and having a large following in the local press."

At a meeting of the Sunset Club, the Reverend Herrick Johnson, D.D., president of the McCormick Theological Seminary, indignantly charged, "The opening of the gates on the Sabbath would be going contrary to the best memories and traditions and usages of our national life." Darrow, of course, upheld the contrary view. Those who insisted on Sunday closings based their arguments on "false premises and illogical conclusions," he claimed. The United States government, said the agnostic attorney, was not founded upon the "law of God." At one time, he pointed out, the Church decreed "you must go to church, or be burned at the stake." The church had become more reasonable, Darrow said; now the church insisted simply that "you shall not be allowed to go anywhere else" on Sunday, and that was the reason for Sunday closings. "Is there anything unreasonable about that?" he asked, his voice laced with sarcasm.[1]

It was "simply and purely a religious question," as Darrow saw it. "I say that I have the right to observe that day or not observe that day according to the dictates of my own conscience and not at the command of any person who sees fit to keep my conscience for me. The man who would seek to enforce a religious day upon you or me is of the very same class as those men who three hundred years ago sought to strangle heresy by building fires around heretics."[2]

Thirty-three years later, in the small Tennessee town of Dayton, Darrow would again argue the same theme as he arraigned the constitutionality of the antievolution law in the Scopes case. "If today you can take a thing like evolution and make it a crime to teach it in the public school, tomorrow you can make it a crime to teach it in the private school, and the next year you can make it a crime to teach it from the hustings or in the church. After a while . . . it is the setting of man against man and creed against creed."[3]

By the time the Columbian Exposition closed, having remained open all but one Sunday, it was a "towering success," with an attendance of over twenty-seven million.

Mayor Harrison was in a jovial mood in the closing hours of the fair as he hosted mayors of other cities around the exposition grounds. After a six-year hiatus, Harrison had been reelected to a fifth term. Chicago's first citizen during the expansive eighties again headed the city during the Columbian Exposition which he considered "the greatest educator the world has ever known" and one of his proudest achievements.

Within hours after welcoming his guests "to visit the dying scene of this magnificent exposition," Chicago's popular and picturesque leader fell victim to an assassin's bullet, the first time in Chicago history that a public official was assassinated.

An unexpected visitor had come to Harrison's home identifying himself to the maid as "a city official" on urgent business. As the seventy-two-year-old mayor came toward him, the young man lifted a revolver and fired three fatal shots. The assailant escaped, only to walk into a nearby police station and announce calmly to the sergeant, "I did the shooting."

"What is that?" asked the startled policeman.

"I'm the man who did it. I did the shooting. That's the gun I did it with," he said, handing the gun to the officer. "I am Eugene Patrick Prendergast. I worked hard for Carter Harrison in his campaign. He promised he would make me corporation counsel. He failed to do this and I have shot him." Later, in the inspector's office at the Central Station, Prendergast volunteered more: "I was justified in killing the Mayor. He broke his word with me about track elevation. He betrayed my confidence."[4]

The track elevations in Chicago, popularly known as the "El," were being built at the time of Harrison's assassination. They were an outgrowth of the accidents of public trolleys riding on street-level tracks throughout the city.

Prendergast, harboring resentment over imagined "ill-treatment" by the mayor, had planned the shooting for several days and purchased a $4 revolver for the purpose.

2

Reporters were present when police officials interrogated the twenty-five-year-old admitted assassin. Slouching deep in his chair, his clothing shabby and dirty, the dull-witted Prendergast discussed the tragedy for which he was responsible. He was a small, thin man with receding chin and hairline, his hair trimmed in the pompadour fad of the era. In a lifeless voice he repeated his story: the mayor had betrayed his confidence.

How? the police sergeant asked. Had the mayor broken a promise to appoint him to an office?

"No, sir, that is not it. I want you to understand I am not an office seeker."

The sergeant persisted. "What was it then—corporation counsel?"

The prisoner's vacant face seemed to come to life. "Well," he contradicted himself, "the mayor failed to appoint me to that place—I was interested with track elevation—with the track problem," his blistered lips paused—he shifted uneasily in his chair, then became incoherent. After a while he continued, "I wanted to discharge my duties to the people."

"Did he promise to make you corporation counsel?" the sergeant asked again.

"No, he didn't; but you know I am the only one who could elevate the tracks and the Mayor's failure to appoint me corporation counsel made it impossible for me to elevate the tracks. I wanted to do it, and am the only one in town who could."

"Have you made the question of track elevation a study?"

"Yes, I have."

"Why?"

"Well, I read the papers every day of these accidents, the results of the tracks not being elevated, and I began to study the matter."

"When did you decide to kill the Mayor?"

Prendergast half rose from his chair. Pointing his finger at the officer, he shouted, "Are you trying to make a criminal out of me?"[5]

Several days before the murder, Prendergast had mailed a postcard to Adolph Kraus whom Harrison had appointed corporation counsel. Written in red on the postcard were the words: "I want your job as corporation counsel. If you know what is good for yourself, resign. Prendergast."[6] Instead of acting on the threat, the authorities considered it harmless and took no action, a failure that the *Minneapolis Tribune* later termed "criminal negligence."

Once Prendergast was identified as Harrison's assassin and the blaze of publicity fell upon him detailing aspects of his "eccentric" and "erratic" behavior, newspapers generally tended to label him "insane."

ASSASSINATED BY A LUNATIC

shouted the headline in the *Chicago Herald*.[7]

"Insanity was written all over the man," reported the *Chicago Times*. He looked "stupid and dumb, as if under the power of an opiate."[8]

Dr. Francis W. McNamara, who became chief physician of the Cook County jail, and who earlier had had the opportunity to observe Prendergast, said almost four decades later that the assassin was "one of the most pathetic cases of psychopathic personality that ever came into the history of criminal jurisprudence."[9]

The *Chicago Legal News* disagreed: Prendergast at the time of the assassination "was in a condition of mind to know right from wrong. . . . Had this crime been committed in Mr. Harrison's native state, Kentucky, his murderer would never have reached the jail—and many people would have said Amen."[10]

While the city was plunged into mourning, the assassin continued to insist he had done nothing wrong, that the murder was justified to revenge his "betrayal."

Although Darrow made no public comment on the case, Governor Altgeld, nearing the end of his term, did so and surely reflected his friend's thinking. "This crime," said the governor, "is one of those frightful things which make one shudder. It is one of a kind unhappily frequent in this country. Almost everyday we hear of somebody being killed in the same way by a person scarcely responsible for his action."[11]

The *New York World* responded to Altgeld's remarks with an oblique criticism for his willingness to pardon the Haymarket anarchists: Altgeld "did not forget to lay a foundation for the pardon of the assassin" if Prendergast was convicted by a jury and a petition for clemency came before the governor.

Darrow, whose legal experience had not yet included a murder case, watched the trial developments closely as Stephen S. Gregory handled the defense. Though the newspapers referred to Prendergast as "insane," the jury decided otherwise, and he was sentenced to be hanged.

3

Darrow's family background decreed his antipathy to capital punishment. Clarence had been about seven, he recalled, when Amirus spoke of having gone to see a public hanging held outdoors in broad daylight. "My father managed to get well in front where he could watch the spectacle, but, he told me, when he saw the rope adjusted around the man's neck and the black cap pulled over his head, he could stand no more. My father turned away his head and felt humiliated and ashamed for the rest of his life to think that he could have had that much of a hand in killing a fellow man." [12] Darrow never doubted that killing by the state was a deliberate and barbaric deed, crueler and more vicious than any committed by one individual against another. While he deplored all forms of violence, an individual's act of killing implied a reason, no matter how weak. For the state to kill could only suggest an avid thrust for revenge. "Every kind of human conduct comes from causes, and in order to change conduct the causes that bring it about must be altered or removed." [13] Such convictions accompanied Darrow into his law practice and remained with him throughout his life.

In the Prendergast appeal Darrow saw an opportunity to raise his voice in the courtroom against the death penalty. He volunteered to join Gregory in filing with the court a petition which alleged that the assassin, since his sentencing, "had become and was then insane or lunatic." A hearing on an inquest of sanity was requested.

Under Illinois law, then as now, no one can be found guilty of any crime committed when in a state of insanity. In addition, the law provides that "a person that becomes lunatic or insane after the commission of a crime or misdemeanor, shall not be tried for the offense during the continuance of the lunacy or insanity." If the accused were found guilty and became "lunatic or insane" before judgment was pronounced, the state had to suspend judgment until the criminal recovered. Moreover, "if after judgement and before execution of the sentence such person become lunatic or insane, then, in case the punishment be capital, the execution thereof shall be stayed until the recovery of such person from such sanity or lunacy."

The hearing was granted, and it was decided to retry Prendergast. The new trial began on January 20, 1894. Darrow appeared for the defense with two other Chicago lawyers, S. S. Gregory and John S. Harlan.

In this, his first murder defense, Darrow set the pattern for a modus operandi he would use throughout his career in criminal, labor, and political dissident cases. Criminal cases were relatively new to him, he informed the jury. [14] He had supposed, he told them, that there were "certain tried standards which the ethics of the profession had enjoined upon prosecutors that should be found by honorable men." Was the state so interested in taking a life that "lawyers should travel beyond the truth of and beyond the record and beg the jury to violate their oaths for the sake of giving 'justice a victim,' as these gentlemen put it?" He accused the state of using an argument that "would not be warranted amongst savages."

Even this early in Darrow's career, prosecutors warned juries against his extraordinary oratory and pleading. "It has been said," his voice rose dramatically, "that I would work upon your sympathies [and] that by art and device I would seek to conjure you to go beyond your duty, to violate the law to cheat justice of a victim. I shall not do it. If the evidence we have presented here is not sufficient for you gentlemen, in this age and generation, to say that it will be an inhuman spectacle to lead this man to the gallows, then the responsibility is with you and not with me."

Throughout the trial, even as the veniremen were being chosen, Prendergast continued to exhibit irrational behavior. To the defense team, the only issue before the jury was the state of their client's mind, and they rested their case on the testimony of a battery of expert witnesses. "You are asked, gentlemen, to ignore the evidence, to ignore experts, to ignore professional men, to ignore civilization and your conscience, to hide behind someone else," Darrow said as he derided the contention of the prosecution that the jury could "excuse itself by affirming the verdict of the previous jury which had found Prendergast sane and guilty."

Darrow cautioned the Prendergast jury: "It is not for me to say, and it cannot be for you to find what are the facts as to the former trial in this case. That is a sealed book, and [the prosecution] had no right to refer to it, but they chose to do it and that you gentlemen might see fit to escape from the strength of this case by shielding yourself behind 12 other men who acted from motives that we cannot fathom. Between this poor boy and the gallows stands this jury, and it must be by your consent that his life shall be blood."

Thirty years later, pleading before a lone judge for the lives of Leopold and Loeb, two young men charged with kidnapping and murder, Darrow would use an almost identical approach to the responsibility of decision when he said, "Your Honor, If these boys hang, you must do it. There can be no division of responsibility here. It must be by your deliberate, cool, premeditated act, without a chance to shift responsibility." [15]

To the Prendergast jury: "You have been asked to ignore all the learning and all the science of the past. You have been asked to forget all the humanity of the civilization which the years of progress and enlightenment have given the world. You have been asked to do all this for the sake of giving the law a victim."

For Leopold and Loeb: "Your Honor stands between the past and the future. You may hang these boys; you may hang them by the neck until they are dead. But in doing it you will turn your face toward the past." [16]

Darrow could bring tears to the eyes of judges and jurors and could himself sob as he pleaded for mercy and understanding. But sarcasm and a biting wit were also his weapons, and he used them readily. In the case of the mayor's assassin, Darrow charged the district attorney with calling to the stand physicians who were not experts in mental disease: "The reason [the prosecution] have introduced in this case doctors without name and without reputation is because they could not get any other to seek to swear away this boy's life.

"Talk of experts! Can it be a man lives in Illinois so ignorant that he does not believe that special skill is necessary in treating of diseases of the mind."

He turned to the medical witnesses the state had placed on the stand and depicted Dr. Davis as a man with "a long history, all, of course, backward. He has had a standing in his profession, but he is perhaps 80 years old, and he comes here as a relic of some forgotten age."

Or Dr. Bluthardt, another medical witness for the state: "If he had on a white apron, we would all take him for a butcher. He looks like it. He testified like it."

For Leopold and Loeb: "*[Dr.] Krohn, who by his own admissions, for sixteen years has not been a physician, but has used a license for the sake of haunting these courts, civil and criminal, and going up and down the land peddling perjury."* [17]

Concluding his plea in the Prendergast appeal, Darrow wooed the jury. His voice was soft: "I would like to have said much more, for I believe in this case as my very life, and I feel it is not only important to this boy, but that your verdict will go toward making history. It will count for civilization or barbarism."

Despite the effective defense presentation by Gregory, Darrow, and Harlan, the jury found Eugene Patrick Prendergast neither insane nor a lunatic and upheld the death penalty.

The high courts turned down further appeals, leaving two other avenues open: Gregory appeared before Federal Judge Peter S. Grosscup for a writ of habeas corpus, while Darrow rushed to Springfield to plead for clemency before Governor Altgeld.

The governor, however, had been called out of town. As Darrow waited to see Joseph B. Gill, the lieutenant governor, a young man came into the waiting room. He explained to the secretary that he was there to talk to the governor about Prendergast who would be hanged the next day unless the governor issued a reprieve.

Darrow, sitting nearby, overheard the conversation. Curiosity aroused, he inquired about the newcomer's interest in the Prendergast case.

"None, except that I don't want to have him, or anybody hanged."

On Darrow's worried face, prematurely wrinkled, appeared suddenly "a smile as winning as a woman's."

"Well, you're all right, then," Darrow exclaimed as they clasped hands. [18]

The secretary then introduced Darrow to the young man—Brand Whitlock, a member of the governor's administration who in ten years would become mayor of Toledo, Ohio. Whitlock was present when Darrow pleaded in vain with the lieutenant governor, and he waited with the now despondent attorney until Darrow's train left at midnight for the return to Chicago.

Darrow and Whitlock discovered that they shared not only a common social and philosophical outlook but an interest in writing and in the realism and social visions of Tolstoy and other Russian authors as well as Thomas Hardy and William Dean Howells. When Darrow left Springfield, sick with his failure to obtain clemency, he carried with him the manuscript of an unpublished Whitlock short story. Through his new friend, Whitlock—who was also to become a prominent American writer—met Howells, the country's major literary critic and editor, whom he had long admired not only for his literary talents but for his stand on clemency for the Haymarket anarchists. With Howell's interest and encouragement, both public and private, Whitlock's literary career began to unfold. [19]

Gregory's efforts in the Prendergast case proved equally fruitless: the writ of habeas corpus had been denied. "Justice" acted swiftly. The next afternoon, Friday, July 13, 1894, nine months after the assassination of Mayor Harrison, Prendergast died on the gallows.

Although the affair ended disastrously—"I can't stand to have a client put to death by the State"—Darrow could take some pride in the effort he had put forth. The hanging of Prendergast only strengthened his opposition to capital punishment. Whatever viewpoints he may have felt it necessary to revise during his life, this belief remained steadfast: the taking of a life by the state is wrong; all life is worth saving.

IV

"I Must Resign"

1

THREE million American workers unemployed. Wages drastically cut. Cries of hunger and want. More than six hundred bank failures; thirty thousand miles of railroad operated by seventy-four corporations in receivership. Profits sharply curtailed.

This was the United States in 1893 after years of a bustling economy during which the business cycle peaked, with rampant speculation on the stock market, and recklessly overextended industrial production.

Labor, acknowledging the depressed economic conditions, submitted without protest to the stringent measures management enforced. Workers naively expected that, as the economy improved, former wages and jobs would be restored. Though business showed some improvement the following year, it declined to give up some of the economic advantages acquired during the depression. Labor responded with an explosion of strikes and disturbances.

Early in 1894 Jacob S. Coxey, Populist and successful businessman, led a straggly march of men from northeastern Ohio to Washington, D.C., to demand that Congress pass a public works program of road construction to create jobs for the unemployed. When the demonstrators reached Capitol Hill and "General" Coxey began to speak, he and two of his lieutenants were arrested for trespassing.

The year 1894 also witnessed a violent coke strike in Fayette County, Pennsylvania, where a state of civil war existed between strikers and deputy sheriffs on the company's payroll. The strike was quickly broken when the owners imported black workers from the South to scab. The turmoil of the aborted strike had barely subsided when the nation was confronted with the "Debs Rebellion": George Mortimer Pullman and the railroads pitted against Eugene Victor Debs and the American Railway Union.

2

Pullman, one of the most creative industrial giants to appear on the turn-of-the-century American scene, made a unique contribution to travel with the invention and development of the Pullman sleeper, a railroad coach that converted to a bed at night, with a folding upper berth and an adjustable lower berth. With a capital of $20,000 saved from working at a variety of jobs and businesses, this thirty-three-year-old son of a poor western New York State mechanic built his first Pullman car in 1865. Success came easily. Railroad sleeping cars until then had been archaic and uncomfortable. Pullman, a superb designer, had an arrogant confidence in his product, and he was determined to build sleeping facilities for the railroad as comfortable and luxurious as those on steamboats. His cars, developed without regard for cost in both design and production, received an instantaneous acceptance from the public. The praise he received convinced him he had added a new dimension to American civilization.

Sitting in his mansion on Chicago's Prairie Avenue, one of the most opulent streets in America, Pullman looked out of his windows at Millionaires Row. He dreamed of building a "model town" for his employees around the factories of his Pullman Palace Car Company on the Far South Side of Chicago. Each morning as he walked to his downtown office at Michigan and Adams with his neighbor, the merchant Marshall Field, he spoke of his dream city.

"The working people are the most important element which enters into the successful operation of any manufacturing enterprise," he expounded.[1]

The architect Solon Spencer Beman was hired to bring the town of Pullman to life. "We decided to build," Pullman explained, "in close proximity to the shops, homes for workingmen of such character and surroundings as would prove so attractive as to cause the best class of mechanics to seek that place for employment in preference to others"[2] and would exclude "all baneful influences. There are no brothels or other objectionable houses; no such places of resort."[3]

Using a blend of Queen Anne–style architecture and a type of Gothic,

Beman designed a theater and a hotel, a public library, and 1800 houses in "industrial eclectic," all ostensibly for the workers. But the $3 annual fee for the use of the library kept out the workingmen, and the price of the theater tickets was beyond their Pullman salaries. Rents were 20 to 25 percent higher than those in the surrounding areas. By June 1881, the town had a population of 654, and by November of that year 1725 people lived there.

In *The Story of Pullman,* a publicity pamphlet prepared for distribution at the 1893 World's Fair, the writer extolled the company town as "a perfectly equipped town of 12,000 inhabitants, built out from one central thought to a beautiful and harmonious whole. . . . A town, in a word, where all that is ugly, and discordant, and demoralizing, is eliminated, and all that inspires to self-respect, to thrift and to cleanliness of person and of thought is generously provided."

Life in the model town, however, had deep undercurrents of unrest. There was another side beyond the "front" with its large airy cottages, beyond the hotel where liquor was served to the Pullman executives but forbidden to the workers. It was the greater part of the town where the employees lived in apartments of two or three or four rooms with one water faucet for each five families and one toilet shared by two or more families, and beyond these the small wooden shanties where a year's rent almost covered the cost of the shanty itself.[4]

The bubble of surface serenity and quiet exploded fourteen years after the founding of the "model" company town. Grievances were the same as those that had provoked other strikes across the country during this period: the company's refusal to restore the wage cuts of the depression era. Pullman had reduced wages an average of 25 percent between September 1893 and March 1894. Yet rents for the houses where his employees were forced to live and prices in the stores where they had to buy remained the same. An angry striker cried, "We are born in a Pullman home. We are fed from a Pullman shop, taught in a Pullman school, catechized in the Pullman church, and when we die we shall be buried in the Pullman cemetery and go to a Pullman hell."[5]

When newspaper reporters asked the Pullman general manager in late April 1894 about rumors of an impending strike, he deprecated them: "We have not been cognizant of dissatisfaction among our men."[6] Two weeks later he advised George Pullman, "Everything quiet; men all at work. Seems to be great relief among them that no strike has taken place."[7] Pullman himself, with singular insensitivity to the plight of his employees, would observe, "As in the best of regulated families there is liable to be an occasional unevenness among us. There must be differences in our colony once in a while."[8]

The next day, however, newspapers told a different story: "A great strike is on at Pullman";[9] and twenty-four hours later the company posted signs at the entrance gates: "The works are closed until notice."[10]

Mark Hanna, the outspoken Republican political boss who had described the town of Pullman as an "outhouse," responded when he heard its builder praised: "Oh, Hell! Model ———! Go and live in Pullman and find out how much Pullman gets sellin' city water and gas ten per cent higher to those poor fools! A man who won't meet his men half-way is a God-dam fool!" [11]

And Finley Peter Dunne, a political satirist and the creator of the mythical character Mr. Dooley, summed up George Pullman in the words of Mr. Dooley: "He has th' whiskers iv a goat without displayin' anny other iv th' good qualities iv th' craythur . . . 'tis a sound to drive ye'er heart cold whin a woman sobs an' th' young wans cries, an' both because there's no bread in th' house . . . But what's it all to Pullman. He cares no more f'r thim little matters iv life an' death thin I do f'r O'Connor's tab." [12]

3

Twenty-four years younger than Pullman, Eugene Victor Debs was the son of Alsatian immigrants who had come to America at mid-century. In Terre Haute, Indiana, the Debs family opened a grocery store where they earned "a modest income." The older Debs had been schooled in the Romantic literature of France and Germany, and he passed on to his son a love of Hugo, Voltaire, Racine, Molière, Goethe, and Schiller. To these young Gene added a new hero—the revolutionary Tom Paine. Inspired and challenged by Paine's century-old call, "These are the times that try men's souls," Debs, too, would sound such clarion calls.

At the age of fifteen he went to work for the railroad and soon became a train fireman. Debs loved the trains. Even after he left the railroad out of respect for his mother's concern over the lack of safety measures, his allegiance to it remained. Attending the first meeting of the Terre Haute branch of the fledgling Brotherhood of Locomotive Firemen, he became a charter member of the local as well as its first secretary, working nights and weekends for the union. Before long he became the full-time secretary-treasurer of the union as well as editor of its periodical, *The Magazine*. Together with his younger brother Theodore, he started a lifetime of social action and agitation. He summarized his life's philosophy more than twenty years later when he was convicted for opposing World War I: "While there is a lower class, I am in it; while there is a criminal element, I am of it; while there is a soul in prison, I am not free." [13]

Darrow would say of Debs, "There may have lived sometime, somewhere, a kindlier, gentler, more generous man than Eugene Victor Debs, but I have never known him." [14]

Debs considered the major problem facing the railroad worker to be a lack of cooperation among the various craft unions. Instead of cooperation, mutual rivalry prevailed. Each trade had its own union; each was exclusive unto its own craft. Debs remembered when, in 1892, the switchmen in Buffalo struck for shorter hours and more pay, and the railroad brotherhood refused to aid them. Because the strike did not have the support of all the railroad workers, it collapsed. As long as the railroad workers were organized as crafts, Debs believed, as long as labor in general was organized in trade unions rather than on an industrial union basis, the worker would be the loser.

Debs had been with the Brotherhood of Locomotive Firemen almost from its inception; he had helped to organize the Brotherhood of Railroad Brakemen, the Switchmen's Mutual Aid Association, the Brotherhood of Railway Carmen, and the Order of Railway Telegraphers. In June 1893, his inspiration and drive created the American Railway Union, an industrial union of all railroad workers; Debs was elected its first president, at a monthly salary of $75. The ARU was the answer to brotherhood officials who "were perfectly willing that we should have a firemen's union, but they were not willing for us to have a union that would unite all employes in the service in the equal interest of all." [15]

Almost immediately the new union won several minor strikes, but its first big battle, in the spring of 1894, involved the Great Northern Railroad, which had cut wages for the third time within a year. Unless the company restored wages, the ARU warned, the workers would strike. When the company ignored the warning, the men walked off their jobs, and not a train moved on the Great Northern. Within eighteen days the union members returned to work victorious—"97½ per cent" of their demands had been granted.

Within months after this victory the Pullman workers turned to the American Railway Union for help in their strike.

4

The strike at Pullman had been in effect about a month when the ARU held its first biennial convention at Uhlich's Hall in Chicago. The Pullman strike dominated the deliberations. Many of the delegates made trips to the nearby railroad town, talked with the strikers, and returned to urge that the convention endorse a boycott of Pullman cars. Despite newspaper accounts referring to the forty-year-old Debs as "dictator" of the union, he failed to convince the aroused delegates to delay action. The union was still young and too inexperienced, Debs believed, to tackle the giant sleeping-car manufacturer in a struggle which might be lengthy and attended by hardships. Furthermore, the ARU did not have sufficient strike funds for a prolonged fight. Debs believed, too, that it was possible to settle the dispute without resort to a strike.

The convention, however, was stirred by the desperation of the strikers. With credit no longer available to them in Pullman stores, some were starving.

The high rents forced many of the families to move in together, so that overcrowded homes stood in stark contrast to vacant Pullman houses. A Pullman clergyman appeared before the convention and, pointing a finger at Debs, cried out, "In the name of God and humanity, act quickly." [16]

A delegation from the convention called on the company to suggest arbitration but was rebuffed by the second vice-president, Thomas H. Wickes. "We have nothing to arbitrate," he declared. His response left the ARU with one choice: they voted to boycott Pullman cars. [17] Debs, deferring to the judgment of the convention, agreed but cautioned against violence.

Slowly gathering momentum, the boycott against Pullman cars spread. Union men refused to work on trains to which Pullman cars were attached. As each ARU lodge voted to support the boycott, Debs sent his instruction: "Commit no violence." [18] By the end of June nearly 125,000 men had joined the boycott. Twenty railroads were involved, though companies not hauling Pullman cars were unaffected.

Despite Debs's warnings against violence, cars were burned in the railroad yards of Chicago and other cities. Admittedly, the strike paralyzed Chicago, a major distribution center. No evidence, however, was ever submitted to any government commission that proved the officers of the ARU participated in, or advised, "intimidation, violence, or destruction of property."

Management regarded the strike as an attack on corporate control—it was labor flexing its muscles. George Pullman saw it as a challenge: either the railroads would be permitted to manage their own business, or they would be taken over by Debs and the ARU. [19]

With the boycott almost a week old, the railroads obtained an injunction in the federal courts. Edwin Walker, counsel for the Chicago, Milwaukee & St. Paul Railroad Company and also for the General Managers Association, was appointed special attorney for the government. Years later, Darrow acidly mocked the appointment: "The government might with as good grace have appointed the attorney for the American Railway Union to represent the United States." [20]

The injunction enjoined the ARU from "compelling or inducing by threats, intimidation, persuasion, force or violence, railway employes who refuse or fail to perform their duties." Federal troops entered the dispute. Darrow's friend, John P. Altgeld, now governor of Illinois, protested to President Grover Cleveland and questioned his action. The troops were "entirely unnecessary" and "unjustifiable," objected the governor. "Waiving all questions of courtesy, I will say that the State of Illinois is not only able to take care of itself, but it stands ready to furnish the Federal government any assistance it may need elsewhere." [21]

Cleveland retorted that "Federal troops were sent to Chicago in strict accordance with the Constitution and laws of the United States, upon the demand of the post office department that obstruction of the mails should be removed, and upon the representations of the judicial officers of the United States that the process of the Federal courts could not be executed through the ordinary means, and upon competent proof that conspiracies existed against commerce between the States."[22]

Still, the governor was not satisfied. He demanded the withdrawal of federal troops. Cleveland tersely replied that in "this hour of danger and public distress" discussion should give way "to active efforts on the part of all in authority to restore obedience to law and to protect life and property."[23]

Altgeld's unpopular exchange of letters with the president of the United States gave his critics fuel to rekindle their assault on him. They reiterated their previous attacks; once again he was called a "defender of lawlessness," a "champion of anarchy." The arrival of the troops increased the tension and violence. Spectators charged that the federal troops provoked many of the incidents, but the injunction—and the troops—defeated the strikers.

On July 7, 1894, with the strike and boycott still in full force, Debs and other principal officers of the ARU were arrested for violating the injunction, which *The New York Times* described "as a veritable dragnet in the matter of legal verbiage, one of those peculiar instruments that punishes an individual for doing a certain thing, and is equally merciless if he does not do it, so it is difficult to understand how the strikers can maintain their present policy and at the same time evade its operation or escape its influence."[24]

Shortly afterward a grand jury indicted them for conspiracy to obstruct the mails. "Let the mail trains through," the union lawyers had advised the strikers, but because the railroads attached mail cars to every train including those pulling Pullman cars, there was a delay in the mails.

5

Clarence Darrow, at his desk at the Chicago & Northwestern, found himself in complete sympathy with the strikers. He detested the use of labor injunctions and "had a deep-rooted feeling for the men against whom the injunctions were issued."[25] He now faced an ethical dilemma. With Eugene Victor Debs leading the American Railway Union strike against the Pullman company, a circumstance which also affected the Chicago & Northwestern, how could he continue as counsel for the railroad? How could he, who wanted the strikers to win, continue to act on behalf of the road? The strikers, he admitted, were no better than their employers and were "often selfish and unreasonable, but I believed that the distribution of wealth was grossly unjust, and I sympathized with almost all efforts to get higher wages and to improve general conditions for the masses."[26] Yet, Darrow rationalized, his duty as attorney for the Chicago & Northwestern was to the road. While pondering the question, he was named to a committee of representatives of all the roads to assist during the strike.

Clarence immediately went to Marvin Hughitt,[27] president of the Chicago & Northwestern, and offered his resignation. Hughitt turned him down, though he agreed to remove the attorney from the committee. If further developments caused any embarrassment on either side, it was decided, the matter of resignation would be reconsidered.

Meanwhile, in the grand jury hearings on the conspiracy charge, the judge left the jury no alternative but to indict Debs and his fellow union leaders. He had explained to the jury that the railroads had a right to the service of each of its employees until the employee himself decided to quit, and any action to induce him "under any effective penalty or threat . . . to the injury of the mail services or the prompt transportation of interstate commerce" could be considered a conspiracy.[28]

As a labor sympathizer, Darrow had expressed to Henry Demarest Lloyd an interest in Debs's indictment. Lloyd suggested to Debs that Darrow be invited to join his defense, and Debs immediately turned to the Chicago & Northwestern attorney. As he would in many of the major cases he undertook, Darrow debated with himself about taking the case: "I knew that it would take all my time for a long period, with no compensation; but I was on their side, and when I saw poor men giving up their jobs for a cause, I could find no sufficient excuse, except my selfish interest for refusing." He could not "justify my strong convictions with a refusal to aid them in their contest."[29]

With the decision made, he again went to Hughitt. "I must resign," he said, explaining his decision to join with S. S. Gregory in the Debs defense.

Hughitt, who admired Darrow and his legal talents, offered no objection this time but suggested that Clarence continue in the railroad's employ at half salary. He would be expected to handle only such matters as were mutually agreed on, an arrangement that continued for many years.[30] Darrow then became the attorney for Debs and at the same time a partner in the law firm of Collins, Goodrich, Darrow & Vincent in the Rookery Building.

6

Historians writing on both the Prendergast and Debs trials have given insufficient credit to S. S. Gregory. It was he who succeeded initially in postponing Prendergast's execution by obtaining a writ of habeas corpus at the last moment on the basis of the assassin's insanity. In the Debs case it was Gregory who made the preliminary motions and cross-examined witnesses at the hearings. Darrow's senior by eight years, he was an independent and courageous lawyer. Eventually he would become president of the Chicago Bar, the Illinois Bar, and the American Bar Association. Darrow described Gregory as "one of the best lawyers" he had ever known, emotional and sympathetic, devoted to the principles of liberty, always on the side of the poor and oppressed—and, he added wryly, "In spite of all this, he had a fine practice, and his ability and learning were thoroughly recognized."[31]

At the government's table with Walker on the opening day of the Debs contempt trial was U.S. District Attorney Thomas E. Milchrist. As Milchrist prepared to call his first witness, Gregory asked for a jury trial: "We do this because both by the word of the government counsel and the word of the court this proceeding is under the act called the Sherman anti-trust law. We hold that the act so far as it authorizes this proceeding is clearly unconstitutional unless trial is by jury. It provides that the commission of certain acts shall amount to a misdemeanor punishable as such. A trial by jury is guaranteed by the constitution to determine whether our clients are guilty of such misdemeanor."[32] Under the Sherman act, the possible punishment was a fine and imprisonment, Gregory pointed out.

The government counsel did not reply to Gregory's motion, but Judge William A. Woods did. He denied it, explaining that "if this proceeding were brought directly under that act there would be no doubt of the right of trial by jury. But this proceeding is not brought directly under that act; it is not technically a criminal proceeding, hence the right to trial by jury does not exist."[33]

The government claimed through witnesses and through telegrams from ARU locals that union officials had violated the court's injunction. The defense offered no rebuttal. Instead, arrangements were made for oral arguments.

Milchrist opened for the government. "I have never known four more dastardly criminals coming into a court of justice than these men. I venture to predict—but I hope my prediction will not come true—that thousands of women and children will cry for bread this winter on account of the actions of the directors of the American Railway Union. These men claim to be champions of liberty. Champions of liberty indeed! These men who have set themselves up as the champions of liberty have brought misery and bondage upon thousands of homes, and had it not been for the firmness and patriotism of the president of the United States the results of their actions would have been far more serious. The American wage-workers should be left to their own judgement in their disputes with their employers and should not be dictated to by professional agitators and street loafers."[34]

Darrow had been ready for Milchrist's attack. He responded with sallies that caused the prosecuting attorney to "turn red in the face."[35] "Mr. Milchrist says that in all his career as a public prosecutor he had never seen more guilty men than those now at the bar. I have always noticed in cases of this character that the public prosecutor invariably declares the defendant then before him to be guilty of the most heinous offense that has ever come to his knowledge. These respondents have been abused by a man whom political accident put in power. His words were gratuitous insults.

"There are various kinds of cowards. It was not brave for this man Milchrist to stand in court where accident has placed him and heap vituperation on these men who cannot reply. That certainly is not bravery."

Milchrist interrupted Darrow: "I will not take lessons from you in professional ethics."

Darrow snorted, "You ought to take lessons from someone." [36]

Darrow told the court that every man in free America had the right to decide for himself whether to leave his job for either good or bad reasons, that no court had the right to put a citizen in a condition of servitude, and that even an unjust reason for quitting work is not "a matter of judicial interference." The court, he argued, had not enjoined the defendants from participating in a strike but simply prohibited them from committing violence. [37]

Judge Woods took three months before rendering a sweeping victory for the prosecution. He found all the defendants guilty of violating the injunctions, and on January 8, 1895, they entered the McHenry County jail at Woodstock, Illinois—Debs to begin his six-month sentence, the others a three-month sentence each.

Among Debs's many visitors to the jail at Woodstock was Victor Berger, the Milwaukee Socialist, who brought him Marx's *Das Kapital* and other Socialist writings. The labor leader emerged from prison a convert to Socialism, and for twenty-five years he remained an evangelist for Socialism. His experience had convinced him that the only hope for labor lay in political action plus unionization.

Following Judge Woods's verdict, the defense attorneys immediately applied to the U.S. Supreme Court for a writ of error, which was denied. A hearing, however, was held on a writ of habeas corpus. Darrow was joined in the Supreme Court appeal by the distinguished lawyer and statesman, Lyman Trumbull, who in 1868 had been one of the few Republicans in the U.S. Senate to vote against the impeachment of President Andrew Johnson. Trumbull, a close friend and associate of President Lincoln, was eighty-one when he offered his services in the Debs appeal without compensation except for traveling expenses.

Trumbull denied that Debs and his co-prisoners had engaged in conspiracy. He argued that "refusing to work for a railroad is not [a] crime, and, though such action may incidentally delay the mails or interfere with interstate commerce," it was not against the law.

Darrow addressed himself to the issues raised in the original trial on whether the Sherman Anti-Trust Act applied to unions and whether workers could legally organize. The "clear purpose" of the act, he claimed, was "to apply to combinations in the shape of trusts and pools, these modern devices that are controlling the necessities of life and the welfare of the people. In no place is there any mention of any labor organization or strike or boycott." He insisted that neither the union nor its officials had been connected with an unlawful act. "If men could not do lawful acts because violence might possibly or reasonably result, then the most innocent deeds might be crime. To make men responsible for the remote consequences of their acts would be to destroy individual liberty and make men slaves. . . . If it is lawful for men to organize and in accordance with the organization to cease labor, they cannot be regarded as criminals because violence, bloodshed or crime follows such a strike." [38]

He conceded that "strikes are deplorable, and so are their causes," yet men who participate in the strike hope that when better social relations are established strikes and any other form of warfare will be unnecessary. "But under the present conditions of industrial life," Darrow continued, "with the present conflicting interests of capital and labor, each perhaps blindly seeking for more perfect social adjustments, strikes and lockouts are incidents of industrial life. They are not justified because men love social strife and industrial war, but because in the present system of industrial evolution to deprive workingmen of this power would be to strip and bind them and leave them helpless as the prey of the great and strong." [39]

On May 27, the U.S. Supreme Court delivered a unanimous opinion: writ of habeas corpus denied.

To Willard L. King, a Chicago attorney who lectured on the Debs trial at Amherst College some sixty years after the Supreme Court decision, the In Re Debs case was not of landmark status. He pointed out that the *Harvard Law Review,* which reports all cases of any significance, had not mentioned it at the time. King believes that were it not for the attack on the Supreme Court by radicals and revolutionaries, the Debs case "would never have found a place in American history." [40] Yet *The New York Times,* which was far from being a radical newspaper, had referred to the injunction as being so broad that it was a "gatling gun on paper!" [41] At the same time, the chairman of the legal committee of the General Managers Association, on learning of the Supreme Court decision, wired the attorney general: "I congratulate you with all my heart on the Debs Decision. The Supreme Court seems to agree with you that 'the soil of Illinois is the soil of the United States.'" [42]

Governor Altgeld countered that the "decision created government by injunction." He insisted that a jury trial would have discharged the defendants. Darrow always believed that with this decision the Supreme

Court strengthened "the arm of arbitrary power. It left the law so that, in cases involving strikes, at least, a man could be sent to prison for crime without trial by jury."[43]

7

As the contempt trial had progressed, the United States Strike Commission appointed by President Cleveland opened hearings on the Pullman strike. The commission heard testimony from August 15 to August 30 in Chicago, and on September 26 in Washington, D.C. The commissioners listened to twenty witnesses summoned on behalf of the American Railway Union, eleven on behalf of the Pullman employees, twenty-nine for the Chicago, Rock Island & Pacific Railway, one for the Illinois Central Railroad, and one for the General Managers Association. In addition, sixteen witnesses were called to testify for the Pullman Palace Car Company.[44] Both Debs and Pullman appeared before the commission.

Debs summed up his beliefs: "If railroad corporations and other corporations and employers of labor generally had treated their employes fairly and justly I doubt if there would today be a labor organization in existence. I think the conclusion is inevitable that every labor organization is traceable to the injustice, the oppression, the tyranny of the employing classes."[45] He shocked the commissioners by voicing the then radical philosophy that there should be government ownership of the railroads.

The commission then turned to Pullman. After permitting him to read into the record a statement praising the town of Pullman, the commissioners began to question him. He finally admitted that in 1893, during the financial crisis, while the wages of his employees were cut, the company paid out stockholders' dividends in excess of $2,800,000.[46] There had been no reductions in the salaries of officers, managers, and superintendents.[47]

"Did the Pullman Company during its years of prosperity ever voluntarily increase the wages of any class or all classes of employes?" asked a commissioner.

"Not specially on account of prosperous business."

The commissioner pressed: "But it has never increased the wages of its employes voluntarily?"

"Certainly it has not increased them any other way."

"It has never divided any of its profits with them in any shape or form?"

"The Pullman company divides its profits with the people who own the property," Pullman declared righteously.[48]

The commission's final report absolved the union of any violence. It noted that "few of the strikers were recognized or arrested" as part of the mob of "hoodlums, women, a low class of foreigners, and recruits from the criminal class" which destroyed the cars.[49] Critical of both Pullman and the General Managers Association, the commission claimed that "a different policy would have prevented the loss of life and great loss of property and wages occasioned by the strike."[50] It questioned "whether any legal authority, statutory or otherwise, can be found to justify some of the features of the association"[51] and said it was "satisfied that if employers everywhere will endeavor to act in concert with labor; that if when wages can be raised under economic conditions they be raised voluntarily, and that if when there are reductions reasons be given for the reductions, much friction can be avoided." Urging employers to consider employees as "thoroughly essential to industrial success as capital, and thus take labor into consultation at proper times,"[52] it recommended a system of conciliation and arbitration and the recognition of labor unions.

8

In early January 1895, sixteen days after Debs and the other defendants began serving sentences for contempt, the conspiracy trial opened in the federal courtroom of Judge Peter S. Grosscup, this time before a jury. Each morning, escorted by two deputy sheriffs, Debs traveled fifty-five miles to Chicago to spend the day in court. Each evening he was returned to the Woodstock jail.

Again at the defense table sat Darrow and Gregory; for the prosecution, Walker and Milchrist. Opening statements by Milchrist and Darrow indicated that both sides considered this a case of far-reaching significance—"a historic case" Darrow would call it.

Milchrist argued that the telegrams sent by the union officials first to "boycott the Pullman Cars" and later to declare a strike against all railways hauling Pullman cars had led to "disturbance and violence." He told the jury: "We will show you that by reason of the advice given by the defendants disturbance and violence resulted in Chicago. We will show a proof of this conspiracy that these men directed not only the men who were members of the American Railway Union, but we will show you hundreds of telegrams that all persons were told to strike and that they would be protected by the American Railway Union, whether they were members of that organization or not."[53]

Darrow's opening statement hinted at his defense strategy. Milchrist is a "humane man," but, said Darrow, he misled the jury when he suggested the U.S. government was prosecuting the case and the railroads had nothing to do with it. "I undertake to state that Mr. Milchrist is but the puppet in the hands of the railroads to persecute, not prosecute, these defendants."

Darrow denied any conspiracy to obstruct the U.S. mails. He conceded the mails were delayed, but not because of any conspiracy on the part of the defendants. "The mails were delayed as a result of a conspiracy hatched and carried out by the general managers to hold up as a club over the men, to convict them and bring them to terms. You are here to determine whether [any one of the defendants] engaged in a conspiracy."

He then discussed the philosophies of the defendants and the position of all workingmen. "These men formed themselves into an organization to meet the organization of their masters, the general managers. Mr. Milchrist says the men had a right to strike; if they had, that ends this case.

"We will show you," Darrow continued, "that the defendants advised over and over again not to interfere with the mails and to abstain from violence. But, counsel tells you, you must convict these men because they advised the strike, and because of that, they are guilty of obstructing the mails! They cannot trace to these men an illegal act."

The defense lawyer became the accuser: "You will see that the proof presented by the government will be of acts brought here to inflame your minds to convict these men in order that their union may be destroyed by the men who are pursuing them.

"These men are not conspirators—these men are not criminals," Darrow stressed again and again. "You and I may disagree with them, may say that what they did was unwise, but when the record is made up, that of men laying down their tools out of sympathy for their fellowmen as we saw last summer was one of the proudest sublimest spectacles in the world. Men have a right to strike; these men did nothing more."[54]

Nearly three decades later, in his defense of twenty Communists charged with advocating the overthrow of the government by force, Darrow would use a similar argument: "Greater love has no organization than that it will lay down its tools in sympathy with its fellow-man.

"I may do something for myself and I am entitled to no credit for it, but when I will risk privation and want and financial loss for the sake of bettering the conditions of the rest, who I feel are suffering injustice, then I am entitled to credit. The man who fights for his fellow-man is a better man than the one who fights for himself."[55]

Darrow decried the conspiracy laws as the favorite club of the tyrants of the world. He continued to agitate for their repeal all through his life. In the Debs trial Darrow was determined to show that his clients, far from taking part in a conspiracy, had acted openly when they boycotted the Pullman cars and refused to haul them. He admitted that trains were stopped. By whom? He suggested the question be asked of the general managers.

Darrow's plan in his defense of Debs and the American Railway Union was to broaden the issue, to accent and to expose the social and economic roots that went into creating the problem of strikes and discontent. He proposed to contrast the two protagonists—Debs and Pullman.

Debs, called to the stand first, was an effective witness for the defense as he related his involvement with the American Railway Union. He traced the role of the ARU in the Pullman strike, its commitment to obedience of the law, and its objective "a unification of all railroad employes for their mutual benefit and protection." Speaking in a quiet, even voice, he admitted that the primary object of the boycott was to aid the Pullman strikers, but once started it brought to the fore the hidden conflicts between the railroads and their employees. He maintained that he had always counseled against violence.

Was the Pullman strike called as a result of his advice?

"No, it was done contrary to my advice," responded Debs.

On February 6, a deputy marshal called at Pullman's office with a subpoena for him to appear as a witness in the Debs trial. Pullman, however, had disappeared. The *Chicago Tribune,* in a curious defense of the railroad magnate, explained Pullman's unwillingness to go on the witness stand: "It is not pleasant for a person who is at the head of a great corporation, who has many subordinates and no superiors, and who is in the habit of giving orders instead of answering questions, to be interrogated by persons who are unfriendly to him, and who may put disagreeable inquiries which he has to reply to civilly."[56]

The *Chicago Dispatch* saw it differently: "George Pullman is a plain American citizen, nothing more and nothing less. He is rich, influential and powerful, but before the law he stands, or should stand, upon precisely the same plane as the humblest of his employes."[57]

One week after a deputy first began the search for him, Pullman, accompanied by his attorney, appeared in court. They went into the judge's chambers where the industrialist explained he had not come earlier because no subpoena had been served on him. "I assure the court that I was not aware that I was contravening a law, and I greatly regret that appearances argue I was acting in opposition to the court."[58] Once he saw the newspaper accounts of his disappearance, he said, he returned from New York to Chicago. Judge Grosscup accepted the apology.

By then, however, the trial was over. One of the twelve jurors had been taken ill. The defense, recognizing that the jury was sympathetic to Debs, suggested that a new twelfth juror be impaneled with the original eleven and the record so far be read to him. The judge questioned the legality of such a procedure, rejected the suggestion, and discharged the jury. Within the year, the district attorney quietly entered nolle prosequi on the records.

No wonder the government had determined to drop the suit: the strike, the trials, the imprisonment of ARU officers for the contempt citation left the union shattered. Released from prison, Debs attempted to revitalize the American Railway Union, but a continually decreasing membership defeated his efforts. In 1897 the ARU was dissolved. Out of the ideals of the defunct union was born the Social Democracy of America, with Debs among the founders of this forerunner of the Socialist party of America.

9

Darrow never recognized the Debs case as defeat. In a lecture on industrial conspiracies in 1913 at Portland, Oregon, he insisted that the Debs case had not been lost. "It is not quite fair to say that I lost that case, because he was indicted and fearing he might get out on the indictment the judge issued an injunction against him. The facts were the same as if a man were suspected of killing somebody and a judge would issue an injunction against him for shooting his neighbor—and he would kill his neighbor with a pistol and then they would send him to jail for injuring his clothes in violation of an injunction. Well, they indicted Debs and they issued an injunction against him for the same thing. Of course, we tried the indictment before a jury, and that we won. You can generally trust a part of a jury anyhow, and very often all of them. But the court passed on the injunction case, and while the facts were just the same and the law was just the same, the jury found him innocent, but the court found him guilty."

In his autobiography, too, Darrow asserts that the Debs case "resulted in victory for the accused."[59] In the legal sense, of course, this is not so. The U.S. Supreme Court, on appeal, upheld the lower court's verdict of conviction in the injunction case. In the conspiracy indictment, no decision had been reached. The defense had learned, however, that at the time of dismissal the jury stood eleven to one for acquittal.

Darrow's reasoning in claiming victory in the Debs case reflects the attitude of militant labor men who hold that no strike is ever lost, that each is an experience from which labor can learn. Each strike teaches the need for solidarity and prepares it for the next battle. So it can be said of the Debs trials. Labor learned that "the courts are the bulwark of property, property rights and property interests, and they always have been. I don't know whether they always will be."

10

Darrow's defense of Debs established him as a leading labor attorney on the national scene. To his philosophical radicalism was added the role of radical lawyer. He became the movement lawyer as well as a criminal attorney. His reputation burgeoned among the poor, the weak, the misunderstood. His office was filled with representatives of labor unions, political dissidents, relatives of men and women charged with criminal offenses from petty larceny to robbery to murder. All sought his help, and seldom were any turned away. If there was money for his fee, he took it. If not, he worked without a fee. Almost half of the cases he undertook in his lifetime were without payment.

V

Out of the Political Arena

1

BY the time the Republican party met at its 1896 convention in St. Louis, William McKinley had been assured a first-ballot nomination as the party's candidate for president of the United States. Mark Hanna, the Ohio political boss, had earmarked an enormous budget, well-directed publicity, and early and effective organization to make McKinley the sure choice of the party.

The Democrats, meeting in Chicago several weeks later, set the nation on a new political course. Reading out of the party the conservative thinking of President Cleveland, the delegates turned down a motion commending the president for "honesty, economy, fidelity and courage."

The influential figure at that convention, John Peter Altgeld, "gave to that body its distinctive character and directed its course into radical channels."[1] The platform reaffirmed the principles of justice and liberty; freedom of speech, press, and conscience; equality before the law; and "the faithful observance of constitutional limits." That last phrase was Altgeld's answer to President Cleveland and the president's actions during the Pullman episode in which the federal government intervened in what Altgeld believed was a state's right.

According to Louis W. Koenig, Bryan's biographer, "The old myth that

William Jennings Bryan captured the Democratic nomination in 1896 simply by sweeping the delegates into their decision by irresistible oratory dies hard." Koenig agrees that the "superb 'Cross of Gold' speech, one of the great political addresses of all time, had its indispensable place in an enterprise of many parts"—but, he insists, the nomination was actually the result of "a perfect blend of oratorical brilliance, political finesse and sheer luck."[2]

The thirty-six-year-old charismatic Democratic congressman from Nebraska orchestrated the audience, and they responded with cheers and shouts, rising in unison to give him fresh bursts of applause each time he emphasized a point.

Bryan, tall, slender, sincere, plunged into his theme amid cheers of "Bryan! Bryan! Bryan!" "The humblest citizen in all the land, when clad in the armor of a righteous cause, is stronger than all the hosts of the error. I come to speak to you in defense of a cause as holy as the cause of liberty—the cause of humanity." That cause was free coinage of silver in the ratio of sixteen units of silver to one of gold. By a return to this bimetallic gold and silver standard, more money would be circulated and economic conditions made more favorable for the people. To Bryan, the question of silver pitted good against evil, the masses against Wall Street.

And then his concluding words, his clarion call: "Having behind us the producing masses of this nation and the world, . . . we will answer their demands for a gold standard by saying to them: You shall not press down upon the brow of labor this crown of thorns, you shall not crucify mankind upon a cross of gold."

Governor Altgeld listened attentively as Bryan spoke. When he and Darrow discussed the convention the next day, Altgeld commented quietly, "It takes more than speeches to win real victories. Applause lasts but a little while." Then, with a quizzical smile, "I have been thinking over Bryan's speech. What did he say, anyhow?"[3]

Darrow, pessimist and skeptic, knew it didn't matter what Bryan had said. An audience at a political convention only wants to be told what it already believes, and to that desire Bryan had responded. His nomination to head the Democratic party ticket in 1896 had significance for both farmer and labor: for the worker it could signal the beginnings of political power and social change; for the farmer it was a fight against the transgressions of industrialism.

Altgeld, a candidate for reelection as governor, convinced a reluctant Darrow to run for the U.S. Congress. Because his district was overwhelmingly Democratic and he believed that Bryan and Altgeld would easily carry the ticket there, Darrow campaigned neither for them nor for himself. Instead, he traveled outside his district on behalf of the other Democratic candidates.

The Republicans, it is estimated, spent between $3½ and $7 million in a campaign managed by the Machiavellian Cleveland industrialist Mark Hanna. In the final days before the election, the party poured money into Illinois to disrupt the Democratic organization. Consequently, Illinois, including the City of Chicago, voted overwhelmingly for McKinley. The final count: McKinley 7,105,000; Bryan 6,503,000. Altgeld, though running 10,000 votes ahead of Bryan in Illinois, nevertheless lost the election.

Darrow was defeated by 300 votes. "Even one day in my district amongst my friends would have assured my election," he explained his loss, "but I cared too little for the position and felt too sure. So I gave all of my time to what seemed doubtful States."[4]

2

Relieved to be out of the political arena, Darrow gladly returned to a full-time law practice and to his avocation of lecturing and writing. He had found that active politics required a sacrifice of political independence, a sacrifice he begrudged. Furthermore, he had a disdain for politicians; most of them he considered schemers and factionalists, with too much pragmatism and not enough idealism. He identified more closely with literary figures, with those who symbolized a universality of man and a sensitivity to life's trials, with writers like Tolstoy, Omar Khayyám, Walt Whitman, Robert Burns. Many of these he eulogized in a group of essays published in *The Persian Pearl* in 1899, or in a series of lectures.

Darrow felt a kinship with Khayyám who believed that man was not essentially bad, only weak and unable to overcome his inherent human faults for "the rules and conditions of his being were as fixed and absolute as the revolutions of the planets and the changing seasons of the year." Khayyám mirrored Darrow's own pessimism which saw all men as "hopeless captives."

But with Walt Whitman, too, Darrow somehow found an emotional tie. No pessimist, Whitman "must live or die because of his philosophy of life and the material he chose from which to weave his songs."[5] Whitman's writing "is remotely allied to the wild chanting of the primitive bards, who looked about at the fresh new marvels of earth and sky and sea, and unhampered by forms and rules and customs, sang of the miracles of the universe and the mysteries of life."[6]

Robert Burns was no pessimist, either. Clarence saw him as the teacher of "the brotherhood of man, the kinship of all breathing things"; the world was made "a brighter, gentler, kindlier place because you lived and loved and sung."[7] He sympathized with the rebel Burns and understood his dreams. Burns, he said, "stood on a serene height, where he looked upon all the strife and contention of individuals and states, and dreamed of a perfect harmony and universal order, where men and Nations alike should be at peace, and the world united in one grand common brotherhood, where the fondest wish of each should be the highest good of all."[8] That day was as distant to Burns as it was to Darrow, but each waited patiently for it to come.

In *Resist Not Evil,* his arraignment of violence and punishment published in 1902, Darrow found Tolstoy the only author he knew whose philosophy of nonresistance was based on Matthew 5:39 — ". . . whosoever shall smite thee on thy right cheek, turn to him the other also." Twenty years later, however, Darrow was not so enthusiastic. While he reaffirmed Tolstoy as a great literary artist, he questioned man's capability of ever reaching a state of nonresistance.[9]

3

The aftermath of the political campaign of 1896 found Altgeld at the age of forty-nine no longer politically ambitious, no longer a seeker of power. In an effort to recoup his financial losses, he returned to the serious practice of law. Darrow soon persuaded the former governor to join the lucrative partnership he had entered into with William O. Thompson soon after the Debs trials. In a gesture of respect and admiration, the two partners made Altgeld the senior member in the new law firm of Altgeld, Darrow & Thompson.

4

Clarence worked long hours in his office and in the courtroom. Almost every night he attended meetings, always intellectually stimulated by the discussions and the men and women he met. The women especially were a revelation to him. Social workers, newspaperwomen, artists, writers, they were activists who, like Clarence, found the city vibrant and exciting. Forerunners of the later feminist movements, they had outgrown the strictures of their Victorian generation and mocked it boisterously. They had causes to espouse and were stirred by political and social movements. On evenings free of meetings, he wrote the pungent essays and poignant short stories for which he was gaining a small but loyal following. He occasionally spoke to audiences eager to hear him discourse on Tolstoy or Nietzsche, on literature, on social as well as political and economic problems, always with pessimism and understanding, always with disarming simplicity and whimsical humor, probing for the weaknesses of society, the frailties of human nature.

Jessie, the love of his youth who had listened avidly when he held forth at the Kinsman debates, whose gentle gaiety was so beguiling to him then, had grown into a quiet, mature woman, wanting only to be enveloped by her home, her son, and her husband. She was not prepared for her life in the big city, nor for the man her husband had become, and she remained completely untouched by the ideas and philosophies and theories which so excited Clarence. Except for a mutual interest in their son Paul, there was nothing to hold them together, and they drifted further and further apart. She made no demands on his time. Hospitable to Clarence's friends whenever he brought them home, she politely served refreshments and then retired, uncomfortable amidst the sparkling repartee, literary critiques, and radical philosophies. She hungered for the close ties of the small communities from which she had come.

Clarence began to spend less and less of his free hours at home. Since Jessie was loath to leave the house for any length of time, he began to vacation alone, always writing regularly to Paul. His relationship with his son remained one of the close ties of his life.[10] In a handwriting which would become more illegible as the years passed, he wrote from the spa at Mount Clemens, Michigan, to the eight-year-old Paul: "Dear little boy: I will be home on Sunday or Monday. I am better than when I went away. Have taken a bath every day. The water has salt and iron and lots of other things in it. It is so heavy that you can't sink in it and when you come out your ears are full of salt. When I come back I will see if I can not get some one to give you some lessons on the fiddle. I think you ought to learn to play."[11]

Clarence and Jessie were divorced quietly after nineteen years of marriage.

5

In his autobiography, Darrow sums up his relationship with his first wife in a short paragraph: "Soon after I was twenty-one years old, while I was living in Ashtabula, Ohio, I married Miss Jessie Ohl, whose parents were neighbors and friends of our family. Of this marriage, my son Paul was born. Later in life we were divorced—in 1897. This was done without contest or disagreement and without bitterness on either side, and our son has always been attached to both of us, and she and I have always had full confidence and respect toward each other."[12]

That they "always had full confidence and respect toward each other" is attested to also by family members. They would meet at Paul's home on occasions involving Paul's young family and seemed genuinely happy to see each other. Jessie, remarkably enough, understood Clarence very well. She apparently never harbored any ill feeling and followed his career with great pride.[13] She recognized his restlessness, his need to be free, even his need for a totally different kind of marriage partner. When he asked for a divorce she gave it to him, although she cared very much for him and it was painful for her. Divorce, relatively rare in the 1890s, carried a stigma. Since they both feared his career might be jeopardized if she instituted divorce proceedings against him, which would tend to show him at fault, Jessie urged Clarence to be the one to file the necessary papers.[14]

In his petition for the divorce he charged that she "wilfully deserted and absented herself from [C.D.] without any reasonable cause, for the space of two years and upwards, and has since continued and yet continues to absent herself."

He made provisions in the divorce settlement that Jessie would receive from him "not less than $150 per month" during her lifetime and the house, "free of all encumbrance," which they had shared at 4219 Vincennes Avenue.[15]

For his part, Darrow always suffered some guilt about the divorce. His sensitivity made him painfully aware of the unhappiness he was causing her, but his unrest was too strong, his hunger too intense, and he needed to gratify his yearnings to be part of a bigger world.

Jessie told Irving Stone that about a year after the divorce, in a depressed and emotional mood, a tearful Clarence came to her lamenting that the divorce had been a mistake.[16] Jessie subsequently married Judge Brownlee, of Ashtabula, before whom Darrow had tried several cases.

Had Clarence and Jessie remained in the small Ohio town, most likely they would have remained together, a satisfied small-town wife and a frustrated lawyer not quite knowing what it was he was missing.

6

Because two people are married to each other does not mean they develop alike, Darrow would say as he discussed the need for easier divorces. Sometimes the ultimate difference between husband and wife is so great as to be intolerable. "Marriage is too intimate a relationship to admit of great differences in tastes and desires."[17]

"Men and women should not live together unless they find pleasure in each other's company as the relationship brings either pain or pleasure. There is no neutral ground. Uncongenial marriages are a source of constant irritations," Darrow believed, "and often are indirectly the cause of one or both of the parties abandoning all hope and effect to make the most of life."[18]

"I'm in favor of divorce," he would jest, "because it prevents murder."

Perhaps Darrow was explaining himself and his own divorce when he wrote that in any relationship human beings are "rarely the same at forty as they were at twenty." Ideals change, ambitions change, knowledge increases, and as a result "it is almost impossible for the mature person to realize how he could once have been interested in things, thoughts, feelings, and ambitions that he had in his youth."[19]

Soon after the divorce Jessie and Paul sailed for Europe. Clarence rented a room at the Chicago Athletic Club on Michigan Boulevard for a short time, then made several other moves before settling into the Langdon Apartments on Chicago's Near West Side. Since it was situated close to Hull-House, the settlement center founded by Jane Addams in 1889, many of the settlement house workers lived at the Langdon. Here Darrow met Gertrude Barnum, who would become an organizer for the International Ladies Garment Workers; Helen Todd, the daughter of a wealthy Minnesota miller; and Armanda Johnson, a young college graduate who had been appointed by Addams as a deputy garbage collector when Addams had been named garbage collector for the Hull-House district. Francis Wilson, Jessie's cousin and later one of Clarence's law partners, who would later become chief justice of the Illinois Supreme Court, shared an apartment with him.

Life at the Langdon was an exciting experience. Clarence's new friends were well aware of his oft-repeated intentions of never again falling into the clutches of marriage. He emphasized often that faithfulness was no virtue and that the sheer physical enjoyment of sex was not to be denied. Somehow, his enthusiasm, his wit, his idealism, his pungent observations on the passing scene, and even his pessimism all combined to make him "strangely handsome." His friend Brand Whitlock described his looks as "a sort of beautiful ugliness." Whatever, there was about him a sexual magnetism that enthralled most women, and he found no lack of companions for his pleasurable pursuits.

Free love had become a way of life for certain radicals. Emma Goldman, the anarchist firebrand who had been interrogated after President McKinley's assassination, was its foremost protagonist, and she decried the notion that marriage and love are synonymous. "Marriage and love have nothing in common; they are as far apart as the poles. No doubt some marriages have been the result of love. Not, however, because love could assert itself only in marriage . . ."[20]

"Can there be anything more outrageous," she asked, "than the idea that a healthy, grown woman, full of life and passion, must deny nature's demand, must subdue her most intense craving, undermine her health and break her spirit, must stunt her vision, abstain from the depth and glory of sex experience until a 'good' man comes along to take her unto himself as a wife?"[21]

Many of the literati and the political dissenters who lived at the Langdon advocated free love. Although Clarence's new friends were not political followers of Goldman, they agreed with her that love did not need the approval of either church or state but flourished mainly in freedom.

Clarence, comfortable in the political dissident movement of the times, confident and at ease with women, proclaimed his belief in free love and vowed he would never again be bound by the institution of marriage. Completely on his own for the first time in his forty years, he relished his newfound freedom.

More than one of the "liberated" women he knew would have willingly given up the independence she so volubly espoused to become the second Mrs. Darrow, but Clarence was having too good a time and rejected any thought of a formal alliance.

At the Langdon he became the center of a circle of devotees—a sort of "household God," a visiting student to the cooperative clubroom sarcastically described him. Unlike the others, Rosa Perdue saw him as a "dangerous man to be entrusted with power,"[22] and his radical ideas were to be shunned.

Many evenings in his apartment, his worshiping guests sitting at his feet, he read aloud from Voltaire and Robert Burns, from Tolstoy, Marx, and Nietzsche.

VI

The Robin Hood of the Courtroom

1

BY the turn of the century, only a little more than a decade after his arrival in Chicago, the name of Clarence Darrow had become synonymous with civil liberty and criminal justice, with a liberal practice of the law. He might be fighting quiet court battles, or sensational cases which placed him at the center of the storm and made page one newspaper headlines; or he might be lecturing on literature and debating topics of social significance; or leading a protest on the lack of seats in the city's streetcars, wearing, with the riders, badges stating bluntly, "No seats, no fare."

His sense of social consciousness, of social awareness, was pulling him in a multiplicity of directions. He had to open the windows on perception, on compassion, and the understanding of each person in trouble who came to him. How did it happen? he wanted to know. Why did it happen? How can we prevent it from happening again? Always it was a plural obligation: *we* are all responsible for one another. We all bear the shame for society's failures.

On what grounds should the guilty be judged? he asked himself. On strict adherence to the law? Or must one first consider the causes that led to the crime? Are the guilty as entitled to a defense as the wrongly charged? What is a "just" punishment? "It is plain that our present method of dealing with crime is a failure, for it takes no account of cause and effect, but acts entirely from hatred and fear and vengeance."[1]

Some of Darrow's reformer friends eyed with skepticism and dismay his defense of bribers and political rascals. These could hardly be "the poor and the weak," the victims of society who never had a chance.

The dichotomy also bothered Darrow. When Ellen Gates Starr, who had helped Jane Addams found Hull-House, criticized him for undertaking a case she considered morally wrong—obtaining favorable amendments for a street-car company franchise—Darrow, in an extraordinarily frank letter, confessed he did it for the money. He had a compelling need for friendship and for adulation. Sensitive to criticism, particularly from friends, he needed to justify his actions. Judged "by ordinary commercial and legal standards of ethics," he explained, he had done no wrong; every lawbook and instructor of law "teaches that all clients have the right to have their case represented."

He conceded, however, that this would be no justification in her mind nor, he admitted, was it in his. "I do not care a cent for all the ordinary rules of ethics or conduct. They are mostly wrong. I am satisfied that judged by the higher law, in which we both believe, I could not be justified, and I am practically a thief." Continuing to chastise himself, he added, "I am taking money that I did not earn, which comes to me from men who did not earn it, but who get it, because they have the chance to get it."

But there was an explanation, he rationalized: "I have taken their ill gotten gains and have tried to use it to prevent suffering. . . . I have defended the poor and weak, have done it without pay, will do it again. I cannot defend them without bread. I cannot get this except from those who have it."[2]

This Robin Hood of the courtroom could have further pointed out that the adversary principle under which the courts operate entitles each defendant to the best possible defense and that the attorney is an advocate, not a judge or jury. Just like the physician, who is not decried because he attends a "criminal" or an "undesirable," so, too, the lawyer should not be condemned when he represents an unpopular client or cause.

"Often," Darrow said, "my clients did not do the things with which they were charged; sometimes they did do them, and then I tried to make the courts and juries understand the reasons why."[3]

He disliked the technicalities of the law. His way was to use the facts to make judges and juries feel a larger sympathy for his clients. And he nearly always succeeded.

2

If the Prendergast execution disturbed Darrow, the indictment of a fourteen-year-old boy and his foster mother for murder was even more distressing as he interpreted the state's demand to be not for justice but for vengeance.

On May 22, 1898, five years after the Prendergast case, Thomas George Crosby shot and killed a deputy sheriff who had a court order to evict Mrs. Marjorie H. Crosby, his foster mother, from her home.

Mother and son were arrested and charged with murder. Darrow and ex-Judge William Prentiss appeared as attorneys for the defense. The trial opened April 26, 1899, to a capacity courtroom attracted by the unusual circumstances of the case. Mrs. Crosby testified that when the mortgage on her house was foreclosed she had consulted a lawyer who arranged for her to stay in the house an additional two months, even advising her to shoot anyone who tried to get her out earlier. "He asked if I had a gun and when I said I had 'Well then use it!' he said," Mrs. Crosby stated.

She denied she told her son to use the gun. "I never thought that little boy would ever be left alone in the house. I didn't know he had the pistol."[4] When the deputy sheriff and several of his colleagues came to the house demanding entry, Thomas told them his mother was away and refused to admit them, warning he would shoot if they came closer. When they tried to enter, Tommy fired.

The state's attorney, because of the youthfulness of the boy, did not ask for the death penalty, but he informed the jury that under Illinois law it could be imposed.

Defense Attorney Prentiss eulogized the youth in his final argument, concluding, "We will not send 'Tommy' Crosby to a reform school. He does not need and has never needed such discipline. He is a good boy and a Sunday school student. If all boys were like Tom Crosby there would be no need for reform schools, jails or penitentiaries."

Two women spectators began to applaud loudly, and soon the entire courtroom was in an uproar. The judge ordered the women to be held in custody in the anteroom. Before court adjourned at noon he reprimanded them and then released them.[5]

Darrow employed a different approach from his cocounsel. He gambled as he told the jury that death for the young boy would be preferable to imprisonment among hardened criminals because in jail he would only learn more about violence and crime. He added that if anyone should be on trial it should be the attorney who had advised Mrs. Crosby that she had "a right to shut all intruders out of her house by locks and chains and keep them out at any cost. If she had that right she had the right to keep them out by force of arms," Darrow reasoned.[6]

The jury deliberated overnight, and after prolonged argument brought in a manslaughter verdict against Mrs. Crosby and freed her foster son. The defense called it a "weak kneed compromise, utterly unjust and reprehensible." The state commented, "Even as the verdict reads, it is a victory for law and order. The jury brought in perhaps the best verdict they could, all things considered."[7]

3

In Oshkosh, Wisconsin, several years after the Pullman strike, the woodworkers at the Paine Lumber Company, the country's largest manufacturers of sashes, doors, and blinds, walked off their jobs, demanding higher wages, abolition of child and woman labor, recognition of the Amalgamated Woodworkers International Union, and a weekly paycheck.

Like George M. Pullman, George M. Paine, too, refused to meet with the union representatives. If the men had a grievance, he said, they could "come alone to our office, and then we will talk. . . . I will not meet your union; I will not meet your committee."[8]

But when a Paine employee who had worked in the mills almost a decade, earning a dollar and a quarter a day, asked his foreman for more money, he was told, "Go to hell, God damn you. I can get a damn sight better than you are for a dollar and a quarter a day."[9]

Another worker requesting a raise was ordered to "get out of here or I'll give you a raise in the pants."[10]

During the fourteen-week strike, a warrant was issued against Thomas I. Kidd, general secretary of the union whose headquarters were in Chicago, and George Zentner and Michael Troiber, picket captains of the strike in Oshkosh. They were accused of a "criminal conspiracy" to injure the business of the Paine Lumber Company.

The defendants were brought to trial on a complaint by the district attorney, since Wisconsin law required no indictment. Darrow was asked to represent the three union men.

District Attorney H. Quartermass objected to Darrow's presence, labeling him an "outside" attorney. At the same time, Darrow objected to F. W. Houghton, special prosecutor appointed to assist the district attorney, because Houghton had participated in a mass meeting to form the Law and Order League and had joined it at that time.[11]

Darrow's defense tactics were easy to anticipate as he questioned each prospective juror regarding his attitude toward labor unions, picketing, and strikes in general.[12]

Throughout the trial the defense attorney emphasized that the State of Wisconsin was not the real complainant, and he charged George Paine, head of the lumber company, with being the force behind the prosecution. Darrow's contention was inadvertently strengthened by Quartermass himself on the first day of the trial when Paine appeared in the courtroom and the district attorney rushed up to him, warmly shook his hand, and led him to the prosecutors' table. Darrow derided this action in his summation: "When George M. Paine lent his august presence to this room, which place, although the temple of justice, was scarce enough to hold him—when in all his majesty and splendor he sat down beside Mr. Houghton, instead of out in the vulgar crowd where his workmen were herded; before he was placed on the stand Brother Houghton turned to him and shook him warmly by the hand. It was the only witness that he shook by hand or whom he seemed to know. I thought he would have been glad to have licked the dust from Paine's boots, had he been given the opportunity to perform this service." [13]

Darrow warned the jury that "these employers are using this court of justice because in their misguided cupidity, they believe that they may be able to destroy what little is left of the spirit of independence and manhood which they have been slowly crushing from the breasts of those who toil for them."

Ordinary men are brought into a criminal court because they are bad, but Thomas Kidd is here because he is good. Darrow's emphasis was sharp: "If Thomas I. Kidd had been mean and selfish and designing, if he had held out his hand to take the paltry bribes that these men pass out wherever they find one so poor and weak as to take their dirty gold, this case would not be here today."

In his own trial fifteen years later he approached his defense in a similar manner: "I am not on trial for having bribed a man. . . . I am on trial because I have been a lover of the poor, a friend of the oppressed, because I have stood for labor for all these years." [14]

Darrow in the Kidd case noted that Paine, the lumber baron, testified that he had attempted during the strike to get Kidd out of town. He wound up, however, "by consulting the district attorney to see how they can keep him here."

The cause of the woodworkers "is one that is very, very near to my heart," Darrow told the jury. Kidd had dared to come to Oshkosh, to interfere with the "holy calling of men who simply wish to get money." These men want to make an example of Kidd, and so the jury is asked to send him to jail.

Confronted again by the evils of the conspiracy law as he had been in the Debs trial, Darrow, the son of a woodworker, told the Kidd jury, "Whenever a king wanted to get rid of somebody, whenever a political disturber was in someone's way, then they brought a charge of conspiracy, and they not only proved everything he said, but everything everyone else said and everyone else did. . . . It was in those old days, even after courts commenced to protect the rights of individuals, they invented the crime of conspiracy."

Emotion dismissed caution as Darrow pointed at the prosecutor: "How Brother Houghton's mouth would have watered if he had been given a chance to convict Thomas Paine for daring to proclaim the rights of man!"

As he spoke, the defense lawyer noticed Special Prosecutor Houghton taking notes, and he was assailed by doubts. Had it been a mistake to mention the agnostic Paine? What were the religious affiliations of the jurors? Would the mention of the agnostic Thomas Paine, whom President Theodore Roosevelt had called "a dirty little atheist," affect their verdict?

He decided to brazen it out. "I see Brother Houghton has made a note of what I say," he continued, "and as near as I can read it from here it is something about Thomas Paine." He had not identified any of their religions, Darrow told the twelve jurors, but "whether you are Protestants or agnostics, or Catholics, or pagans, or Paine men," he hoped his reference to the author of *The Rights of Man* would not prejudice their decision.

Darrow interrupted his plea briefly to turn on the district attorney: "Shame on you, Brother Quartermass. You are a better man than [to prosecute this case]. You should never have allowed George Paine to invade your office and use the State of Wisconsin for this unholy purpose. Because I want to say again that you are not a bad fellow at all. It is George Paine that I am after."

Darrow's style of pleading had now reached fruition. His summations not only contained pleas for mercy, he also reflected on what the jury's decision would mean to history. "Men do not build for today," he philosophized; "they do not build for tomorrow. They build for the centuries, for the ages; and when we look back it is the despised criminal and outlaw, the man perhaps without home or country or friend, who has lifted the world upward and onward toward the blessed brotherhood which one day will come."

And Darrow concluded, "It has fallen to your lot, gentlemen, to be leading actors in one of the great dramas of human life." Their verdict, he said, would "be a milestone in the history of the world, and an inspiration and hope to the dumb, despairing millions whose faith is in your hands."

It took two days for the defense attorney to finish his summation. On November 2, 1898, the jury, out fifty minutes, balloted twice and returned a verdict: "Not guilty."

The Oshkosh trial had lasted three weeks. Darrow received a token fee of $250 and the union's promise to publish his summation in pamphlet form and distribute it among its members.

4

From the very moment William Randolph Hearst came on the journalistic scene in 1887, controversy surrounded him. In those early years he was known as "the champion of the rights of all, the foe of privilege and monopoly, and friend of all who labor and are heavy laden."

He preached public ownership and democracy. He fought street railway as well as gas monopolies, and his newspaper muckraked the beef trusts. In 1896

Hearst, like Darrow, supported Bryan for the presidency of the United States, and in 1904 Darrow would second the nomination of Hearst for vice president at the Democratic party convention.

Historically, however, Hearst is remembered not only as a yellow journalist but as the man who started the Spanish-American War. He has been termed a charlatan, a "forerunner of American Fascism,"[15] antilabor, and antiprogressive.

About the time Altgeld joined Darrow in his law practice, the firm had been hired by Hearst to incorporate his newspaper, the *Chicago American,* and in the fall of 1900 the paper had one of its first legal encounters involving the publishing of a cartoon and a news report critical of a ruling by Circuit Court Judge Elbridge Hanecy.

The Fortieth General Assembly of Illinois had, three years earlier, voted to legalize the consolidation of ten out of eleven gas companies in Chicago into the People's Gas, Light and Coke Company. Neither the public nor the press had made any outcry over the legislation.

The *American,* which had not been in existence in 1897 when the law was passed, now began to urge that the constitutionality of the law be tested. The issue caught the public's attention, and as a result of newspaper and public pressure, quo warranto proceedings were initiated questioning the authority under which the utility company exercised its franchise. The state's attorney appeared before Judge Murray F. Tuley in Circuit Court and obtained leave to file the information in the proceedings. The gas company, through its attorneys, went before Judge Hanecy and moved that Judge Tuley's order be vacated. Judge Hanecy listened to arguments from both sides, then ruled the Gas Act constitutional. The formation of the trust, he decided, did not jeopardize any public rights.

Hearst's *Chicago American,* an afternoon newspaper, reported on the decision released that morning and criticized it as definitely prejudicial to the public interest. Furthermore, the *American* accused the gas trust of being "scoundrelly through and through, and has its faculty of knowing upon whom it may depend." The cartoon showed a caricature of Judge Hanecy "with his arms behind his back and hands outstretched, palms out."[16]

To Hanecy, the article and cartoon not only attacked the court but "were of a graver nature. They are a bold threat and a defiant statement to every other Court that may have to do with any case that this newspaper or its managers may be interested in."[17] He cited the editors with "constructive contempt," that is, contempt of the court outside the courtroom.

The firm of Altgeld, Darrow & Thompson represented the newspaper in the hearing. Judge Hanecy appointed a special prosecutor to handle the case. On the opening day of the trial, Altgeld asked for a change of venue which was denied, as was also his request for a jury trial. The hearing proceeded.

The former governor recalled to the court that he too had been a victim of newspaper attacks when in office, and he expressed surprise at the judge's sensitivity to the published articles. Yes, they were indiscreet, Altgeld admitted, but they did the judge no harm.

Hanecy was not to be mollified. He sentenced the editors to a period of up to forty days in jail. "To overlook the assault on the court would be cowardice," he said. "A fine would be inadequate." [18]

Francis X. Busch, former law school dean of De Paul University in Chicago and a former corporation counsel of the City of Chicago, had been a young court reporter at the trial. He recalled Judge Hanecy as "the only tyrant on the bench" he had ever encountered in his more than half century at the bar. "I had never experienced in a courtroom that which happened in that courtroom."

Hanecy was impatient as Darrow argued. The judge tried to stop him: "You might as well know, Mr. Darrow, what you are saying is going into one ear and out the other."

Darrow's unorthodox retort was in keeping with the irritation he felt toward the judge: "I'm not surprised, Your Honor. Maybe it's because there's nothing to interfere with the passage, Your Honor." [19] Surprisingly enough, he was not charged with contempt.

In that same case Darrow cited authorities who had, in earlier proceedings, acted in opposition to Judge Hanecy's decision. He produced a law book with a flourish to give it added importance. Then he said, "Now, Your Honor, I want to cite this specific case which resembles the one at bar in four important respects: one, it is a contempt case; two, it's a constructive contempt case; three, it was an appeal from the Honorable Elbridge Hanecy; and four, it was reversed by the Supreme Court as I expect this case to be." [20]

After Judge Hanecy sentenced the newsmen, Altgeld and Darrow appeared before Circuit Court Judge Edward F. Dunne on a writ of habeas corpus. On December 3, 1901, Darrow delivered "a fervent plea for the freedom of the press and freedom of speech." Prominent lawyers of the city crowded the courtroom. To the reporter of the *Chicago American* covering the story, Darrow's "peroration was the strongest appeal for the preservation of American liberty as guaranteed by the constitution that had been heard in a courtroom for many years."

The judge, who had been pacing as Darrow started to talk, stopped, sat down, bent forward, his gaze fixed on Darrow whose voice shook with emotion: "These defendants are prosecuted today, not because they have committed contempt of this court, not that; but because they have dared to speak for the poor and weak, who could not speak for themselves.

"No man ever undertook to help the poor and the weak and no newspaper ever undertook it without suffering the penalties of their rash and thankless acts."

Darrow approached the plea in the newspaper contempt case as he had in many of his labor cases, and as he would continue to do throughout his life: it was always the cause.

"I care for these defendants only for these great causes they represent. The principles involved in this case lie at the foundation of the country that we love. They are the moving spirit of all the progress of the land." [21]

In the Kidd case three years earlier he had told the jury he was not appealing to them for Kidd but rather for "the long line of despoiled and downtrodden people of the earth. . . .

"Gentlemen, the world is dark; but it is not hopeless. Here and there through the past some man has ever risen, . . . willing to give the devotion of his great soul to humanity's holy cause." [22]

In the Haywood, Moyer, and Pettibone trial a few years later: "Mr. Haywood is not my greatest concern," and he warned: "Don't be so blind in your madness as to believe that when you make three fresh new graves you will kill the labor movement of the world." [23]

Darrow saw no contempt in the *Chicago American* case, and, furthermore, he believed a judge should be above criticism. "Perhaps he is not, but he ought to be.

"It needs no strong arm of the law to enforce respect of the court. You cannot compel respect of the court by the keys of the County Jail, you can compel fear, but fear is one thing and respect is another."

Looking up at Judge Dunne, Darrow suggested that if some morning the judge found all the newspapers in Chicago praising him, "instead of sending out to buy each one of those papers and paste it in a scrap book, you ought to cite all of the publishers for contempt of court, because this conduct has a tendency to make you stand by your opinion.

"But if it is a contempt in one way it is in another. Still I have never heard of a judge setting out to get any newspaper man because he praised his opinion or approved the law that the court announced from the bench.

"Of course, if you praise it helps one side, if you blame it helps the other, under the theory of these contempt proceedings, which are really contemptible proceedings, because the judge ought to be above a proceeding for contempt." [24]

Judge Dunne handed down his decision at ten o'clock on Saturday morning, December 7, 1901. He held that "public officials, executive, legislative and judicial, have always been and always will be subject to criticism because of their official acts. It is one of the incidents and burdens of public life."

Furthermore, Judge Dunne agreed with Darrow's contention, "There is no good reason why a judge should have a different law applied to him than is applied to a president, a governor or a member of the legislature." [25]

The newspapermen were set free.

Unfortunately, Darrow's classic defense of freedom of the press is now largely forgotten. Its only record lies in the yellowed, brittle pages of the *Chicago American*, which published it originally.

5

Many stories circulate about Darrow. Some may be true and some are probably greatly exaggerated, but apocryphal or not, all illustrate how people saw him—the gadfly, the iconoclast, the fearless defender.

In another case before Judge Hanecy, the judge snapped at Darrow during his plea: "Your time is running." Darrow, unperturbed, pulled out his watch, looked at it, checked to hear if it was running, smiled, turned first to the judge: "Why, so it is, Your Honor," and then faced the jury. "Gentlemen of the jury: God created the world in six days, but no lawyer on earth could start to argue this case in ten minutes. When you get to your jury room, you can stay as long as you want to. You take your time; argue it out among yourselves; whatever you do will satisfy my client and me."[26]

In one of Clarence's earlier courtroom battles in Ohio, he was opposed by a bearded older attorney who continually referred to the young lawyer as "my beardless adversary." Clarence made no objection to the epithet. He waited until his summation to reply to it: "My opponent seems to condemn me for not having a beard. Let me reply with an anecdote: The king of Spain once entrusted a youthful liege with an important messaage to the court of a neighboring monarch. The neighboring monarch flew into a rage and cried, 'Does the king of Spain lack men that he sends me a beardless boy?'

"The young ambassador answered, 'Sire, had my king but known you imputed wisdom to a beard, he would have sent you a goat.'"[27]

Clarence won the case.

Busch, during his days as a court reporter, covered hundreds of trials in which the greatest advocates participated. All of them except one, he said, "placed their chief hope of success in the courtroom in a thorough pre-trial preparation and put but little reliance upon their inspiration to handle unexpectedly difficult situations. The exception was Darrow. Darrow's preparation might or might not be thorough depending upon the intricacies of the case, its importance, and his associates in the trial. Darrow, however, was a courtroom genius, and I have witnessed the repeated triumphs of that genius in the cross-examination of witnesses whose direct testimony came to him as a total surprise."[28]

6

In early March, Altgeld spoke at a mass meeting in Joliet, forty miles west of Chicago, on behalf of the Boers. He denounced Great Britain's treatment of the small South African country as another example of the strong taking advantage of the weak, but concluded on an optimistic note: "I am not discouraged. Things will right themselves. The pendulum swings one way and then another. But the steady pull of gravitation is toward the center of the earth." For forty-five minutes he held his audience spellbound and finished to enthusiastic applause, which followed him as he walked offstage. As he reached the wings he staggered and fell. [29]

At midnight Darrow was called to the bedside of his gravely ill friend. Before he arrived Altgeld was dead. Clarence brought the body of his beloved law partner and friend back to Chicago and made arrangements for the funeral on March 14, 1902. He and Jane Addams, whom the governor had long known and admired, spoke at the ceremony.

So important was Altgeld in Darrow's life that in his autobiography he inserted in its entirety his funeral eulogy, which began: "In the great flood of human life that is spawned upon the earth, it is not often that a man is born. The friend and comrade that we mourn today was formed of that infinitely rare mixture that now and then at long, long intervals combines to make a man. John P. Altgeld was one of the rarest souls who ever lived and died." [30]

7

In 1901, Alabama adopted a constitution typifying the South's determination to disfranchise the Negro. It set such standards for the right to vote as education, regular employment, ownership of property valued at $300, and a war record. That same year, out of 135 lynchings in the United States, 107 of the victims were black; Booker T. Washington's autobiography, *Up from Slavery,* appeared; and Darrow, long before the world heard the slogan "black is beautiful" and understood that the Negro must assume his rightful position as a human being, told a Negro audience in a black Chicago church that he rejected any plan for bettering the human condition which did not teach man "his own integrity and worth; you must make each man and each woman understand that they are the peer of any human being on earth." He was discouraged, however, about the ability of the white race to change. "When I see how anxious the white race is to go to war over nothing, and to shoot down men in cold blood for the benefit of trade . . . when I see . . . how the colored race is particularly subjected" to injustice and oppression, "I admit I am pessimistic."

He urged it on his audience that when white men insult blacks "on account of your inferior position they also degrade themselves when they do it. . . . You may be obliged many times to submit to this, but it must always be with the mental reservation that you know you are their equal, or you know that you are their superior, and you suffer the indignity because you are compelled to suffer it, as your fathers were once compelled to do; but after all, your soul is free and you believe in yourself, you believe in your right to live and to be the equal of every human being on the earth."[31] The "I Am Somebody" program among blacks could not have said it any more effectively in the 1970s than Darrow did in 1901.

Often Clarence recalled his own upbringing in the Western Reserve of Ohio, the effects on his childhood of growing up surrounded by abolitionists: of hearing about Garrison, Foster, Pillsbury, and others who gave their lives and their reputations to travel up and down the country agitating for the abolitionists' cause; and of John Brown "who loved the poor black workman" and struck a blow in defense of the Negro.

Like Dr. Martin Luther King, Jr., in the 1960s, Darrow too had a dream. Like King, he did not believe in the law of hate. He believed in the law of love. "I would like to see a time when man loves his fellow-man, and forgets his color or his creed. We will never be civilized until that time comes."[32]

8

Leon Czolgosz, a young Hungarian-American, joined the long line of admirers in the Temple of Music at the Pan-American Exposition in Buffalo, New York, September 6, 1901, waiting to shake the hand of President McKinley. As he approached the president, Czolgosz raised his right hand which appeared to be bandaged but in actuality concealed a revolver. He fired two shots, critically wounding the president, who died eight days later. Soldiers and Secret Service men immediately captured the assassin.

Though Czolgosz confessed he had been influenced by anarchist teachings, he insisted that he alone bore the responsibility for his act. The authorities attempted to implicate Emma Goldman and other "notorious" anarchists. "You wanted to help her in her work, and thought this was the way to do it," the authorities suggested to him. Despite Czolgosz's flat contradiction, "She didn't tell me to do it!"[33] Emma Goldman and Abraham Isaak, an anarchist editor, and his son and several other anarchists were arrested as police attempted to link them to the murder of the president of the United States.

The overwhelming hysteria that had engulfed the country immediately after the assassination had by now coalesced in a move to erase the anarchist "menace."

Darrow was in Hanover, New Hampshire, visiting his son Paul, a student at Dartmouth College. He had read a newspaper account of the arrests and knew that Jane Addams of Hull-House had visited Isaak in jail. Darrow hastily wrote to Addams praising her for the visit and expressing the belief that the anarchist editor was "perfectly innocent of any crime" and "in great danger of suffering" for his radical opinions, which "right or wrong are for the . . . improvement of the world.

"I never knew Emma Goldman," Darrow continued, "but there is not the slightest excuse for her arrest." Then Darrow used a line of reasoning which he had already begun some years earlier and which he would continue throughout his career—that although he did not want to get involved, he felt it was his duty and he had to ease his conscience. He said the same thing when he dropped his change in the beggar's extended cup: he was "buying 10¢ worth of relief" from his conscience.

He was reluctant to get into the fray of defending the Isaaks, but "I do not see anything else to do and shall not avoid what seems to me to be my duty. . . . I have no right to try to save myself when the injustice is so great as here. . . . It may be necessary for every friend of justice to use all our influence in every direction including raising money, for if they try to convict it will be a hard and dangerous fight under the law as it now exists."

He warned, "If a jury believes that a speech of Miss Goldman's . . . or a speech of mine or any other persons caused the shooting they can hold such persons guilty," and, he promised, "I shall be ready to do all I can for them."

He predicted, "I may be unduly alarmed but I feel that the powers of capital will try to stamp out all radical thought and utterances and will go to any length to accomplish it. Some lawyer not connected with the radical movement could do more to help them," he advised, "if we could only get such a lawyer, but it must be a good one and one with the wisdom of the serpent and the gentleness of the dove, and this is a rare combination—for lawyers."[34]

As it turned out, there was nothing to implicate the Isaaks, Goldman, and the other anarchists in the assassination, and they were released shortly. Darrow breathed a sigh of relief. He would be spared, even if briefly, the rigors of another page-one legal battle.

The execution of Czolgosz added fuel to Darrow's stand against capital punishment. Neither the prompt hanging of Prendergast, who had killed Mayor Harrison only a few years earlier, nor the swift execution in 1881 of Charles J. Guiteau for the murder of President James Garfield had deterred McKinley's assassin.

9

In the early 1900s, the great steel magnate Andrew Carnegie founded the Carnegie Institute with a gift of $40 million to encourage "investigation, research, and discovery, and the application of knowledge to the improvement of mankind."

Clarence thought the mere accumulation of such excessive wealth obscene, even though some of it eventually was directed to the public good. Troubled by the manner in which such wealth was attained, he never reconciled himself to the few having more than enough while the many could barely subsist. As he observed financial empires merge and enormous wealth become concentrated into fewer hands, he offered some unexpected—and unconventional—advice to the inmates of the Chicago Cook County jail on "legitimate" and "illegitimate" ways of robbery.

Invited by the warden to speak on crime and criminals, he watched as the prisoners marched into the jail's assembly hall, grumbling in the expectation of another boring sermon. Week after week the gray-uniformed men reluctantly listened to a priest, a minister, or a rabbi harangue them about their sinful ways and urge their redemption, their moral regeneration.

The man who stood before them this time, however, was not a clergyman but a prominent attorney. In his mid-forties, rumpled suit, a thick lock of hair carelessly falling over one eye, Darrow was the antithesis of the carefully groomed, righteous-speaking theologians who had preceded him at earlier lectures.

His opening remarks startled his listeners. "I really do not in the least believe in crime. There is no such thing as a crime as the word is generally understood."[35] The men leaned forward. The heresy continued. There is no distinction between the "real moral conditions" of the people in or out of jail. "[You in jail] can no more help being here than the people outside can avoid being outside." One thumb hooked into his galluses, the other hand extended to emphasize his thought, Darrow expounded his philosophy on crime and criminals acquired more than a score of years earlier when he first read Judge Altgeld's revolutionary book, *Our Penal Machinery and Its Victims*.

Like Altgeld, and like a vast group of forward-thinking penologists today, Darrow insisted that poverty and slums and lack of opportunity are the primary causes of crime, that the poor make up the vast majority of the prison population, that the causes of crime must be studied rather than ways of punishment. He argued that prison without rehabilitation is futile, that capital punishment as a means of alleviating crime is senseless and innately cruel.

"Be good" and you will "get rich and be happy," Darrow told the inmates, his deep voice with its slight rasp heavily laced with sarcasm. "Of course we know that people do not get rich by being good, and that is the reason why so many of you people try to get rich some other way, only you do not understand how to do it quite as well as the fellow outside."

Try the way of the Carnegies, the Morgans, the Rockefellers, or the gas trust and the beef trust, he advised. "They charge me one dollar for something that is worth twenty-five cents. . . .

"Some of you are here for obtaining property under false pretenses—yet I pick up a great Sunday paper and read the advertisements of a merchant prince—'Shirtwaists for 39 cents, marked down from $3.00.'"

The inmates laughed when he accused them of being less than "angels. . . . You are people of all kinds, all of you doing the best you can—and that is evidently not very well." They cheered when he suggested "there ought to be no jails," that there is only one way to cure crime and "that is to give the people a chance to live. If every man and woman and child in the world had a chance to make a decent, fair, honest living, there would be no jails and no lawyers and no courts." Jails "do not accomplish what they pretend to accomplish. If you would wipe them out there would be no more criminals than now. They are a blot upon any civilization, and evidence of the lack of charity of the people on the outside who make the jails and fill them with the victims of their greed."

With Darrow's concluding words the prisoners marched back to their cells, stunned at the barrage of unorthodox ideas hurled at them. "Too radical," complained one shocked listener to his bewildered fellow prisoners. "Much too radical." [36]

Darrow's friends agreed that the speech was too radical—for that audience. Such theories, they admonished him, should be voiced only to a very selective audience. When Darrow published his address, he wrote in the introduction, in a flash of whimsy, "Realizing the force of the suggestion that the truth should not be spoken to all people, I have caused these remarks to be printed on rather good paper and in a somewhat expensive form. In this way the truth does not become cheap and vulgar, and is only placed before those whose intelligence and affluence will prevent their being influenced by it." Quixotically the pamphlet sold for five cents.

Although time has dulled the shock of Darrow's remarks, his ideas seem quite contemporary as the last quarter of the twentieth century continues to struggle with the problems of law and order, punishment and rehabilitation, morals and ethics. His thinking is reflected seventy-five years later in a graffito scrawled on the outside of a former women's jail now housing a library in Greenwich Village, New York: "Prisons are the concentration camps of the poor."

VII

"Steadfast Champion of People's Rights"

1

ALTGELD'S death left Chicago's liberals and radicals disconsolate. Without his leadership the city seemed dimmed. Clarence, "lonely and dreary," missed his friend desperately. Altgeld's wise counsel and reasoned thinking had always had a sobering effect on the more impetuous, emotional Clarence. His "spiritual and intellectual son," the governor considered the younger man, and in truth he was just that.[1] Many of Clarence's ideological commitments had been born in Altgeld's thinking. They had fought the same battles: waged war together against capital punishment, chosen the same side in the Pullman struggle. They almost always regarded events from the same vantage point. Darrow loved having Altgeld in his office. He was soothed by the mere presence of his quiet, thoughtful friend. The governor's causes touched a responsive chord in Clarence's breast, and each time Altgeld set forth on a speaking engagement he left with Darrow's blessing.

Altgeld's memorial, as it is for most men, consisted of the battles he fought, and the few he won. The issue of municipal ownership of utilities in Chicago had been important to him, and he had crusaded vigorously for it. Spurred by his activities and those of many of the city's liberals, including the Socialists and Henry George's Single Tax group, a Voters League was organized to

secure the election of candidates for the state legislature who would be pledged
to this platform.

The league drafted Darrow, a prominent advocate of this policy, as the
candidate from the Seventeenth District, which included the Nineteenth
Ward where the Langdon Apartments, at 456 Desplaines Street, were located.
Roughly bordered by Van Buren Street on the North, Sixteenth Street on the
south, Laflin Street on the west, to a branch of the Chicago River on the east,
the district comprised an area of approximately fifteen square miles.

Illinois voting procedure elects three members to the state legislature from
each district; generally the majority party nominates two and the minority one.
Under this arrangement the voter can either cast his ballot for two of the
candidates or all three, or "bullet" his three votes to a single aspirant.

The prospect of being able to do something positive about municipal
ownership and adequate accident compensation, to which he was also
dedicated, appealed to Darrow. He turned to the Democratic party for slating.
He was on close personal terms with many of the Democratic leaders and
assumed they would honor his request once he agreed to run. But the
Democratic party had other ideas and other candidates in mind. "Too late,"
they turned him down. "We are already committed."

Having made up his mind to run for office, Darrow refused to allow this
setback to deter him. He filed a petition to run as an independent on a public
ownership platform, pledging himself to the initiative and referendum, public
ownership of public utilities, nomination by direct vote of the people, and
home rule for municipalities.

Darrow's attitude in seeking elective office was almost capricious. He seems
never to have wanted completely either of the two offices for which he ran. In
the 1896 election, when he was a candidate for the U.S. Congress, he spent
all his time traveling around Illinois for other Democratic candidates and made
no effort for himself in his own district. This time, in 1902, he eschewed the
conventional campaign rhetoric and told his listeners exactly where they stood
with him: "I told them why I was running, and that it was their fight just as
much as mine. I notified them that if elected I would not ask for a job for any
one or bestow any favors that I would not grant if I were not a member."[2]

The Democrats had slated a saloonkeeper and a minor politician; the
Republican side offered "a ward politician" and a young lawyer named Charles
Erbstein who would be associated with Darrow in a number of criminal trials.

On election eve, November 1, 1902, the *Chicago Daily News* endorsed
Darrow as a man of "great ability," adding that he would make an excellent
representative and urging the voters to "'plump' three votes for Darrow."
While the *Chicago Tribune* never endorsed him, three days before election it
predicted a Darrow victory.

When the returns were counted, the *Daily News* noted that "the independent vote made itself felt in Cook County."[3] Darrow captured 11,692 out of the 29,225 votes cast in his district. The two Republican winners received 6849 and 5282, respectively. Both the Democratic candidate who polled 4204 and the independent Erbstein whose votes totaled 1198 were defeated.

2

Six months earlier, in May 1902, 147,000 miners in the anthracite coalfields had gone out on strike, demanding a 10 to 20 percent increase in wages, an eight-hour day, and union recognition. A strike two years before had resulted in a 10 percent pay increase, but the settlement then had been influenced by Mark Hanna, industrialist and Republican party chairman, who convinced the operators that McKinley's election would be worth more than a 10 percent wage increase. The 1900 settlement, however, satisfied neither the operators nor the union. The operators, prepared for a long, determined fight to destroy every vestige of union power, resented the political pressure that had been exerted upon them. On the other hand, the miners won only a few of their demands and were denied union recognition. The final insult came in April 1901 when the operators extended the 1900 wage rate for another year, to April 1902.

In February 1902, John Mitchell, president of the United Mine Workers of America, invited representatives of the railroads and coal companies operating in the anthracite fields of Pennsylvania to a joint conference of miners and operators, the object of which would be "the formation of a wage scale for the year beginning April 1, 1902, and ending March 31, 1903."[4]

Within a week replies arrived. Typical was that of George F. Baer, president of the Philadelphia and Reading Coal and Iron Co.: "This company does not favor the plan of having its relations with the miners disturbed every year. The proposition to unsettle all the labor conditions of the various anthracite districts each year by holding a conference between persons who are not interested in the anthracite mining and cannot have the technical knowledge of the varying conditions at each colliery is so unbusinesslike that no one charged with the grave responsibility of conducting industrial enterprises can safely give countenance to it."[5]

The Philadelphia and Reading president further asserted that the experience of the operators since the 1900 agreement had been unsatisfactory. "There cannot be two masters in the management of business," he declared flatly and charged the issue of union recognition with creating a "divided allegiance."

Baer then detailed an analysis of the results of his company's 1901 operation which showed, he claimed, that the efficiency of his company's mines decreased one million tons because the contract miners worked only four and a half to six hours a day and the number of tons produced by each miner decreased from 11 to 17 percent.

W. H. Truesdale, president of the Delaware, Lackawanna, & Western Railway Company, went further than Baer when he advised Mitchell that the Delaware employees "are well satisfied with their present rates of wages, their hours of work, and the general conditions under which they perform their work for us. They are prosperous, contented, and we believe recognize that they have been fairly and equitably dealt with on all questions that have been brought to the attention of the management by representatives acting in their behalf."[6]

A letter from E. B. Thomas, board chairman of the Erie Railroad, New York, calculated that the miners' productivity between April and October decreased 12 percent; the mines suffered at least 102 interruptions of work because of unwarranted demands and agitation by members of the United Mine Workers.[7]

Four months later, with no solution in sight, President Theodore Roosevelt stepped into the impasse. In a precedent-shattering move, he asked Carroll D. Wright, commissioner of labor, to investigate "the causes and conditions accompanying the present controversy between the anthracite miners of Pennsylvania and the coal operators."

Baer was among the first to be interviewed by Wright. The mining president appeared sincere and thoughtful as he told Wright that "we honestly believe that, so far as we know ourselves, we are men of as good consciences and as great intentions as anyone; that we have the interests of labor more at heart, because we are brought in daily contact with it, and that we have the interest of business and the prosperity of the country more constantly before our eyes than all the members of the Civic Federation and the philanthropists put together. We can help to destroy the prosperity of the country by meeting the foolish demands of those who are asking for more than it is in our power to give." Baer imputed to the miners a lack of discipline since the last strike. He said that with the confidence of the union behind them they worked only when they pleased, and "we have no control over them."[8]

John Markle, of G. B. Markle & Co., representing the independent mine operators, insisted they could not be expected to arbitrate with "the Anarchist who, with torch in hand, goes through a street to burn up buildings," and "there is not a whit of difference" between what the anarchists do and what Mr. Mitchell's organization endeavored to do in the anthracite fields.[9]

The operators unanimously rejected the union's invitation to a conference. On March 14, 1902, they posted a notice at each colliery:

"The rates of wages now in effect will be continued until April 1, 1903, and thereafter, subject to a 60 days' notice.

"Local differences will, as heretofore, be adjusted with our employees at the respective collieries."

Again Mitchell requested a meeting "for purpose of discussing and adjusting grievances which affect all companies and all employees alike."[10] Again the operators declined to meet.

The union revised its original demands: now the miners offered to settle for a 10 percent pay increase and a 10 percent decrease in the working day. They also agreed to a binding arbitration, that is, to accept the decision of an arbitration board.

Rejected.

With all avenues to a settlement closed, the union's executive committee instructed union members to "abstain from working beginning May 12," when they would elect representatives to a convention opening May 14 to decide whether or not work should continue under the present conditions. Of the 811 votes cast at the convention, 461¼, or 57 percent, were in favor of a stoppage; 349¾ voted against.

With the vote, miners throughout the anthracite area left the work sites. As the strike spread, newspapers, usually on the operators' side, featured stories dramatizing the union's use of violence—stoning and dynamiting of scabs' homes, shooting nonstrikers on sight, blowing up buildings, creating a reign of terror in the anthracite region.

Mitchell fought the charges time and again. "It would appear that the men who constantly risk their lives working in the bowels of the earth were a lawless class," he said. "Statements of the burgess and chiefs of police prove that there have been less infractions of the law and fewer arrests during the time the strike has been in progress than for a like period preceding it."[11]

As in the Pullman strike, the union's leadership repeatedly warned its members against using violence, and although there were sporadic outbursts, generally there were few disturbances.

Inevitably, fear of a coal famine arose, and the price of coal jumped from $5 to $6 a ton to $15 to $20 in the Eastern cities. The 1902 off-year election was not far off. Senator Henry Cabot Lodge of Massachusetts advised President Roosevelt that there would be grave political consequences unless something were done about the strike before the first week of November.

The general tone of the operators replying to the union was offensive, and public opinion, which originally favored the operators, now turned against them. Baer's statements in particular were antagonistic and vindictive. Most of the clergy in the region, particularly the Catholic priests whose Church had the greatest membership, supported the strike. Newspapers across the nation became proponents of arbitration, as did the governor of Pennsylvania and some of its judges. The operators, adamant, refused to move from their antiarbitration stand.

Strikers hung scabs in effigy, ostracized nonstrikers, boycotted businesses and professional men who serviced nonunion workers, and publicized an "unfair list." President Charles W. Eliot of Harvard, although calling the scab an "American hero," also noted that as an educator he instinctively sympathized with any movement which would "uplift the race." He included labor unions in that category.[12]

As the cool days of the fall season arrived, hysteria gripped the country. The press urged President Roosevelt to appoint an investigative commission. The operators opposed government intervention and insisted they would never accept another compromise such as in 1900. But hospital and school coal bins began to empty. With anthracite coal the most widely used fuel for heating, the poorer people, especially those in the metropolitan areas, were in a particularly vulnerable position.

Conditions convinced the president he had to act, and on the first day of October he wired John Mitchell and the heads of the anthracite mining companies to come to Washington on Friday morning October 3 "in regard to the failure of the coal supply, which has become a matter of vital concern to the whole nation."[13] At the meeting in the nation's capital, the president reminded his guests that, of the three parties affected by the anthracite strike, "I speak for neither the operators nor the miners, but for the general public.

"As long as there seemed to be a reasonable hope that these matters could be adjusted between the parties it did not seem proper for me to intervene in any way," he explained. "I disclaim any right or duty to intervene in this way upon legal grounds, or upon any official relation that I bear to the situation; but the urgency, and the terrible nature of the catastrophe impending for a large portion of our people in the shape of a winter-fuel famine impels me, after much anxious thought, to believe that my duty requires me to use whatever influence I personally can bring to end a situation which has become literally intolerable."[14]

He urged "an immediate resumption" of the operations in the coal mines without delay as he appealed to the patriotism of the operators and the union and "to the spirit that sinks personal consideration and makes individual sacrifices for the general good."

Mitchell accepted first. Born into a mining family, he had gone to work in the mines at age twelve when he was one year under the legal age. Three years later he joined the Knights of Labor, a militant labor union. In 1894, when he was twenty-four, Mitchell walked out on strike with 125,000 miners at the call of the United Mine Workers. Fired when the strike ended, he went to work for the union, eventually rising to the presidency. At the meeting called by Roosevelt, the UMW president again offered to meet the operators in an attempt to adjust differences, but the operators remained adamant. Again Mitchell suggested that the president appoint a tribunal to arbitrate the strike and promised the union's willingness to accept a binding arbitration.

Baer read his response from a prepared text: between 15,000 to 20,000 men remain at work in the mines, he said, "and they are abused, assaulted, injured and maltreated by the United Mine Workers. There is a terrible reign of lawlessness and crime. The duty of the hour is not to waste time negotiating with the fomenters of this anarchy and insolent defiance of law."[15]

John Markle was next. He asked President Roosevelt "to perform the duties vested in you as the President of the United States, to at once squelch the anarchistic conditions of affairs existing in the anthracite coal regions by the strong arm of the military at your command."[16]

Truesdale reiterated his stand: he would resist and oppose and combat, physically and mentally, the objectives and purposes of the UMW. He asserted that one-sixth of the membership in this "illegal organization" were between the ages of fourteen and twenty, "their young, immature minds poisoned with the most dangerous, anarchistic, distorted, wicked views and errors concerning the rights of citizenship and property that any one can possibly conceive of; all taught the teachings and practice of the officers, organizers and apostles of the United Mine Workers' Association."[17]

Mitchell renewed his offer of arbitration. In reply to charges by the operators that the miners had so far during the strike committed twenty murders, he offered to resign if they could prove who the guilty miners were. "Mr. President, the truth of the matter is, as far as I know, there have been seven deaths, unfortunately. No one regrets them more than I do. Three of them were committed by the coal and iron police, and no one else has been charged with them. God knows the miners do not escape being charged with everything done there."[18]

When President Roosevelt placed the question of arbitration before the operators, they again unanimously answered, "No."

The strikers voted to continue the walkout until their demands were met.

3

The stalemate was not broken until ten days later when the mine operators, left with no choice but to accept arbitration, suggested to the president of the United States that he name a commission "to whom shall be referred all questions at issue between the respective companies and their own employees, whether they belong to a union or not, and the decision of that commission shall be accepted by us."[19] They further suggested that the commission include an officer of the engineer corps of either the military or naval service of the United States, an expert mining engineer experienced in the mining of coal and other minerals and not in any way connected with coal mining properties, a judge of the U.S. Court of the Eastern District of Pennsylvania, a prominent sociologist, and somebody actively involved in mining and selling coal.

Roosevelt acted immediately in gathering his nominations. He submitted a list of names which was immediately accepted by the operators: Brigadier-General John M. Wilson, U.S.A., retired, late chief of engineers, as the officer of the engineer corps; E. W. Parker, Washington, D.C., expert mining engineer; Judge Gray, Wilmington, Delaware, for judge of a U.S. Court; E. E. Clark, Cedar Rapids, Iowa, grand chief conductor of the Order of Railway Conductors of America, to fulfill the request for a sociologist (President Roosevelt assumed that for the purpose of such a commission the term "sociologist" meant somebody who thought and studied deeply on social questions and practically applied his knowledge); Thomas H. Watkins, Scranton, Pennsylvania, acquainted with the mining and selling of coal. He also added to the commission Bishop John L. Spalding, Peoria, Illinois, and Carroll D. Wright, commissioner of labor, who had made an earlier investigation at Roosevelt's request.

On October 16, 1902, President Roosevelt informed Mitchell of his nominations and requested union approval. "It is a matter of vital importance to all our people, and especially to those in our great cities who are least well off, that the mining of coal should be resumed without a day's unnecessary delay," the president urged.[20]

Events moved fast. On October 21, the union accepted the nominations and authorized Mitchell to represent them in the arbitration. Henry Demarest Lloyd, a lawyer for the miners, suggested to Mitchell that Darrow's sympathies toward labor and his experiences in both the 1894 Pullman case and the 1898 Kidd case made him an ideal chief counsel for the anthracite arbitration. Mitchell readily agreed. In the midst of campaigning for state representative, Darrow received the invitation to represent the United Mine Workers in arbitration proceedings. It was, he felt, impossible for him to pass up an opportunity to aid the union's cause.

The formal hearings of the commission opened in Scranton, Pennsylvania, on November 14, 1902. The eve of the first hearing heard the usual pronouncements from counsel on both sides. "It is going to be a fight to the finish," promised Darrow; David Wilcox, attorney for the Delaware & Hudson Co., vowed, "We intend to concede nothing."[21]

Attorneys for the nonunion miners appeared at the opening session requesting permission to present their side. Later in the hearings Darrow would scornfully accuse them of working for the operators, who had a battery of twenty-four lawyers on their payroll, including those representing the nonunion men.

In Darrow's workbook for the anthracite arbitration are included all the documents relating to the 1902 strike, both during the arbitration proceedings and preceding them. Darrow, who always spoke extemporaneously in his summations, used the workbook as a reminder. "Rebut," he scrawled in his loose-flowing, almost indecipherable handwriting after many of the prepared statements of the mineowners and their lawyers.

During the three months of hearings Darrow presented 241 witnesses to develop the union's case. Always sensitive to human suffering, he combined impersonal statistics with the human aspect of the controversy and dramatically led his witnesses to relate the horrors of life in the mines. A spectacle of pathos unfolded in the parade of witnesses: breaker children who never saw daylight as they picked the slate from the coal and breathed the foul air of the mines; wives and mothers who talked of illness and poverty.[22]

Twelve-year-old Andy Chippie, son of a miner killed in the Markle mine, went to work in the breaker before his legal age. In his childish voice he recounted how he was held liable for his dead father's $88.17 back rent, and instead of his wages of forty cents a day he received a rent-due statement with the balance outstanding.

According to the *Literary Digest,*[23] the story which aroused the most sympathy was that of Henry Coll, a fifty-year-old miner who worked for Markle & Co. Coll sat "aged and bent" on the witness stand, both face and hands scarred by falling coal.

"I worked for Markle & Co. for nineteen years and lived in one of the company houses until a few days ago, when I was evicted. My family consisted of my wife, my two adopted children, my own son, and my mother-in-law, who is said to be one hundred and two years old, and who has been blind many years."

"Were you ever hurt in the mines?" asked Darrow.

"Hurt? I haven't a whole bone in my body. My skull was fractured, an eye put out, and one leg is as bad as a wooden one.

"Once I was hurt so badly that I was laid up for a long time. The other miners contributed money, and Mr. Smith, the superintendent, gave $50. The money was all turned over to the company store and kept there to pay for my rent and groceries. All charges against me were deducted from the collection."

"You say you adopted 2 children?"

"Yes, one of them was the child of a miner who died on the same day that the mother was buried. He left 2 children. James Gallagher took one and I took the other. We couldn't see the little ones starve."

"When did you first know that you were to be evicted?"

"Well, I had a 6-day notice, but I could not believe that that would be enforced, for I had been there so long and I owed rent only during the strike; but one day Sheriff Jacobs came and told me that I would have to get out. I told him my wife was sick with tonsillitis and it would be dangerous for her to leave the house. I asked him for one day's time. He said he would see Mr. Markle, and started up the road. I saw him stop and speak to Mr. Markle, and then he returned and said: 'You can not have five minutes now.'

"My people were carried out. My old, blind, mother-in-law was carried down-stairs and taken by the deputies to a home 2 blocks away. My wife went out in the rain and tried to gather the household goods and pack them into barrels. It was raining and I was sure she would get worse, but I had to go to Hazleton and find a home for them. I found a house, such as it was, and I got my family into it, but my wife got worse.

"I didn't have money for a doctor and she wouldn't go to the Miners' Hospital. She got so bad that I finally arranged with a doctor. My wife and I were to see him, for we didn't have enough money to ask him to call. I gave him a dollar on account, but he gave it back to me. She grew worse and worse, and the other night she woke up and said: 'I'm choking.' I gave her some medicine, but she sprang to my arms, and while I looked she died." Coll's voice choked in sobs.

Judge Gray, who had been pacing up and down as the man told his story, turned sharply. "Died?" he asked.

"Yes, dead. I buried her yesterday." The old man's head dropped and he sat unable to speak for a minute. Then he added quietly, "And her mother may be dead now for all I know."

"That is all," said another defense lawyer, who had taken up the examination and stopped the testimony.

"Yes," said Judge Gray, "that is all, and it is enough."

Mitchell read a formal statement justifying the miners' demands for a 20 percent pay increase, a 20 percent reduction in the hours of labor without a reduction in earnings, a system by which coal "shall be weighed and paid for by weight wherever practical," and union recognition.[24]

Wayne MacVeagh, an attorney for the operators, tried time and again to get Mitchell either to endorse the violence and boycotting in the region during the strike or to condemn the local leaders and the union. Mitchell always replied, "In my judgement violence never contributed to the success of a strike. Our experience as an organization demonstrates conclusively that discipline can be maintained where trade agreements exist."[25]

So effective was Mitchell as a witness and so adept at parrying the questions during cross-examination that MacVeagh could not resist complimenting the UMW president: "You are the best witness for yourself that I ever confronted."[26]

4

As the hearing proceeded, Darrow, at Lloyd's suggestion, wrote to Louis D. Brandeis, a prominent Boston lawyer who fourteen years later became a U.S.

Supreme Court Justice. He asked Brandeis for help as "we have decided to make an aggressive move" and attack "the extortionate charges for anthracite freight rates as compared with bituminous; the legal and economic wrong in the union of mining and transportation; the relations of over-capitalization to low-wages, etc." He invited Brandeis to give this argument before the commission. Brandeis responded immediately. Although he would be pleased to confer with Darrow, without compensation "other than the satisfaction of having aided a good cause," he had a case assignment for trial and could not be in Scranton in time. Instead, he sent a "law memorandum" which he believed would be of some interest to the miners' attorney.[27]

Based on some of Brandeis's research, Lloyd requested permission from the commission "to complete our offer of proof that, through the natural monopoly of anthracite coal in these valleys, and the unnatural monopoly of mining, transportation, and marketing wages of labor and other conditions are unnaturally depressed. . . ." He wanted to discuss profits and exorbitant freight rates. The commission decreed such matters outside the scope of the inquiry.

The hearings continued until the Christmas break and resumed in Philadelphia on January 9, 1903, when the operators and the nonunion miners presented their case company by company. "We shall produce evidence showing that the whole coal region was in the control of the mob, especially in August and Sept., and was completely terrorized," promised the nonunion attorneys.[28]

5

The case against the union miners began.

John J. Williams, nonunion miner: "A big cobbler struck me in the back, knocking me down, and two shots were fired. Then I was struck in the head with a club and fell dazed."[29]

William Jenks, of Wilkes-Barre, swore he had been impaired for life when he was attacked by a mob and suffered the rupture of an artery in his left kidney. "The doctors tell me that I can never be well again, although I had never been sick in my life before."[30]

John Luckie, from Cooper Hill near Wilkes-Barre, said the strike ruined his business and he was forced to give up his butcher shop to take a job cleaning up around the breakers.

In cross-examination, Darrow tried to show that the railroads and mine operators paid Luckie's transportation and expenses to come to Philadelphia, but Judge Gray objected. The operators had a "perfect right to send witnesses here at their own expense if they so desired," he declared.[31]

George Fort, a docking boss in one of the Wilkes-Barre collieries, testified that the UMW at its Hazleton convention in 1901 ordered all docking and loader bosses to withdraw from the union.

Wiping his glasses vigorously, Darrow jumped to his feet: "How do you know that the Hazleton convention adopted such a resolution?"

"The district superintendent of the Lehigh Valley Coal Company told me so."

"He told you that unless you came back with your withdrawal card on a certain date you couldn't go to work, didn't he?"

"Yes, sir."

"Then you quit," shouted Darrow, "because your employer ordered you to, not because the union forced you to withdraw, didn't you?"

"Well, yes. I guess I did."

Mitchell explained to the commission that the resolution passed at the convention was not an order, but it was permission for the bosses to withdraw honorably if they so desired. "The reason for its adoption was that the operators had declared war on union bosses, and as they were not miners strictly speaking, the organization thought it wise to let them exercise their own discretion."

After listening to the explanation, Judge Gray observed, "That puts an entirely different construction on the evidence of this witness."[32]

The mineowners had built a major portion of their case upon wage tables showing averages earned over a period of years. In a few brief moments of carefully worked out strategy, Darrow demolished the evidence by exposing the data submitted as fictitious. His attack was swift and sure.

From time to time as he listened to hours of statistics being read off, he would voice a casual objection, but he saved his major attack for the final presentation when George Baer's company, the Philadelphia and Reading Coal and Iron Co., presented its figures.

With J. P. Jones, Baer's chief paymaster, on the stand, Darrow recalled that figures were to be given for seven collieries. "Do you know about the one you dropped out?" The question came in a dangerously low tone.

"I believe it shows the less average."

"It is one of the very lowest?"

"Yes, sir."

"And the three that you put in its place were three of the very highest, were they not?"

Jones consulted his papers. "They show very good averages, Mr. Darrow."

Now Darrow moved in, methodically and deliberately destroying the data. "There are thirty-seven collieries. We have here the five highest." Of the nine chosen to be used as models, Darrow thundered, "You have got seven above the average."

The witness stammered a weak excuse, but Darrow was not to be put off. "Mr. Jones, there are only four per cent of the men in Indian Ridge colliery who got as much money as you set down as the average earnings of the whole colliery, and ninety-six percent got less, is not that true?"

"I presume it is."

The commission impeached the wage tables of all the mines. Darrow had destroyed whatever credibility any of the data might have had.[33]

During the week of February 9, final arguments began, and the counsel for the various operators made their preliminary statements in a courtroom buzzing with noise and confusion. George Baer, prime spokesman for the operators, gave the closing summation in a talk lasting two hours and twenty minutes. An overflow crowd, including many of the city's most prominent citizens, jammed the court in anticipation of hearing Baer excoriate the union.

The *Chicago Daily News* whimsically exaggerated in its editorial page: "President Baer draws such a good crowd that the vaudeville managers may be after him presently."[34]

There was no sound as Baer read from a carefully prepared document in which he listed all the difficulties and expenses of operating a colliery. From time to time he would lay down the manuscript, look directly at his audience, and his voice would rise several octaves in outrage as he charged the union with violence and a lack of responsibility.

He said, "I think it is generally conceded that the marvelous progress of the past century is due to the general acceptance of the theory that under the action of individual liberty, maximum efficiency and justice would be secured. Political freedom and individual freedom have marched side by side. The individual was given free scope within sound rules of law to exercise all the powers he possessed to improve his condition and advance himself in life."

Calling Mitchell a "mistaken leader," Baer derided the eight-hour day, and opposed union recognition. "Ten hours is not an unreasonable length of time for man to work in the breakers of the anthracite coal fields." He maintained that the anthracite miners get "fair wages; that they compare most favorably with the general wages of the country, and that men willing to work honestly and exert themselves do earn, annually, sums in excess of the average."

And then, to the complete surprise of the defense and the commission, Baer reversed himself and proposed that the miners be paid on a sliding scale to be regulated by the price of coal. He offered an immediate increase of 5 percent retroactive from November 1, 1902, to April 1, 1903, after which the new scale would become effective. He vowed that wages would not fall below the present standard.[35]

"Why couldn't Baer have said so nine months ago?" asked the *Chicago Daily News*.[36]

Baer conceded that, in a dispute between capital and labor, it was commendable that the human race took the side of the weak against the strong. He would not find fault, he said piously, even though the criticisms against him were harsh.[37]

Several times while Baer spoke applause broke out, to be promptly suppressed by the chairman.

Baer's summation was as arrogant as his earlier response to a Wilkes-Barre citizen who had urged him to terminate the strike. His advice then was not to be discouraged because "the rights and interests of the laboring man will be looked after and cared for, not by the agitators, but by Christian men to whom God, in His infinite wisdom, has given the control of the property interests of the country."

In his anthracite workbook, Darrow pasted an undated clipping from an unidentified newspaper which questioned Baer's words under the headline,

IS PRESIDENT BAER GUILTY OF PLAGIARIZING FROM A KING?

The newspaper quoted the Socialist candidate for governor of Pennsylvania who cited a remarkable similarity in the sentiments and language of the Baer letter and those of George III of England at a time when the American colonists were talking about rebellion against the mother country. King George in 1775 said, "The rights and interests of the American colonists will be looked after and cared for, not by the agitators and rebels, but by the kind Christian gentlemen whom I, as the direct representative of God, have appointed to look after my lands in the Western World."

"George the Last" Darrow dubbed Baer in the margin alongside the clipping.

A newspaper editorial, commenting on Baer's summation, noted that "Mr. Baer omitted the 'divine right' argument this time."[38]

6

The crowd that gathered to hear Darrow's closing arguments was even larger than that for Baer, and hundreds had to be turned away. Lloyd wrote to his wife, "He began . . . with the sympathies of the Commission I thought, perhaps jealously, almost openly against him. But he closed with their undivided interest and admiration."[39]

A summation by Darrow had become a dramatic event as he employed his skills of persuasion. The cause of the miners became his own personal cause. Ordinary language turned to sheer poetry as he pleaded for an end to the scandal of children working in the coal mines, or lashed the operators with scorn for their indifference to the miners' hardships and poverty.

Despite Darrow's request not to be applauded because it distracted his attention, a request repeated again and again by Chairman Gray, outbursts of applause were "frequent and vigorous."

In his black, three-piece suit with bow tie, the lock of hair tumbling over his forehead, he began slowly, softly: "I have heard my clients, one hundred and forty-seven thousand workingmen who toil while other men grow rich, men who go down into the earth and face greater dangers than men who go out upon the sea, or out upon the land in battle, men who have little to hope for, little to think of, except work—I have heard these men characterized as assassins, as brutes, as criminals, as outlaws, as unworthy of the respect of men and fit only for the condemnation of the courts.

"I know that it is not true. . . .

"These are men, men like any others, men who, in the midst of sorrow, travail and severe and cruel crisis, demeaned themselves as nobly, as bravely, as loyally as any body of men who ever lived and suffered and died for the benefit of the generations that are yet to come. . . . I shall apologize for none of their mistakes, and excuse none of their misdeeds. But I do say it does not come well from their accusers to call them criminals. . . .

"Gentlemen," he said, ". . . you can do just as you please about recognizing the union. If you do not recognize it, it is because you are blind and you want to bump up against it some more. It is here. It is here to stay."[40]

In the Haywood murder trial, four years later, he again warned, "Don't be so blind, don't be so foolish as to believe you can strangle the Western Federation of Miners when you tie a rope around his neck. Don't be so blind in your madness—as to believe that when you make three fresh new graves you will kill the labor movement of the world."[41]

The operators, Clarence said in the anthracite hearings, are smarter than the miners, they say so themselves, and counsel for the miners will admit it. "They have got all sorts of advantages of us. Their social advantages are better, their religious privileges are better, they speak the English language better. They are not children. They can hire good lawyers and expert accountants, and they have got the advantages of us in almost every particular, and we will admit all that."

"Except the lawyers," murmured the chairman, looking directly at the defense attorney.[42]

"Oh, they have got the advantage there. We are not worrying so much about the lawyers as we are about the commission."

Darrow accused Baer of willfully fomenting the strike. "The man more responsible than any other [for the strike] comes before this commission and says the operators will do exactly that which these men demanded nine months before, and which he and his companions, in their blindness, their ignorance, and their stupidity refused. Why did not Mr. Baer go to Mr. John Mitchell nine months ago as he came to the commission today?"[43]

He spoke of his own dreams: "A universal republic, where every man is a man equal before his Maker, governor of himself, ruler of himself and the peer of all who live; where the work of the trade union is done and trade unions have melted and dissolved. And I love trade unions, because I believe they are one of the greatest agencies that the world has ever known to bring about this time." [44]

He summarized: "This contest is one of the important contests that has marked the progress of human liberty since the world began."

He had used a similar approach in the Debs case: "This is a historic case," he said then, "which will count much for liberty or against liberty."

To Darrow, history was the story of a constant struggle for human freedom: always two sides pulling in opposing directions—one holding to the status quo, the other working toward social and economic progress.

Darrow spoke for more than eight hours. At his conclusion the commission temporarily suspended the session since the enthusiastic applause gave no indication of subsiding. Spectators crowded around the labor defender to offer congratulations. [45]

Lloyd would write to his wife: "Many of the capitalist women were quite carried away. One confided to Darrow, 'I am convinced now if never before.'" [46]

The *Philadelphia North American* called Darrow's summation "the very blood and marrow of the claims and evidence presented by the Mine Workers" and "one of the most remarkable that has been heard in recent years." [47]

And a *Chicago Daily News* columnist commented wryly in retrospect, "If President Baer thought that by conceding everything he could head off Darrow from making a speech he does not know Darrow." [48]

The commission went into executive session to study the more than ten thousand pages of transcript and the vast number of exhibits and statistics. On March 18, 1903, it delivered its report to President Roosevelt, a report which recommended a 10 percent pay increase, a nine-hour workday with the same wages as paid for a ten-hour day prior to April 1902, and overtime in excess of nine hours in any day to be paid at "a proportional rate per hour." [49] The commission, however, did not "consider that the question of the recognition of the United Mine Workers is within the scope of the jurisdiction conferred upon it." [50]

"The men have not got all they ought to have had, but they certainly have won a notable victory," commented Lloyd. [51]

The *United Mine Workers Journal* voiced the thinking of most labor people: "A good decision" despite the lack of union recognition.

In historical terms, the anthracite arbitration hearings set a precedent for government to become directly involved in labor-capital disputes. Never before had a United States president brought these two forces together in compulsory and binding arbitration.

7

The practice of the law alone was never sufficient for Darrow. His interests were broad, his energies endless. On many occasions when he had a free evening or Sunday he slipped away from the pressure of commission work to speak to a small group on such topics as Tolstoy, Whitman, literature, or Omar Khayyám.

"Not all the world is beautiful, and not all of life is good," he would lecture on literature to an enthralled audience of Jews or Russians or blacks. "The true artist has no right to choose the lovely spots alone and make us think that this is life. He must bring the world before our eyes and make us read and learn. As he loves the true and noble, he must show the false and bad. . . . He must think, and paint, and write, and work, until the world shall learn so much and grow so good, that the true will all be beautiful and all the real be ideal." [52]

Once, during the anthracite hearings, Philip Edward Mosely, secretary of the Interstate Commerce Commission, and Kellogg Durland, social worker, went to hear Darrow speak on Tolstoy. They had heard of his power as an orator, but they were determined not to be swayed by him.

Tolstoy, said Darrow, found "no refuge in blind creeds, whether of the church or state. He boldly stood in the clear light of day, with his feet upon the earth, unbound by the traditions of the world in which he lived, and took counsel of his conscience and his judgment and of nothing else." [53]

Mosely and Durland sat stonefaced for more than an hour as people all around them interrupted frequently with enthusiastic applause. "Suddenly I found myself making as much noise as anyone else," Durland confessed. "Glancing at Mosely, I saw that he was clapping his hands together with great vim. Our eyes met, and we laughed sheepishly." [54]

8

Another development in Darrow's professional life occurred during the anthracite hearings. A group of Chicagoans—friends, labor people, news-papermen, many representatives of the Altgeld forces—came to Philadelphia to urge Darrow to run for mayor of Chicago in the coming election against the incumbent Mayor Carter Harrison, who was expected to run for a fourth term.

The boom had started about a year earlier when the *Chicago Tribune*, immediately after Clarence's overwhelming victory for state representative, reported, "A union labor party which will come out in support of Clarence S.

Darrow as an independent candidate for mayor next spring has been launched."[55] Darrow, however, rejected the proposed candidacy. His ready response to those who pressed him to run was that not only was he not interested but he had too many radical ideas to stand any chance of being elected. The Socialist party, slating its own candidate, discouraged him. The party claimed that those who were promoting him needed his political prestige in order to make a respectable showing in the mayoralty election. Darrow's supporters, the Socialists charged, were trying to destroy the Socialist movement, since many voting for Darrow would otherwise vote the Socialist ticket.[56]

The Draft Darrow for Mayor movement quieted down briefly, only to revive with his success at the anthracite hearings. By the time the victorious attorney returned to Chicago, the movement had advanced astonishingly among the working class and the radicals. Darrow for Mayor buttons, made up by a group of his followers, were widely distributed.

Labor sponsors of the welcome-home meeting at which Darrow, Lloyd, and Mitchell would speak became worried that the evening might turn into a political rally rather than an expression of thanks to the champions of the miners. More than five thousand people showed up in near-zero weather to welcome them. The orchestra played "The Star-Spangled Banner." Thunderous applause and a sea of waving hats and handkerchiefs greeted the heroes as they appeared on the stage of the Auditorium.

Lloyd spoke first. Recalling the tumultuous welcome given to Debs when he returned from his six-month imprisonment at Woodstock, he compared the difference between the Debs celebration in the "dim and dingy" old Battery D armory and this one at the Auditorium, "the finest and largest assembly room in America." He commented on the change in public opinion which at one time held the worker solely responsible for a strike.

He paid homage to Darrow. At the side of Debs and at the side of Mitchell, Lloyd said, "stood the same steadfast champion of rights of the people, Clarence S. Darrow, that rare bird, a lawyer whose first love is love of justice, and who remains true to his first love."[57]

Cries of "our next mayor," "Darrow for mayor" rose in a crescendo of applause throughout the Auditorium. Darrow paid no heed to the chanting as he went directly into the purpose of the meeting.

"We are here tonight to congratulate Mr. Mitchell, his associates and ourselves on the great struggle, the greatest industrial struggle the world has known." The miners, he said, "looked starvation squarely in the face and entered in the greatest conflict which industry has ever seen and they have won. They won not by their own strength for they were weak and poor. If they had been unaided by their fellow workmen and fellowmen throughout the United States, the whole valley would have been turned into a howling wilderness within 30 days."[58]

Referring to the conditions in the anthracite regions, Darrow pointed out that the mine operators were the masters, the miners the servants. The miners saw in John Mitchell "the first ray of light in their dark lives."

Darrow the agitator never missed an opportunity to espouse the cause of trade unionism. The problems in the mines and the problems of capital versus labor could be met only by the organization of workingmen. "Labor unions are by no means perfect. They, too, are monopolistic and good is not always found there. But it is the greatest instrument for the upbuilding of character. The labor union is not the last step. It is not the ideal but the instrument helping toward the ideal. There will be a time in the destiny of the human race when the home of the dreamer will be realized, a time when there will be no unions, when they have done their work. We are living in a state of war, with capital on one side and labor on the other."

This credo became part of the preamble of the Industrial Workers of the World founded two years later and supported by Darrow. "The working class and the employing class have nothing in common."

The labor union will have concluded its work, Clarence told the cheering audience, when there are "no longer rich and poor, no longer master and slave. Then will men be neighbors in universal brotherhood—the fondest dream of all in the interest and good of all."

Mitchell, a "pure and simple trade unionist," lacked the vision and revolutionary fervor of Darrow. He saw trade unions as raising "the standard of our manhood, of our womanhood, and of our childhood." Labor and capital "can sit down together in honest conference and tell the truth," and Mitchell believed, idealistically, that conflicts could be settled amicably.

The reception over, Darrow was again pressed to announce his availability as a mayoral candidate. "I am going to look the situation over and then I will know what to do," he told his friends as he boarded a train for Springfield to be sworn in as a state legislator. Maybe when he came back to the city he would have a definite statement, he said, but at the present time he had nothing to say. "My friends are coming to me today in large numbers and I am getting much information. I certainly feel gratified at the consideration shown me," and he promised to listen to all who wanted to talk to him.[59]

9

For more than a week Darrow listened and considered the candidacy. Then came the announcement: He would not run for mayor. The statement surprised every political circle in Chicago. The local labor men, especially, were shocked and disappointed. They had regarded Darrow's candidacy as a certainty.

The *Chicago Daily News* approved his decision. "Mr. Darrow has done right in recognizing the obligations that rest upon him to do his best in the public position which he holds.

"It is to be supposed, furthermore, that Mr. Darrow realized that some of the influences which were exerted to induce him to become a candidate for mayor were more interested in making a tool of him for the injury or aid of other candidates than in helping him to get elected," the paper noted perceptively.[60]

It is possible that Darrow, too, recognized he was being used. Certainly the labor movement was split over his candidacy, and the Socialist leaders opposed it. Despite his explanation, other factors played an important role in his final decision. His ego never took too kindly to losing. Although he was tempted by the mayoralty and found it hard to turn down the possibility, he certainly understood the strength of the competing Mayor Harrison forces. The odds, he realized, were not in his favor, even though some Democratic party stalwarts had endorsed him.

Insisting that his decision was irrevocable, Darrow left for Springfield where, on February 18, 1903, he became a member of the Illinois House of Representatives, sworn in by Justice Carroll E. Roggs. Members of both the Republican and Democratic parties applauded as he took the oath.

The most important lesson Clarence learned in Springfield was that an independent cannot succeed—he can help to kill bad bills by battling vigorously and aligning the publicity on his side, but there is no way that a lone legislator can get a bill passed.[61]

He took responsibility for the passage of only one law—to raise the limitation on the amount of recovery for deaths caused by negligence. Originally the law imposed a $5,000 limit, but the cost of living had increased since then, and "I introduced a bill to remove the limitation, leaving it in the hands of the jury. When I offered the bill, the grafters pledged their support but I knew better. I had never intended to leave the amount open." He eventually amended the bill to a maximum of $10,000 and it passed. Darrow would note in his 1932 autobiography that "the cost of living has so greatly increased that the amount should again be raised."[62]

During his two years in the legislature he also helped pass the Municipal Ownership Bill, as he had promised, and the Child Labor Law. He always tried, sometimes successfully, to kill those bills that increased penalties and defined new crimes.

They were lonely days and nights for him in Springfield. "Come *down please*. Come down and stay over two trains," he pleaded with Henry Demarest Lloyd. "I am very lonesome without having seen you for so long and then I am rather blue."[63]

He was relieved when his term ended.

10

While Darrow was still a state legislator, word filtered into the United States of a particularly heinous massacre of Jews at Kishinev, in the south Russian province of Bessarabia. Early in April 1903, for three days and two nights a wild mob unrelentingly attacked the Kishinev Jews. Aided by the local police and the militia, the pogromists tortured and murdered them: babies were torn apart, men butchered, women mutilated, and girls raped. Police deliberately handed over to the crazed rioters Jews who defended themselves. Attempts by Jews to get aid from the czar's government were frustrated as operators of the state-owned telegraph wires refused to send the distress messages. Eventually, a wire did go through from a railroad station far from Kishinev, and within thirty-six hours "as if by magic murder and robbery ceased at once."[64]

Anti-Semitism, as manifested at Kishinev, was fostered by the local government. Leaders of the mob included scores of "distinguished government officials," professionals, students, and the son of a prominent judge. The casualties of the three-day massacre totaled between 45 and 60 dead; more than 600 seriously injured; between 1500 and 1600 shops and buildings damaged, looted, and destroyed; 2000 families homeless; and 12,000 homes ruined.

On April 18, 1903, almost a thousand people jammed the Star Theater in Chicago, a few blocks from Hull-House, to protest the massacre. Jane Addams, Darrow, and Peter Sissman, who a decade later became Darrow's law partner, headed the rostrum of featured speakers.

Miss Addams told the meeting, "We are here to express our disapprobation of Russia's cowardice in failing to protect her citizens from massacre. Perhaps the saddest part of this all is that it has broken down the sentiment that all over the world was leveling ranks and obliterating race prejudice."

Darrow often voiced protest against disabilities imposed on blacks, against lack of civil liberties for dissenters, against injustice to labor. Now, the Kishinev atrocities aroused his ire. He not only condemned what happened in Russia but took a world overview and charged the United States with prejudice. He said the czar could, if he wanted, point to the burning and lynching of Negroes and to discrimination against Jews not through the nation's laws but by its tolerance of prejudice. "Were Rockefeller or Morgan a Jew, we would rally against them, finding their personal flaws as racial flaws."[65]

"Jews are derided not only in Russia, but Chicago and all over the United States. There is no apologist in all the land for those who committed the massacres. The U.S. can do nothing to halt this persecution of Jews in Russia: the one weapon at hand is moral suasion. Even from this calamity some good may come." Darrow, the pessimist with hope, suggested, "The Jew may be better treated and better appreciated in the time that is to come." [66]

He never admitted, however, that the establishment of a homeland for the Jews might be the answer. Twenty-four years later he debated the issue of Zionism with Rabbi Stephen S. Wise, who argued that Jewish nationalism was more than a reaction to anti-Semitism.

The case for Zionism, said Rabbi Wise, is found in the discovery by Jews in the last three decades of the nineteenth century "that a people which has no home of its own, is welcome nowhere; that in order that a people may enter in the full heritage of life, together with all other peoples, it must have a home, it must have a center, it must have a country of its own; it must live and think and feel in the terms of freedom and self-determination, the things for which you and I bled and fought during the years of war." [67]

In the whimsical style which enchanted audience and juries, Darrow responded that if Zionism is good for the Jews, well and good. As far as he was concerned, he didn't think it was. He displayed a lack of prophetic vision when he dismissed Palestine's potential as an agricultural or industrial land, and observed that "the Jews are not given to cultivating the soil, even if it is good land, but they are too smart to want to dig it there."

He questioned the practicality of establishing a Jewish homeland in Palestine. "I have many friends who are Zionists. I think a great deal of them. I love the idealist. I cannot help being a dreamer myself. Neither can I help waking up. It would be all right to dream if you were not obliged to wake up.

"Some of these men . . . I don't know one of them that I don't like because I know it has an idealistic reason back of it, I know it, Rabbi Wise is an idealist, several of the Jews, my friends in the city, are idealists—they all are—but when you go out to raise money from a great number of people, millions and millions, for a proposition that is absolutely impossible, a proposition which goes against space and time and the laws of nature, I tell you, you cannot do it, and many of you will be bound to regret that you ever undertook such a foolish thing."

Rabbi Wise answered, "Instead of mocking tonight the passion of a people who believe they must have a home, they want a home, most of them, they have no place to live. . . . They are homesick. From all over the world they are saying . . . 'I am going home; I am going home.' . . .

"The Jews made Palestine the land of fulfillment. It is still the land of promise," insisted Rabbi Wise.

Persecuted peoples were Darrow's business. Again in 1933 he would voice his protest against the persecution of Jews, this time in Germany under

Hitler. He was not as optimistic as he had been in 1903. "There is one thing that seems to have been made pretty clear by this terrible movement against the Jews, originating in Germany and closing, I don't know where. I don't know that it will ever end. So far as I can read, and understand about the Jews, they have been persecuted by almost all people on the face of the earth! And still, they have lived through it, and perhaps have been stronger. But it is a terrible test for any people to go through!

"Mr. Hitler is not the only man who has engaged in the laudable purpose of persecuting the Jews!" he sarcastically told a forum at the Washington Boulevard Temple in Chicago. "The thing which shocks me and the rest of the world is that at this stage of life, when many people have thought that human beings were growing more intelligent, when we believed that men and women were broader and more understanding and more liberal, there should come a man with the power and strength to make a warfare upon a race out of the clear sky; and the most destructive warfare, as I read of it, that has ever been carried on against the Jew!"

He recalled his first experience with Jews, more than sixty years ago, in a little country town. "We seldom saw one; that, I believe, is why we didn't like them. I happened to be born in a family which had no religious prejudices, and who believed in freedom for all men, but I heard the same stories at school that all the other children heard. I came to look upon them the same way. It was a long time before I . . . knew the debt that civilization owes to the Jews! It was a long time before I knew the debt that liberality and freedom owe to Jews! You don't need to leave your seat to find that out. You can test it anywhere! Let any meeting be announced, in any part of Chicago or New York, or any big city in the United States, when a body of people are called to protest against injustice and wrong; where they are called upon to unite for liberty; and you will find that meeting is largely made up of Jews! And it makes no difference whether they are protesting for a Jew or a Gentile; whether they are protesting for a Socialist or for a Communist, you will find them there and everywhere raising their voice for freedom. And if we took them out of our community there wouldn't be anything left in the way of protest meetings in this country. They are strong in every organization that stands for human liberty. They are strong in every movement for freedom."

Stressing that the Jew has stood not only for freedom of the Jew but for all men, Darrow told a cheering audience, "I would hate to see the Jews banished from the country in which I may ever live." The last people to betray freedom would be the Jews: "In every great cause for human liberty, they have always fought, not only in the case for human liberty, but in the cause of equality. They have stood against wealth and power and influence, and stood for the common man. That is why I am for them! That is why I know we need them! That is why I know the world needs them."[68]

Again, as in his Kishinev speech, he looked upon anti-Semitism as part of a worldwide illness. As long as injustice prevails against a people or any religion, no one is safe, he insisted. It was this world theme that governed Darrow's lack of interest in Palestine as a homeland for the Jews and his conviction that Zionism was not the answer.

VIII

"I Cannot Find Time to Write"

1

THE decade surrounding the turn of the century witnessed Chicago's greatest flowering. The city of incredible vices and virtues throbbed with cultural ferment as it became a mecca for social and cultural movements. The architecture of Louis Sullivan, Dankmar Adler, Frank Lloyd Wright, Daniel Burnham and John Root, and others led the country in bold and original design. In 1882 the skyscraper was born here: the ten-story Montauk Block, set on a newly conceived foundation of concrete and steel railroad ties. From this beginning developed the era of the skyscrapers, which included, in Chicago, the sixteen-story Unity Block built in 1892 by John Peter Altgeld.

The city grew fast, and if the new structures sometimes rose next to wood-planked sidewalks, few objected. In due time, concrete would replace the wood. The shanties and the other dull, undistinguished buildings clustered around the new architecture would soon be demolished and replaced with walls of stone.

The finest journalists in the country appeared in the pages of such daily Chicago newspapers as the *Tribune, Daily News, Inter-Ocean, Evening Post,* and the *Record.* There were Eugene Field and George Ade and the young

Theodore Dreiser. Finley Peter Dunne, the political satirist, mocked both the national and the local scenes in his Mr. Dooley series.

Literature was nourished by fictionists like Opie Read, Hamlin Garland, Frank Norris, Floyd Dell, Henry Blake Fuller, George Barr McCutcheon, and Edith Wyatt, and by the poets Harriet Monroe, Wallace Rice, and William Vaughn Moody. Theodore Thomas led a first-rate symphony in the acoustically perfect Auditorium until his death in 1905 when Frederick Stock took up the baton in the newly constructed Orchestra Hall. Lorado Taft exemplified the sculpture of the city. Paderewski, Melba, Hofmann came to perform before small but appreciative audiences.

Chicago burgeoned from the Renaissance-styled Art Institute, with its old masters and "moderns," to Jane Addams's Hull-House, where the highest principles in settlement work made it a center for social reform; from the new University of Chicago to the Essanay Studios, a brash gamble at putting together film in which the characters seemed to be moving—"movies," bringing Charlie Chaplin, Gloria Swanson, Wallace Beery to the whole country.

Audiences thrilled to a myriad of theater offerings—from *The Merchant of Venice* to *Charley's Aunt*. Julia Marlowe and Lillian Russell came to perform, and the Barrymores, Drew, and Eddie Foy.

The bold innovations of Chicago's industrial giants had created a glorious metropolis soon after the immense destruction left by the 1871 fire. There was no peace in the new Chicago, no repose, only a tremendous vitality that coursed through the city and gave it many faces—surely sensual and crude and grasping, but also intellectual and sensitive and imaginative.

Beyond the elegant confines of tree-lined Michigan Avenue and Prairie Avenue were poverty and misery, sweatshops and child labor, and labor unrest. The caldron simmered, periodically erupting.

The White City Club on the South Side was one of the small intellectual oases that had begun to proliferate throughout the city. Its membership roster included many of the creative talents of Chicago—writers, artists, sculptors, musicians. After repeatedly declining invitations to speak there, Clarence finally agreed to read his essay on Omar Khayyám. For him the Persian poet— so often seen as licentious and imprudently daring—was a fellow social critic who believed that "the so-called sins of men were not crimes, but weaknesses inherent in their being and beyond their power to prevent or overcome." [1]

Clarence, raising his voice in the human cry for love, sympathy, and understanding, believed, as Omar had, that "every jail, every scaffold, every victim—is a monument to . . . cruelty and blind unreasoning wrath," [2] and he used Khayyám's *The Rubáiyát* to rage against prevalent ideas of crime. The lawyer and the poet each accused the world of a lack of social responsibility and jabbed at its bigotry and oppression. "There was then, as now," said

Darrow, "the master with all the false luxury that idleness could create in that land and time; there was also, as to-day, the hopeless slave, whose only purpose on the earth was to minister to the parasite and knave; and both of these, master and man alike, were helpless prisoners in the schemes and devices, the machinery and inventions, the worthless appendages and appliances that bound and enslaved them, and that have held the world with ever increasing strength to the present day."[3]

He finished to applause, with the audience rising to its feet. As many gathered around him at the lectern, he spied his friend John R. Gregg, creator of the shorthand system, coming toward him. With Gregg were his wife and an attractive young woman whom they introduced to him as Ruby Hammerstrom. The meeting was not particularly momentous: the customary "pleased to meet you," but something about the auburn-haired Ruby captured Clarence's fancy—a vivaciousness that he found stimulating and exciting. He wanted to see her again. She refused. As the weeks passed, she continued to resist his importunings.

Women. There were many in his life who desired his favors. He enjoyed each one as he relished his freedom from marriage. Many women courted him with an eye to becoming the second Mrs. Darrow, but Clarence would not be corraled.

Ruby's elusiveness intrigued him. He could not know that she had fallen in love with him that first night, or that she was engaged to a New York stockbroker. Clarence's personal reputation, too, was no secret. Coming from a very religious, conventional background, sixteen years younger than Clarence, she was far removed from the radical, dissident freethinkers with whom he was now associated, and he was vocal about his intention never to marry again.

Eventually she agreed to meet him for dinner with Mrs. Gregg. The forty-two-year-old lawyer, witty, urbane, put himself out to impress her. Soon her engagement was broken, but four years passed before they were married. Occasionally her work as a writer for the Chicago Evening Post took her out of the city, but more often it was his travels that separated them. He spent months in Philadelphia and Scranton at the anthracite miner arbitrations, then back and forth to Springfield during the two years there as a legislator.

Just before the marriage license bureau closed on Saturday morning, July 16, 1903, Francis Wilson, with whom Clarence still shared an apartment in the Langdon, in order to avoid publicity arranged to obtain a license for Clarence and Ruby. Wilson and Ruby's brother were the witnesses as they went before Judge Edward Dunne who, with little fanfare and minus the conventional "for better or for worse" and "until death do you part," pronounced them Mr. and Mrs. Clarence Seward Darrow.

Since Ruby's parents were vacationing in Europe, the Greggs arranged a quiet champagne wedding breakfast for the newlyweds, after which they raced to the Englewood station on the South Side to board a three o'clock train for Canada on the first lap of their trip to Europe, leaving a chagrined press corps waiting in vain for interviews at the Union Station downtown. [4]

The honeymoon took them to Toronto, Montreal, and Quebec, where they boarded a small freighter for Europe. While the hero of the courtroom suffered spell after spell of seasickness, which kept him in his berth most of the time, Ruby read aloud to him Thomas Watson's *The Story of France*. Once ashore, they visited England, Holland, Germany, Austria, Switzerland, and France, and returned to the States, sailing from Liverpool, nearly three months later.

2

It was on their honeymoon that Clarence completed *Farmington*, a fictionalized autobiographical account of his youth. A nostalgic portrait of a small town seen through the eyes of a child, it is pure Americana and as much a slice of mid-nineteenth century America as Mark Twain's *Adventures of Huckleberry Finn* and *The Adventures of Tom Sawyer*. Underlying its 277 pages, however, is the deep pessimism that Darrow never could throw off.

The book ends with the poignant confession: "All my life I have been planning and hoping and thinking and dreaming and loitering and waiting. All my life I have been getting ready to begin to do something worth the while. I have been waiting for the summer and waiting for the fall; I have been waiting for the winter and waiting for the spring; waiting for the night and waiting for the morning, waiting and dawdling and dreaming, until the day is almost spent and the twilight close at hand." [5]

Farmington recalls that children's lives for generations, until emancipated by the more permissive spirit of the 1950s and 1960s, were dominated by "don'ts" and "nos." When the game became most exciting, there was the call to come home: "time to eat," "time to study," "time to clean up." Parents were always saying "no" when at least sometimes they could have said "yes." Even when it came to desserts, Clarence complained, the custom was to eat it last. He could never understand why the pie could not be eaten first, why he should challenge fate and the possible change of his taste buds. What if he should die suddenly and thus be denied the best part of the meal?

Abe C. Ravitz, in his book *Clarence Darrow and the American Literary Tradition*, suggests that *Farmington* is a forerunner of Sherwood Anderson's *Winesburg, Ohio*, and the series of "books which erupted in the early 'twenties and drew attention to the anti-village school, whose celebrated leaders Sinclair Lewis and Zona Gale penned major contributions (*Main Street* and *Faint Perfume*) to establish the popularity of this thematic concern." [6] Oscar Cargill, too, believed *Farmington* is part of "the revolt from the village." [7]

Darrow's book, however, is both a love letter to his childhood and a much more complex indictment of the "prejudices and conventions" inherent in the environment of the nineteenth-century small towns. *Farmington* received little recognition from the reading public; most reviewers dismissed it as a "charming" sketchbook. But it is much more than that. Its carefully drawn characters offer an insightful assessment of warped lives, unfulfilled dreams, quiet despair. Darrow understood "that the smaller the world in which we move, the more impossible it is to break the prejudices and conventions that bind us down." [8]

Whereas Mark Twain's classics of boyhood are books of action, *Farmington* is philosophical. With poetic appeal and sensitivity, Darrow exposes himself in depicting the influences that shaped his dreams. It is again Darrow's proclamation that man is shaped by forces over which he has no control. Asked how close to autobiography *Farmington* was, Darrow replied, "Pretty close. . . . Anyway I have given a picture of my father there." [9]

A review in the prestigious *Dial* said that *Farmington* "is a book for boys, for women—but above all, it is a book for men who have once been boys." [10] A modern critic has called the book "the heart and soul of Darrow; a portrayal of the early influences of his life." [11] Irving Stone in his Darrow biography describes *Farmington* as "perhaps the only one of his dozen books which achieves the artistic symmetry and perfection for which he longed." [12]

Hamlin Garland, novelist, dramatist, and critic, had urged Darrow to rewrite *Farmington*. Garland felt that, though the book's theme was "great," Darrow had not "made the fullest use of it." Darrow rejected the idea. "My time is so taken by other work that I cannot find time to write the books I have in mind." Garland was convinced, however, that a rewrite of *Farmington* would be "worth more than all" Darrow's work in defense of "criminals and fools." [13]

3

Returning from their honeymoon, Clarence and Ruby stayed for several weeks at the Victoria Hotel on Michigan Boulevard where they hosted many of Clarence's "bewildered friends," who found his marriage an irony and could not forget how insistently he had professed the delights and advantages of free love. From the Victoria, Clarence and Ruby moved back to the Langdon, adding to Clarence's original bachelor apartment the apartment below in "duplex-fashion." Wilson had moved out before their return.

Ruby came of a "moderately prosperous" Swedish family. An only daughter with six younger brothers, she had not been trained for outside work, since a woman's place, her parents believed, was in the home. The strongly independent Ruby left at eighteen after a family row. She came to Chicago where she worked as a journalist, a career she gave up to devote herself solely to Clarence.

Nevertheless, eleven years later, in a by-lined article in the *Chicago Tribune* headlined "A bas [sic] 'Courtesy!' Viva 'Equality,'" she advised women not to "register themselves 'weaker vessels' by asking men to be kind to them." If women do so, she warned, they must "expect men to regard themselves as bigger and better beings being wheedled into making charitable concessions like giving up their seats in cars, and entire roomfuls bobbing out of their chairs like jumping jacks because a woman enters."

She saw only one way for women to go. Her husband's influence was present in her advice: "Teach and train women to develop healthy bodies and minds, give the working women better hours, better pay, better conditions, better opportunities to breathe and branch forth into a class of women that will not need to wearily appeal to the mercy of men for a corner of a car to collapse into.

"Educate the leisure-women to rise above their idiotic fashions, . . . and perhaps it will not torture them to stand awhile and let exhausted laborers rest meantime."[14]

4

The summer after Ruby and Clarence were married they went to the Colorado mountains when the courts closed and there enjoyed hiking, climbing, being together. Ruby exhilarated and challenged him. She was bright and quick, well read, and not afraid to express her opinions, but she was not as aggressive as the New Women with whom he had been associating.

That summer, too, in the Colorado mountains, Clarence wrote his only novel, *An Eye for an Eye*.[15] The book opens: "When Hank Clery left the switch-yards in the outskirts of Chicago he took the street car and went down town. He was going to the county jail on the north side of the river."

The story, however, is not about Hank but about his friend, Jim Jackson, condemned to death for murdering his wife. He sits in his grim cell on the day before his scheduled execution, waiting and hoping for a reprieve from the governor. His friend Hank Clery waits with him. As Jim tells Hank the story of his life and in a humble monologue recounts the events of the night of the murder, they can hear in the background the scaffold being built and heavy sandbags dropped to test the strength of the rope.

The orphaned Jackson had started to work in the Chicago stockyards at the age of fourteen: "I never liked that work; I used to see so much killin'." From the stockyards he went to work for the railroads, first as a freight house unloader and then as a switchman, a job which would give him "more air and not be quite so confinin'." There is a strike, and Jim recalls how he "hit a scab over the head, but he was comin' to take our job. I never thought it was so awful bad to hit a scab who was takin' another man's job. Of course I know some of 'em are poor and have families, but so have the strikers got families and we was strikin' to help all the poor people. If you read the newspapers and hear what the judges say you would think hittin' scabs was worse'n murder."

Clarence's dilemma asserts itself through Jackson. "I don't s'pose it's just right, but I don't hardly see what else is to be done. . . . Now it seems to me there's lots of things worse'n hittin' scabs." The glimmering of a social conscience rises in the uneducated Jim Jackson. Darrow, through his protagonist, can't resist propagandizing. "If I was one of them packers I know I'd give a lot of meat to poor people instead of fixin' every way I could to make 'em pay so much, but the rich people don't seem to think there's anything wrong about that, but it's awful to hit a scab or to strike."

Blacklisted after the strike Jim changes his name and goes to work in the yards again where he sees a friend and fellow switcher killed by a train. "I somehow got scared and couldn't switch any more. So I quit the yards" to become a potato peddler.

Coming home from work on the night of the murder, Jim decides against going into a saloon for a drink. The same amount of money will buy a steak for supper and make his wife feel "pleasanter and liven her up a bit. We hadn't been gettin' along any too well for some time."

He brings the steak home and soon "smelt" it "fryin'." When he sees his wife reach for the teakettle to pour water on the meat he gets "mad" because "that wan't no way to fry a steak."

They begin to argue. The child is put to bed and the argument turns increasingly bitter, feeding on frustrations that have nothing to do with the steak. Mrs. Jackson hysterically calls Jim a coward and dares him to kill her. "Why don't you do it? Kill me! You miserable dirty coward!"

Darrow emphasizes man's lack of free will and the part played by fate in leading Jackson to the gallows. He married a girl he had never paid attention to until "the time she got that red waist and done her hair up with the red ribbons. I don't know anything about how it was, but they seemed to ketch my eyes and I commenced goin' with her"; poverty led to quarrels; they wanted to separate but the settlement house worker and the priest to whom they turned for help advised against divorce, and furthermore, they didn't have the $50 the lawyer charged.

Deterministic elements led to the tragedy. Darrow builds his case: if Jackson's future wife had not worn the red blouse on the day she did, Jim would not have been attracted to her; if on the day of the murder Jim had bought whiskey instead of a steak, there would have been no quarrel. If the poker had been in the kitchen where it usually was and not in the living room where they were arguing, Jim could not have reached for it and struck the fatal blow; if he had not had an incompetent lawyer, he would have had a better defense; and finally, if there had not been a crusade against crime at the time Jim committed his act, the pressure for conviction would not have been so great. Jackson tells his friend, "I never intended to kill anybody but somehow everything just led up to it, and I didn't know I was gettin' into it until it was done, and now here I am."

Does the specter of capital punishment lessen crime? Darrow propagandizes with Jackson's confession: "If ther'd been forty scaffolds right before my eyes I'd have brought down that poker just the same." To Darrow the answer was obvious.

An *Eye for an Eye* predates Theodore Dreiser's celebrated *An American Tragedy*. Both books depict life as brutal, painful, and sad. Dreiser attacked the problem as a novelist, Darrow as a polemicist holding that ideas are more important than words. In this powerful sociological novel, Darrow confronts the basic struggle for existence. In a momentary insight, Jim Jackson—simple, vulnerable—arrives at a knowledge and comprehension of his life which exceed his capacity to articulate.

As in his courtroom pleas, Darrow advocates understanding and compassion for society's helpless victims caught in the web of poverty and injustice.

Irving Stone believes Darrow, in *An Eye for an Eye*, was "more interested in getting over his ideas than in adhering to an art form."[16] Darrow would have concurred. He believed "that if one has anything to say it is hardly worth while to take the necessary time that is required to make a perfect work of art, and even if you took the time and accomplished it the book would probably not be as good."[17]

Isabel Colbron, in her review for *The Bookman*, said, "If to create an illusion, to attain the effect aimed at, completely and entirely, is literary art, then Mr. Darrow's work is literary art of the highest, in spite of an apparent neglect of all the canons of literary art."[18] Ravitz, writing more than a half century later, asserts that Darrow deserves "a trophy not only for sociological veracity but also for genuine literary achievement."[19] Despite large sections where the writing blurs and rambles, there are parts beautifully and sharply written. Overall, the sense of realism is pervasive.

That sense of realism also runs through the many short stories he wrote. "This story is about Little Louis Epstine, aged nine years," is the way Darrow started "Little Louis Epstine," which appeared in *The Pilgrim* in 1903.[20] "As might be guessed, Louis was a Jew." Louis had only one hand. How he lost it "is a matter quite outside of this story."

Louis, a newsboy from Chicago's Maxwell Street ghetto, lived with his mother. One day, she bought him a "nice warm cap that pulled down over his ears, and cost twenty-five cents." This gesture awakened in Louis an awareness of "how good" his mother was, and he realized for the first time "how hard she worked, what poor clothes she had, how she never went to a circus or killed a rat in the gutter, or had any kind of fun."

Suddenly Little Louis feels very tenderly toward his mother. Determined to show his love, perhaps more pity than love, he resolves to buy her a gift. He had seen a string of red glass beads in the department store. He had also seen the price marked on the beads: forty-eight cents.

Louis saves his pennies, and a week before Christmas he has thirty-five cents. This particular morning, the coldest of the winter, Louis leaves for newspaper alley to pick up his papers. His mother warns him to keep his coat buttoned. "Gee, ain't this cold!" says Louis as he leaves the house. His ragged coat hardly keeps him warm. Few people are on the street. Many times that morning he thinks of going home, but there are the glass beads he wants to buy, and he has his papers to sell. He can't get "stuck" with them; there are no return privileges.

He remains on the street until all his newspapers are sold and gets home at his usual time. Soon his remaining hand begins "to feel queer—it was all prickly and numb." His mother puts cold water on it, but it still aches. She calls a doctor who looks at it, shakes his head, says Little Louis had better go to the hospital, he is afraid "they must cut off the hand, but they would ask the doctor at the hospital first."

The mother comforts her son, he will be well again, she says, and she and his brothers and sisters will be good to him and take care of him. Louis admits he knows this. It is no solace. It is so close to Christmas and he doesn't have the money he needs. When his mother asks what he means, Little Louis Epstine blurts out between sobs his plans for getting the beads for her.

Darrow created "Little Louis Epstine" as an antithesis to the conventional Christmas tale where all ends well in the best of all possible worlds. In this story as in his others, Darrow stresses the cruelty of life, its poignant hopelessness, and the brutal struggle for survival. It is "a Christmas carol for muckrakers."[21]

So strongly did Darrow feel about "Little Louis Epstine" that he had the first page of the story, as it appeared in *The Pilgrim*, reproduced in his autobiography thirty years later.

Always in Darrow's fiction he depicted his heroes as losers. Always there is the implicit pathos of their lives, of futility, of overriding doom. Over all his writing can be detected his own feelings for his characters, his own sense of identification with them and with mankind generally. These stories, which today appear exaggerated and sentimental—even a bit trite—are the beginnings of the proletarian school of writers which flourished in the 1920s and 1930s.

5

In the fall, on their return from Colorado, the Darrows moved into a large apartment in a newly completed building on Sheridan Road on Chicago's North Side. Here they entertained frequently, from the most distinguished names in Chicago to its most modest citizens, Clarence delighting in his books, paintings, his friends, his young wife. He enjoyed reading aloud to their guests, his mellifluous voice rising and falling to the words of Tolstoy and Voltaire, or it might be William Dean Howells's prose, the satire of Finley Peter Dunne, or the poetry of Heinrich Heine and Omar Khayyám.

Ruby was happily learning to share the life of a successful attorney and meeting new and varied personalities. One of the strengths of their long marriage would be that she never ceased to hold Clarence at the center of her world, the only permanence, never hesitating to follow wherever his work and interests led. Serving him became her major interest. Despite the fact that she had had a career of her own before their marriage, such single-minded devotion and attention to her husband seem strangely outdated in light of the new breed of "liberated" women beginning to appear in the early twentieth century with their demands for sexual freedom and equality.

For his part, Clarence depended on her and was grateful for her ministrations and her attention to the minutiae of everyday living. He was, however, an independent spirit who needed room to go his own way, something Jessie had understood and been able to make her peace with in a way that Ruby never accepted. Although the marriage gave satisfaction to both of them, as the years passed, Ruby suffered many uneasy moments and some jealousy, much of it amply justified.

Preston Bradley, minister of the Peoples Church in Chicago and a longtime friend, believed Darrow saw women from the perspective of a conquest. "I don't think there was very much morality involved. Clarence liked women and he did have affairs and that I know. But they were always moment by moment, none of them very serious. He was proud of his prowess." [22]

6

The same year Clarence married Ruby, he became associated in a law partnership with Edgar Lee Masters, poet and attorney. The two men could not have been more dissimilar. Although their talents meshed, their personalities totally contradicted each other. Masters—the poet of *Spoon River Anthology*, still to be written—was quarrelsome, egotistical, cynical, and reserved. He excelled in the myriad details of legal appellate work. He loved humanity but only in the abstract. Darrow, friendly and outgoing, hated the sin but never the sinner. In appearance, too, there was contrast: the easygoing Darrow in his careless dress, and the precise, immaculately tailored Masters.

The differences, however, held promise of a balanced business association. Darrow brought in the clients and made courtroom appearances. Masters, highly logical and well organized, researched and briefed the cases and remained in charge of the office. Yet, from the start, perhaps because they went into it for the wrong reasons, the partnership was doomed. Masters, whose primary interest was literature, intended his association with Darrow to lead to financial independence so he could shake himself free of the law and devote himself to writing. He soon discovered that Darrow was less interested in making money than he was in defending the just cause. Furthermore, Darrow's catholic interests—lecturing, debating, writing—cut into his law practice. He needed Masters to hold down the fort and do the mundane jobs while he wandered in search of windmills to conquer.

The poet, struggling for recognition, must have felt tremendous hostility as the accolades poured in on his partner, while he sat in the office researching legal precedents and writing briefs. By the time the firm was dissolved eight years later, Masters was beside himself with tightly controlled fury toward Darrow, an emotion he seemed to hold onto, with one brief exception, the rest of his life.

The two had met in 1898 when each had law offices in the same building in downtown Chicago. After their breakup, Masters insisted he had been "instrumental" in having Darrow appointed attorney for the receiver of a bankrupt building and loan association. "When the time came for us to settle our fees, this criminal lawyer resented my demands and grabbed the larger share of the money, though I had done most of the work," he complained.[23]

Masters described the formation of the partnership in his autobiography written twenty-five years after the firm was dissolved, but he never mentioned Darrow by name. "This criminal lawyer . . . who was well known in Chicago, and as much feared and disliked as Altgeld himself," invited Masters to become a partner. He "was not in good odor in Chicago," Masters wrote, "and that made me fearful about listening to his proposal to join his firm."[24]

Despite his own hostile feelings toward Darrow and those of his father-in-law who considered Darrow "immoral" and "an atheist and an anarchist . . . and doubted his sincerity and his honesty of mind," Masters accepted the offer. The firm reportedly earned $25,000 to $35,000 annually for each partner. "I was making more money than I ever had made," Masters reflected; "I was making it to have leisure for poetry! What a mirage through which to be laboring to the perfect good!"[25]

Darrow, too, gave no indication of his association with Masters either in his autobiography or in any of his writings. He rarely mentioned him in conversation. Many years later, however, in Honolulu during the Massie trial, reminiscing with a friend about the early years in Chicago, he said, "Masters used to be in my office—we were partners for a time. He did some fine things. But he seems to have been embittered, somehow."[26]

That was as much as he ever said on that subject. He seldom spoke pejoratively of others behind their backs. He preferred instead the soft thrust, the barb, in direct confrontation.

Abram Adelman's law office was on the same floor as that of Masters and Darrow, and he knew both men. In his frequent conversations with them he never heard Clarence express any ill will toward his partner. "Darrow," recalled Adelman, "was by nature a man who didn't deal in malice and wasn't subject to it. Darrow dealt in philosophical generalities rather than person- alities. Masters, though a gifted man, was given to fits of anger and malice."[27]

Some of the antagonism on Masters's part was obviously based on finances. He resented Darrow taking to the lecture platform instead of attending to business in Chicago. "He was doing little of the work of the office; and my own burdens were heavier in consequence."

Perhaps he had some justification. There was the time Darrow was to present the closing argument in a personal injury suit against a railroad. Everything was going favorably for the client. But Darrow did not show up for the final plea, and a distressed Masters had to face the jury. The client lost. Darrow had gone to Cincinnati for a debate.

Masters also claimed "this criminal attorney" didn't know how Masters felt toward him until he read Masters's poem "On a Bust" in *Songs and Satires,* published in 1916, five years after the dissolution of their partnership. Even then Darrow gave no indication that he recognized Masters's feelings.

Despite the poet's contention that his wife "feared" and "disliked" Darrow, she turned to him to represent her in divorce proceedings, which certainly furthered Masters's antagonism and resentment.

To Masters, Darrow was "more like Lincoln than anyone I have ever known." This was no compliment because he thought Lincoln "mannerless, unkempt, and one wonders if he was not unwashed." He considered Lincoln a "slick and crafty politician." His letters to Carter H. Harrison, Jr., the former mayor of Chicago, and to Altgeld's biographer Harry Barnard, both written in 1938 after Darrow's death, are venomous outpourings of hatred.

Yet, in 1922, with no explanation for the momentary change, Masters wrote about Darrow:

> In all my days I have found
>   No sadder man, gladder in his sadness.
> I have found no man who went his way
>   With less excuse or reason fashioned for himself
> of going at all; and no man

> Who believed more in truth and good will
> Though he backed them only with their own
> Self-evident need for being.[28]

7

The partnership of Darrow, Masters & Wilson (Darrow's former Langdon roommate had joined the firm shortly after its formation) handled a variety of cases—from representing strikers against injunctions to arbitration and criminal and civil cases as well as arguing constitutional law before the U.S. Supreme Court.

As an aftermath of the assassination of President McKinley, the U.S. Congress for the first time enacted legislation to exclude aliens because of their beliefs. The law, passed in March 1903, also provided for the exclusion and deportation of "anarchists, or persons who believe in or advocate the overthrow by force or violence of the Government of the United States, or of all government, or all forms of law."

That same year John Turner, an English anarchist who acted as an organizer for the Amalgamated Union of Shop Assistants and Warehousemen and Clerks of Great Britain, came to the United States to deliver lectures in some of the large cities and to collect material for a series of articles on trade conditions in the States for *Grocer,* a journal published in London.

On October 23, 1903, Turner spoke at a mass meeting on "Trade Unionism and the General Strike," in which he gave a historical survey of the trade-union movement and pointed "out that as the organization of both employer and worker developed, when strikes did occur, they became more sweeping in their operations and would be likely to culminate in a general strike or lock-out of the wage earners."[29]

At the conclusion of his talk Turner was arrested under a warrant issued four days earlier which specified that his presence in the United States was proscribed by "An Act to Regulate the Immigration of Aliens in the United States."

Turner was transported to Ellis Island where he was locked in a nine-foot-by-six-foot cage and held for deportation.

Protest meetings against Turner's arrest were held in a number of cities. The *Independent* had asked in an editorial, "How many Americans know that a law of the United States forbids admission to this country of any person 'who disbelieves in or who is opposed to all organized government, or who is a member of or affiliated with any organization entertaining or teaching such disbelief in or opposition to all organized government'?"[30]

Darrow and Masters, retained to argue the unconstitutionality of the law before the U.S. Supreme Court, went to Washington where they presented a 187-page brief in which they not only argued the unconstitutionality of the law but gave a historic review of various cases involving free speech previously judged by the high court. They also presented arguments in favor of free speech by such political philosophers as Locke, Mills, Madison, Jefferson, and Spencer. Turner, they argued, was a philosophical anarchist and did not come under the meaning of the statute. Darrow's plea, backed up by Masters's research, exemplified the team they made. The research of the brief showed Masters at his best, while Darrow, as a pleader, was superb. For a time the plea was sold as a definitive brochure on freedom of speech.

"It is the boast of historians that Hamilton, Jay and Madison in the Articles which were afterwards published under the title of the 'Federalists' persuaded the states under the confederation to withdraw therefrom and to adopt the present Constitution. A new government was thereby formed. The Declaration of Independence announces it as a self-evident truth that the people have the right to abolish old governments and to institute new ones. And yet this act of 1903 seeks to inhibit beliefs in or advocacies of the overthrow of the government of the United States. If it be a right to abolish old governments and to institute new ones, the means of such abolitions cannot be absolutely wrong when the abolition itself may be justified. And hence the necessity for liberty of belief and speech upon this subject."[31] The Darrow-Masters team contended that the 1903 law abridged freedom of press and speech and that Congress had no right to pass such a law. That Turner was an alien was inconsequential. If Congress could not pass a law prohibiting or abridging speech, it did not have the competency to limit the right of freedom of speech for anybody, including aliens.

The Court, in an opinion read by Chief Justice Melville W. Fuller, rebuffed all the arguments of Turner's counsel as it held that an alien in the country does not have the protection of the First Amendment rights to freedom of speech.

Current Literature would have the last word, which could well be that of Clarence Darrow on the Turner case: "The case against Count Tolstoy, if he came here, would be as clear as the case against Turner. . . . We must keep true to Jefferson's maxim that error is not to be feared when truth is left free to combat it."[32]

Or as Darrow would tell the jury in the Chicago 1920 Communist case, "I want to take my chances by leaving every man free to bring his contribution to the world; by leaving every man free to express his thought; by leaving every man free to throw his opinions into the great crucible that we may work it out. . . . I ask you to say that men shall be free, and if in the open discussions between free men my clients triumph, well and good; they ought to triumph; and if they are wrong their theories must go down."[33]

IX

"I Speak for the Poor, for the Weak"

1

A call from the Western Federation of Miners to defend three officials in a murder trial at Boise, Idaho, disrupted the Darrows's idyllic life in the gracious North Side apartment. Clarence accepted, and Ruby began to make arrangements for the trip. She put their furniture in storage, packed, and left with Clarence for the West.

For the past decade, labor troubles had plagued the rich mining district in Idaho's Coeur d'Alene, an area only twenty-five miles long and from one to five miles wide. A bitter strike over union recognition erupted in 1899, with mineowners and their private detectives and scabs on one side, the union and its sympathizers on the other. Clubs. Guns. Dynamite. Class war—and it was taking place not in the large industrial centers of the East as Marxian theorists anticipated but on the mining frontiers of the West. Reflecting the basic characteristics of the frontier with its potential for violence, the Idaho struggle between capital and labor—the status quo versus union recognition and a bigger share of the rewards—was class conflict with total chaos on both sides, each absolutely determined to achieve victory.

Union miners armed with rifles were pitted against armed nonunion men at the Bunker Hill Company mills where the miners had earlier placed dynamite.

Two men died in the resulting explosion; property damage exceeded $250,000. Insisting that the entire county was in a state of insurrection, the operators turned to Governor Frank Steunenberg for help. Because the Idaho National Guard was on duty in the Philippines, Steunenberg asked President McKinley to send federal troops.

The president complied immediately. The federal militia, excessively punitive in rounding up the union miners, confined them in "bullpens," a euphemism for the barbed-wire camps into which they were thrown. Steunenberg, fearful that violence would erupt again when the militia left, requested they remain as long as necessary. He approved a "permit system" instituted by the military to allow the miners to return to work only if they renounced union membership.

The miners, who twice had helped elect Steunenberg on the Populist ticket, branded the governor a traitor and held him mainly responsible for the mass arrests and prolonged detention of their members. After eight months a truce was called, order restored, and the troops withdrawn. The governor retired to Caldwell in 1900 at the completion of his second term, where he lived quietly, a respected and popular member of the established community.

Almost six years later, early on the evening of December 30, 1905, as Steunenberg opened the gate to his home, a bomb attached to it exploded. He was dead within twenty minutes. His murder outraged the citizens of Idaho, and most of them held the miners' federation responsible.

The authorities acted immediately to cut off all areas of escape for the perpetrators. Strangers in town were suspect and were questioned extensively. Governor Frank R. Gooding announced a $10,000 reward for the apprehension of the assassins, and the Steunenberg family added $5000.

Two days after the explosion, police arrested Tom Hogan, who had been in Caldwell several months spending money freely and evincing particular curiosity about Steunenberg's personal habits. On several occasions Jack Simpkins, a Western Federation of Miners official, had been seen with him.

An Oregon sheriff, visiting in Caldwell at the time of the explosion, recognized Hogan as Harry Orchard, an itinerant miner from the eastern district of his state. A search of Orchard's hotel room turned up evidence linking him with the governor's death. He was charged with the murder and transferred to the Boise jail.

Soon James McParland, a Pinkerton detective, was assigned to the investigation. Determined to break the federation which he considered a terrorist organization involved in the murder, McParland took over. He was fanatically antilabor and had been instrumental in destroying the Molly Maguires, a secret organization of miners engaged in violent tactics to protect themselves against the brutality of the mineowners and their hired detectives. The group disintegrated in the early 1880s after several of their leaders were convicted of murder and executed. McParland claimed Orchard was only a tool of the WFM and recommended that he be taken from the Caldwell jail and held in solitary confinement at the state penitentiary in Boise.

McParland visited Orchard there after ten days. They discussed the Molly Maguires and their trials. McParland named persons who had turned against the defense to save themselves. Orchard, unaware that his visitor was a Pinkerton detective, complained about being transferred to Boise.

McParland now began to spin a web of intrigue designed to convince Orchard to turn state's witness. He explained to Orchard that he had been transferred to protect him from those who had hired him to murder Steunenberg and now intended to kill him. He flattered him, called him "a great criminal," and played on his vanity. Three days later, the Pinkerton detective again visited Orchard and warned him the state had enough evidence to hang him, while those really responsible would go free. If Orchard took his advice, McParland suggested, "you will not be hung. If you do not you will be hung in very quick order as the state is ready to prosecute as soon as Court convenes."[1] He continued his efforts to seduce the prisoner. Did Orchard believe in an all-seeing and Divine Power? he asked. Did he believe in a Hereafter? "Yes, yes," Orchard did believe. He believed that "it was my duty to tell the truth, regardless of consequences to myself or anybody else." The "reborn Christian," as he would have been tagged in the 1970s, felt he owed it "to society, to God, and to myself." When Governor Gooding made an unprecedented visit to his cell, Orchard told him that his only thought now was to achieve peace with his Maker.

Orchard's confession took three days to record: twenty-six murders, including the killing of fourteen nonunion miners at Independence, Colorado, in June 1904, as well as planting the bomb which killed Governor Steunenberg. He had been paid by the "Inner Circle" of the Western Federation of Miners to dynamite and murder. He implicated William D. Haywood, militant secretary-treasurer of the union and of the one-year-old Industrial Workers of the World; Charles H. Moyer, WFM president; George A. Pettibone, a Denver businessman who previously had been an active WFM member; and Jack Simpkins, a member of the union's executive board. He also named Steve Adams, a miner, as his frequent accomplice.

Simpkins disappeared, never to surface again. The fact that Haywood, Moyer, and Pettibone were in Denver was an obstacle, but one McParland would overcome. "Owing to the fact that neither of these parties has been in Idaho during this conspiracy we cannot say that they are fugitives from justice, and we may have considerable trouble in extraditing them. However, we are perfecting plans by which we hope to get them into Idaho in a legal manner, where there is little doubt but we can convict them," McParland reported to Governor Gooding.[2]

The legal maneuver called for McParland to leave for Denver on Sunday afternoon, February 10, while State's Attorney Hawley, a former WFM attorney, immediately initiated plans to extradite Haywood, Moyer, and Pettibone. Adams, if located, would be kept under surveillance until the three had been arrested, at which time the state would request his immediate apprehension on the charge of being an accessory before the fact in Steunenberg's murder.

Eight days later the arrests were made, Haywood in a rooming house near union headquarters, Pettibone at his home, and Moyer at the railroad station as he was leaving for Kansas to visit the Smeltermen's Union. All were taken to the Denver County jail and held incommunicado. When a member of the union's law firm looked for them there, the jailer denied they were in the jail. "From this it will be seen," McParland wrote to his headquarters, "the Sheriff carried out his instructions to the letter." [3]

The three men first learned the charge against them when the sheriff whispered to Haywood, "They are going to take you to Idaho. They've got you mixed up in the Steunenberg murder." [4]

Then came the race for the Idaho border. At five o'clock the next morning Haywood, Moyer, and Pettibone were taken from the jail. "We drove along the quietest streets, each of us in a separate carriage with three guards," Haywood described the scene. After a stop at the Oxford Hotel they came to the station where "a train was ready and waiting. We stepped aboard and were off for Idaho. We were going at a terrific speed. The engine took on coal and water at small stations and stopped at none of the larger towns along the route. When we arrived at Boise we were put into separate conveyances. . . . We drove to the penitentiary. There was the sign over the gate: Admittance twenty-five cents, but," with a stab at ironic humor, Haywood added, ". . . I was admitted without charge." [5]

In the Idaho penitentiary, the three were placed in murderers' row. McParland had accomplished his mission.

The day after the extradition, Adams was arrested at Haines, Oregon. Taken to Boise, he was immediately placed in a cell with Orchard, who urged him to confess to a series of criminal acts and to lay the blame on the top echelons of the union. McParland came, this time to talk with Adams. The state had to convict Haywood, Moyer, and Pettibone, and Simpkins, he told him. They needed Adams to corroborate Orchard's confession. If he refused, he would be taken to Colorado and charged with the murder of two claim jumpers. If he agreed to turn state's evidence, then he need only be a witness in the Colorado murder trial, not the defendant.

McParland left, and Adams was returned to Orchard's cell. Again the persuasive argument by Orchard for Adams to back up his story. Confused and frightened, Adams finally confessed that both he and Orchard had committed acts of violence at the request of the federation's Inner Circle.

A jubilant prosecution prepared for trial.

Immediately, the state moved Adams to a cottage on the prison grounds where he lived with his wife, although they remained incommunicado from the outside world.

2

Edmund F. Richardson, WFM attorney and one of the leading lawyers in the Northwest, rushed from Denver to Boise. He filed habeas corpus proceedings in the Idaho Supreme Court. Denied. He appealed to the U.S. Supreme Court which agreed to hear arguments.

3

On December 3, 1906, Justice John M. Harlan, speaking for the majority of the U.S. Supreme Court, ruled that the officers involved in the extradition had "proceeded throughout this affair with no evil purpose and with no other motive than to enforce the law," and affirmed the decision of the lower courts.[6]

A lone justice, however, dissented. Justice Joseph McKenna argued that the officers of the state exerted "illegal power" and "deprived the accused of a constitutional right." The justice went further: "Kidnapping is a crime, pure and simple. It is difficult to accomplish, hazardous at every step. All the officers of the law are supposed to be on guard against it." Then he asked, "But how is it when the law becomes the kidnapper, when the officers of the law, using the forms and exerting its power, become abductors?" and he concluded: "Our criminal jurisprudence will not need for its efficient administration the destruction of either the right or the means to enforce it. The decision in this case at bar, as I view it, brings us perilously near both results."

4

With the adverse decision, Clarence Darrow was retained. He was probably the only lawyer in the country "intellectually equal to the requirements of the case," commented Max Baginski, in the anarchist publication *Mother Earth*.[7]

When Steve Adams's uncle reported to the defense that Steve had been coerced into a confession and would repudiate it if he could be assured of a defense, Darrow promised to act as his attorney "as faithfully as for the rest" if Steve would send for him.[8] Adams repudiated his confession. His attorneys obtained his release from the Boise jail on September 8, 1906, on a habeas corpus writ. Immediately, Shoshone County, Idaho, authorities arrested him and transported him to Wallace to stand trial for the 1904 murder of Fred Tyler who had jumped a claim belonging to a friend of Adams.

5

The Adams case was part of the state's overall strategy to convict Haywood, Moyer, and Pettibone. If he were found guilty in the Tyler murder, the state intended to offer him a commutation or a pardon in exchange for testifying against the three union men.

Both Richardson and Darrow went to Wallace for the Adams trial which opened in early February. State's Attorney Hawley, who would prosecute the Haywood case, also represented the state in the Adams trial, together with Henry F. Knight, the local prosecutor. Knight, in his opening statement, said Tyler took up a timber claim in the spring of 1904 in "the new country" near the St. Joseph River. On or about August 10, on his way home after fishing, he stopped to share supper with a neighbor before continuing on to his own cabin. He never reached his cabin. His body was found in the timber by surveyors, a bullet hole in the back of the skull. The state said Adams confessed he had been in the area and committed the murder.[9]

To provide some shock effects for a trial that did not promise too much excitement, the prosecution kept on its table during most of the trial, in full view of the jury, a pair of badly decomposed overalls allegedly belonging to Tyler, his hat, undershirt, handkerchief, fish sack, bottle container, tobacco box, and hair that fell from the skull when lifted. Tyler's bones, the prosecution noted, were in the unopened box. His "shattered, dried, weather-beaten skull," however, was introduced in evidence and held up to the jury by the deputy sheriff who described the wounds in detail.

McParland, testifying against Adams, denied he had put the defendant through the third degree or made any arrangement for Adams and Orchard to be assigned to the same cell. He did, however, admit to having visited the cell from time to time to learn if Adams would corroborate Orchard's confession; he admitted taking Adams into the "inner room of the warden's office" where he gave him a cigar and reiterated his friendship. He made arrangements for them to be served a "nice" luncheon. McParland, insisting that the state "always acted fair with those who acted fair by it," got Adams "mellow and ripe" and convinced him to tell all, but he never threatened or held out inducements, McParland testified.[10]

To back up its case, the prosecution read Adams's confession in which he admitted to membership in the federation and claimed to know Haywood, Moyer, and Pettibone intimately. He said they told him to contact Jack Simpkins in Wallace, Idaho, "about some business connected with Steunenberg." Simpkins offered him $300 "to get rid" of two claim jumpers and also told him the union wanted "to get" Steunenberg. Adams's confession said he killed Tyler for the money.

The judge admitted the confession into evidence subject to the jury's determination that it was obtained without duress.

Adams appeared calm and self-possessed on the witness stand in a courtroom "packed to the door." He described his arrest at his uncle's ranch near Baker City, Oregon, how he had been thrown in jail overnight, then taken to Boise and kept in a cell with Orchard for a week. During this period Orchard told him he had confessed to the Steunenberg murder and implicated both the WFM and Adams. He advised Adams to corroborate the testimony so the conviction of the WFM officials would be secured. "Save yourself," Orchard urged him.

Adams further testified, "McParland led me on step by step and showed me all that he wanted me to say, with the idea of making a strong chain of evidence to convict the officers" of the federation.[11]

On the stand, Adams repudiated his confession in its entirety.

Prosecutor Knight summarized, "The question for the jury to consider in this case is whether the alibi for the defense shows in any way that the defendant was in another place at the time Fred Tyler was ruthlessly shot down."

Both defense attorneys presented summations. Richardson called Adams "only a pawn in the great game that is being played." Referring to the private house which the state fixed up for Adams and his wife on the prison grounds, he said, "It is not and never has been customary to take a self-convicted victim from his cell the moment his confession has been made, place him in a nice room and send for his wife and family."[12]

Darrow reminded the jury that "there is not a man in this courtroom who really cares to take Steve Adams' life. It is not for him, a humble, almost unknown workman, that all the machinery of the State has been set in motion, and all the mines and the mine owners of the West have been called to their aid. Not that. It is because back of all this, and beyond and over all, there is a great issue of which this is but the beginning. Because, beyond this case, and outside of this courtroom, and out in the great world, is a great fight, a fight between capital and labor, of which this is but a manifestation up here in the woods and the hills."[13]

Hawley in his response described Darrow's address as sounding like a refrain from a "street corner orator." He said, "The state does not wish to see an innocent man hung. . . . Steve Adams is not a cat's paw in our hands and we are trying this case upon its merits."[14]

The jury deliberated two days but remained hopelessly deadlocked. The defense, unable to get Adams released on bail, left Steve sitting in the Wallace jail and set off for the Haywood trial.

6

Arriving in Boise on April 26, 1907, eight days after his fiftieth birthday, Clarence and Ruby rented a cottage on the edge of the city where Clarence could get away from the "tension and congestion of people" and then return to his courtroom responsibilities in the Haywood trial "with new zeal."[15] Moyer and Pettibone would be tried separately.

The *Idaho Statesman* reported that Richardson, "the leading attorney for the defense, will follow Mr. Darrow to Boise within a few days."

Each lawyer considered himself to be the "leading attorney." This controversy simmered quietly throughout the Adams and then the Haywood trials, and only after the Haywood verdict did it become public. Yet, on November 6, 1906, three months before the Adams trial opened, Darrow had written to Haywood, Moyer, and Pettibone that he could not stay in the trial if Richardson were directing its course. "I would not have undertaken the case on those terms in the first place, and can not do it now." In the letter, addressed to "My dear friends," Darrow noted that Richardson "is undoubtedly an able man and has been with you for a long time and it seems to me that he should be retained and that I shall be allowed to withdraw."[16] But the defendants were not ready to release either Darrow or Richardson. In addition to Darrow and Richardson, the Haywood defense included Fred Miller of Spokane, a WFM attorney originally retained to represent Orchard before his confession. In 1920 he would represent Sacco and Vanzetti. Other defense attorneys were Edgar Wilson, an ex-congressman from Idaho, and John Nugent, later U.S. senator from Idaho.

For the prosecution: Hawley, and William E. Borah, participating for the last time in his career as an attorney before assuming his duties as the newly elected U.S. senator from Idaho.

The judge: Fremont Wood, a Down East Yankee described by the prestigious magazine *Current Literature* as radiating "the square deal. To begin with, he bulks big. He has a massive head, solidly set on broad, square shoulders topping a powerful body. His eyes are keen and kindly, and have the twinkle in them that shows he knows how to laugh."[17]

The court sessions were only one aspect of the case which kept it at top press coverage. Protest meetings and demonstrations around the country added to the ferment. *Mother Earth* editorialized, "Only energetic action on the part of organized labor will free the imprisoned leaders of the Western Federation of Miners."[18] The U.S. Supreme Court ruling notwithstanding, there were many who insisted the prisoners had been kidnapped from Denver, and they used the dissenting opinion of Justice McKenna to augment their claim.

President Theodore Roosevelt added to the tempest with the publication of a private letter to James S. Sherman, Republican congressman from New York. Intended to clarify a totally unrelated matter, it inadvertently incensed not only radicals and unionists but thousands of other citizens with its injudicious prejudgment of the case. Edward H. Harriman, the railroad magnate, had informed the press that Roosevelt wanted him to raise $250,000 for the Republican party in New York State. Denying the charge, the president authorized the publication of certain letters he had written which he believed would absolve him. The letter to Sherman was in the group. In it, Roosevelt condemned Harriman for his "cynicism and deep-seated corruption which makes the man uttering such sentiments, and boasting, no matter how falsely, of his power to perform such crimes, at least as undesirable a citizen as Debs, or Moyer, or Haywood."[19]

Led by Debs, tens of thousands throughout the country donned buttons reading, "I am an undesirable citizen."

The president's statement became an issue at the trial when one of the talesmen admitted he had read it. Two already accepted as jurors insisted the remarks would not influence them. Objecting when the defense questioned a talesman about Roosevelt's comment, the prosecutor shouted, "I will be glad to eliminate Roosevelt if you will. He was brought into the case by the defense."

Richardson disagreed. The president had come in by himself. "He is 2,000 miles away and he writes letters."

Darrow interjected, "He was brought in by his own butting in."[20]

According to *Current Literature,* neither the socialist clamor, nor the demonstrations, nor the "kidnapping" of the defendants "sufficed to draw general attention to this *cause célèbre* until President Roosevelt recently published his notable letter."[21]

7

The *Idaho Statesman* noted on the opening day of the trial that its progress "will be watched with interest by the eyes of the civilized world." As reporters and magazine writers from all parts of the country converged, the paper reported their arrivals: Perkins of the *Portland Evening Telegram;* George Kibbe Turner of *McClure's Magazine;* Tierney of the *Denver News,* Kennedy of the AP. More than fifty special correspondents came. The telegraph company installed ten additional circuits to handle the millions of words which would be sent during the trial.

Debs, touring the country in defense of Haywood, Moyer, and Pettibone, wanted to come to Boise to cover for the Socialist weekly newspaper, *Appeal to Reason,* what he considered "the greatest legal battle in American history."

According to Haywood, Darrow refused to let him come because the attorney wanted "to be recognized as the most prominent person in the trial"[22] and felt Debs would take the limelight from him.

Haywood misjudged Darrow. The attorney considered the Boise case a political trial, and his modus operandi would not have permitted him to keep Debs away to gratify his own ego if it would help the cause of his defendants. Furthermore, Darrow adored Eugene Debs, whose cause had changed the direction of Darrow's life: "There may have lived some time, some where, a kindlier, gentler, more generous man . . . but I have never known him. Nor have I ever read or heard of another."[23]

A more accurate explanation is in a letter from Richardson to Debs urging him not to come, as his presence as a radical labor leader "would do more to injure the cause of the defendants than help."[24] Moyer and Pettibone, also representing the conservative views of the Western Federation of Miners, agreed with Richardson.

8

Thursday morning, May 10, 1907. Judge Wood pounded his gavel to open the first session of the Haywood trial in the District Court of Ada County. The crowd, smaller than anticipated, found the courtroom uncomfortably warm. The special electric fans promised had not yet arrived.

The bailiff escorted Haywood to a seat at the side of his younger daughter in the same row of chairs in which his family sat. A large man, Haywood well deserved his sobriquet of "Big Bill!" His huge hands, as they lay in his lap, still showed the ravages of his early years in the mines. One of the founders of the Industrial Workers of the World (the "Wobblies"), Haywood believed in the power of direct action, the general strike, and the preamble of the IWW constitution: "There can be no peace as long as hunger and want are found among millions of working people and the few, who make up the employing class, have all the good things of life.

"Between these two classes a struggle must go on until the workers of the world organize as a class, take possession of the earth and the machinery of production, and abolish the wage system" so that the new society can be built "within the shell of the old."

McClure's Magazine described Haywood as "a type of the man not unfamiliar now in America, equipped with a good brain, who has come up struggling and fighting, giving blows and taking them, who knowing deeply the wrongs of his class, sees nothing beyond."[25]

9

Selection of a jury was arduous and long drawn out. Reporters noted the contrast in the techniques of Richardson and Darrow. The former sat as he questioned in a "vigorous, emphatic" manner, his voice strong enough to be heard in the farthermost corners of the courtroom. Darrow, on the other hand, leaned over the talesman as he interrogated, his voice soft and confidential, as if only the two of them were in the room. His manner was seductive and designed to lull the juryman into confessing his prejudices. It was a device that Darrow employed successfully throughout his career, and seldom was he surprised by a juror's reaction to trial events.

Unfamiliar with the legal phraseology required in Idaho courts, Darrow challenged with the words "for real prejudice." Before the judge could correct Darrow, Nugent, the Boise defense attorney, interjected the correct formula: "We challenge the juror for actual bias in that he is prejudiced against the defendant William D. Haywood." Darrow would smile; the judge would rule.

Prejudices. Hardships. Knowledge of the case. All hampered selection. It took fifteen days before the court finally impaneled the jury: nine farmers, a real-estate agent, a builder, a foreman of a street railway company—eight Republicans, three Democrats, one Prohibitionist.

10

While the jury was being impaneled, a selective number of newspaper people were invited by Governor Gooding to interview Harry Orchard. For more than sixteen months the state's star witness had been held incommunicado when, to the surprise of the judge and the lawyers on both sides, stories about Orchard appeared in the newspapers. He was quoted as insisting that "I have nothing in particular to say but I might say that anything I may have said I said on my own free will and accord after taking plenty of time to deliberate."[26]

Newspapers across the country carried the stories. Much was made of Orchard's appearance. "Whatever the Harry Orchard of Dec. 30, 1905 may have been, men who look like Harry Orchard of May 16, 1906 are men who tell the truth. There is a conscience, beyond those blue, unfaltering eyes of his," wrote O. K. Davis of the *Chicago Tribune* and *The New York Times*.[27]

Judge Wood was incensed that Gooding had permitted the interview. He ordered an investigation and asked the attorneys for both sides to comment. All agreed the interview was highly "improper at this time."

Richardson noted that "the governor of this state who had done things which have been questioned throughout the entire United States, if not the civilized world," brought to the penitentiary representatives of the press who were biased "upon the side of the prosecution."

Darrow bitterly added his accusation: "Of course there can be but one purpose of this joint reception of the governor and his friend, Mr. Orchard, and that was to influence this case at this time."

The next morning the incident was whitewashed when the county attorney reported that his investigation found no improper motive. He explained that there had been speculation regarding Orchard's mental and physical health, and correspondents had long requested interviews with him. The governor consented as a matter of public news.

11

Prosecutor Hawley, who became governor of Idaho a few years later, made the opening statement.[28] At a nod from Judge Wood, he rose from his seat and moved confidently toward the jury, his words cold and deliberate. "It is our purpose, gentlemen of the jury, to show that the death of Steunenberg was the result of a conspiracy, an understanding and collusion between the leaders of the Western Federation of Miners and other persons," he began. "We claim that the leaders of this union are responsible for this outrage and it will be our purpose to prove them so. We will show that the leaders of this organization have been responsible not only for the death of Steunenberg but scores of others besides."

Darrow jumped to his feet. "The death of others" had nothing to do with the case. "The Court cannot tell at this time whether the statement is objectionable or not," Judge Wood said, overruling Darrow's objection.

Hawley explained that it was not the purpose of the state to prove that Haywood, Moyer, and Pettibone were there when the crime was committed even though they were charged with having thrown or exploded the bomb. "Our object," he said, "will be to show that from the very inception of the Western Federation of Miners there has existed a conspiracy among its leaders—its inner circle. The leaders have employed desperate criminals from time to time to do away with those who may have been selected for one reason or another for disappearance and who have run counter to their interests."

Again Darrow was on his feet: Hawley's address was "a mere piece of rhetoric" solely to prejudice the jury. "I would like to suggest to the court," said Darrow, "that I have no desire to call counsel to task—"

Hawley shouted, "I object to any suggestions to the court from counsel."

In a drawl which only added spark to an already excited district attorney, Darrow said, "Oh don't be so particular."

"Don't you be so particular about interrupting me," raged Hawley.

"I will interrupt at any time the interests of my client demand it," retorted Darrow. "If the attorney will be calm for a minute I want to make arrangements to except to the statement and I want to co-operate for an orderly trial."

"We will meet you half way on that," agreed Hawley.

"Now," Darrow turned to the court, "we insist that the state has no right to make proof in this trial to all of the alleged disorderly or unlawful acts of the Western Federation of Miners which it is declared extend all over the western country. We are not trying anyone here but W. D. Haywood and the charge is the murder of former Gov. Steunenberg."

The prosecutor claimed that the WFM "traded in blood, had hired assassins as its needs seemed to require and had raised by assessments from time to time an emergency fund from which were squandered large sums for personal uses and for the retention of the best legal talent to defend those of its members who were accused of crime. The killing of Steunenberg was not the primary object to the main conspiracy but was merely accidental to it."

Hawley repeated Orchard's confession to McParland. "We will call this gentleman to the stand," he added.

"Which gentleman?" Darrow asked in seeming innocence.

"You may think these remarks are very cunning but they are out of place here and if you keep them up you will be repaid in kind," Hawley retaliated furiously.

Darrow appealed to the court. "I merely asked which gentleman he meant."

"I referred to James McParland," shouted Hawley, "a terror to evil doers in this western country, a man whose presence is a guarantee of good order. You have probably encountered him before in defending your client."

As Darrow started to respond, the judge indicated for him to sit down.

Hawley's opening address ran one hour and twenty minutes before the parade of state witnesses started.

12

The forty-one-year-old Orchard was the star witness for the state. Dark hair combed smoothly, red mustache neatly outlining his upper lip, the short, stocky Orchard calmly moved to the stand. His expression was frank and peaceful as he submitted long narrative replies to Hawley's questions.

He was the "repentant Christian" atoning for his sins.[29] "Harry Orchard is not my true name. I have gone by that name for about 11 years. My true name is Albert Horsley." He admitted he was a bigamist who had deserted his children. He briefly summarized his background up to the time he arrived in the Coeur d'Alene area. From then on it was a detailed description of murders, dynamiting blasts, and "an unsuccessful attempt to blow up a gang of nonunion miners." He said both he and Adams had assassinated an operators' detective for which they were each paid $100 by the Inner Circle of the WFM. Haywood—he nodded toward the defendant—had paid him several hundred dollars for the depot explosion at Independence. Haywood and Pettibone had also wanted him to kill Governor Peabody, Steunenberg's predecessor. Orchard on the stand spelled out all the crimes he had detailed in his autobiography, recently published in *McClure's Magazine*.[30]

Aghast, courtroom spectators listened to him coolly relate the events leading to the Steunenberg murder. "I was in the salon of the hotel playing cards and I came out into the lobby and saw Mr. Steunenberg talking to another man. I went over to the post office and asked if there was any mail for me and when I came back he was still there. I went up to my room and got the bomb. I took it and started up to his residence as fast as I could walk—as fast as I could go—and I placed the bomb at his gate in such a way that when the gate was opened, as it was fastened to it with a string, it would explode. When I was going back about two blocks and a half further toward the hotel—I met Steunenberg. Then I ran as fast as I could to get back to the hotel."

Orchard added that "there had been an understanding between Pettibone and Haywood and Moyer for a good while that when I get done with this business they would give me money to buy a ranch."

Richardson cross-examined. Though Darrow had planned to do so, he yielded with the proviso that he be allowed to decide the conduct of the trial after Orchard's appearance.

Clarence was critical of Richardson who reexamined the witness on every detail of his direct testimony, a technique Darrow considered "futile" as "most witnesses repeated on cross-examination the story already told." Richardson's "loud voice and antagonistic manner" were "somewhat lacking in subtlety." Still, Clarence credited Richardson with "laying the foundation for the impeachment of Orchard, by unbiased witnesses, regarding many statements made in direct examination."[31]

After twenty-six hours under cross-examination, Orchard broke down in tears. "I began to think about my past life and the unnatural monster I had been," he sobbed, "and I didn't care much what happened to me. I was afraid to die, too, for I came to believe the grave did not end it all." He paused to wipe the tears from his eyes. He knew he "would be forgiven if I truly repented and I decided to make a clean breast of it all." He had "never been in doubt of having been forgiven from that moment."

It was a dramatic performance worthy of the greatest actor. Although the defense doubted Orchard's sincerity, some were moved to believe him. Harvard University's Professor Hugo Muensterberg, a distinguished psychologist who came to Boise to study Orchard's mind, was swayed enough to declare flatly that he believed the confession.

"Far from being the furtive weasel of a man that his story would lead one to expect, Orchard was well-set-up, bluff, with an apparent open manner," observed Haywood.

13

When the judge denied the motion by the defense to acquit, Darrow made his opening statement: "We have to take the bloom from the peach but we will prove that Harry Orchard never committed half the crimes he boasted of on that witness stand."

The defense lawyer stood before the jury, his foot resting on the rail that served as a footrest for those jurors in the front row. "It is a shame to tear down his story—to take from him all that glory—but there will be something of a recompense for him," he promised disdainfully. "We'll prove conclusively that he is the most monumental liar that ever graced a witness stand.

"We will show that Haywood, Moyer and Pettibone—none of them—ever had any connection with this man Orchard in a criminal matter."

"A good speech," reported *The New York Times*. "He speaks most of the time in an ordinary conversational tone, stepping back a little when he soars to brief flights of oratory or wants to lend vigor to his words by using more voice." [32]

All through the trial Boise seethed with excitement. Kendrick Johnson, a ten year-old in Boise at the time, recalled that "through the eyes of a small boy, the excitement was intense. The constant talk of danger fired my imagination and I saw dynamiters under every hedge and behind every tree." [33]

Almost a hundred witnesses offered to testify for the defense, and more than seventy-five did, including Moyer and the defendant Haywood. On the stand Moyer denied any discussion with Orchard regarding criminal acts.

14

"William D. Haywood," called the bailiff. Big Bill promised to tell the truth, the whole truth, and nothing but the truth. Darrow examined. [34] In a low voice Haywood related his background. Both his father and stepfather worked in the mines as he did from the age of nine.

"Did you ever have a hostile feeling for Steunenberg?" asked Darrow.

"No sir. I regarded him the same as any politician who could be swayed by capitalist influence."

Haywood explained that the WFM was active in politics to the extent that it was interested in electing candidates favorable to labor unions. The federation had also worked for the enactment of better ventilation, the eight-hour day and child labor laws.

William Borah, as special prosecutor, cross-examined Haywood for four hours during which the defendant successfully parried most of his questions. Asked whether he agreed with the sentiments expressed in an article in the *Miners' Magazine* which referred to Steunenberg as "a hireling and a traitor," Haywood responded, "As far as sentiments of that kind directed against Steunenberg personally are concerned I can't say I entirely approved of them, but as regards him officially I did then and do now endorse them. I regarded Steunenberg and you, Senator Borah, in the same class."

The *Rocky Mountain News* reported that Borah "grilled the witness with a merciless tongue, always framing his question as to convey the impression that a loaded gun in the shape of the documentary evidence was at hand to confound and route Haywood and his attorneys. Momentarily the spectator looked for the long promised sensations but they did not materialize." [35]

C. P. Connolly, writing in *Collier's*, believed, however, "that at the close of the case for the defense, a much stronger chain of evidence had been forged against Haywood than the prosecution had succeeded in welding." [36]

15

The open windows and the electric fans furnished little relief to a sweltering courtroom as State's Attorney Hawley started his summation. He had been suffering from stomach distress for several days, yet, the *Idaho Daily Statesman* reported, he made "an address that will go down in the history of court proceedings as one of the greatest of its kind." [37]

Every seat in the courtroom was occupied as Hawley reviewed the testimony of witnesses for the defense and denounced them all as perjurers or at the least as unintentional liars. Only persons prejudiced in Haywood's favor, he claimed, would have disputed Orchard's testimony. Hawley's sincere manner, his air of honesty, impressed the jurors. The discomforts of the hot weather, the beads of perspiration running down their faces, were forgotten; they seemed transfixed by his words. He gestured as he spoke, sometimes sitting on the state's table only a few feet away from them.

"Harry Orchard," Hawley predicted, "will be fiercely attacked in the arguments of the attorneys for the other side"; they will call him a liar. "But, gentlemen, there is some mysterious but powerful influence back of this confession . . . the saving power of divine grace working upon his soul and through him to bring justice to one of the worst criminal bands that ever operated in this country. Orchard's faith is now in God. He is a Christian. He has told his story that justice may reign and he fully expects to bear the punishment that law demands. Orchard told you with tears in his eyes, with voice hushed, that he told his story because he knew it was a duty he owed God, himself and humanity." [38]

Hawley spoke for nearly eight hours, over a two-day period. "Gentlemen of the jury, I tell you frankly, if I did not believe in my heart that Haywood was guilty I would so state. I wish I could find some way by which I could conclude from the evidence that I was satisfied of his innocence, because I would a thousand times rather have a man vindicated than to have him dragged through the mire and dirt of a conviction, but we can come to but one conclusion and that is he is not only responsible for this atrocious murder, but that for more than a score of other murders that have been proven here is he equally responsible." [39]

Haywood exhibited no emotion as he listened quietly, sometimes taking notes on a small pad or whispering to one of his attorneys.

16

It had been decided between the two leading defense attorneys that Darrow would follow Richardson in summation. On Monday, July 22, one of the hottest days of the year, Richardson opened. The temperature rose to a furnacelike intensity; the whirring fans created barely a ripple in the heavy air of the courtroom. From the early troubles in the Coeur d'Alene to the explosive murder of the governor, Richardson recited the history of the Western Federation of Miners.

Then he turned to Orchard: "An accomplice is a man who takes part in a crime. In this case the accomplice is the man who actually committed the crime. There is no charge that the defendant was there. He did not fire the bomb—and nobody claims he did." Richardson emphasized that a jury must not render a verdict of guilty on suspicion or "probable" guilt. He stressed that even the charge against Haywood accused him only of advising, aiding, and abetting Orchard and that the defense disproved those charges, too.

As Hawley had predicted, the defense attacked Orchard's conversion to Christianity. Richardson called Orchard "a cheat. His religion is a sham, assumed to bolster up a confession made before he ever thought of adopting such a cloak.

"It has not been his religion that prompted this damnable, false confession. No," Richardson shouted, "it has been another motive. He is endeavoring to swear away the life of yonder noble, wife loving, child loving man, so that he himself, may save his own crime smirched, carcass from the scaffold." [40]

The following day, Darrow began his address to the jury, a summation delivered in four sessions, over an eleven-hour period. [41] He held his eyeglasses by the nosepiece as he gestured toward the jury. In his first sentence he indicated that he considered this more than a criminal case: though it was important to Haywood as well as to Moyer and Pettibone who were still to be tried, and to Haywood's family and friends, it was even more important to society as a whole and in particular to the labor "movement which represents the hopes and wishes and the aspirations of all men who labor to sustain their daily life."

Darrow lost no time in focusing on one of his favorite themes: the rights and the protection of labor. He would crucify Orchard's reputation to protect those rights. Walking back and forth before the jury, he would pause periodically and lean forward as if speaking in confidence. "I sometimes wonder whether here in Idaho or anywhere in the country, broad and free, a man can be placed on trial and lawyers seriously asked to take away the life of a human being upon the testimony of Harry Orchard."

For three hours he castigated the star witness for the state. "I have the greatest respect for any religion or any code of ethics that would do anything to help man, whatever that religion may be," he said, admitting that his feeling for religion was probably different than that of Hawley or Borah. He derided Orchard's conversion. "I undertake to say, gentlemen, that if Harry Orchard has religion now, that I hope I never get it. I want to say to this jury that before Harry Orchard got religion he was bad enough, but it remained to religion to make him totally depraved." Orchard was a "monstrous liar . . . bred to cheat and to lie," the deserter of his family, a rogue who "went out into the world and covered himself with mud and dirt and crime until he was revolting in the sight of God and man."

Despite the fact that he did not understand "the purpose of that mysterious power which molded Harry Orchard's brain," Darrow said he had always fought the taking of a human life by the state and he would not ask for Orchard's life. "And if the time should ever come that somebody pronounced against him the decree of death and nobody else asks to save his life, my petition will be there to save it. I do not believe in man taking away the life of his fellow-man."

Darrow would repeat that theme in the Leopold and Loeb case almost two decades later when he told the judge, in his defense of the two boys charged with murder and kidnapping, that "all life is worth saving." [42]

His voice hoarse, his eyes tearful, Clarence talked about the defendant Haywood as he concluded his summation late on Thursday afternoon. "I have known him well and I believe in him. God knows it would be a sore day to me if he should go upon the scaffold. The sun would not shine or the birds would not sing on that day—for me. It would be a sad day, indeed, if any such calamity would come to him. I would think of his wife, of his mother, I would think of his children, I would think of the great cause that he represents. But gentlemen, he and his mother, and his wife and his children, are not my chief concern in this great case. If you should decree that he must die, ten thousand men will work in the mines and send a portion of the proceeds of their labor to take care of that widow and these orphan children, and a million people throughout the length and breadth of the civilized world will send their messages of kindness and good cheer to comfort them. It is not for them I plead. Other men have died in the same cause in which Bill Haywood has risked his life. He can die if this jury decrees it; but, oh, gentlemen, do not think for a moment that if you hang him you will crucify the labor movement of the world; do not think that you will kill the hopes and the aspirations and the desires of the weak and poor."

His wrinkled gray suit jacket fell open. He shrugged his shoulders, stretched his hands toward the jury beseeching them to save not only his client but all those "who toil with their hands. . . . Gentlemen, it is not for him alone that I speak. I speak for the poor, for the weak, for the weary, for that long line of men, who, in darkness and despair, have borne the labors of the human race."

Haywood's sobbing wife in her wheelchair added an overwhelming poignancy to the emotional scene Darrow had created. The defendant, his face drained of color, sat rigid. His mother agitatedly fanned herself with a palm leaf. Then the tears rolled down her cheeks and soon she, too, buried her face in her hands. "The picture of despair, his elbows on his knees and his chin in his palms," Mrs. Haywood's father did not cry, but his face "was alive with emotion and his eyes were glued to the floor."[43]

The press generally saw Darrow's summation more as a passionate statement of his own views of society than as a plea for his client. In a powerful and emotional denunciation of Orchard and of Hawley for believing Orchard's story, Darrow, they felt, filled his speech with invective, vituperation, denunciatory humor, and pathos, but not with argument for Haywood.

17

Borah closed for the state. He was soon to take his seat as the Republican senator from Idaho, which he would represent for thirty-three years. A political maverick from the day of his inauguration to his death, he opposed much of President Woodrow Wilson's progressive legislation but supported most of the New Deal program initiated by another Democratic president, Franklin D. Roosevelt.

In contrast to the working-class spectators in the courtroom during Darrow's summation, the elite of Idaho came to hear Borah. Mrs. Steunenberg, widow of the assassinated governor, sat in the courtroom for the first time. Hundreds stood on the lawn, under open windows, to hear the plea.[44]

"Gentlemen," opened Borah, "I am not going to undertake to make a speech nor to talk to you, but I am simply going to talk with you about the evidence in this case." His voice quivered as he referred to "some twenty odd crimes. . . .

We are not fighting organized labor. We are not fighting the weak and the poor. Neither are we here to consent that organized labor shall be a shield to crime. This is not a fight on organized labor—it is simply a trial for murder."

Pausing dramatically to look first at Darrow and then at the jury, Borah said he wanted to discuss "some of the startling doctrines of Mr. Darrow. This is not for the purpose of attacking the man personally. Personally, I like him very much but I do not like his doctrines as given to this jury. If Haywood felt as his counsel feels, who speaks for him, if this is the creed of the W.F.M., why should they not kill and murder?"

The special prosecutor recalled the night ex-Governor Steunenberg was murdered. In a lyrical cadence he talked of the drifting snow, the cold and merciless chill, the blood upon the white earth. "I saw Idaho disgraced and dishonored—I saw murder—no, not murder—a thousand times worse than murder. I saw anarchy displaying its first bloody triumph to Idaho. I saw government by assassination pointing to the mangled form of Frank Steunenberg, the broken family, the blood bespattered home, and saying to all—look, look and take notice!" He warned, "Here is the fate of all who do their duty to their State and the government. I thought over that night again. I said to myself, Thou living God, can time or the arts of counsel unteach the lessons of that hour? No, no; for the sake of all that good men hold near and dear let us not be misled, let us not forget, let us not be falterers in this great test of courage and heroism.

"In the court of your conscience," Borah told the jurors, "the verdict must be worked out and I must leave it all with you. Yet I hesitate to close. This matter lies nearer to my heart than anything in my whole life. Nevertheless, I can but turn the matter over to you for your final action. Thanking you for the State for your long and devoted service and bidding you have courage for your final great duty, I leave the State's interests with you."

Darrow considered Borah's address "the fairest and the ablest I have ever heard from counsel in a great murder trial."[45]

The next morning, following Borah's plea, Judge Fremont Wood instructed the jury. Most of his instructions pertained to the law's presumption of innocence, the burden of proof, corroboration, reasonable doubt, and circumstantial evidence. Most important were Instruction 34, in which the judge said, "Under the statutes of this state a person cannot be convicted of a crime upon the testimony of an accomplice unless such accomplice is corroborated by other evidence," and Instruction 36, "Corroborative evidence . . . must tend to connect the defendant with the particular offense upon which he is now on trial."[46]

After listening to more than ten weeks of testimony, the jurors filed out to decide the verdict, and Haywood was taken back to jail. A hung jury was the most favorable decision either side hoped for. Richardson, satisfied he had done his best, went home to sleep.

For Darrow, however, sleep was impossible. As the jury deliberated, he walked the streets, fearful of Haywood's fate. Where the lives of his clients were at stake, Darrow's first reactions were always emotional, before reason and legal thinking took over, and even then emotion permeated his intellectual approach. Yet, the issue of "why" a crime was committed was almost as important as saving his client, because if he could find the reasons behind the crime, then others could be saved from the fate of those he was defending. It was idealistic and often hopeless, but all his life he continued to look for the "why."

Often he came to the Boise jail "down in the mouth and worried." Pettibone would try to cheer him up: "You know, it's us fellows that have to be hanged!"; and Haywood would suggest that "when things got gloomy at the office" and Darrow wanted to be cheered up he should "come down to the jail."[47]

Always in a murder case the same refrain: "I can't stand a client to be executed, I can't stand it!"

At seven o'clock Monday morning, July 29, 1907, word came that the jury had reached a verdict. The judge was notified, the attorneys were called, the defendant was brought into the courtroom. The jury foreman handed the envelope to the clerk: "We, the jury, find the defendant, William D. Haywood, not guilty."

Emma Goldman, Alexander Berkman, and Hippolyte Havel, famed anarchists, savored the victory. They wired President Roosevelt: "Undesirable citizens victorious. Rejoice."

Said Borah, the "good men and true of the State of Idaho have passed upon the case and that disposes it so far as the State of Idaho and Haywood are concerned."

Theodore Roosevelt, however, did not agree. "There has been a gross miscarriage of justice, to my mind, out in Idaho at the acquittal of Haywood. I suppose the jury was terrorized, but it is not a pleasant matter from any standpoint."[48]

The *New York World* editorialized: "The state failed to prove its case. . . . The trial and the verdict must be a sad blow to an army of Socialist agitators and demagogues who were looking for a martyr to their cause and thought that they had found one in Haywood."[49]

The trial and the verdict, said the *New York Press,* "is a triumph for the American law that its due process was preserved in the heat of the bitter and ruthless conflict just as if the scene of the trial had been not Boise but Boston."[50]

The Haywood trial cost the State of Idaho $95,000, of which the Pinkerton agency received $30,000, Hawley $30,000, and Borah $5000.[51]

All through the trial there had been rumblings of disagreement between Darrow and Richardson. Each court session was followed by a stormy scene between the two lawyers. With the verdict in, the conflict became public.

Richardson complained that Darrow was headstrong. His great fault in the Haywood trial was that he was a Socialist and inclined to put the interests of the party over that of his clients. He would never again be associated with Darrow in a lawsuit. Darrow, on the other hand, found Richardson "very hard to get along with. He was very egotistical, arrogant, and exceedingly jealous. We could never travel double again. If Richardson is retained I will not be back in Boise."[52]

Radicals and labor men approved of the way Darrow had conducted himself and believed his plea largely responsible for the acquittal. When it came down to a choice between Richardson and Darrow, they retained Darrow. A few days after the trial, Darrow and Haywood attended a labor reception in their honor in Denver. A crowd of ten thousand cheered their arrival as they rode in an open carriage drawn by six white horses followed by a procession of labor sympathizers. At the Albany Hotel a committee of one hundred representatives from labor organizations paid homage to them.[53]

18

Ruby and Clarence returned to Chicago. But only briefly. Within two months the State of Idaho was ready to prosecute both Pettibone and Adams, and the Darrows returned to Boise.

As he prepared for the trials, Clarence came down with the flu. Before he was fully recovered, his left ear developed an insistent pain which increased in intensity as the days passed. His physicians diagnosed it as an infection "in grave danger" of developing into mastoiditis. The pain became intolerable. In the middle of the night Ruby had to send for the only ear specialist in Boise, Dr. Charles Hudgel, who admitted Clarence to the local hospital where he lanced the ear. On October 6, newspapers reported that Darrow had left the hospital "too soon" after the operation "and had a relapse." The doctors warned him against participating in the forthcoming trials. Adams, however, had repudiated his confession because of his confidence in Darrow, and Clarence felt a responsibility to continue. "If Adams lost it meant his death, or his surrender to the State, which would further imperil the lives of Moyer and Pettibone," he said.[54]

The state had requested a change of venue in the Adams trial to Rathdrum, a small town about sixty miles northwest of Wallace, scene of the first trial. Surrounded by farm country, with few miners or laborers, Rathdrum was less cognizant of union problems than Wallace where many mines were located and the ongoing struggles between miner and operator intensified.

The journey from Boise to Rathdrum covered a long, circuitous route through Washington State, where the Darrows stopped off in Spokane to consult an ear specialist.

The constant pain never let up. Before they left Boise, Dr. Hudgel prepared them for the trip and for their destination, which had no medical facilities. He gave them some medical instruments with detailed instructions on keeping the eardrum open and irrigated regularly and directions for sterilizing the instruments each time. All Clarence's energies were devoted to fighting the agony. The trip was a nightmare for the suffering Clarence, and for Ruby, who spent hours sterilizing the instruments to irrigate the ear.

The Spokane specialist delivered the same opinion as Dr. Hudgel—it might be mastoiditis, but it was too soon to tell and definitely too soon for surgery. He recommended hospitalization since such infections generated fever which, if not attended to immediately, might well prove fatal. He warned Darrow that he was risking his life by his determination to defend Adams.[55]

19

The Adams trial opened early in November with Clarence at the defense table. He would later describe the time in Rathdrum as "one continuous orgy of pain." He and Ruby lived in a private home near the courthouse. At night he slept with a hot-water bag which Ruby reheated hourly. When the pain became unbearable, they resorted to the hypodermic needle which Ruby filed "to the slimness of hairs with finest emery-paper; the instrument had to be boiled, the needle, and the tablespoon that held the needle while it was being sterilized, as well as the liquid and codeine; the outfit assembled with sterilized gauze so that no fresh infection would be added to whatever it was that I already had."

The days and the weeks merged. The pain did not subside, nor did the nature of the illness exhibit itself.

20

All through the trial Adams sat beside his attorneys, chewing gum and twirling a lead pencil, his eyes shifting from one part of the courtroom to another.

It had been difficult to find an unprejudiced jury. The previous Adams trial in Wallace and the earlier Haywood case had received wide publicity and laid a groundwork of opinion. In the end, however, a jury of "mostly farmers, who said that they had no opinion, and could render an impartial verdict" was assembled.

McParland again testified for the state. He had urged Adams "to make a clean breast of the affair as he would feel much better and it was a debt he owed the state and to law and order—and that he was a tool and he admitted it. I used the Bible stories of David and Paul as an illustration of what fitted a man of crime, and that he might be redeemed."

"By whom?" asked Darrow.

"By God, of course," McParland said.

"You did not tell him that you would forgive him?"

"I have not the power of absolution," replied McParland. "I told him that I believed the state would be fair."[56]

In his summation Darrow reiterated much of his earlier plea for Adams. He again called the trial "remarkable" and "unprecedented" in the annals of prosecution. Adams, he said, "is being tried because he went back on McParland and repudiated his statements. They thought McParland could use him to hang Haywood but he could not. They want to use him to hang Moyer and Pettibone, but they can't do it."[57]

The jury began deliberations at eight-thirty on Saturday evening. After five ballots taken over nine hours, with no change in the count—eight for acquittal, four for conviction—the hung jury was dismissed and Adams returned to the penitentiary.[58] Eventually he stood trial in Colorado on a charge relating to a strike in that state. He was acquitted and disappeared from the labor scene.

21

With the Adams trial concluded, Darrow and Ruby left for Portland, Oregon, where he received treatment for his infected ear. It did not help, and he was advised to see a noted ear specialist in San Francisco. Again, observation and treatment. Again, the doctor doubted the mastoid was infected but could not say where the pain came from and advised care and attention.

A telegram notified Darrow that Pettibone was scheduled for immediate trial. Unable to obtain a continuance, he prepared to leave for Boise despite the doctor's warnings that the trip might be fatal to him. "But Pettibone thought it might be fatal to him if I stayed," so Ruby and Clarence boarded the train to Boise. Upon arrival Clarence went directly to St. Alphonsus Hospital. Again, the source of the infection could not be identified.

A newspaper, which had been detailing the progress of his illness, now sought a last interview, as he was reported near death. Never at a loss for a quip, Darrow said he "wasn't really ready" and promised to call the newsman "as soon as the grim reaper started his job in earnest."

22

He appeared in the Boise courtroom about three days before the Pettibone jury was impaneled. Edgar Wilson, who had been part of the defense team during the Haywood trial, had examined most of the talesmen, with Darrow completing the choices.

During Hawley's opening statement, Darrow moved a chair in front of the jury box where he sat taking notes. In consideration of Darrow's illness, and because the testimony was essentially a repeat, both state and defense agreed to accept some of it in depositions.

Darrow did most of the cross-examining of the witnesses. Harry Orchard again appeared as star witness for the state and repeated his testimony in the Haywood trial. Darrow decided to forgo questioning Orchard on his direct testimony as he saw no advantage to the defense in having the jury hear again Orchard's accusations against the union officials. Instead, he probed the witness's mind, leading him to recount the details of his crimes.

Orchard appeared chastened as he recited a list of bombings and murders committed without regard to the innocents involved. He told how he had deserted his wife and child and never given them another thought. The jurors, sympathetic after the prosecution's portrayal of him as a penitent sinner, drew back "in horror and disgust."[59]

The cross-examination tested the limits of Clarence's endurance and brought him near collapse. Now Pettibone, too, joined Darrow's doctors in urging him to withdraw, but he insisted on making a short statement to the jury.

There was no doubt, when Darrow started to speak the next morning, that he was a very sick man. He spoke in a barely audible voice, each word enunciated in pain. The jurors strained to hear as he informed them he was withdrawing from the case. Within a few hours, he was on his way to the hospital in Los Angeles.

On the strength of his cross-examination and the mood it had created among the jurors, his associates decided not to offer evidence and to waive argument.

Pettibone was acquitted. While in jail awaiting trial he had contracted tuberculosis. He died shortly after being released. Finally, the case against Moyer was dismissed, and he resumed his activities in the Western Federation of Miners.

The Executive Board of the WFM, however, ousted Big Bill Haywood as secretary-treasurer because they disapproved of his militancy as a Socialist and as an official of the anarchist-syndicalist IWW. His later years were marked by activism in labor strikes and in fighting U.S. entry into World War I. Sentenced for interfering with the war effort, he jumped bail and fled to Russia to prison where he died on May 18, 1928, disillusioned with the political regime for which he had held such high hopes.

23

The Los Angeles hospital stay was as frustrating as the other hospital visits. The doctors could not determine the reason for the pain. As Darrow was leaving to return to Chicago, a swelling appeared over the entire area back of his ear, the symptom the doctors had been looking for to confirm their speculations of mastoiditis, and he was rushed back to the hospital for surgery. Had the crisis occurred a few hours later, when he was on the train far from medical attention, it could have cost him his life. The experience only reinforced Clarence's argument that man has no control over his fate. "In the language of the court," he explained, "'I got a continuance.'"[60]

24

A few months after the Pettibone acquittal, Harry Orchard appeared before Judge Wood to change his plea from "not guilty" to "guilty." Before passing sentence on Orchard, the judge reviewed both the Haywood and Pettibone trials. He believed Orchard's testimony because "I am of the opinion that no man living could conceive the stories of crime told by him and maintain himself under the merciless fire of cross-examination by leading attorneys of the country, unless upon the theory that he was testifying to facts and circumstances which had an actual existence in his own experience." Since, however, he had no alternative but to impose the death sentence, he recommended the Pardon Board commute Orchard's sentence to life imprisonment.

Regarding the murder of government officials, Judge Wood warned, "I want to take the opportunity of this solemn occasion to say to the associates in crime of this defendant that they cannot by such acts terrorize American executives and prevent them from performing their plain duties, and they cannot prevent American courts from declaring the law as they find it."[61]

The Pardon Board followed the judge's advice. Orchard remained a privileged trustee in his little house on the grounds of the Idaho prison until his death on April 13, 1954. To the end he "ostentatiously" practiced his religion.

The cost of the trials practically depleted the union's treasury, and Darrow settled for $35,000,[62] most of it dissipated by his illness. In addition, the Panic of 1907 wiped out much of his investment and savings. He returned to Chicago with debts which took over a year to repay.[63]

X

At Home in Hyde Park

1

IN Chicago's Hyde Park, a twenty-minute train ride from Clarence's downtown office, Ruby found a large, airy, nine-room flat on the top floor of a six-story apartment building at 1537 East Sixtieth Street. Only a few blocks from the University of Chicago whose towers could be seen from its windows, the apartment also overlooked the tree-lined parkway along Sixtieth Street known as the Midway, and the panorama of Jackson Park and Lake Michigan.

The furniture came out of storage, and before long the apartment took on the "unostentatious . . . solid, comfortable, leisurely air" of the Darrows themselves. The large, high-ceilinged rooms with solid oak beams and "predominating color of red" helped "to give an impression of warmth."[1] Clarence liked the color red.

The master bedroom, at the south end of the apartment, had windows on three sides. The library took up the entire north end. From its uncurtained windows on a clear day the unobstructed view of Chicago's Loop ten miles away delighted Clarence. The walls of the library were completely lined with books which spilled out of the bookshelves. They overflowed onto chairs, tables, and windowsills, with piles of them stacked on the floor around the edges of the room.

Here Ruby and Clarence remained for over thirty years. To the apartment on the Midway came professors and writers and intellectuals, scientists and philosophers, young and old, to exchange ideas as Clarence debated with them and challenged their thinking.

Hamlin Garland, who had known Darrow for many years, recalls dining at the Darrow home shortly after they moved in. Clarence was "as grave and even more bitter than his writing indicates." He read aloud some of his own unpublished short stories called "The Law's Delay" which Garland considered "intolerably gloomy and savage but powerful. . . . His writing is too monotonous in tone, too bitter in quality, too pessimistic of outlook to succeed, but it has a protest which it is well to consider." [2]

2

At a protest meeting in 1908 where Clarence spoke, Helen Todd introduced him to Mary Field, another Hull-House social worker. The label "social worker" always tempted Darrow's cynicism, and he gave vent to some lighthearted teasing about the profession's accomplishments. With a jovial sense of humor, Mary, twenty-one years his junior, parried his thrusts with barbs of her own. Clarence was delighted.

As they continued to meet they found a common political ideology. Unlike many of the radical women he knew, she was "witty and mischievous" about her anarchist ideas "instead of philosophical." [3] The stage was set for a relationship which continued until his death.

Mary was a rebel. A 1900 graduate of the University of Michigan, she had turned her back on her strict Victorian upbringing and rejected all formal religious and political authority. She came to Chicago to do social work, first at the Chicago Commons, a slum settlement house, then with Jane Addams at Hull-House.

Five years remarried when they met, Darrow was not averse to treading "the primrose path." William Allen White says he did so "not idly but with zeal and a deep conviction of . . . rectitude." Darrow "was not an indiscriminate petticoat chaser, nothing like it; but he loved, like the wind, where he listed."

Undoubtedly there had been an affair at the start. Looking back at the relationship, Mary's younger sister Sara said of Mary, "Yes," she had an affair with Darrow, "and she never forgave herself." [4]

"The sex part was evidently short-lived and the relationship settled into a deep friendship." [5] By 1911 Mary was deeply in love with Lemuel Parton, a San Francisco newspaperman. They were married in 1913, "one of the truly happy marriages I've ever seen," says their daughter, Margaret Parton. "Lem was totally accepting of Mary's lifelong love of Darrow, and came to share it, I think."[6]

Clarence influenced Mary profoundly, turning her from social work, which he insisted was only a salve on society's conscience, to a strong interest in the labor movement and eventually a new profession of labor reporter.

Mary moved to New York late in 1909. "As this move seemed to me a little inexplicable, and as Mother had always been vague about it, I went to see Ida Rauh Eastman, who had been Mother's room-mate in Greenwich Village," Mary's daughter wrote. "Ida, who was an actress in the first plays at the Provincetown Playhouse, at ninety-one still had a Sarah Bernhardt sort of voice as well as a wry and poetic memory.

"'Why did Mother leave Chicago?' I asked her.

"'I think it had something to do with that lawyer-fellow—you know, that one all the women were in love with. What's his name? Darrow, yes that's it. I think she was unhappy about him and wanted to get away so she came to New York.'

"'But Ida, she always told me she loved him the way a disciple loved Jesus.'

"Ida snorted. 'Maybe. But she loved him about nine other ways too,' she said dryly."[7]

Margaret asked her mother once, "Were you in love with him?"

"In a kind of way," Mary answered slowly. "Not the way I loved . . . Lem— but more like the way the disciples loved Jesus. He was such a *great* man! Like Freud, with the compassion and tenderness and understanding of Jesus. And yet he was anything but Christlike."[8]

Just before the McNamara trial in 1910, Darrow wrote to Mary in New York: "I miss you all the time. No one else is so bright and clear and sympathetic to say nothing of sweet and dear. . . . Am tired and hungry and wish you were here to eat and drink with me and talk to me with your low, sweet, kind, sympathetic voice."[9]

Talking to her daughter about the letter more than forty years later, Mary said, "Anybody reading these words would think that Darrow was passionately fond of me. And in a way, he was. But he could be mean as the devil, too. He asked me once to meet him downtown for dinner. An awful rainstorm came up and I had to get back to my flat. Darrow gave me a nickel for carfare—he wouldn't think of putting me in a taxi. He was awfully stingy."[10]

"Stingy." Masters complained of Darrow's niggardliness, too. Perhaps the key is in a letter to his friend Fremont Older, editor of the *San Francisco Call*, written probably in 1910: "I never have been able to get over the dread of being poor and the fear of it," he confessed. Then, almost in envy, "You have passed that with the rest seemingly without an effort."[11]

Yet, Mary notes Clarence gave freely when she expressed concern over Mother Jones, the militant organizer of the coal miners union. "He pulled a wad of rumpled money out of his pocket and told me to buy her some woolen underwear. It came to almost $100."[12]

Gertrude Barnum, his social worker friend from the Langdon days, also spoke of his generosity to her fund-raising appeals for various labor causes. Victor Yarros, a law associate, said, "He helped many financially as well as professionally."[13]

3

Darrow's letters to Mary, a collection running from 1909 through 1930, portray a lonely, sad man, often anguished and bitter. He talks about mutual friends, experiences they shared, recommends books. He discusses his writing and encourages her in her writing. His fears and longings poignantly fill pages in his almost undecipherable handwriting. "No sooner do we plant our feet on something that seems like solid ground than we find the sand shifting under us and we look for something else":[14] "Life is horribly cruel and the trouble is there is no way out of anything."[15]

Strangely, he never mentions Ruby even though the women knew each other. He asks about Mary's husband, about their daughter. He writes about his son and granddaughters. In some of the letters he suggests that Mary write care of his office or a next-door neighbor. Occasionally there is a "naughty story . . . about a girl, a virgin with a great and growing curiosity who finally managed to get it satisfied and remarked to a friend . . . that it was the most over advertised experience she had ever known."[16]

Mary Field came to Chicago to observe the Leopold and Loeb trial, but was unable to get into the courtroom because of the crowds. She asked Darrow for help. For reasons of his own, he made no effort to ease her difficulties, and she returned to New York.[17]

Ruby believed that Clarence severed relations with her from that time onward because he had tired of her aggressiveness. She was wrong. Ruby undoubtedly recognized Clarence's especial feeling for Mary, and she was particularly bitter against her, so much so indeed that she implored Irving Stone when he was writing Darrow's biography not to immortalize her in Darrow's life. She suggested that if he allowed Mary to "embroider" her relationship to Clarence he should also get a long list of the other "ladies-in-waiting."[18]

Ruby trails through Mary's diary over the years. "Darrow comes without his legal prosecutor." "Helen Todd and I talked of Darrow and the curious fear he has of Ruby, the power she has over him to humiliate, to betray." "Against the collective woman Darrow rages as he would like to against the little piss ant wife whose pettiness and jealousies have galled him for years."

"She was the kind of woman," Mary said of Ruby, "who would say, after some friend had left the room, 'Such a nice girl. Pity she never washes under her arms.'"

Once at dinner with Ruby and Clarence, Fremont Older, and Lincoln Steffens, Mary made some witty comment. Clarence laughed: "Mary, you're an awful clever girl. You're the cleverest woman I ever knew."

"You're the thousandeth!" Ruby "chirrped," adding, "No, maybe the thousandeth and one woman he's told that to!"

"According to Mother," says Margaret, "Ruby always chirped or whined." [19]

Mary was hard on Ruby. There were others who saw Ruby in a different light. To Marcet Haldeman-Julius, Ruby had "a quick, reaching mind. She is naturally reserved . . . not from aloofness but from a deep temperamental shyness . . . her emotions are rich and true." [20]

"If ever there lived a solicitous and loving wife," said George Jean Nathan, it was Ruby. "She watches over Clarence, day and night, like a baby, and Clarence delights in it. . . . Without Ruby, he would be completely lost—and he knows it. . . ." [21]

Preston Bradley, liberal Chicago minister and a friend of the Darrows, "liked Ruby. She was no fool. She understood Clarence, and she was really the last word for him, and what she said went." [22]

4

Unknown to Ruby, Clarence put up the security that enabled Mary and Lem to purchase a nineteenth-century brownstone town house at 7 Charles Street in the Greenwich Village district of New York City. Many times when he came to New York for lectures he would dine with them or they met him with other friends for dinner, sometimes with Ruby.

Once, when he came to New York for a lecture without Ruby, Mary noted in her diary that Clarence lectured on "Personal Freedom," "that which he has no knowledge of." [23]

Margaret remembers great excitement whenever Darrow appeared at the Parton home for a dinner party. The preteenager would curtsy to the assembled guests, who might include Lincoln Steffens, Sinclair Lewis and Dorothy Thompson, Carl Sandburg, Theodore Dreiser, Norman Thomas, Charles and Mary Beard, labor leaders, editors, scientists, artists. There were always discussions about economics, graft and corruption, Russia and what had happened to all the old radicals. Sandburg sang ballads and played his guitar, Darrow read aloud; there were charades, in jokes, and much laughter. [24]

Margaret remembers Darrow "as a large creature sitting in a big wicker chair holding forth—lots of talk, laughter." She does not have fond childhood memories of him, nor of his influence over her mother. "Loving and optimistic," Mary was a good foil for Darrow, but as the years passed she sometimes imitated Darrow's "cynicism, the despair, the arrogance." Mary "had a first-class mind until she met Darrow," her sister said, "and after that she had a second-class imitation of Darrow's mind."

The child Margaret always approached Darrow tentatively, in awe of the huge man her mother obviously adored. She remembers Carl Sandburg singing ballads to her, Fremont Older swimming with her, Sinclair Lewis taking his dinner plate from the adult table and bringing it over to her corner. But not Darrow: she later writes in her autobiography, "One had the impression . . . that if you couldn't be clever and amuse him it would be best to melt into the shadows behind the piano." [25]

Once Margaret asked Darrow to autograph a page of a book on which Babe Ruth had already inscribed his name. Clarence smiled as he wrote, "Clarence Darrow, Pinch Hitter." He read the inscription aloud and "everyone laughed so much that I realized it was another of their adult jokes which I didn't understand and went away unnoticed. Somehow, with Darrow I always felt like a thing, an object rather than a living person who happened to be a child." [26]

Judge Dwight McKay of the Circuit Court of Cook County, whose father and Clarence were old friends, has more tender memories of Darrow. [27] Many times Clarence and Ruby dined at the McKay home. Both families often took motor trips together. "Neither Darrow nor my father owned a car, but they could always borrow one. We used to drive to Egg Harbor, Wisconsin, up beyond Green Bay. Invariably, when Darrow drove we'd end up in a ditch. He would talk and look at everything but what he was doing and he'd end up in a ditch, and then we'd sit there waiting for a team of horses to come to pull us out. While we were waiting he'd be telling stories. It didn't bother him that we were in the ditch."

When the Darrows came to the McKays for dinner, Clarence always read stories to the children. "He knew we had the *Rutabaga Stories* and he would ask for the book. Both my brother and sister and I could read a little, and we knew enough to know that, even though he pretended to be reading a story to us, he was making it up. He had the ability to get right to you and keep you occupied and interested."

5

Hysteria flared up in the East European Jewish community living around Hull-House when, in 1908, the Russian government attempted to extradite Christian Rudovitz, a Russian revolutionist living in Chicago.

"It is impossible for anyone unacquainted with the Russian colony to realize the consternation produced by this attempted extradition," said Jane Addams. "One old man, tearing his hair and beard as he spoke, declared that all his sons and grandsons might thus be sent back to Russia; in fact, all of the younger men in the colony might be extradited, for every high-spirited young Russian was, in a sense, a revolutionist." [28]

The thirty-five-year-old Rudovitz, a Lutheran born "on the Doblen estate, Courland, of Lettish nationality," joined the Russian Social Democratic party in September 1905 "because there was a revolution there." Together with his comrades he participated in raids to "expropriate" arms for the revolution. Through its spy system, the imperial government learned the identity of the leaders of the revolution, arrested and tortured them, and summarily executed them.

Rudovitz had attended the meeting where the party voted to kill three spies as part of an organized effort to overthrow the imperial government. In late fall 1907, he fled to the United States, where he settled in West Pullman, Illinois, and worked as a carpenter until his arrest on the complaint of the Russian consul in Chicago, who on behalf of the Russian government requested his extradition.

Insisting he was a political rufugee, Rudovitz requested asylum. Jane Addams and many of the settlement workers at Hull-House as well as Federal Judge Julian Mack interested themselves in the case. Darrow, Peter Sissman and Charles C. Hyde of Northwestern University appeared before U.S. Commissioner Mark A. Foote to represent Rudovitz.

Martin Jurow, another Russian revolutionist, was the chief witness for Rudovitz. Jurow told the commissioner that his own two brothers, twelve and sixteen years old, had been tortured when they refused to divulge his hiding place.

The purpose of the military organization of the Social Democratic party, Jurow explained, "was to overthrow the present government and establish one by the people. We robbed the Barons and disarmed the soldiers. We broke into houses and stole guns and ammunition.

"We adopted resolutions that those who give evidence against our leaders should be killed."

He then explained that the three who had been slain by the revolutionary group were "spies who had given information which led to the punishment of our leaders." [29]

In his closing argument before Commissioner Foote, Darrow charged that "Czar Nicholas II is plotting to reach the hand of despotism into the United States and drag back, no man knows how many, political offenders of Russia.

"If the crime was committed in Russia and it was not a political offense then it is the duty of this court to return him there for trial. We have admitted that he was in that meeting and that he voted and that three persons were killed."

To Darrow, the passions that moved Rudovitz and his comrades were similar to the "same eternal ideal that inspired that band of men who were the great-great-great grandfathers of the daughters and the sons of the American Revolution who went out and burned houses and cut throats and shot on sight.

"This is not an ordinary crime," Darrow insisted, as he would in his defense of the McNamaras three years later. "An ordinary crime is not one affecting a whole nation or a whole class of people. This case affects an entire class. The smallest part of it is that it may mean death to this accused man if he is sent back to Russia."

William C. Rigby, representing the Russian government, objected. "It is not to be assumed that this defendant will be punished by death."

"Well," Darrow retorted, "we disagree with you on that. If his punishment is not death it would be a sentence to Siberia and that would mean worse than death. There are perhaps 200,000 exiles of the Russian revolution and probably half of them are in the U.S. and the Russian government seeks to reach out its arms to this republic and seize whom it will among the men who have sought America as a political asylum."

Darrow could not resist the temptation to remind the commissioner that America had been created by political exiles, that America had been born in revolution.[30]

Commissioner Foote disagreed with the defense's contention and recommended to the State Department that Rudovitz be extradited to Russia.

The case was appealed to the secretary of state. Darrow and Sissman again were counsel for the accused, along with William J. Calhoun, constitutional lawyer. The appeal brief insisted, as had Darrow and Sissman earlier before the commissioner, that at the time the spies were killed there was "a political uprising throughout the Baltic provinces and [it] extended over a large portion of the Russian Empire." Every act of which Rudovitz was accused was "directly connected with, incidental to, and formed a part of the political disturbance."[31]

Among his last official acts as secretary of state before he took his seat as a U.S. senator from New York, Elihu Root decreed that Rudovitz's crime was a political offense and, therefore, "under the terms of the treaty in effect between the U.S. and Russia since 1893" he was not extraditable. Root held that the acts of violence were "inextricably connected with the revolutionary activity."[32]

When news of the secretary of state's ruling was flashed to Chicago from Washington, D.C., many communities burst into spontaneous celebration. The settlement workers in Hull-House who had made Rudovitz's struggle for liberty their own were exultant. The *Chicago Daily News* reported that "in the Jewish quarter, where there are many persons who fear the far-reaching hand of the Russian police quite as much" as Rudovitz in the county jail, the news "caused general rejoicing."[33]

"It is certainly true," Jane Addams commented after the victory, "that if the decision of the federal office in Chicago had not been reversed by the Department of State in Washington, the United States government would have been committed to return thousands of spirited young refugees to the punishment of the Russian autocracy."[34]

XI

Dynamite!

1

IN 1910 the Democratic party won by a landslide in the off-year election. For the first time in eighteen years the Democrats constituted a majority in the U.S. House of Representatives and would, with the cooperation of insurgent Republicans, control the Senate as well. In addition, the victory included eight traditionally Republican governorships in twenty-six states. Woodrow Wilson, who would become president of the United States in two years, had resigned as head of Princeton University to campaign on the Democratic ticket and be elected governor of New Jersey.

More than a decade of intensive muckraking had made clear to the nation the need for legislation in such areas as food and drugs, child labor, insurance, politics. America moved toward reform. Although almost at their ebb tide, the muckraking magazines continued to expose social and economic ills and political corruption. An English writer visiting America observed the mood of the country: "Never has there been such an example of a nation sitting in judgement on itself as America."

In Chicago, forty thousand clothing workers went on strike, sparked by a walkout of sixteen women who suffered from low wages and long hours and charged petty persecution by overbearing foremen. They demanded a closed shop and the establishment of a mechanism to settle labor disputes. The object of the walkout was Hart, Schaffner & Marx, a manufacturer of men's clothing. After four months, the bitterly fought struggle ended with a signed agreement between HS&M and the United Garment Workers Union[1] which established a three-man arbitration board. The union named Darrow its representative; the company appointed its attorney. Although the two lawyers were to have named a third, for the next several years they successfully settled all disputes by themselves.

The labor movement had a different experience on the West Coast. San Francisco was a union city, but Los Angeles developed into a mecca for the open shop, encouraged by General Harrison Gray Otis, publisher of the influential *Los Angeles Times*. The virulent antiunion stand of this one newspaper was a major factor in the labor wars which beset Los Angeles.

And then, early one morning in October of 1910, the *Los Angeles Times* building exploded, killing twenty men, and antiunion forces accused labor of placing the bomb.

Though aware that some of its leaders and rank-and-file members had no qualms about using violence to gain what they considered justifiable demands, the American Federation of Labor immediately issued a statement disclaiming any connection with the bombing. Anton Johannsen, who later became a vice-president of the Chicago Federation of Labor, an AFL affiliate, was for a time implicated in the bombing. He stated the case for the direct actionists: "Before the union began to use dynamite their men lived on starvation wages, some of them on less than $400 a year, with families! If they say: 'we want light on the activities of union men,' I say: 'All right, but light up the Steel Trust also. Light up both labor and capital.' Put on the search lights, and we are willing that our sins should be compared with the sins of the employers."[2]

Soon after the *Times* blast, police found unexploded bombs near the homes of *Times* publisher Otis and of F. J. Zeehandelaar, an official of the antiunion California Merchants and Manufacturers Association.

Otis was not in the city at the time of the *Times* bombing. Upon his return he adopted the same outraged posture as his editors. "Oh, you Anarchic scum," he editorialized in the paper, "you cowardly murderers, you leeches upon honest labor, you midnight assassins, you whose hands are dripping with the innocent blood of your victims, you against whom the wails of poor widows and the cries of fatherless children are ascending to the Great White Throne, go, mingle with the crowd on the street corners, look upon the crumbled and blackened walls, look at the ruins where are buried the calcined remains of those whom you murdered. . . ."

The *International Socialist Review* retorted sarcastically that, even were Los Angeles to be destroyed by an earthquake, Otis would lay the responsibility on the unions.[3]

Some labor writers suggested that Otis had had the dynamite planted to "frame" organized labor. Eugene Victor Debs, for one, espoused this view and wrote in the *Appeal to Reason,* "I want to express my deliberate opinion that the Times and the crowd of union haters are the instigators, if not the actual perpetrators of that crime and murder of 20 human beings."[4]

A few of labor's friends speculated that, though unionists may have thrown the bomb, Otis was morally responsible for "goading" unionists into violence.[5]

"You hear talk of the hateful baiting which breeds hate," wrote Frederick Palmer in the muckraking magazine *Hampton's,* "of a man of power and position using his newspaper weapon with such venom in beating down his enemies that he created the elements which could find no voice except nitroglycerin to answer the dynamite of Otis's language."[6]

Otis had not always been antiunion. When he became editor of the *Los Angeles Times* in 1882, a year after the founding of the newspaper, nothing in his background indicated any antagonism to unions. There was, indeed, evidence to the contrary: at age fifteen he walked off a job on the *Rock Island Courier* in Rock Island, Illinois, when the owner refused to recognize a union. As a journeyman in the U.S. Government Printing Office, he held a membership in the Typographical Union. During his early years with the *Times,* the unions of the printing trades were allowed to meet in the *Times* offices. By 1890, as the newspaper became financially secure and prestigious, its editorials moved away from Otis's initial prolabor position. Otis complained that unions attempted to "dictate" to management; he labeled them "insufferable despotism . . . odious to freemen,"[7] and dismissed his earlier stance as a "youthful indiscretion."[8]

His antiunion feelings crystallized during the 1890 strike against the four daily L.A. newspapers, and he became the most powerful spokesman for the open shop. Through his efforts the city became the citadel of antiunionism on the West Coast. By 1910 he was insisting that, of all the "splendid material assets" of Los Angeles, "none is so valuable . . . as her possession of that priceless boon, industrial freedom," which meant the open shop. He heaped upon the unions all the hostility and venom he had developed against them through the years. Virtually paranoid, Otis drove around in an armored car with a small cannon mounted on it. His "American Plan" blacklisted union members and cut off balky employers from materials and credit.

Described as "a fighter, quarrelsome and intolerant, choking with the spleen of his fight long after he has lost or won," Otis aroused "all the dregs of any opposition by his unfair tactics and his vicious stabs. He is not without strong followers and powerful enemies. In a public way he has given and taken brass-knuckled blows. He has used splendid power with utter irresponsibility. He is vain and pompous. Froth and fume, and love of epaulets and power and titles, are parts of his make-up."[9]

The *Times* labeled the bombing the "Crime of the Century" both in its news stories and on the inscription of a plaque dedicated a year later to the victims of the blast which hung in the *Times* building lobby.

Rewards for the apprehension of the criminals were offered by various sources—Los Angeles Mayor George Alexander, the Los Angeles Board of Supervisors, the Merchants and Manufacturers Association, and the California State Legislature as well as the California State Building Trades Council and the General Campaign Strike Committee.

While authorities were investigating the *Times* bombing, the labor front in Los Angeles remained quiet. Then suddenly, several months later, on Christmas Day 1910, an explosion partially wrecked the strikebound Llewellyn Iron Works. Again labor was accused, and again labor vehemently denied complicity.

Now, a simultaneous official investigation of the *Times* and the Llewellyn Iron Works bombings began. To head this investigation, District Attorney John D. Fredericks appointed L.A. Police Chief of Detectives Samuel L. Browne. The Merchant and Manufacturers Association hired Earl Rogers, a prominent West Coast criminal attorney, and provided him with a staff of assistants. Mayor Alexander, fearful that his administration would be discredited unless the crime was solved swiftly, named William J. Burns, head of the detective agency bearing his name, as a special investigator.

Neither the *Times* nor the Merchants and Manufacturers Association favored the appointment of Burns because he had been an adversary of Rogers during an earlier graft investigation in San Francisco; nor did Burns like the idea of being associated with Rogers. He accepted the assignment only with the understanding that his "activities and discoveries be kept secret."[10]

2

Within months, Burns and his agents had their first suspects—James B. McNamara and Ortie McManigal. Determined to find out from whom they were getting their orders and money, Burns allowed the two men to commit a few more dynamiting "jobs" before he arrested them in Detroit. In their possession at the time of the arrest the detectives found a large supply of dynamite and percussion caps. McManigal confessed to various bombings and implicated James B. McNamara, a confirmed unionist, and his brother, John J., secretary-treasurer of the Structural Iron Workers Union. Then, with the Indianapolis police, Burns invaded a meeting of the Structural Iron Workers Union executive board, seized John J. McNamara, and brought him before a justice of the peace who ordered his extradition to Los Angeles.

In the meantime, Ortie McManigal repeated to Los Angeles authorities the confession he had made earlier to Burns. He told of a series of dynamite and bombing plots. John J. McNamara, he said, was the controlling genius who originated each "job" and James B. McNamara placed the dynamite, including the dynamite that wrecked the *L.A. Times* building.

According to McManigal, J.J. had become convinced three years earlier that only through the use of dynamite could the ironworkers win their struggle with the Erectors' Association. McManigal's own agreement with J.J. called for a $200 advance upon undertaking a dynamite job. Although he had not participated in the L.A. bombing, McManigal admitted responsibility for the blast at the Llewellyn Iron Works as well as hundreds of similar assignments.

In Los Angeles, John J. McNamara, the union official, reasserted his innocence. He addressed a statement to organized labor throughout the United States and asked the public to withhold judgment until "a full and fair defense had been afforded."[11]

James B. McNamara remained silent.

Despite McManigal's confession and the implication of guilt surrounding the McNamaras, organized labor rallied to the brothers. They shouted "frame-up," and compared it to the Haywood, Moyer, and Pettibone labor case three years earlier. The American Federation of Labor president, Samuel Gompers, came to see the brothers in jail and pledged union support.

A delegation of labor officials visited Clarence Darrow and spent an evening persuading him to undertake the defense. The fifty-three-year-old Darrow urged them to retain a younger, less tired man. The delegation adamantly insisted that only he—with his very special labor experience and his compassion for the workingman—would have a chance to save the indicted brothers. Finally, Darrow reluctantly agreed to be chief defense counsel.

The American Federation of Labor set up a defense fund "to insure a proper defense, a fair and impartial trial. Eminent counsel have been engaged," the AFL telegraphed its locals.

Darrow anticipated a budget of at least $350,000. He explained that counsel would have to move to Los Angeles for the preliminaries and remain there for the duration of the trial, and that associate counsels and investigators would have to be employed, defense witnesses brought to Los Angeles, and provision made for an indefinite stay. The union locals responded generously to the appeal for funds.

Committed to the McNamara defense, Clarence and Ruby sublet their apartment, put their furniture in storage, and again boarded a train for the West. Darrow took with him John Harrington, who was a lawyer and also an investigator for the Chicago City Railway. Masters remained in the Chicago office, although he and Darrow would never again practice law together.

3

On arrival in Los Angeles, Darrow immediately sought associate counsel and soon hired LeCompte Davis, a leading L.A. trial lawyer; Joseph Scott, an attorney of wide acquaintance in the city; and former Indiana Judge Cyrus F. McNutt, a legal scholar whose judicial decisions had marked him as sympathetic to labor. Job Harriman, candidate for mayor of Los Angeles on the Socialist ticket, was already involved in the case as the union lawyer.

Leasing a whole floor of office space in the Higgins Building, Darrow hired Bert Franklin, a Los Angeles detective and former deputy marshal, to join Harrington in investigating potential jurors.

On July 6, 1911, nine months after the bombing, the McNamara brothers, charged with the murder of the twenty victims of the *L.A. Times* blast, appeared in court and entered pleas of "not guilty." The defense requested a December trial date. The prosecution argued for October 1. The judge set October 11.

Both labor and management looked upon the trial as a battleground in the ongoing labor-capital war: Darrow representing labor and the unions versus Captain John Fredericks, the prosecuting attorney and proponent of law and order. The importance of the trial brought a record number of journalists to cover it.

4

October 11, 1911. The sheriff escorts the McNamara brothers, handcuffed to each other, from the county jail to the door of the courtroom where the deputies form a barrier around them as their handcuffs are removed and they are led to the defense table.

Five minutes later Clarence Darrow arrives with Ruby. Other members of the defense team follow.

District Attorney Fredericks, approaching the judge's bench, suggests "that the defense should elect whether it desires to try both of these defendants together or severed."

"Severed," Darrow says. "We will sever."

"Then, Your Honor," responds Fredericks, "in that case we will try J. B. McNamara first and J.J. next." The decision had been reached by the state after countless meetings between the district attorney and Detective Burns. Fredericks had favored beginning with J.J., the union official, but Burns disagreed. He argued that since James B. McNamara had placed the dynamite he should be the first to stand trial.[12]

5

Shortly before the trial, Mary Field had come to Los Angeles from New York with assignments to cover the McNamara trial for several periodicals, including *Bridgeman's Magazine,* a labor journal. As a friend of the defense, she helped to investigate the veniremen.

Borrowing a horse and buggy, she would take her six-year-old niece driving. As they passed the home of a potential juror, Mary would stop the horse, take the child by the hand, and knock on the door. "My little girl has to go to the toilet," was the routine introduction. "May she use yours?"

While the lady of the house led the child to the outhouse, Mary was invariably left alone in the living room. Following Darrow's instructions, she would check to see if there was a Bible on the living-room table and inspect the books and magazines in the room.[13] Darrow, who believed a man was in part what he read, relied on such reports.

6

James B. McNamara, the lone defendant, watches as jury selection proceeds. The pace is slow, the questioning of the veniremen detailed.

While his brother John J. McNamara remained in county jail awaiting trial, the ironworkers' union reelected him secretary-treasurer, and from the AFL convention the brothers received a telegram signed by its president, Samuel Gompers: "By unanimous vote of the convention it directed me to send you the assertion of the delegates of their belief in your innocence of the crime with which you have been charged, and to pledge to you our continued moral and financial support to the end that your innocence may be established."[14]

At the same time, Detective Burns, speaking with reporters, insisted that "overwhelming evidence" existed "to convict the McNamaras with any sane jury."

"Out in Los Angeles," editorialized *Current Literature,* "a trial for murder is proceeding that, it is estimated, will cost nearly one million dollars and may take several months to finish. The famous Moyer and Haywood trial in Idaho, that aroused such bitter recriminations, has a close analogy in this McNamara trial in Los Angeles. One of the McNamaras is secretary of the Structural Steel and Iron Workers' Union. The other is his brother. . . . All over the country labor unions have been appealed to for funds to conduct the defense. The principal attorney for the defense, Clarence S. Darrow, of Chicago, who acted in the same capacity for Moyer and Haywood, says this fund, at the opening of the trial on October 11, amounted to $120,000. William J. Burns, the detective who furnished the evidence on which the indictments were obtained, asserts that to his positive knowledge the fund amounts to over one million dollars."[15]

7

The tempo accelerated in the frenzied Los Angeles mayoral campaign. The Socialist party, with Job Harriman as its candidate, could almost taste victory. Backed by the Central Labor Council, Harriman, also a defense attorney in the McNamara case, ran ahead of the other candidates in the primary, although he did not receive the majority necessary for election. Of the 45,500 votes cast, more than 20,000 voted for him; the incumbent Mayor Alexander polled 16,800; and the Republican candidate, Mushet, about 7500. The unexpected strong showing of the Socialist ticket led to an unprecedented uniting of anti-Socialist and antilabor forces in Los Angeles in preparation for the runoff election on December 5.

Organized labor, which overwhelmingly supported the McNamara lawyer, marched in a massive parade wearing Harriman buttons and chanting, "Register your protest against the McNamara frame-up!" "Harriman for mayor!"

Both defense and prosecution admitted the relationship between the McNamara trial and the mayoral election. The prosecution wanted to use the trial to discredit labor before the election, while the defense desired to postpone a verdict or any adverse testimony until after the election.

Lincoln Steffens, the noted muckraker and an old friend of Darrow's, came to cover the trial for a group of twenty-one newspapers. He arrived as attorneys were struggling to complete the jury selection. Recognizing the possibility that the McNamaras were indeed guilty, he reasoned that if they had set the bomb they and their counionists must have suffered desperately to resort to the use of dynamite, and he excused the violence as "a social manifestation of a condition."[16]

He obtained Darrow's permission to visit the brothers in prison. He had come to Los Angeles, he told them, not so much to cover their trial as to write the story of the abuses suffered by labor that "set them off on an organized policy of dynamiting." Ignoring the fact that they had already pleaded not guilty and that the whole labor movement had taken up the fight for their innocence, he said that he wanted to use their case as "an inquiry into the wrongs done labor, and so to get at the causes of class hate. . . . It's a doubtful experiment and a risk for you, but it's got to be done sometime. Why not now?" he asked. "Why not help me dig up on the side—while the legal case is going—the case of labor against capital as a parallel, as a background to the case of California versus the McNamaras. I might be able to show why you turned to dynamite, but I can't—I won't—do it without your permission." [17]

John shrugged. "Why not?"

To which Steffens responded, "Because while I don't mean to, of course, I might make a blunder that would give something away and hang you." [18]

"If you could do what you propose I'd be willing to hang," said James B. Turning to his brother: "It's for that that we have been working . . . to force attention to the actual conditions of labor." [19]

Steffens reported the conversation to a deeply troubled Darrow, who adamantly refused to consider a change of plea. His duty was to save his clients from the death verdict, he argued, and furthermore, he was not only representing the brothers but also acting for organized labor which had hired him.

In truth, however, Darrow had begun to have his own doubts about his clients' innocence. His investigations could find no contradictions in McManigal's confession. Moreover, he had intimations that the state had substantial evidence and was building a strong case. He confided his concern to Fremont Older, editor of the *San Francisco Call,* who was a friend of labor, and to LeCompte Davis and to Steffens. He asked Davis, a close friend of District Attorney Fredericks, to talk confidentially with him about plea bargaining. [20]

8

Jury selection continued. Each day a deputy sheriff brought witnesses into the courtroom to identify J. B. McNamara as having been at a certain location at a specific time. "No man on earth whose conscience was not free could stand the strain of seeing every day new links forged in the chain that would inevitably bind him to the murderer's chair," commented a prominent Los Angeles lawyer who attended court every day and was familiar with the evidence against the younger McNamara. "It is a wonder to me that J.B. stood the ordeal as long as he did." Often the defendant recognized a prospective witness who came into the courtroom. And then he would turn to Darrow as if to say, "There's another one, Clarence. That fellow knows me." [21]

During this period, Darrow and Steffens spent a weekend with E.W. Scripps, veteran newspaper publisher, at his ranch near San Diego. A few days of rest and relaxation had been planned for the weary Darrow, with no mention of the McNamaras. Scripps, however, sensed a depression and a restlessness about the attorney: Darrow wanted to talk about the case, what it meant to him and to the labor movement. He wanted to discuss violence in the labor struggle. Was it futile? Was its use ever justifiable even to bring progress?

Scripps welcomed such an exchange. He had just completed an essay, his latest thesis on "Belligerent Rights": a defense of force and dynamite by labor as its only weapon against the hostile employers who control the jobs, who have the press at their command as well as the bar, the legislators, the governor, the police, the militia, all the power of the state.[22]

Darrow, lost in contemplation, reflected that he almost wished for a settlement out of court. His clients were never just cases to him, particularly where the death penalty was in question. He became emotionally involved and agonized over the possibility of an execution, and the specter of capital punishment always haunted him. Over and over he cried, "I can't stand a client of mine to be hanged."

As Steffens and Darrow had breakfast the next morning on the train back to Los Angeles, the muckraker asked Darrow whether he really wanted an out-of-court settlement.

"Oh," Darrow brushed aside the idea, "it is impossible."

"I think not. I think I could work it out, if you'd let me." Steffens outlined his plan—an approach modeled on the golden rule where the brothers would plead guilty and receive lesser sentences, the state would agree not to prosecute other union men connected with the case, and both labor and management would meet around the bargaining table to settle their differences.

"Do you think for one moment that the local employers would consent to let those prisoners go?" Darrow challenged Steffens. "And if they did, would the eastern employers who have suffered from dynamite let them?" Darrow knew intimately the history of class struggle, of the open versus the closed shop; he was aware of the sociological forces that had instigated the dynamiting of the *Times* and the indictments that followed. "It's impossible. Impossible," he repeated.

Attempts at plea bargaining in a labor case were unusual then. Generally a labor defense charged "frame-up," as it had been doing here. But Darrow, recognizing the strength of the state's case, desperately sought a solution to save the lives of his clients, and he reluctantly consented to let Steffens begin negotiations. He insisted, however, that he must not be implicated for fear that it would prejudice the defense.

Within several weeks a representative of the defense visited the district attorney and indicated the defense's readiness to plead James B. McNamara guilty, with the understanding that he would be given a life sentence and charges against John J. dropped.

Fredericks stubbornly refused. "I will never consent to take the little one and let the big one escape. J.J. must plead guilty," Fredericks insisted.[23]

"J.J. will never plead guilty," retorted the defense.

J.B. offered to "swing" if the state would release his brother.

Fredericks repeated: J.B. must plead guilty to the *Times* bombing and receive a life sentence; J.J. must admit to the Llewellyn Iron Works dynamiting and get ten years.

Finally, after much wrangling, the defense agreed to the terms set by the state and began arrangements for a change of plea.

In the meantime, a shocked public learned from newspaper reports that on November 28, 1911, in broad daylight on one of the main streets in Los Angeles, Bert Franklin, former deputy U.S. marshal and now chief detective for the defense, had been arrested while "paying off" $4000 to a prospective juror in the McNamara trial.

9

Friday morning, December 1, 1911. At the opening of the morning session the prosecuting attorney requested a continuance until afternoon. "I have never asked for a continuance before and would not do so unless it was of vital importance," Fredericks said.[24] The defense seemed relieved when the request was granted.

For days reports had been circulating that a new development in the McNamara case was about to unfold. The continuance only added more suspense to the excitement and speculation. Outside, reporters surrounded the district attorney. Did this mean new evidence? New indictments? New arrests? What effect would Franklin's arrest have on the McNamara case? Fredericks responded that he had not told the court and would certainly not comment to reporters. "All I can say is that it is important, otherwise we would never have requested the continuance."[25]

10

Friday afternoon, December 1, 1911. Reporters head for the reserved section in the courtroom as court buffs and friends of the McNamara defense scramble for seats. The corridor overflows with spectators straining to get in. Darrow, weary and resigned as he absentmindedly chews on a pencil, slumps in his chair at the end of the defense table. A tense LeCompte Davis sits beside him, while Joseph Scott paces nervously around the inner rail of the courtroom.

To the surprise of the courtroom audience, deputy sheriffs escort both John J. and James B. McNamara into the courtroom. As the door to the judge's chamber opens, Fredericks walks out slowly, his face pale. His chief deputy, W. Joseph Ford, is already sitting at the state's table.

Judge Walter Bordwell strides swiftly from his chambers to his bench. He bangs the gavel to emphasize the court's words: "People versus James B.

McNamara. Is the defendant in court?" The momentary silence is ominous. A friend moves toward Darrow. "I am tired; so very tired and sorrowful," the attorney murmurs.

Davis approaches the bench. "Your Honor," he says, "the defendant is in court. In the case of the People versus James B. McNamara that is now on trial, may it please the Court, after a long consideration of the matter and final consultation between counsel and the defendant, we have concluded to withdraw the plea of not guilty, and have the defendant enter in this case a plea of guilty" to the murder of Charles Haggerty, one of the twenty men killed in the *Los Angeles Times* explosion.[26]

Pandemonium breaks out. Charles Yale Harrison would aptly describe the scene as "a psychical explosion."[27]

Davis continues: "A like course we intend to pursue with reference to J. J. McNamara, in the case of the people against him, wherein he is charged with having destroyed the Llewellyn Iron Works, or with having placed dynamite at the Llewellyn Works."

The judge calls the defendants to the bench. "Do you plead guilty or not guilty?"

Each defendant answers, "Guilty." From the courtroom audience comes a painful cry of anger, anguish, and disbelief. That one word—"guilty"—will rock the labor movement and disillusion and embitter tens of thousands of men and women who had looked upon the McNamaras as martyrs in labor's struggle for unionization, better working conditions, and higher wages.

Adjusting his glasses, the judge focuses on the defendants who stand before him. "I will appoint the time for pronouncing the judgment in this case at 10 o'clock A.M., December 5, 1911, which is next Tuesday."

Darrow seems to have aged during the proceedings. The lines in his face appear more deeply etched, his shoulders stooped, his eyes agonized. On the way out he stops to speak to the reporters. "There was no way out of it. We have been working since a week ago last Monday with the officers. I would never have allowed him—I mean J. B. McNamara—to plead guilty if there was any other way. My fight from now on will be to save my two clients all I can."[28]

Outside, Harriman buttons were lying discarded in the gutters; the waiting crowd was hostile. Only hours before they had hailed the attorney as their hero. Now they were shouting epithets and making threatening gestures. His old friend Billy Cavanaugh, now a policeman, was alarmed. He took hold of Darrow's arm. "Come with me."

"No," Darrow shook him off. "No, Billy, I shall go down the street with the crowd. I have walked with them to the courthouse when they cheered me, and I shall go back the way I came."[29]

Much to his surprise, his office in the Higgins Building was filled with people who had come to shake his hand and congratulate him on the "brave fight" against impossible odds. "Prominent lawyers, newspapermen and visitors from all parts of the country expressed their confidence in the ex-chief counsel for the defense and assured him that calamity howlers who now attacked him were very much in the minority."[30]

11

James B. McNamara issued a statement. "I may swing, but if I do, it will be for a principle. They could never have got me to the gallows on evidence but I was afraid that poor old John might get it because of my fight for life.

"Poor Darrow, Scott and Davis are all in. They felt mighty bad about this. I told them that I must save John and told them to go see the district attorney and arrange to have me swing if they would let John—who could not help himself—off. The talk dragged a bit, but I turned the trick today. I pleaded guilty."[31]

The prosecution claimed that it had held all the evidence necessary for conviction weeks earlier and had expected the defense to ask for a compromise—the defendants to plead guilty in exchange for lesser sentences. It insisted that the defense changed its plea only after Franklin was charged with bribery.

Not true, Darrow countered. "We purposefully drew out the examination of jurors several days after the negotiations were completed" so that the arrangements for a change of plea could be made in secrecy.

A disbelieving Samuel Gompers decried the McNamara confession and denounced the brothers and their attorney. "This unexpected self-conviction is nothing more than the failure of two individuals to live up to the high principles of organized labor and cannot reflect just condemnation upon the cause of labor as a whole. The American Federation of Labor is a law-abiding institution," Gompers cried.[32]

General Otis of the *Times* gloated. "The result of the confession of the McNamara brothers in open court is a great triumph for truth and law. It vindicates our contention. It is proof of what we suspected from the outset— that this unexampled crime was either inspired by organized labor, or was done by desperate members of organized labor, who knew beforehand that they would have the sympathy of their lawless fellows."[33]

Harriman, campaigning for mayor, loudly voiced his objections to the change of plea and said he had not been consulted in the decision. While the newspapers headlined his association with the McNamara defense, his campaign manager denied that the affirmed guilt of the brothers would have any ill effects on the Harriman campaign.

"PATRIOTS WILL WORK ALL THE HARDER FOR THE DEFEAT OF HARRI-

MANISM" READ a seven-column headline in the *Los Angeles Times* on December 3, 1911.

12

Tuesday, December 5, 1911. The largest crowd ever to attend a criminal trial in Los Angeles County blocks the corridors on the day the McNamaras appear in court for sentencing. From seven o'clock until ten in the morning when court convenes, hundreds of curious men and women fill the entrance to the courtroom in the Hall of Records.[34]

Special officers and a squad of policemen patrol the inside and the outside of the building. Only county officials, well-known lawyers, and those with special passes are admitted. The press is barred, too, unless they show credentials; even these do not always help as more than five hundred claim to be newspaper people.

Everyone who enters the Hall of Records is searched for concealed weapons. To help solve the security problem, the judge and the lawyers on both sides agree to move the proceedings to Department 12, in the Hall of Justice, so that the prisoners do not have to pass through the streets but can enter the courtroom directly from the jail.

The defense attorneys, silent as the prisoners enter, remain so throughout the sentencing. James B. McNamara, nervously chewing gum, glances around the room. His hands toy with the watch chain dangling from the vest of his black suit. John J., also dressed in black, appears more composed. Captain Fredericks moves toward the bench. Judge Bordwell speaks first: "This is the time set for the sentencing in the People versus McNamara." Fredericks interjects that J. B. McNamara had given him a statement the previous day asking that it be read to the court.

In the statement J.B. affirms he had placed a suitcase containing sixteen sticks of 80 percent dynamite in Ink Alley, a part of the *Los Angeles Times* building, and that these exploded at one o'clock in the morning. "I did not intend to take the life of anyone," J.B. stresses. "I sincerely regret that these unfortunate men lost their lives, and if the giving of my life could bring them back I would freely give it. In fact, in pleading guilty to murder in the first degree, I have placed my life in the hands of the state."[35]

Fredericks points out to the judge that there are at least two sentences which the judge can impose, each equally severe: one, the death penalty; the other, life imprisonment. "However, in the minds of a great many persons, and possibly in the mind of the defendant the sentence of imprisonment for life would be considered possibly in some degree a less punishment than the punishment of death. There has been no dickering nor bargaining in this matter," the prosecutor adds. However, counsels on both sides are aware "of the usual custom of granting some degree of consideration to a defendant who has pleaded guilty—not on the ground of mercy, but on the ground of service to the state. This defendant has pleaded guilty. By so doing he has settled that which for all time in the minds of a great many would have been a doubtful question. He has saved the state, and he has served the state in other ways; and it is my judgment that some small degree of consideration should be extended to him because of that fact." Captain Fredericks steps back from the bench. [36]

Judge Bordwell turns to James B. McNamara. "There is very little or no ray of comfort, Mr. McNamara, in the assertion by you that you did not intend to destroy life. The widows and orphans and the bereaved parents will look upon that statement at this time as a mockery. The circumstances are against you in making any such claim. A man who would put sixteen sticks of 80 per cent dynamite in a building full of combustible materials—I say that a man who under such circumstances would place a dynamite charge of that quantity in such a building, in which you as a printer knew that gas was burning in many places, and in which you knew there were scores of human beings toiling, must have had no regard whatever for the loss of his fellow beings. You must have been a murderer at heart." [37] The only reason the court will not impose the maximum penalty of death upon the gallows is because it believes it to be the "better part of wisdom to do otherwise.

"You shall be confined in the State prison in San Quentin for and during your natural life," Judge Bordwell sentences the twenty-eight-year-old James B. McNamara.

Now it is John J., union official, who stands before the bench. Captain Fredericks explains that the defendant pleaded guilty to placing dynamite, nitroglycerin, and other chemical compounds in the strikebound Llewellyn Iron Works, with the intent of destroying the building. Fredericks again cites the precedent for extending some "small consideration" in the matter of penalty.

"All I would suggest," says Fredericks, "is that the court take into consideration the probable life remaining to this defendant, and leave him, at the end of his term, a few years of freedom. I believe it is a wise policy of the state, when a man surrenders himself, gives up and pleads guilty, that some small consideration should be extended."

Judge Bordwell ignores Fredericks's comments. "You have heard the Court's remarks to your brother, and in no small degree, sir, they undoubtedly apply to you," the judge lectures. "And as in his case, the fact that the court may not mete out to you the extreme penalty of the law is in no degree due to my doubt that you merit it, but simply appears to be the part of wisdom to do otherwise. The judgment the court now pronounces upon your plea of guilty to this charge is that you be confined to the state prison at San Quentin for the period of fifteen years."

Sheriff's deputies hurriedly take the two men to their cells in the Los Angeles County jail. A few days later they are moved by Pullman car five hundred miles to San Quentin where they start their prison terms.

13

Former President Theodore Roosevelt, reflecting the mood of the nation, wired Burns: "All good American citizens feel that they owe you a debt of gratitude for your signal service to American citizenship." [38]

Two weeks later, Roosevelt asserted that "murders committed by men like the McNamaras, although nominally in the interest of organized labor, differ not one whit in moral culpability from those committed by the Black Hand, or by any band of mere cutthroats, and are fraught with an infinitely heavier menace to society." [39]

Yet, many sensed the desperation which had led to the McNamaras' action. A young minister in New York City, John Haynes Holmes, saw the McNamaras as "useful soldiers of a cause" and "not criminals in an ordinary sense." Bill Haywood understood: "My heart is with the McNamara boys as long as they are fighting against the capitalists."

The Survey: A Journal of Constructive Philanthropy, published by the Charity Organization Society of the City of New York, published a symposium in which Louis D. Brandeis asked why men like the McNamaras "believe that the only recourse they had for improving the condition of the wage-earner was to use dynamite against property and life? Certainly it was not individual depravity.

"Was it not because they, and men like them, believed that the wage-earner, acting singly or collectively, is not strong enough to secure substantial justice?

"Is there not a causal connection between the development of these huge, indomitable trusts and the horrible crimes now under investigation?" Brandeis wanted to know. [40]

In the same issue of *The Survey,* Edward A. Filene, founder of the famous Boston department store bearing his name, advised "every employer who wishes to do his share towards solving the issue between capital and labor to encourage the better and stronger class of his employees not only to join the labor organizations but to take active and effective part in their work. From unions so constituted much help will come for the rightful settling in the most lawful way of the great questions involved in the relation of employers to employees." [41]

In response to public demand, President William Howard Taft created the U.S. Commission on Industrial Relations to investigate the Los Angeles tragedy, since so little was known about the structural ironworkers trade, the men who worked in it, and their adversary, the Erectors' Association.

14

Four years after the McNamara trial, the commission published the results of its study in a 192-page pamphlet on the National Erectors' Association and the Bridgemen's Union. The study described the structural ironworkers' job as less skilled than that of most other building tradesmen but considerably more dangerous. "The trade does not look inviting to the man on the street," nor does it look attractive to the "home-loving married man" as the work requires travel from job to job. Most of the ironworkers had simply "drifted" into the industry. The business agent of a Pittsburgh local verbalized the opinion of many when he remarked that the union had made mistakes, but "what can you expect of us? A lot of irresponsible bums can't be expected to be diplomats."[42]

The study pointed out that the adversary of the Bridgemen's Union had shortened its name in 1906, three years after its formation, from the National Association of Manufacturers and Erectors of Structural Steel and Iron Work to the National Erectors' Association. Originally, its principal purpose had been to negotiate with the International Association and Structural Workers Union regarding hours and wages and to deal generally with the union. The year it changed its name, however, it also changed its course. It announced a new objective in Article III of its seven-article constitution and bylaws: The aim "shall be the institution and maintenance of the Open Shop principle in the employment of labor in the erection of steel and iron bridges and buildings and other structural steel and iron work."

For the first time the country became aware of industrial conditions in the structural iron industry. The study accused both groups—the employers and the employees—of intermittently using physical force to win temporary advantages for itself, although permanent industrial peace eluded them.[43]

Underlying the conflict was the open shop which the union considered not only an obstacle to progress but a jeopardy to gains accrued by the union. Labor, therefore, was firmly committed to fighting the principle of the open shop. On the other hand, the employers considered the open shop to be in their best financial interests. It gave them the freedom to conduct their operations as they desired, without regard to employee rights, and thus resulted in increased profits.

"Only the recognition by each side of the rights of the other" can lead to industrial peace, and "both sides must agree on what those rights are and define them by mutual consent," concluded the study.

15

The dynamiting to which the McNamara brothers had confessed was no reckless conspiracy but rather a deliberate act by the defendants, capping one of the bitterest and most violent conflicts in American labor history. It was but another facet in the struggle for unionization in Los Angeles, an episode in what Big Bill Haywood called "the class war." It was the struggle of the haves against the have-nots; the workers on one side and the employers on the other; on one side the International Association of Bridge and Structural Workers, on the other side the National Erectors' Association.

While controversy raged around the confession, another development occurred. Bert Franklin, Darrow's chief detective in the McNamara case, pleaded guilty to jury bribery charges and implicated Darrow. Earlier, Franklin had told newspapermen that, if called as a state's witness, he would reveal all he knew, and he bragged, "Though I don't expect immunity, I'm positive I will never spend a day in the penitentiary."[44] He was right; his only punishment was a $4000 fine, the same amount he allegedly offered each juror.

Again and again, in a slowly mounting tide, items began to appear in the newspapers—at first subtly, then more openly—that Darrow might face indictment for jury bribery as a result of the McNamara case and that the change of pleas was prompted by the anticipated Darrow indictment.

16

The McNamara compromise so laboriously hammered out was broken the day the judge sentenced the brothers. He lashed out at Steffens, denying that the change of plea was due to his efforts. He reiterated the theme of the district attorney and the detectives for the state, that the "attempted bribery of jurors in the J. B. McNamara case were [sic] the efficient cause of the change of pleas which suddenly brought these cases to an end."[45]

Steffens's experiment with the golden rule failed dismally. The "righteous judge who never erred or sinned" denounced the McNamaras; and instead of the gospel of love, hate and revenge took over, Steffens said.[46]

Several days later Darrow issued a more detailed statement in which he repeated that he had entered the McNamara case with great reluctance and only "after the most earnest persuasion." If in his agreeing to plead the McNamaras guilty his motives had been misjudged, he could only say he had "acted unselfishly and from devotion alone.

"I do not beg anybody's friendship or sympathy in this matter. I have the consciousness that I have done everything that I could do, and have acted in the way that is best for all in this world wide conflict. If anything more is asked from me by either side they will find me ready when the time comes."[47]

But he was not as cavalier about the possible indictment as he tried to appear. Late one rainy evening in Los Angeles, a tearstained, bedraggled Clarence appeared in Mary Field's doorway. He did not say a word as she opened the door and he walked past her to the kitchen. Slumping down in a wooden chair, he pulled a bottle of whiskey out of one pocket and a gun from the other. Carefully, he placed them both on the table in front of him.

The scene unnerved Mary. The gun was totally out of character for this man who so volubly eschewed violence, and despite his campaign against prohibition Darrow rarely drank. Sensing his anguish, Mary brought two glasses and he poured a shot for each of them.

"Mary, Mary, I can't stand it. They're going to indict me for bribery. I can't stand it." He cradled his head in his hands and wept. He talked of suicide as he fingered the gun. "I can't stand the disgrace."

Mary talked to him softly and tenderly far into the night. When he was calm, he rose, put the half-empty bottle in one pocket, the gun in the other, and walked slowly out into the rainy dawn.[48]

Many years later, in discussing the bribery case, Mary reflected, "Darrow believed in saving lives. I think that if he thought bribery was the only way to keep the boys from being killed, he would have felt justified in using it."[49]

17

Speculation and rumors regarding Darrow and the McNamara jury bribery continued to grow. Darrow told newsmen he was "not so thick-skinned or blunt-witted as not to have taken cognizance of the fact that many persons are coming as near as they dare to accuse me of bribery."[50]

Concerned over the rumors, Steffens wanted to include Darrow in the McNamara compromise agreement, but the lawyer rejected the suggestion. "They can have me to try, if they'll let these prisoners off."[51]

Even had Darrow agreed, it is doubtful the prosecution would have consented since they were determined to "get" him because of his strong labor support.

"My conscience is clear," Darrow said. "I have fought a hard fight, have borne my burden bravely and would do the same thing over under like circumstances. Of course I feel saddened to think that I am the object of bitter attacks, but my main sorrow is for something greater—a burden of others.

"Any man who fights for an issue that has great opposition is hailed with enthusiasm by at least one side, if he wins. If he is, because of circumstances of which he has no control, a loser, he is open to attacks from all sides."[52]

XII

Darrow Needs a Lawyer

1

TWO months after the McNamara confession, a grand jury in Los Angeles returned two indictments against Darrow: one charged that on November 28, 1911, he "willfully, unlawfully, corruptly and feloniously" gave $500 to George N. Lockwood, who was being considered for the jury, with the promise of another $3500 if, when accepted, he would vote for an acquittal in the case of the People versus J. B. McNamara. The second indictment, similar to the first, named Robert F. Bain, already chosen for jury duty, as the subject of the attempted bribery. If convicted, the defense lawyer faced a maximum $5000 fine and/or five years' imprisonment on each charge.

Now Clarence Darrow, one of the best legal brains in the country, needed the services of a defense attorney.

"Get Earl Rogers," friends in California urged.

Clarence was well aware of Rogers's reputation as the best criminal lawyer on the West Coast and of the colorful and dramatic courtroom exploits which had earned him fame and notoriety. Darrow had considered inviting him to join the McNamara defense, but, because Rogers had already played a prominent part in the *Los Angeles Times* investigation, legal ethics would have disqualified him.

Clarence and Ruby traveled to the San Joaquin Valley where Rogers was in the middle of trying a "big will" case. They spent a day in the courtroom observing him in action. Impressed with his performance and with his acumen, the Darrows asked Rogers to handle Clarence's defense, and he readily accepted. "He felt he had been slipping somewhat and that he needed Darrow almost as much as Darrow needed him," wrote Rogers's biographers. "His ego told him that his selection to defend the nation's acknowledged premier criminal lawyer would naturally place him in Darrow's class."[1]

Today, the very fact that Rogers had been involved as special prosecutor in the *L.A. Times* bombing investigation would make it difficult for him to undertake the Darrow defense. Criminal Attorney F. Lee Bailey believes "such a feat of switch-hitting would probably be prohibited as a clear case of conflict of interest."[2]

The indictment so devastated Darrow that he could hardly summon the strength to prepare for the fight ahead. Applauded and fawned upon for years by labor, he now turned to the unions for financial help. For the most part they refused, condemning him for having "betrayed" the McNamara brothers as well as the union cause. Gompers also turned down Darrow's appeal for money. He added that, although the unions had been badly misled by the McNamaras and their counsel, he did not believe that Darrow would resort to bribery.[3]

Yet, there were individual unions that did offer assistance. An early client, the United Garment Workers in Chicago, came to his aid. The rank-and-file membership of many of the smaller unions pooled their nickels and quarters. A Mr. Meyers sent a $5 money order, followed by one for $3. Darrow returned the $3. "I want you to know I appreciate it, how good you were to send it, but I feel that it is wrong to take so much from a man who must work as you do."[4]

Although the bribery charge almost crushed him, he was even more disturbed that some of his friends believed him capable of betraying the McNamaras in order to save himself from the charge of jury bribery. He wrote to Debs, the Socialist labor leader whom he had defended in 1894, asking him to "do something to bring the old time people to my support. It is awfully hard to be deserted in this crisis by those who should stand by me."[5]

Debs replied that although he was "exceedingly touched and pained" by Darrow's words, there was a strong feeling against Darrow among Socialists. Debs expressed it as delicately as he could.[6] "You may think it very cruel on the part of your former staunch friends and admirers that they are now lacking in sympathy when you most need it, but perhaps you are not entirely blameless and they are not wholly at fault.

"I know you will allow me to be as candid with you as I would be with a brother. It appears that there was some investigation at Chicago recently as to certain facts in your record, conducted with a view to getting at the truth, and that the report was anything but flattering to you. Among other things it is charged that in consideration of a fee you went over to the Harvester Trust in some case in which a school fund was involved and that you succeeded in beating the school fund out of a large sum due it for the fee you obtained for such service from the rich owners of the trust."

This charge against Darrow had cropped up time and again. Darrow admitted that he had represented the company in a tax hearing at which he suggested a compromise, but he insisted he had done nothing morally or legally wrong.

There was another reason for the Socialists' unhappiness with Clarence, Debs said: his "espousal of the cause of Merriam the Republican in the recent municipal [Chicago] campaign had about as much as anything else to do with the Socialists and others having concluded that you loved money too well to be trusted by the people."

Debs said he had been "shocked" when Clarence retained "such a notorious corporation corruptionist and all around capitalist retainer as Earl Rogers. . . . When I read that you had retained him I first concluded that it surely was a mistake but upon second thought I saw in this report what seemed to me the seriousness of your situation and the extent to which you were driven to engage the lead-wolf to escape the pack. . . ."

Then followed words of encouragement: Be "strong enough . . . ," Debs urged his friend, "to stand alone and to face the world unafraid. . . . The good there is to your credit no amount of gratitude or indifference can wipe out. You have fought on the right side . . . even if you have made mistakes and in the end the summing up will be to your everlasting credit."

For a time reports circulated that compromise overtures were being made by the Darrow defense. To all these rumors Darrow angrily retorted that "no such action has been or will be considered by me."

2

Many evenings the group of steadfast labor friends gathered around Darrow, spending the time in camaraderie and a display of their loyalty. Mary Field described one such evening while Darrow was awaiting trial:[7] The labor official "Tvietmoe loomed the biggest among us—'The Viking' they call him, and such he is. He looks down on the group through heavy-lensed glasses that magnify his eyes so that he looks like an owl. His face is a complex of strength and gentleness, of indomitable will and kindness, of power and of tolerance.

"Johannsen. 'The Spirit of Labor.' Tvietmoe's face is a mask. Johannsen's is like a clear lake reflecting hate, love, high purpose and low cunning. His laugh, big, uproarious, contagious, is ever spilling from him as the foam runs over the edge of a schooner of beer. Telling his obvious jokes, unrefined, uncultured. Yet dominated by the love of freedom.

"There were others there: Morton, the editor of *Freedom,* and lesser satellites. And Darrow, poor broken Darrow, looking like an oak that has been cleft by a lightning bolt. For a time he forgot his pain.

"Tvietmoe paced the room, his big thumbs looped in the armholes of his vest, something of the elephant in his stride, something of the panther in his eyes.

"He quoted 'Battle Cry' by Neihardt:

> More than half beaten, but fearless,
> Facing the storm and the night,
> Breathless and reeling, but tearless
> Here in the lull of the fight;
> I who bow not but before thee
> God of the Fighting Clan,
> Lifting my fists I implore thee,
> Give me the heart of a man!

"A thrill ran through us all. We felt the bravery, the defiance, the sheer purpose of the man.

"'God!' said Johannsen, breaking the strain. 'That's a God damn son of a bitch of a poem! Pass the whiskey.'

"So they all drank. Even Darrow drank. His great spirit somewhat revived.

"Then Tvietmoe sat at a little table with Morton. Morton read, dramatically gesticulating, a translation of Bjornson's *Beyond Human Power,* while Tvietmoe followed the translation in the original.

"As Morton read, his voice thundered the protest of the strikers in the play, wheedled the part of the ministers and boasted the replies of the millowners. And Tvietmoe's face, usually a blank wall of emotional control, played the passions of the play—sympathy, hatred, appreciation."

Morton read until after midnight when they left to go home through the empty streets.

"'Fighting the fight is all,' said Tvietmoe. 'Goodnight!'"

Johannsen's laugh echoed through the cool night air.

And Darrow, enveloped again in his despair, his eyes moist, sorrowfully trudged home.

3

On the eve of the trial, Fredericks for the state and Rogers and Darrow for the defense issued statements to the press.

According to the district attorney, "The evidence against Darrow is convincing. It does not rest upon any one or two witnesses. It is just as convincing as the evidence in the McNamara case. It will be my duty to ask a jury not only to find Darrow guilty, but to recommend that he be sentenced to confinement in the state penitentiary."

Rogers stressed, "Evidence founded upon the word of an informant who has pleaded guilty to a felony is not good. The district attorney's case against Darrow is framed upon such structure. Bert Franklin, the chief witness for the state, was an employee of the forces behind the prosecution a long time before he was arrested. Other witnesses relied upon by the District Attorney were being paid to betray."

"If it were the case of a client," said Darrow, "I would say without reservation that the evidence would prove my innocence. Maybe I am too sanguine because it is my own liberty at stake; but I am confident that a jury will acquit me. I am innocent of bribing either of the two McNamara jurors who received money from Detective Bert Franklin."

4

Sensationally newsworthy events were taking place during the weeks of the trial. Both Republicans and Democrats held presidential nominating conventions, Theodore Roosevelt bolted the GOP, the Germans began preparing for World War I. Yet Darrow, always colorful and controversial, made "good copy," and most newspapers across the country reported his trial in detail. Since the Debs trial eighteen years earlier, Darrow's image had been as an honest defender of the poor, the weak, and the unpopular. The unexpected charges against him shocked the nation, which eagerly devoured accounts of the trial. The press set up direct lines for immediate coverage from the courtroom to their newsrooms. Each newspaper assigned a reporter to write the story and a telegrapher to send it out on the wires.

As in the McNamara case, Fredericks and Ford represented the state. At the defense table with Rogers sat Jerry Geisler, Horace Appel, and Judge McNutt, who had also been a defense attorney in the earlier case. Soon after the Darrow trial started, failing health forced Judge McNutt to withdraw. He died during jury selection. Geisler, a law clerk in Rogers's office, researched the fine points of the law for this case.

Appel, a Mexican Jew with a vast command of accented English, not only helped with the examining and cross-examining but, brazenly displaying his contempt, goaded the district attorney and the prosecution staff to the limits of their endurance.

Presiding in the Superior Court of the State of California, in and for the County of Los Angeles, was the Honorable Judge George H. Hutton.

5

May 15, 1912. An electric fan vainly tried to cool the courtroom as the May sun poured through the stained-glass skylight, illuminating the inscribed words: Justice, Law, Government. A dejected Darrow sat at the defense table directly under the word Justice.

After the first group of veniremen had been seated in the jury box, Fredericks explained the case. He spoke quietly with an air of supreme confidence. "In a general way the People of the State of California are plaintiffs, and Clarence Darrow is the defendant, and it is charged that during the progress of the trial of the People versus McNamara, Mr. Darrow, the defendant in this case, offered a certain bribe specified in the indictment to one Lockwood, who was a juror summoned in that case."

Wearing the same rumpled gray suit he wore during the McNamara trial, Darrow brightened during jury selection. Sitting at the defense table beside Rogers, he seemed to enjoy "a witty sally or a bit of humor in the answer of a talesman."[8] The shame and suffering so apparent during the indictment proceedings were well hidden for the moment, although he soon reverted to his earlier depression in an emotional seesaw that persisted throughout the trial as he drifted between occasional periods of confidence and plunges into despair. From time to time Rogers would nudge his client as a reminder to change his desolate expression.

Lincoln Steffens described Darrow during this time: "At three o'clock he is a hero for courage, nerve, and calm judgment, but at a quarter past three he may be a coward for fear, collapse, and panicky mentality. He is more of a poet than a fighting attorney. He is a great fighter, as he is a good lawyer. His power and his weakness is in the highly sensitive, emotional nature which sets his seething mind in motion in that loafing body."[9]

Mrs. Darrow, wearing a simple-styled dress and a sailor hat trimmed with a green ribbon, anxiously scanned the face of each prospective juror trying to learn his sentiments toward her husband.

Nine court days after the first talesman was questioned, a thirteenth juror in the case of the People of the State of California versus Clarence Darrow was selected, to act only if one of the original twelve became incapacitated. The Darrow jury consisted of three ranchers, two orange growers, three realtors, a lumber dealer, a cement contractor, a carpenter, a transfer man, and the thirteenth, a hotel man.

6

Within thirty minutes after the jurors were sworn in and the indictment read, Fredericks began his opening statement. Abusive and vituperative, it set the tone for the state's mood. He started by explaining the nature of the indictment against Darrow, "that he offered a bribe, gave a bribe to George N. Lockwood.[10]

"We will show you that Clarence Darrow, the defendant in this case, employed the detectives who were used in the defense of that case; we will show you that among the detectives employed by the defense was Bert Franklin; we will show you that Bert Franklin was in the employ of Clarence Darrow, and we will show you that he was not in the employ of anyone else during his work in that case. We will show you that there was also employed by Mr. Darrow a man by the name of Harrington, a detective from Chicago.

"We will show that Bert Franklin went to Mr. Lockwood, whom he knew, and offered him a certain sum of money if, when he was called as a juror, if he succeeded in passing the examination and getting to be sworn as a juror, offered him a certain sum of money if he would vote not guilty. That in doing this, we will show you that Bert Franklin was doing it at the instance and request, and under the directions of this defendant, Clarence Darrow. We will show you that that money was a part of the money that was sent to Clarence Darrow by agents who were employing Mr. Darrow for the purpose of defending the McNamaras. We will trace that money from that fund into Mr. Darrow's hands.

"We will show you that immediately upon the arrest of Mr. Franklin, Mr. Darrow went on his bail and went on his defense and got him out of jail temporarily. We will next show you that that act on the part of Clarence Darrow was one of a series of efforts to prevent justice in that [McNamara] case by paying money, hundreds of dollars, to other jurors and to witnesses who were witnesses for the People against the defendant."

Darrow, totally crushed by the personal onslaught, fumbled with a cigarette paper, his face flushed and haggard as he looked down at the floor.

Every seat in the courtroom was occupied. In the corridor a horde of spectators pressed against the barred doors. Fredericks reiterated: "We will show you gentlemen, by evidence here, that this defendant endeavored to defeat and obstruct justice in this case.

"We will show you that in the same endeavor to obstruct and defend justice he paid money, hundreds of dollars, to witnesses who were witnesses for the State."

Defense Counsel Appel jumped to his feet. "We object to that statement."

Ford interjected, "To avoid interruption, we will stipulate that every part of

the argument may be deemed to be excepted to by the defendant on the ground
that it is misconduct."

Appel, in a resentful rejoinder, "We certainly are not taking advice from
you."

From time to time during Fredericks's vitriolic outpouring, Ruby leaned
over and whispered to her husband, placed her arm across his shoulders,
stroked the back of his neck.

The district attorney pressed his allegations: "In the same case for the same
purposes that he paid this money to Lockwood, he paid money to witnesses to
leave the State, to get them out of the State, and he paid money to witnesses
for the State for the purpose of having them not testify. Then he brought
agents here for the purpose of corruptly influencing our witnesses." He paid
large sums of money "to bring people here, to Los Angeles, to work upon
McManigal and persuade him, by offering him inducements, and bribes, to
change his testimony and to refuse to testify for the State."

"Misconduct," shouted Rogers, but Fredericks was not to be stopped until
he concluded: "I think, gentlemen, that, in a general way, that will be the
outline of the prosecution. I have tried to state it to you coldly, without
appearing to argue it, and I congratulate you now upon being able to start in on
the trial."

The *Los Angeles Times,* interpreting Fredericks's opening statement, labeled
Darrow "the director-general in a wholesale bribery plot."[11]

7

The procession of state witnesses started. George W. Lockwood:[12] policeman two years, constable three years, in charge of Los Angeles City prisoners
five years, in the sheriff's office four years. Prodded by the questions of the
state's attorney, Lockwood recounted his story. Although he had known
Franklin for a dozen years he had not seen him for at least a year until "awful
late" on Saturday night, November 3, 1911, when Franklin appeared at his
home unannounced to discuss the McNamara case. "It is late and I am awful
tired," Lockwood had apologized to Franklin and promised to visit the
investigator at his office in Los Angeles the following week.

When Lockwood showed up at Franklin's office, Franklin explained that he
was working for the McNamara defense and wanted Lockwood as a juror in
the case. Shocked by Franklin's effrontery, Lockwood said that such a
suggestion from Franklin made him ineligible as a juror.

"Can I talk with you about the case?" Franklin asked.

"I said 'yes sir,'" Lockwood testified. Franklin noted that he and Lockwood
"had gone along through life until we had aged perceptibly without properly

using our heads," that it was time both of them acquired sufficient funds for their old age.

"As near as I remember," Lockwood testified, "Franklin said he had not the slightest doubt but what if I was a juror in that case and heard the evidence, . . . I would, of my own free will and accord, from the testimony, bring in a verdict of not guilty."

Franklin repeated time and again that there was no evidence against the McNamaras, "except such as had been manufactured," and in an incredible display of guile said that the only reason he offered Lockwood money was out of friendship.

Franklin promised Lockwood $500 before he entered the jury box. From $2000 to $2500 would be placed in escrow for him pending the outcome of the trial. Lockwood asked for a few days to think over the proposal.

When they met again, Franklin told Lockwood he had already "fixed" one juror on the McNamara panel, and he implicated Robert Bain.

By this time Lockwood, however, had decided he wanted no part of the scheme and reported it to the district attorney who suggested that Lockwood pretend to accept Franklin's offer. From then on Lockwood acted with the "knowledge and advice" of the district attorney.

At another meeting, when Lockwood questioned the logistics of the payments, Franklin assured him there would be no difficulties. Captain C. E. White, whom they both knew, would act as the intermediary. The plan called for Lockwood to meet White on the corner of Los Angeles and Third at nine o'clock on Tuesday morning, November 28, 1911, to collect the first payment.

Lockwood's testimony set the scene for the bribery. At no time did the defense question the accuracy of his description. What they vigorously denied throughout was the claim that Darrow was part of the scheme.

On the appointed morning, Captain White turned over to Lockwood a $500 bill and showed him a roll of additional bills. At the same time a man "rode up on a motorcycle and stopped there close to us, and I dropped the $500 bill on the ground and stopped to pick it up," Lockwood testified. They saw Franklin across the street and walked over to him. "We were just this side of the corner on Third, and Franklin remarked, 'Don't look around, don't look around,' and used a word I don't care to use unless compelled to in this presence."

Fredericks asked, "What do you mean?"

"Well, he said, 'The sons-of-bitches,' just in that way, and he said, 'Don't look around.' And then he says, 'Let's get out of here.' And we started and walked up, he and I, side by each, to the corner of Third and Main. Then we walked north on Main where the jog in Third Street goes west, and as we approached that place, I saw a man come across the intersection, and Bert said to me, 'Wait a moment, I want to speak to this man,' and I turned around, just as the two met, and at that point Mr. Browne (the chief of detectives) put out his hand, and separated them."

"Separated Franklin and the man that came to meet him? Who was that man that came there and met Franklin?" Fredericks asked.

"I have learned since that it was Clarence Darrow."

When the afternoon session ended, Judge Hutton informed the jury that they were "sequestered and living apart from the general community in order that you may keep your minds entirely free from any evidence, free from any newspaper statements, any newspaper headlines, from any comments by passers, or from any other persons."

8

Lockwood was on the stand when court opened the next morning. The prosecutor had only a few more questions before cross-examination. "Mr. Lockwood, during the time that you have discussed here and the transactions and the talk you had with Mr. White and Mr. Franklin, state what was your purpose."

"Wait a moment," objected Defense Attorney Appel. "No objection," Rogers intervened.

Lockwood answered, "My idea was that a great crime was being perpetrated—"

Appel interrupted: "We don't want speeches, Your Honor."

Fredericks: "I think he is answering it."

Lockwood: "I will say, my idea was to prevent what I considered a great crime." Furthermore, he intended to turn the money over to the district attorney as evidence.

Fredericks: "Cross-examine."

Rogers moved from the defense table toward the witness stand as he asked, "You say you dropped a $500 bill on the sidewalk. What for?"

"As a matter of showing that the transaction was closed and giving notice to people in waiting that were ready to make the arrest."

"People in waiting. What do you mean by that?"

"Detectives."

"You knew they were there?"

"I knew that they were supposed to be there."

Rogers changed the subject. Did Lockwood consider Franklin a friend?

"Why, as far as I could remember, yes."

"You considered yourself a friend of Mr. White's?"

"Yes sir."

"You thought Franklin was a bad man?"

"I thought he was in a disreputable business, at any rate."

"Did you tell him, 'Bert, this is wrong, you ought not to insult me in this way'?"

"No sir, I did not."

Rogers asked, "Did you tell him, 'Bert, you know that you cannot bribe me; I am not that kind of a man'?"

"No sir."

"Franklin would not have come out that night if the district attorney and you had not telephoned to him?" Rogers asked, referring to Lockwood's earlier testimony that he had called Franklin at the D.A.'s suggestion.

"Possibly not."

Rogers focused on that theme. "Now, at the time Franklin came out in response to your telephone call, you asked him where was Darrow, did you?"

"Yes sir."

"And he said, 'Well, did you think Darrow was coming out here?'"

"I said, 'I sure thought so.'"

"What did he say to that?"

"He wanted to know what made me think so."

"What did you say to that?"

"I said, 'You wanted to know if you should bring the Big One out,' and I supposed that is who you meant."

"You wanted to trap Darrow out there?"

"I had nothing to do with the trapping of Darrow out there at all."

"Didn't you try to trap Darrow out there?" Rogers asked again.

"When he said that he—'Shall I bring the Big One?', I supposed he meant Clarence Darrow."

"And he told you he didn't?"

"He said he didn't mean him."

"And that he didn't mean Darrow at all but that he meant someone else?"

"Yes sir."

"Who did he mean?" asked Rogers.

"Captain White."

Returning to a theme of Fredericks's direct examination, the large denomination of the money passed, Rogers questioned Lockwood: "What did you say about those bills, the size of them?"

"I says, 'A man would have hard work to pass one of those bills.' I think I told him they ought to have been in fives or twos, or something of that kind."

"Why did you say that?"

"Simply filling-in talk, waiting for the arrest to be made."

"Why did you say it ought to have been fives and twos?" Rogers insisted.

Fredericks objected on the ground that the question had been asked and answered. "This kind of witness," explained Rogers, "we are at liberty to cross-examine him thoroughly." The judge overruled the prosecutor's objection and Lockwood answered, "Simply because I was filling in time expecting the arrest to be made any second."

Rogers pursued: "You knew, didn't you, if a man was going to really try to bribe you, he wouldn't use one thousand dollar bills and five hundred dollar bills? You said so, didn't you?"

"The only thought that I had in regard to the size of these bills was simply to fill in time there, until the absolute arrest would take place."

Rogers followed up with, "Then you didn't tell the truth when you said it was all wrong to use thousand dollar bills in a case of that kind?"

To Fredericks's objection Rogers bristled. "An accomplice, framed or otherwise, is subject to cross-examination on all his motives, why he did this, that and the other thing, in every particular."

Again Rogers asked Lockwood why he thought the passing of a five-hundred-dollar bill on a proposition "of that kind was decidedly out of the way, that it ought to have been twos or fives." And again Fredericks objected, noting that the same question had been asked and answered five times.

"Just a moment," Rogers flared. "I know these objections are made simply for the purpose of letting the witness have an opportunity to think, and suggest to him."

The court admonished Rogers, "I do not think you ought to say that."

Fredericks's voice dripped with sarcasm. "Mr. Rogers gives himself too much credit as a cross-examiner."

Rogers shot back furiously, "I have beaten you every time but once."

To which Fredericks retorted that it was because that one time was "the only time we ever had anything" in the way of a good case.

Lockwood tried again to reply to the question: "The only object, the only reason I had for anything there was to fill in the time until the arrest was made."

"You wanted Captain White to be arrested, did you?" asked Rogers.

"I wanted what I considered to be a crime stopped."

Rogers insisted that his question be answered. Fredericks insisted it had been. Judge Hutton ordered Lockwood to be more direct.

"I certainly wanted the arrest made," said Lockwood.

"Of White, didn't you?" persisted Rogers.

"Yes."

"And you wanted the arrest made of Franklin?"

"Yes sir."

"And you wanted Darrow, didn't you?"

"If he was connected with it."

After two days of grueling examination, George Lockwood was excused.

Clarence Darrow, circa 1893. (*Courtesy of the Chicago* Tribune.)

Darrow with son Paul. (*Courtesy of Blanche Chase and Mary Simonson.*)

Jessie Ohl Darrow. Clarence Darrow's first wife and Paul's mother. (*Courtesy of Blanche Chase and Mary Simonson.*)

Darrow with son Paul (*Courtesy of Blanche Chase and Mary Simonson.*)

Dinner celebrating Darrow's acquittal on a jury bribery charge, Los Angeles 1912. Left to right, seated: Darrow (second front left), Ruby and Fremont Older. Standing between Ruby and Clarence is Mary Field. (*Courtesy of Margaret Parton.*)

Lincoln Steffens and Clarence Darrow in Los Angeles, circa 1911. (*Courtesy of Elmer Gertz, Exhibits Chairman, Darrow Centennial Celebration, 1957.*)

Darrow being frisked as he enters the courthouse at the Massie trial in Honolulu, 1932. (*Courtesy of Elmer Gertz, Exhibits Chairman, Darrow Centennial Celebration, 1957.*)

Leaving the Joliet Illinois State Prison after visiting their respective brothers Leopold and Loeb, 1924. Left to right: Mike Leopold, Darrow, and Allan Loeb. (*Courtesy of Elmer Gertz, Exhibits Chairman, Darrow Centennial Celebration, 1957.*)

In Dayton, Tennessee, during the Scopes trial, 1925. Left to right: Darrow; Dudley Field Malone, another defense attorney; and George W. Rappeleyea, the Dayton citizen who was instrumental in setting up the antievolution test law. (*Courtesy of Elmer Gertz Collection, Special Collections Department, Northwestern University Library, Evanston, Illinois.*)

Clarence and Ruby Darrow en route to the Massie trial. Honolulu 1932.
(*Courtesy of Elmer Gertz Collection, Special Collections Department, North-western University Library, Evanston, Illinois.*)

Darrow at a teachers' meeting in Chicago in the early 1930s. Left to right: Illinois State Senator Adelbert Roberts, Darrow, and U.S. Congressman Oscar DePriest. (*Courtesy of Elmer Gertz, Exhibits Chairman, Darrow Centennial Celebration, 1957.*)

XIII

The State's Star Witness

1

DARROW UNMOVED BY BRIBERY STORY TOLD BY FRANKLIN

Star Witness for State Declares on Stand that McNamara Chief Counsel Authorized Passing of Bribe to Juror in Dynamite Case
[*L. A. Record,* Wednesday, May 29, 1912]

Bert Franklin walked to the witness stand as Darrow glanced scornfully at his former employee. Mrs. Darrow, at her husband's side, placed her hand protectively over his.

Assistant District Attorney Ford examined Franklin.[1] Listing his occupation as "private detective," Franklin said Darrow had hired him as chief investigator for the McNamara defense in August 1911.

"Did you receive any directions from Mr. Darrow as to what your duties were?"

"Yes sir. Mr. Darrow said he wished to employ me to investigate all members of the county term trial jury that were in the box."

"Is that all that was said upon the subject?"

"No. He told me just what he wanted to find out about the members of the jury—to find out the apparent age, the religion, the nationality, who their attorney was, what the feelings of the jury were toward union labor; what the feelings of the jury and the opinion of the jury were in regard to the explosion of the *Times* Building, the opinions of the members of the jury as to whether the McNamaras were guilty of the crime with which they were charged."

"Did you receive any directions from Mr. Darrow to investigate the financial standings?"

"Yes sir, their financial condition, their property, and the bank at which they did business, if possible."

"Mr. Darrow give you any directions as to the manner in which you should approach the people?" Ford questioned.

"No sir, he didn't give me any directions. We discussed that proposition, though."

"Did you ever discuss the question of bribing jurors with Mr. Darrow?"

"Yes sir."

"When was the first occasion you discussed the question of bribing jurors?" Ford asked.

"The first time Mr. Darrow and I had any conversation—any direct conversation in regard to bribing jurors—was on the fifth day of October 1911."

"Who was present?"

"Nobody but himself and myself."

"And where was that?"

"On Spring Street between First and Second."

"On the street?"

"Yes sir."

"Just tell the jury what was said at that time with reference to that matter."

"I met Mr. Darrow, Mr. Davis, I think Judge McNutt and Joseph Scott [all attorneys for the McNamaras] but I am not sure, coming out of the Bryson Block. I spoke to them all, and Mr. Darrow and I walked away by ourselves, the rest of them following leisurely behind. Mr. Darrow made the remark it was time for us now to get busy with the jury and that he wanted to see me and talk over the matter in regard to Mr. Bain [already accepted for jury duty]."

"What was said between you and Mr. Darrow about Robert Bain?" Ford wanted to know.

Horace Appel objected that the question "has nothing to do with this case; upon further ground, no foundation has been laid for the introduction of this evidence; that the declarations of the defendant and the declarations of the witness in regard to Juror Bain are immaterial at this time."

Ford admitted that "no foundation has been laid as yet showing the connection of the defendant Darrow with the bribery of Lockwood, but we

avow our intention of connecting the testimony with that and have only
adopted the order and time for convenience. It is a matter discretionary with
the Court."

Objection overruled.

Darrow, the lines of anguish on his face showing "nights of sleeplessness
and worry," studied the jury to see what effect the detective's testimony was
having on the twelve men who would decide his fate.

Franklin testified that the first conversation he had with Darrow about
bribing Bain was on the morning Darrow handed him a check for $1000 when
he learned that Franklin knew Bain "very well." The witness added that
despite the fact he advised Darrow that Bain was antiunion and thus would be
a poor juror, the lawyer insisted he talk with Bain. Darrow said, "'We have
been talking the matter over and have decided that $5,000 would be a proper
amount to pay to the jury, for jurymen.'" Of this total, Franklin said, $4000
would go to each juror and $1000 to him.

"Bain was the kind of a man," Franklin told Darrow, "if he didn't want to
go in that way he would come out and tell me so and that would be all there
would be to it. He said, 'All right, I will give you a check for $1,000.'"

Franklin recounted to the jury his visit to the Bain home. As with the
Lockwood testimony, what follows is the raw material from the court record
and not a novelist's fantasy. "I went to the door and knocked. I did not receive
any response. I came to the front door and Mrs. Bain was at the window and
asked me what I wanted, and I told her that I wished to speak to her and told
her who I was.

"I said, 'Mrs. Bain, this is Mr. Franklin.' Well, she says, 'What Mr.
Franklin is it? Mr. Bert Franklin?' I said, 'Yes ma'am.' She said, 'What can I
do for you?' I said, 'I would like to have a few moments conversation with you.'
'Well,' she said, 'I have just—I was in the bathtub when you knocked at the
back door and I hadn't anything on but my kimona,' and I said, 'Well, I would
like to talk to her a few moments; and she lifted the window and shortly came
to the door and opened it and asked me to come in, which I did. She then went
to the back door and she came back and said that she had locked the door for
fear somebody would come in. I asked her how she was getting along. She said,
'Very well.' I asked her how Bob was. Said, 'Getting along very nicely.'

"I then told her that I used to work with Bob, knew him very well and could
possibly put him in a position to make a little money in his old age, and she
asked me what it was. I then said, 'Mrs. Bain, may I talk to you in a
confidential way?' She said, 'You certainly can, Mr. Franklin. I have known of
you for a long time and you can talk to me about any subject that you wish.' I
then asked her if Bob had been drawn on the jury. She told me that he had;
that a jury summons had been left at the house for Bob and she had given it to
him. I asked her what Bob's feelings was towards union labor. She told me at
one time he had been in favor of it, but that he had had some trouble in the
union and was opposed to union labor. I asked her if she had ever heard Bob

express any opinion in regard to the explosion of the *Times,* as to who was guilty. She told me 'No,' that 'Bob was very quiet and very seldom expressed an opinion.' I again repeated that I thought perhaps I could put her and Bob in the way to make some money that would help them out in their old age, and told her what it was. I told her that I would like to have Bob on the McNamara jury; that I was in a position to pay him five hundred dollars in cash and two thousand dollars when he had voted for an acquittal of the McNamaras. Well, she said, 'Mr. Franklin, you know that Bob is a very honest man.' I said, 'Yes, Mrs. Bain, I realize that. I have always felt so.' But, she said, 'That sounds good to me, and I would like to have Bob consider it.'

"She said she would try to prevail upon him to take the money, or words to that effect."

Franklin returned to the Bain home that same evening. "I said, 'Hello, Bob,'" Franklin testified. "He says, 'Hello, Bert, come in.' I went in the house. He asked me to sit down. He asked me how I was getting along, and I told him very well. I asked him where he was working, what he was doing, and he told me. I asked him if he had steady work, and he said, 'Yes, for the last few weeks.' I asked if she [Mrs. Bain] had spoken to him in regards to me, and he said that she had. I asked him what he thought about the matter and he said he raised some objection when his wife spoke about it, but she had convinced him. I asked him if he would accept $500 in cash with the promise of payment of $2,000 more after the McNamara case was closed and he had voted for an acquittal. He said that he would. I then took from my pocketbook $400 and gave it to him and he accepted it. He asked me at that time what assurance he would have of getting the money, the balance of the money, and I told him there would be no question about that, that his position would be far superior to ours, that we would be compelled to pay the money, if we didn't he could report it. He agreed to that, and then I left."[2]

Franklin added that Darrow continually impressed upon him that he was determined to win the McNamara case, that "it was an important case in his life, and probably would be the last one he would ever try of that importance."

The assistant state's attorney turned to Franklin's attempt to corrupt George Lockwood, in Franklin's words, a "man of character" and of "sterling integrity and a man who would listen to me patiently and on account of our friendship repeat nothing that was said."

Franklin's testimony meshed with that given by Lockwood.

2

The state kept Franklin on the stand for two days, "a cowering rabbit with his foot in a trap." According to the *L.A. Examiner,* he was "uncertain and halting, a wretched witness in the hands of friendly counsel."[3]

Late afternoon on Friday, May 31, Earl Rogers began his cross-examination. In his formal, long-tailed coat which he wore throughout the trial, the
tall, handsome attorney presented a colorful portrait of an engaging, shrewd
personality. He was quick-witted and resourceful as he hammered at Franklin
mercilessly without pause. His voice was vibrant, "like the yell of a band of
painted Comanches, as terrifying as the famous 'rebel yell' of a bristling
battalion. Every word was a blow in the face, every tone a scornful insult,"
reported Joseph Timmons in the *L.A. Examiner*.[4]

"You told Darrow," Rogers punctuated each word, "that if he had not
showed up on the scene at that unfortunate moment that you would have
pulled off your stunt of turning Lockwood over to the police and charging him
with extortion, did you?"

"I did not say that."

"What did you say?"

"I didn't say anything about a stunt."

"What did you say, then?"

"I told Mr. Darrow that if he had not appeared upon the scene at that time,
that particular time, that inopportune moment, if you please, that I would
have turned Mr. Lockwood over to the police—and charged him with
accepting a bribe in the McNamara case."

"So that was your first attempt to get out of your crime by charging
somebody else with it?" accused Rogers.

"Yes sir. I did that, Mr. Rogers, after I had found that Mr. Lockwood had
turned traitor to me, a man who had been his friend for years and I was
playing even. I was doing the very best I could to get out of the scrape that I
was in."

Rogers challenged, again every word puncturing the air. "And still are, is
that so?"

Franklin mimicked Rogers's voice, emphasizing each word as Rogers had. "I
will answer that question and say to you, Mr. Rogers, that I am doing what I
consider the best thing for my wife and family that I have sworn to protect,
and I am going to continue to do it."

"Mr. Franklin," Rogers made no effort to hide his contempt for the witness,
"you told Mr. Darrow that Mr. Lockwood was a man of sterling integrity, did
you not? And at the same time you thought that he would accept money to
perjure himself. You said he was a man of sterling integrity and yet you
thought you could buy him?"

"I thought that I would try it. I told Mr. Darrow, and I repeat it, that if
Mr. Lockwood did not wish to accept the bribe that he would come out like a
man and say so, and that would be all there would be to it, on account of our
friendship."

"As a matter of fact, you went to Mr. Lockwood for the purpose of bribing
him and having at least the expectation that you could."

"I thought I should ask him," responded Franklin. "I didn't think he would take it. I never thought he would take it and I was much surprised when he agreed to."

Franklin's reasoning began to sound like the double-talk in Lewis Carroll's *Alice's Adventures in Wonderland*. Incredulous, Rogers asked, "You thought that if your old friend of years and a man of sterling integrity got $4,000 dangled in front of him that you could induce him to commit perjury, am I right? And yet you thought him a man of sterling integrity? What kind of moral sense have you when you think a man of sterling integrity will take a bribe to sell his soul?"

"Mr. Rogers," answered Franklin, "I am not here to testify to my moral sense that I should have or I would not have done what I did."

3

Mrs. Darrow fans herself in the stuffy courtroom. She directs the cool air first at Clarence and then at herself. Darrow sits slumped in his chair, only his sorrowful, wrinkled face and shaggy head, drawn in between his shoulders, are visible above the top of the table. Though he betrays no change of emotion, Ruby's face mirrors many different feelings as the testimony twists and turns, now for, now against, the defendant.

4

"Now, Mr. Franklin," Rogers thundered at the witness, "you said a moment ago that every man has his weak part. What you really meant to say was that every man has his price?"

"I did not."

"Well then, in Lockwood's case you thought he had the price."

"I didn't think so, no sir."

"You want to say that; you didn't think he would take your $4,000 when you said you would go out and offer it to him?"

"I didn't think he would, no sir, and I told Mr. Darrow I didn't think he would."

"To come down, you wouldn't have gone to him at all and exposed yourself as a jury briber to your intimate friend unless you thought there was some chance of his taking it?"

"I went there to Mr. Lockwood because I believed at that time that he was a man that would stand by a friend and not do what he has done to me; run me into a trap."

"Well, assume for the sake of argument that you did think he would not run you into a trap or expose you—"

"Yes sir."

"Please answer my question. You did think there was a strong chance of his taking the money?"

"No sir, I did not."

"What did you go out for?"

"To see if he would take it."

"You exposed yourself to a crime when you didn't think he would do it."

"I went there to make an offer and for him to either accept or reject it, as he saw fit."

"You knew you were committing a crime?"

"I did, yes sir."

"Why was it, then, without any chance of success, without any thought you could succeed, you committed a crime? Do you think we will believe that?"

"I don't know what you may be able to believe, Mr. Rogers, that is what I did."

In a quiet, ingratiating voice, Rogers asked, "Now, let's see, you are getting something for your testimony?"

"I am not," Franklin answered righteously.

"You are getting immunity for your testimony, aren't you?"

"I have never been offered immunity and I never have asked it."

Rogers cited to Franklin a section of the penal code that provides that when a witness, as in Franklin's case, takes the witness stand and testifies, he cannot be prosecuted. Franklin said he understood the section.

"You went on the stand believing that, didn't you?"

"It never entered my mind."

Fredericks objected to Rogers's rapid-fire questions. He particularly objected to the last question because it assumed "something not in evidence. The witness could be prosecuted for perjury if he committed it."

"Well, he wouldn't be prosecuted," Rogers snapped. "That is certain."

"He certainly would if he committed it," shouted Fredericks.

Franklin joined in: "And there isn't any chance that I would."

Judge Hutton overruled Fredericks's objection. Rogers continued his attacks, repeating that Franklin knew that the moment he took the stand he became immune from further prosecution.

The former detective for the McNamara defense finally admitted he knew that when a witness takes the stand "and testifies to some act of his own for which he might have been prosecuted, that unless that section [of the code] is read it automatically acts and he is immune from punishment."

Rogers smiled. "So you do know you are immune right now?"

"I do, yes sir."

"And when you went on that stand you knew you became immune?"

"I never thought of it when I went on the stand. I had before," Franklin volunteered.

"You had before?" sneered Rogers. "Well, it was in your mind before you went on the stand that you are going to be immune from punishment when you stepped on there and started talking?"

Again Franklin admitted, "If I hadn't known so I wouldn't have gone."

Rogers would not let up. "Then you went on there to get immunity to save yourself?"

"No sir," said Franklin.

"Well, you got immunity for going on?"

"Automatically, yes sir," said Franklin.

"Automatically or otherwise you got immunity now, haven't you, you know it?"

Franklin's tone was surly. "You are a lawyer, you know, I don't."

"You know it too?"

Cornered, with no escape, Franklin finally agreed. "I think that is correct, yes sir."

Judge Hutton adjourned court for the day.

5

Tuesday, June 4, 1912. Franklin remained on the stand until five o'clocl most of the time dodging Rogers's questions relating to immunity. Finally, just before adjournment, he admitted that the assistant district attorney had said, "Bert, we don't want you, we want those behind you."

Franklin identified the "those" when he said Darrow told him the money for the attempted bribery came "directly" from AFL President Gompers. Rogers immediately protested that Darrow would never make such a remark even if it were true.

The witness remained unperturbed. "Then he told me an untruth." Under the barrage of questions and accusations, Franklin displayed a remarkable calm, folding and unfolding a sheet of paper as he responded to the vigorous cross-examination.[5]

In Washington, D.C., Gompers denied he ever gave Darrow money for jury bribery. "Franklin's story is absolutely false, and furthermore," said the labor leader, "I don't believe Darrow ever made such a statement."[6]

In the courtroom Rogers wanted to know whether Franklin had indeed told the press that he never received "a dishonest dollar from Darrow," that Darrow knew nothing of the bribery matter, that he is "too good a man to do anything of that kind, he was most kind hearted, generous, and the best man I ever knew in my life and wouldn't stand for any corruption or dirty work, and he never gave me a dollar for any corrupt purposes in the world."

Rogers repeated the question when he asked whether Franklin had not told Timmons of the *Examiner* that anyone who said he called Darrow a jury briber "was a God damn liar. I may be guilty of all I am charged with, but I am not a damned fool. I certainly am not going to drag an innocent man into this thing."

"I said almost exactly the words you used for Mr. Timmons," Franklin replied, with the exception I am not going to drag an innocent man into this. "I said, 'Mr. Darrow is one of the kindest and best men I have ever worked for' and I repeat it now to his face. He treated me splendidly, and I have no complaint to make." Darrow smiled wryly and bowed his head to acknowledge Franklin's compliment.

Rogers introduced into his questioning the names of several other prospective jurors Franklin attempted to corrupt by bribery, including John S. Underwood, a member of the Employers' Association. Rogers wondered, "It is inconceivable that a man with any soundness of mind, if he were really illegitimately intending to try to bribe a juror and not merely to make a fake play for the purpose of injuring Mr. Darrow, seems to me he would have picked somebody besides a man who had a strike in his own place, it seems to be absurd that Mr. Franklin if he did intend as a matter of fact to bribe a juror, would have picked Underwood. He might as well have picked John Llewellyn" of the Llewellyn works, the plant that had been bombed.

"I thought I would try. I didn't know," Franklin repeatedly responded.

For ten days and almost 1100 pages of direct and cross-, re-direct and re-cross-examinations, Franklin sat on the witness chair eluding, parrying, answering, avoiding questions as lawyers for the defense and for the prosecution monotonously argued, raised objections, withdrew objections, took exception to rulings, and the judge sustained and overruled. For long days Franklin sat on the stand recalling, reliving again and again, explaining his motives and actions, his comments to newspaper reporters, and describing his conferences with Darrow, with LeCompte Davis, with the other attorneys. Finally, Fredericks and Rogers released the witness.

6

Henry H. Flather, cashier of the Riggs National Bank in Washington, D.C., as a witness for the state,[7] identified a list of credits, debits and checks in a McNamara defense ledger. The defense admitted that Darrow endorsed the checks.

Suddenly Darrow jumped to his feet, shouting, "I object to that statement of counsel." A stunned courtroom listened to Appel's explanation of Darrow's outburst: sotto voce—but loud enough to be overheard by the jury—Fredericks had taunted the defendant by insisting that Darrow would not have admitted the endorsement had he not known that the state could prove it. "Now, I know," said the peppery Appel, "the Captain don't mean to do Mr. Darrow any injury. But I just call the attention to that—"

An angry Fredericks interrupted, "Nobody would have heard it. It was a little colloquy between ourselves, and I assumed that the defendant was man enough to have a private conversation with a man he was talking to and not try to bawl it out and make capital out of it, when it meant absolutely nothing, that is what I assume."

Furious at the unexpected assault from Fredericks, Darrow thundered, "I object to that statement, anything he said to me was said for the purpose of influencing someone, and he is nearer the jury than he is to me, and he has no right to make any such remarks."

Fredericks: "I will submit not one man on that jury heard it."

Darrow: "I don't know whether they did or did not, but anyway, you have no right to make that remark."

Appel joined in: "This is not right. That is taking advantage of a man that is here on trial. I dare say, the gentleman probably would not say that to other people, although I have great confidence in Mr. Fredericks and in his manhood, but I don't think it is right. I think it is taking advantage. I think it is cowardly to do that."

Fredericks retorted, "I will take care of my part of it. I am not playing the baby act."

"Well, you are inferring that we are, and I will tell you that I am just as much of a man as you are, I know you and I am not afraid of you." Appel lashed back as he started to move around the table to Fredericks's side.

"Mr. Appel," warned the judge.

Appel: "I have seen—"

Judge: "Mr. Appel! Be seated or I will instruct the bailiff to seat you. Sit down." Judge Hutton said he had not heard the remark, but if he had he would have reprimanded Fredericks for making it as it was entirely out of place. Hereafter, "any remarks made while court is in session must be made to the court," Hutton ordered.

Before he adjourned court for the noon recess, Judge Hutton announced, "There is a matter I want to discuss before you leave. I had not quite disposed of the incident that occurred here a few moments ago. Captain Fredericks should have apologized for the remark. I feel that was his duty. He saw fit not to do so but on the contrary added a remark to which the defendant and his counsel took still further offense and at which the court took offense." He fined Fredericks $25.

Turning to Appel, Judge Hutton censured him also because, instead of accepting the court's promise that further attention would be given the incident, Appel had interrupted the judge to call Captain Fredericks's language cowardly. "This conduct on his part certainly tends to interfere with the lawful proceedings of this court." Appel's fine: $5 for contempt of court.

Appel smiled as he told the court, "Your honor, on behalf of the defendant—we except to the conduct of the court in finding his counsel guilty of contempt of court during the trial of this case, for having the manhood to get up here and defend his client. On behalf of myself I do not find that the court has done anything more than he should do in the finding but on behalf of the defendant I take an exception for whatever benefit he may get from it. As far as I am concerned I think you ought to fine us more."

"He can pay part of mine if counsel feels it will do," commented Fredericks.

Judge Hutton banged his gavel. "Gentlemen, stop this right here. There will be no more comments across the table between counsel. This is not the time or place for facetious remarks."

7

Darrow's own clients sensed a caring and a personal interest that went beyond his defense of a case. Occasionally this quality engendered a loyalty that created problems for the attorney. Clarence was working in his office in the Higgins Building after court hours when his clerk announced a visitor who insisted on seeing him. A large man, dirty and disheveled, followed the clerk into the office.

"George Bissett!" a surprised Darrow greeted the guest warmly.[8] "You are a long way from home; what are you doing here?"

Clarence had first met Bissett in Chicago in 1910 when the younger man's mother pleaded with Darrow to save her son from going to the penitentiary on a murder charge. Bissett, a common laborer with no formal education, was a proselytizing Socialist whose ambition was to start a Socialist newspaper. At the woman's persistence, Darrow had looked into the case and found the original plea in error. At the new trial, with Darrow defending him on a plea of self-defense, Bissett was acquitted. He had only recently learned of Darrow's trouble and had come to Los Angeles to offer his aid, riding freight cars from Chicago.

"George," the weary lawyer remonstrated, "it was fine of you to come all this distance to help me, and I appreciate it more than I know how to tell you, but what did you think you could possibly do?"

"Well," Bissett explained, "I have been here about a week and have been getting a line on Franklin and I found out where he lived, what time he went away in the mornings, and I have some dynamite and I am going to kill Franklin tomorrow when he leaves his home."

Darrow shuddered. "George, you have no idea what you are about to do."

Trying to show his appreciation for the astounding offer while at the same time dissuading his self-appointed "protector": "George, you propose to kill the chief witness for the State against me—in broad daylight. You must be crazy to think that you could do it without being hanged."

"Yes, I've thought of all that," Bissett answered, "but I owe my life to you, and I'm here to take the chance. I want to do it for you."

Darrow embraced the younger man. "I fancy few men have made such an offer of self-sacrifice," he said. "Nothing like it has ever happened to me. But it must not be done!" He assured Bissett he definitely expected to be acquitted and offered him fare to return to Chicago.

Bissett reluctantly gave in. "I'll do as you say but I won't take any money of yours; I never pay railroad fare." He wept as he walked away from the lawyer.

XIV

More Witnesses Against Darrow

1

NOW began a parade of witnesses to prove the state's claim that the McNamara defense had not only bribed jurors but paid "hundreds of dollars to witnesses who were witnesses for the State" and that Darrow was a totally unprincipled lawyer.

Kurt Diekelman[1] was the clerk in the Los Angeles hotel where J. B. McNamara registered as J. B. Brice a few days before the *Times* bombing. Though Diekelman did not make an absolute identification of McNamara, he appeared to be certain enough for the prosecution to assign Burns detectives to watch him.

Burt Hammerstrom, Ruby's brother, also worked for the defense in the McNamara case as an investigator. According to Diekelman, Hammerstrom went to Albuquerque, New Mexico, where Diekelman had moved, to persuade him to·come to. Chicago and away from the influence of the Burns men. The McNamara investigator offered him money and a choice of jobs in Chicago. If he had a girl he could take her with him. "We have found out that you have not positively identified McNamara," Hammerstrom told him. "You would not send an innocent man to the gallows, if there was any chance of saving him. We are trying our best efforts to save this man, he is perfectly

innocent. Don't you think it would be right for you to consider the least doubt
there is and consider that and be on our side?" He promised Diekelman money
to return to Albuquerque if he was not happy in Chicago.

From the time Hammerstrom first contacted him, Diekelman reported their
conversations to Burns operatives. "Hammerstrom was not trying to conceal
you in Chicago?" Rogers asked in cross-examination. Diekelman admitted that
Hammerstrom not only made no attempt to conceal him while in Chicago but
in fact introduced him to many public figures, including ex-Mayor Dunne and
Ed Nockels of the American Federation of Labor.

Diekelman, as a star witness for the state, turned out to be a more valuable
witness for the defense. He described a tug-of-war between the defense and
the state for his testimony. He admitted he could not definitely identify
McNamara and that, while the defense tried to get him away from Burns
operatives, they made no effort to prevent him from testifying.

Ruby, increasingly nervous, her face pale and drawn, paid particular
attention to the Diekelman testimony, which became more complex as it
unfolded. Not only was her husband on trial, but the involvement now
expanded to include the accusation that her brother was guilty of bribery. Her
eyes fastened on the witness, she unconsciously nodded when his replies were
favorable and shook her head in disbelief when the witness uttered words
antagonistic to her husband and brother.

2

Witness for the prosecution: C. E. White,[2] "stakeholder" in the Lockwood
bribery. Franklin and Lockwood had been deputy sheriffs under White:
Franklin the outside deputy, Lockwood a guard. White's testimony was
straightforward. He had acted on the plea of a friend to help two friends and
thus became involved in a felony. There was no question as to his
truthfulness.

Under cross-examination, White said that Franklin promised him "my
financial interests would not suffer if I would consent to act for them." The
district attorney also promised that "if I went on the stand and told the true
story I would not be prosecuted."

Every day increasing crowds of people struggled to get into the courtroom.
Chaos and confusion reigned despite the additional bailiffs assigned to keep
the corridors clear. At the beginning, many labor sympathizers had considered
Darrow a traitor and stayed away, but as the trial continued and reports of the
daily testimony appeared in the newspapers, they became more aware of the
intangibles of the situation and began to understand Darrow's motivations in
pleading his clients guilty. Before long the Central Labor Council of Los

Angeles voted to support him, and many in labor's ranks began to attend the trial sessions.

3

Wednesday, June 12, 1912, 10:00 A.M. Witness for the prosecution: Samuel L. Browne,[3] detective in the district attorney's office and one of the officers who arrested Franklin, White, and Lockwood. He had also participated earlier in apprehending one of the McNamaras. Fredericks wanted to know what Darrow said when he witnessed the arrest of Franklin.

Browne, in his soft Southern accent, responded, "Mr. Darrow spoke to me. He said to me, he says, 'My God, Browne, what is all this?' and I turned to him and said, 'Bribery.' He says, 'Isn't there anything that can be done?' He says, 'This is terrible.' I says, 'I don't know of anything that can be done, you will have to see Captain Fredericks.' He says, 'Isn't there anything you can do?' I says, 'I cannot do anything.' He says, 'If I had known this was going to happen, I never would have allowed it to have been done.' I then said to Mr. Darrow, 'You ought to know Franklin.' He says, 'Franklin came to me,' he says, 'very highly recommended.' I says, 'Mr. Darrow, I don't know what I can do.' He says, 'My God, Browne, this is terrible. You do the best you can for us,' he says, 'and I will take care of you.'"

Of all the detectives who testified for the prosecution only Browne received any consideration from Rogers in cross-examination, although no sense of kindness prompted this treatment. Rogers's laudatory words were intended to build up the defense by showing that, when Darrow talked to Browne at the site of the attempted bribery, he knew Browne was "the man who ran down the perpetrators of the *Times* horror" and "the very man, the very chief of them all, who most was interested in the conviction of the McNamaras." They would show that Darrow recognized Browne as "the man whom he had to fight and whose work he had to combat all the time," and he would never knowingly say anything to the detective that was not in his own best interests.

The prosecution, on the other hand, interpreted Browne's testimony as establishing a direct connection between Darrow and the bribery attempt.

4

As the days passed, the startling contrast in style between Rogers, Darrow, and Appel became more obvious. Darrow, in his baggy gray suit and wilted string tie, leaned toward the unsuspecting witness, repeating his question until a crack in the testimony appeared. A smile would appear on his careworn face, and for a moment he seemed rejuvenated, the burden lighter. He would straighten up, look around to make sure the jury too caught the contradiction, then lean forward again and start over, slowly developing his case, each point born of despair and won by argument of reason and logic.

Rogers, a dandy in his high-fashion trousers and velvet knee-length jacket, tackled his cross-examination as if he were the lead in a melodrama. And that was the way he regarded the courtroom—as a legal stage for his dramatic talents. His flamboyant tactics and his colorful plumage set the tone as he pranced before judge and jury.

Appel, always in need of a shave, his straggly hair begging for a scissors, was a brilliant cross-examiner, although on "this team he acted mostly as a backstop, objecting to the prosecution's objection to Rogers' conduct of the trial," according to the memoirs of Hugh Baillie who covered the trial for the *Los Angeles Record*.[4]

Baillie's recollection is not totally accurate, according to the actual trial transcript. Appel did more than "backstop" Rogers whose frequent absences from the courtroom were always accompanied by rumors—he was ill, or failed to show up because Darrow had refused to pay him an installment on his fee. Rarely mentioned, however, was that during some of these absences Rogers was sleeping off a heavy drunk, although his biographer cautiously admitted that "heavy drinking had undoubtedly been a factor in Rogers' illness."[5]

"Earl Rogers came to us every morning and blackmailed us," said Ruby Darrow. "If we didn't give him money he said he wouldn't go into court that day."[6] Rogers's daughter, Adela Rogers St. Johns, complained that at the time of her father's death, in 1922, $27,000 in Darrow expenses were "still on our books."[7] If so, she does not explain why no legal action was filed to collect this money.

5

Witness for the prosecution: George Behm,[8] locomotive engineer, uncle of Ortie A. McManigal who turned state's witness and made what the prosecution called a "full confession" involving the McNamaras' part in the *Los Angeles Times* bombing. Through Behm's testimony, Fredericks continued to build the case against Darrow as a manipulator of jurors and witnesses.

The McManigal confession was the important link between the brothers and the *Times* bombing. McManigal's wife believed her husband confessed because of fear and threats, and she telegraphed Behm, McManigal's uncle, to meet her in Chicago. Together with John Harrington, investigator for the McNamara defense, they met with Darrow at his home on East Sixtieth Street in Chicago.

Behm testified that Darrow had asked him whether he was a union man and whether he was in sympathy with the labor movement and with McNamara and McManigal. "I told him that I was as far as I knowed of anything about the case." Darrow asked him to urge McManigal to change his testimony.

Fredericks wanted to know what Darrow would do for McManigal if he changed his testimony. Behm said Darrow promised that McManigal would be free, and he would see that McManigal got a good job in Chicago. McManigal, however, refused to be moved.

Fredericks turned to a new avenue of questioning. Had there been any conversation between Behm and the McNamara lawyers on what he should say before the grand jury if he were subpoenaed? Behm said all the lawyers agreed that when "I was called before the grand jury I should not answer any of the questions they asked me any more than my name and my residence."

"Which one of the attorneys, if you remember," asked Fredericks, "instructed you that you should refuse to answer all the questions?"

The answer was explicit: "Mr. Darrow."

6

Darrow started the cross-examination of Behm on the afternoon of Tuesday, June 18. " Now, what other questions were you told to answer or not answer in that case?"

"Well, there was questions that you—that was asked me there that I should refuse to answer before the grand jury, that you told me that anything that I told you to ask McManigal to ask him to change his testimony I should not answer that, I should say, 'I refuse to answer that question. That don't concern the case.' Those were the answers you told me to give the court."

Darrow tried to get the witness to tell about any other subjects he was told "to refuse to answer" or instructed "to lie about."

"I cannot bring anything out now," responded Behm. "Only you told me to deny everything. I will tell you, Mr. Darrow, you had me in so many different ways of lying and telling the truth—"

Darrow: "What else did I tell you to lie about, to use your own language?"

Behm: "Very near every word you told me was to be a lie."

7

Thursday, June 20, 1912. Witness for the prosecution: John R. Harrington,[9] lawyer, hired by Darrow to interview witnesses and research testimony for the McNamara trial, aroused angry tempers and intense emotions the moment he stepped onto the witness stand for the state. Immediately, the defense clashed with the prosecution as to whether

Harrington should be allowed to testify. Appel argued that Harrington's lawyer-client relationship as set forth in the California code of civil procedure made him incompetent to be a witness. Ford retorted that the witness had not been employed as Darrow's attorney nor as a McNamara lawyer.

Judge Hutton ruled against the defense's objection noting that were the McNamaras on trial Harrington would not be accepted as a witness.

Harrington had agreed to testify only if he were given immunity from any charge of jury tampering in the McNamara case. His rotund figure perched on the edge of the chair, he revealed in his musical Irish brogue that Darrow had shown him $10,000 in a roll of bills and told him that if a couple of jurors could be reached James B. McNamara would never be convicted. Harrington warned Darrow against any such attempt as it not only would ruin the case but destroy everybody connected with it, including Darrow himself. Such conduct would be "repudiated by the labor leaders all through the country and by the union people all over," Harrington said he told Darrow.

"What, if anything, did he say further?" asked Fredericks.

"He then says, 'I guess you are right, I won't do it.'" Harrington offered the information that an hour after Bert Franklin's arrest he saw Darrow, who appeared nervous and worried that he would be ruined if Franklin talked.

"Cross-examine," said Fredericks returning to the prosecutor's table.

Rogers strutted before the witness, posturing as he moved. "Mr. Harrington," he began, "do you say that Mr. Darrow told you out at his home that he had a roll of bills that he got at Tvietmoe's bank in San Francisco?"

"He showed me a roll of bills," Harrington repeated.

"A roll of bills," wryly commented Rogers. "Just out of the spirit of bravado, to show you he had the roll of bills, eh?"

"I think it was more buffoonery."

"Buffoonery?"

"Yes sir."

"And he told you he had a roll of bills to buy jurors with, in the spirit of buffoonery?"

Ford: "We object."

Rogers: "He said so."

Ford: "Will you let me make my objections, please." Ford's voice rose in volume.

Rogers: "Yes, go on."

Ford: "I will when you quit commenting and grunting."

Court: "Objection overruled."

Harrington: "He showed me a roll of bills, yes sir."

Rogers: "You said out of a spirit of buffoonery, you mean by that fun?"

"No."

"What do you mean by 'buffoonery'?"

"A spirit of bravado."

"Do you know the difference between bravado and buffoonery?"

Ford protested that the attorney's questions were not suitable as cross-examination. Again the court overruled him.

Rogers continued: "You understand the English language pretty well?"

"Yes sir," said Harrington.

"What do you mean by buffoonery?"

"Just showing how smart he was."

Rogers persisted: "Showing you how smart he was? That he had $10,000 to bribe jurors and show you how smart he was, a kind of a joke?"

"I didn't regard it as a joke."

"Now, don't you know that buffoonery is joking?" asked Rogers. "Do you know the definition in the dictionaries of buffoon or buffoonery?"

Harrington confessed he did not.

"Then, why did you use the word?"

"It is an ordinary word, commonplace word."

"By that you mean what?"

"Bravado."

"Bravado?"

"Yes."

"That he was showing off?"

"Yes sir."

"Didn't you say a while ago it was not bravado but buffoonery?"

"No sir." Harrington refused to be trapped.

Bristling with rage, Rogers changed the subject. "You are testifying for immunity, aren't you?"

"No sir," Harrington shot back.

"You are testifying to get yourself out of a hole, aren't you?"

"No sir."

"You went out there to Mr. Darrow's house, ate his bread and salt and slept in his house, didn't you?"

"Yes sir."

"Now, you go on the stand to supply the missing links, don't you?" Rogers focused on the bribery theme. "Do you mean to say that Mr. Darrow showed you a roll of bills and told you that he was going to bribe witnesses with it, or jurors with it?"

"He didn't use the word 'bribe'; he used the word 'reach.'"

"Was there any reason why he should do that, take you into his confidence?"

"No sir."

"Any reason why he should tell you he was going to reach jurors with a roll of bills?"

"I thought at the time there was."

"What was it?"

"I didn't know but what he might want me to do it. Feeling me out on it."

"Did he suggest to you that you should do it?"

"No sir. I put a damper on that right away."

"What did you say when you put a damper on it?"

"I told him it would be foolish to attempt such a thing; it would be his ruin."

"Was any living human being ever present at any of these conversations between you and Darrow?"

"No sir."

"Then, nobody ever heard Darrow say any of these things to you that you testified to?"

"Not that I know of."

In all the evidence submitted against Darrow, never was there a witness to corroborate another witness on a specific charge. This was especially apparent in the testimony of such "star" witnesses as Harrington and Franklin, and it undeniably weakened the state's case.

8

No sooner had Judge Hutton left the courtroom than Rogers warned Ford, "Don't say I grunted at you."

Ford roared, "I'll say it as often as you do it."

"Then I guess we'll have to settle it like true Irishmen," Rogers hurled his challenge.

Ford suggested their battle be held outside the walls of the courtroom.

"Anywhere you like," snapped Rogers.

Appel, usually in the thick of the altercation, this time acted as a peacemaker as the other attorneys crowded around the two belligerents.

Rogers made the first move toward peaceful relations. "The trouble with us," he said to Ford, "is that we are both hot-tempered."

Ford agreed. "I was as much to blame as you were," he said as he extended his hand, "and I suppose the best thing to do is to shake hands and forget it."

Rogers accepted the gesture.

Reporter Joseph Timmons summarized the courtroom activities of the last several days in the *Los Angeles Examiner:* "Earl Rogers thought Thursday that Assistant District Attorney Ford sneered at him; yesterday, Ford thought Rogers grunted at him." [10]

9

Saturday, June 22, 1912, 10 A.M. The bailiff pounding for quiet could not stop the laughter either of the courtroom spectators or the jurors when Fredericks, quivering with rage, charged that Darrow was "trying to use hypnotism" on Harrington. His hair disheveled, his voice raised several octaves, Fredericks shouted, "We would like Mr. Darrow to keep his seat" and stop moving around the courtroom.

"I have been trying to get this little man to look at me for two days," Rogers explained in reply to the prosecutor's objection. "I have walked over there, I have stood here, and I sat here, and I walked around yonder, and I tried to catch his eye once, and I have never succeeded. I have moved around with the hope and purpose of seeing if I could not get him to look me in the eye or look Mr. Darrow in the eye, and he has never done it."

Fredericks said he had no objection to Harrington "looking" Rogers or Darrow in the eye, but "we maintain Mr. Darrow is attempting to use hypnotism on this witness."

"This is the most childish—" Appel started to say when Fredericks interrupted: "I know what I am talking about."

Judge Hutton observed that, as far as the question of hypnotism was concerned, "it is not a science that this court will recognize."

"It is a science the medical professional recognizes," Fredericks argued.

"There may be such a thing as occasional instances of hypnotism, but it is not a matter that is reduced to a scientific basis, and the court will take no notice of the existence of such a science, it is not recognized as a science."

Fredericks, however, had the last word. "Before we get through, perhaps the court will."

10

When Darrow returned to his office that evening he found a telegram from the labor committee of San Francisco: "Appreciating your magnificent past services to the labor movement and the workers of our country, and reposing the utmost confidence in your integrity," they invited him to deliver the Labor Day oration at Shell Mound Park on September 2. "This year's Labor Day celebration promises to be the largest and most epoch-making in the history of the trade union movement of California, as it will comprise all organized labor, not only at San Francisco but in the Bay counties, and it is therefore sincerely to be hoped that you will accept our invitation of speaking as only you can to the hosts of united labor on the memorable occasion." [11]

The message was encouraging. It meant not all labor had forsaken him, a fear that weighed heavily upon him. Darrow responded with his usual touch of irony. "Very much obliged for your kind invitation. I will be there unless previous and very pressing business keeps me away." [12]

11

The days became riotous not only in the courtroom but on the street. One afternoon the deputy sheriff in charge of the jury knocked down a man who tried to pass among the jurors as they made their way to the hotel after the day's proceedings. In the courtroom, tempers were high, emotions stretched thin. Rogers sparked a flare-up when he demanded that the state make available to the defense a Dictograph transcript recorded in a hotel room between Harrington and Darrow. Robert J. Foster, a representative of the Erectors' Association, together with a federal prosecutor, Oscar Lawlor, had arranged with Harrington to engage Darrow in a conversation to be picked up by a Dictograph and transmitted to another room in the hotel where a shorthand reporter transcribed it. The prosecution refused to turn over the transcript. For four hours the attorneys battled furiously, Ford contending the evidence was "a written communication made to the District Attorney in official confidence and the public interests would suffer by disclosure of it at this time." Appel argued public interest would suffer if an innocent man were convicted by suppression of the evidence.

"There won't be any innocent man convicted," Fredericks barked in a prejudging of the defendant. Ford interjected, "We will not suppress anything," as Fredericks added, "It will come out at the right time."

"Yes, it will come out, as you are coming out," mocked Appel bitterly. "It is all coming out about the efforts and your conduct of the case here is the most prominent part, the suppression of any evidence for public interests."

Fredericks, exasperated, shouted, "I am done, Your Honor, that has got to stop, that has got to stop."

Appel did not hear as he reiterated, "Public interest demands that the paper be given to us."

"Now, stop it," ordered Fredericks. "I have stood this thing just as long as I am going to stand it and I will stand it no longer."

Court: "Captain Fredericks, sit down."

The enraged prosecutor screamed at the top of his voice, "I have stood this thing until I have gotten sick and tired of it. If this is going to be a court of justice let us have a court of justice and if it is going to be a fight, then I will have a fight." He picked up a glass inkwell from the counsel table and raised his arm to hurl it at Appel. Rogers jumped to his side and restrained him.

Judge Hutton admonished both Appel and Fredericks. "Wait a minute. If counsel on either side are so overworked and nervously exhausted as to become hysterical they can say so and the court will adjourn and give them a reasonable opportunity to get over it, but the hysterical outbursts seem to indicate overwrought nerves on both sides. These personal attacks have absolutely nothing to do with the merits of this case, absolutely nothing. Mr. Appel's personal attack upon Captain Fredericks was entirely out of order, and Captain Fredericks's reply was shockingly out of order. The court is amazed. Let's drop the incident." The court ruled against the defense in its demand for the transcriptions.

In his testimony, Harrington said he tried unsuccessfully to get Darrow to implicate himself while the Dictograph was running, but Darrow kept insisting he had nothing to do with the bribery.

12

Thursday, June 27, 1912. Fredericks called Guy Biddinger to the stand.[13] A detective sergeant on leave from the Chicago police force and now employed by the Burns Detective Agency, Biddinger had been one of the detectives who arrested J. B. McNamara and Ortie McManigal in Detroit. The state expected his testimony to prove that Darrow tried to buy information from him for the McNamara defense.

Biddinger claimed Darrow had asked him what evidence the prosecution had against the McNamaras, where it was kept, and whether he could get it for the defense. "I told him that I had the keys that I had taken off of J. J. McNamara when I searched him at police headquarters in Indianapolis; they were the same duplicates of keys McNamara had when he had been arrested in Detroit. He says, 'That is a damn strong piece of evidence against him, I wish you could get hold of that.' I said, 'I have already got hold of it. I have hold of 27 or 28 hotel registers. I have one register where J. J. McNamara signed for his brother as J. B. Brice at a roadhouse outside of Indianapolis at a dinner, and J. J. McNamara's own handwriting.' He said, 'Can you get hold of that?' I said, 'Yes.' He asked me how I would get possession of or get hold of it and I said I was the only one Mr. Burns would trust and he was going to send me out. He wanted to know if I couldn't arrange for a couple of his boys to hit me on the head when I got on the train and take it away from me. I said, 'I will see, I will let you know when I am going out with that evidence.' He said, 'I will bring up some money tomorrow.' I said, 'All right, how much will you bring?' and he says, 'I will bring down $1,000.'"

According to Biddinger, Darrow gave him only $500, apologizing that the defense was "a little short" but would eventually pay the $1000 promised. Biddinger turned over the $500 to William Burns, head of the Burns Detective Agency, for whom he worked.

"Cross-examine," said Fredericks.

13

Judge Hutton was ready to adjourn for the day, but Rogers wanted the jury to be sent out of the courtroom while Biddinger and the district attorney remained. He asked that the court reporter record his statement "outside of the record of the case."

Fredericks said that if it was outside the record of the case he would also leave the courtroom. When Rogers requested him to remain, he said, "Oh, that is different. I will stay on a request."

"Now, what is your statement?" asked Judge Hutton.

Rogers complained that before court opened that morning both Biddinger and Burns called him a "son-of-a-bitch" and, in addition, he accused both men of carrying guns. Burns, he believed, also had a sword cane. "Now, if Your Honor cannot protect me under those circumstances, I want to know it, in order that I may protect myself."

"Mr. Rogers," asked Judge Hutton, "do you say this witness has come upon the witness stand armed?"

Rogers: "He was armed night before last with a 44 caliber revolver and he may have taken it off now."

Biddinger: "I always carry a couple of them."

Rogers: "Have you got them now?"

Biddinger: "I will answer if the court asks me. I won't answer you."

Court: "I will inquire of you if you have come on the witness stand with a revolver on your person?"

Biddinger: "No sir."

Rogers: "Did you have a revolver out there this afternoon?"

Biddinger: "I will answer if the court asks me, I will answer it. I don't care anything about you."

Rogers: "Maybe you will sometime."

Biddinger: "Not at all."

Fredericks interposed: "This seems to be a personal matter—"

Rogers: "It is not a personal matter for an officer of this court to have that kind of a thing happen. I won't have it."

Court: "I assume, of course, that no witness will come into this courtroom with any gun or article of self-defense on his person, either a revolver or anything else, and the court will take very prompt action if anything of the kind occurs."

Biddinger: "When I heard your order I left my guns outside."

14

July 1, 1912. Court had adjourned for the weekend because of the illness of a juror. When it reconvened Monday afternoon, Darrow cross-examined Biddinger, delving into the witness's professional background. Biddinger admitted he did all kinds of detective work. "Shadow work?" suggested Darrow.

"Sometimes shadow work, yes."

"What kind of work is that?"

"Well," explained the witness, "if I didn't know who you was and wanted to find out I would drop behind you until I took you home and I would make a few inquiries; find out who you was, and if I didn't—if I wasn't sure of my man I would follow him."

Darrow wanted the detective to talk about their first meeting. Biddinger said Darrow had been "very anxious to discover who the spy" was in the McNamara defense camp but he refused to tell him. The attorney referred to Biddinger's testimony where he accused Darrow of trying to arrange for "a couple of his boys to hit me on the head" in order to get the evidence for the prosecution which he might be carrying with him.

"Was anything said as to what kind of club it should be?" Darrow asked.

"No sir."

"Or what part of your head you should get hit over?"

"No sir."

"Was there anything said whether the train should be held up and boarded on the desert?"

"No, you said you would have a couple of your boys get on the train with me that night."

"Whereabouts?"

"In Chicago."

"Whereabout was the operation to take place?"

"I hadn't any idea."

"While the train was in motion."

"Yes sir, I suppose so."

"And then they were to take the stuff and jump off the train and leave you there, is that it?"

"I suppose that is the way it was to be."

"You haven't been reading Burns detective stories, have you, and dreaming?" asked Darrow.

"No sir, I have not."

Judge Hutton said sharply, "Don't answer that question."

Darrow questioned Biddinger about their alleged financial arrangements. The detective asked for $5000, but Darrow would go no higher than $500.

"You expected $5000?" Darrow asked incredulously.

"Yes sir."

"For what you had already given me?"

"You was going to give it to me for my goodwill."

"You valued the goodwill pretty high, didn't you?"

"I didn't place any value on it at all."

"All you was doing was getting what you could out of it?"

"All I was doing was trying to trap you," was the vindictive reply.

Darrow admitted he paid Biddinger to secure information which the state had against the McNamaras. He insisted, however, there was no connection between the money paid Biddinger and the crime for which he was being tried.

15

The day before William J. Burns, head of the William J. Burns National Detective Agency, testified, he spoke to a sympathetic audience at the weekly luncheon meeting of the Advertising Club of Los Angeles. He accused Samuel Gompers of being "one of those who has thought himself above the law but he has been taught that all men indeed are equal in this country and that anyone breaking the law must suffer his punishment. I should like to mention names, dates, places, but at the present time I am a witness in the Darrow trial and am, therefore, not at liberty to speak to you as plainly as I should like to." [14]

When Burns took the stand at the Darrow trial to corroborate the testimony of Biddinger, [15] the jurymen straightened in their seats. Their interest in Burns was not so much for the expected testimony as for his colorful personality and the wide publicity he had received when he apprehended the McNamaras. Short, dapper, wearing a gray suit with carefully creased trousers, he was the sartorial opposite of the defendant against whom he was testifying. As he walked to the witness box, the self-assured Burns carried a cane which he carefully placed on the reporters' table.

Rogers's biographers erred when they wrote that "Burns was having little difficulty in offsetting Darrow's queries" so Rogers "immediately came to the rescue by intruding himself." [16] The trial transcript tells a completely different story. Darrow did not handle the cross-examination. Burns, on the witness stand for direct examination, was asked by Fredericks whether John R. Harrington had ever been in his employ. Darrow objected to the question and asked sarcastically, "What are we trying to prove here at this time by this wonderful man?"

Burns shouted, "I object to your referring to me in that way."

Court: "The objection of the witness is sustained."

Darrow: "I withdraw it then, it is not true."

Burns: "Mr. Rogers is telling him not to withdraw anything."

Court: "Mr. Darrow has withdrawn the remark."

Burns: "Your Honor, I want to call your attention to the action of Mr. Rogers."

Darrow: "I withdraw the word 'wonderful.'"

Fredericks: "Let us proceed."

Court: "If there is any affront to you, Mr. Burns, that was contained in Mr. Darrow's remarks, he has withdrawn it. So far as what counsel may do at their table in conferring among themselves, it is not a matter that the court can interfere with unless it interferes with the progress of this trial in some way."

Burns: "Now, if Your Honor please, I would like to at this time call your attention to statements that have been made by Mr. Rogers in this courtroom that I carried a sword cane. It is not true. This man also made a statement I was a suborner of perjury, in the presence of this jury."

Rogers: "I make it again, sir, and do not take it back."

Burns asked for protection from the court against such comment by Rogers.

Judge Hutton responded that a witness on the stand cannot be subjected to derogatory personal remarks. Before court adjourned for the day, Judge Hutton imposed $25 fines on both Rogers and Burns, noting that "apparently there is some personal difference that has existed between Mr. Burns and Mr. Rogers. The witness as such went out of his way to bring up that personal difference. That cannot be done in this court. When that did occur it was the business of counsel to refer that matter to the court for adjustment. That not having been done the court is left no alternative but to declare this personal altercation an unlawful interference with the proceedings of this court."

16

The acrimonious bickering expected between Rogers and Burns during cross-examination the next day did not develop. The session proceeded with extreme politeness and decorum. The "fashionable audience," including many women "attired in their best gowns" and many lawyers who had anticipated an unusually heated session, were disappointed at the calmness. Rogers's voice "had the cooing notes of a dove and Burns was Parisian in his politeness."[17]

"Mr. Burns," opened Rogers, "I propose to cross-examine you fully upon the testimony you gave yesterday. Any differences you and I have I intend to forget in cross-examining you."

Did Burns know that a former manager of his agency in Los Angeles offered to sell copies of reports, payrolls, books, and memoranda to "dozens of persons"? Did he know that Biddinger had tried to trap Darrow? "Yes," he had known both, and he had helped Biddinger after learning that the McNamara defense tried to bribe him. In the public lectures that Burns had been delivering throughout the country since Darrow's arrest and indictment, had he not said that he was determined to get Gompers or words to that effect? No, he never made such a statement. Did he recently, within the past several weeks, tell Lincoln Steffens that first he would get Darrow and then Gompers but that he had to get Darrow in order to get Gompers? The prosecutor objected. The court sustained the objection.

So restrained were Rogers's cross-examination and Burns's reaction that the *L. A. Herald* noted tongue-in-cheek that their joint performance was worthy of the Nobel Peace Prize.[18]

17

The complexities of the trial and the weeks of wrangling exacerbated the situation. Sometimes it seemed reason was obscured as the arguments proliferated and the courtroom battles raged. For several weeks Mrs. Darrow appeared to be on the verge of collapse. Her face pale and drawn, she appeared in court every day, but her self-control was eroding. She sat at the defense table next to her husband, suffering with him as the state presented witness after witness who claimed to be familiar with Clarence's efforts at bribery. Dismayed by the vicious testimony, she tried to spare him as she bent her face to his, whispering words of comfort.

The morning her seat was vacant, newspapers reported that Mrs. Darrow had suffered a "nervous breakdown." It was more than a week before she returned to her usual place in the courtroom.

The state called only a few more witnesses before it completed its case. Several of these talked about Franklin's futile efforts to bribe them. Frank R. Smith, orange grower, told Franklin, "There ain't no use to talk to me because you haven't enough money to buy me." Guy W. Yonkin, in the cigar business, testified he became "very mad" to think Franklin would suggest such a "proposition" to him. A few others, associated with local banks, related money transactions between Darrow and Franklin.

18

Friday, July 5, 1912. All the main characters in the drama except Rogers were present in the courtroom. The thirteen jurors filed into the jury box. Judge Hutton announced he had received a telephone call from Mrs. Rogers that the principal defense counsel was too ill to be present and had suggested the trial be continued to Monday.

The judge agreed. Court adjourned for the weekend.

19

Monday, July 8, 1912. The last witness for the prosecution in its direct presentation, Robert Bain [19] gave the substance of Franklin's bribe offer. "He wanted me to accept a bribe, and under considerable hesitation I finally accepted it, and he was going to pay me $500, and when he went to pay me he only had $400."

Under the agreement Bain would "hold out for acquittal." Yet, he warned Franklin that "if the evidence is strong enough I sure will vote for a conviction."

The topsy-turvy reasoning in this case was evidenced continually by the repeated revelation that Franklin not only made an injudicious choice of veniremen for bribery but also antagonized them by paying less than originally promised.

Day in and day out, for eight weeks, covering exactly 3900 pages of court transcript, the State of California determinedly presented evidence it hoped would convict Darrow. It was not until Monday afternoon, July 8, 1912, that Fredericks announced, "The People rest."

XV

Witnesses for the Defense

1

DARROW had asked his law partner, Edgar Lee Masters, to obtain character references from the Chicago community. Masters grudgingly gathered depositions from a cross-section of Darrow's acquaintances and friends: a former U.S. senator and a current U.S. senator, scores of judges, the mayor of Chicago and several former mayors of the city, the president of the Chicago Bar Association, former prosecutors, the current state's attorney, fellow lawyers, and various businessmen.

Some were in philosophic disagreement with the defendant, others shared his theories about government, economics, and sociology. Both protagonist and antagonist, however, told the same story: Darrow's reputation was unblemished, of the highest caliber.

Earl Rogers, lorgnette neatly balanced on his nose, sat in the witness chair much of the time as he read the depositions aloud. Assistant District Attorney Arthur Keetch, who had cross-examined the character witnesses in Chicago when the depositions were taken, read the cross-examination. The day and a half spent reading the depositions created a welcome hiatus in the trial from the almost constant bickering that pervaded the courtroom.

2

Tuesday afternoon, July 9, 1912. Job Harriman, first witness for the defense,[1] was juxtaposed to Franklin. He did not see Darrow on the day Franklin said Harriman had given money to Darrow; he denied that Darrow had ever given him $10,000 or "any other sum whatever to keep for him for any purpose whatever in any place anywhere" except checks in payment of his fee as a McNamara attorney.

In cross-examination, Fredericks wasted no time in his attempt to show that Harriman's interest in the Darrow case exceeded that of an ordinary witness. He accused Harriman of assisting "to a certain extent" in the attempted bribery of the McNamara jurors, and charged him with knowing about the plan for dynamiting the *Los Angeles Times* building well in advance of the blast. Harriman categorically denied such knowledge.

A series of witnesses for the defense repudiated Franklin's testimony. Tom L. Johnston, attorney:[2] When the defense called Johnston, the district attorney objected on the basis that he had been Franklin's lawyer after his arrest on the bribery charge. Appel argued that a person who confesses his own "misdeeds in court in order to convict another" waives the privilege of lawyer-client relationship "and everything he says to his attorney may be extracted from him in court and everything that the attorney heard from his client may be taken from the attorney as a witness by interrogation here."

Judge Hutton agreed with Appel.

Johnston testified he had informed Franklin that he asked Ford to postpone Franklin's bribery case, but Ford wanted Franklin to confess that Darrow was the one behind the crime. Ford said he was securing sufficient evidence to send Darrow to the penitentiary, and if Franklin would not turn state's witness he could go to the penitentiary with him.

Appel to Johnston: "Upon you saying that to Franklin, did he or did he not say to you then that neither Davis nor Darrow had given him any money to bribe jurors, and that they knew nothing about it, and that he would be a God damned liar if he said they did, and did you not then say to him not to lie about anything but to tell the truth?"

Johnston: "Yes."

Witness for the defense: Peter Pirotte,[3] police officer, Venice, California. Franklin suggested they open a detective agency together in Venice after he got out of his "little trouble." Pirotte asked him, "How are you getting along with that?" "There is nothing to that," Franklin answered. "I am going to get out all right; the district attorney don't want me; they want Darrow." Pirotte said he would talk to him when he cleared himself.

Witness for the defense: George W. Hood,[4] neighbor and lodge brother of Franklin. Franklin told him he received the bribery money from a stranger who "was standing within 30 feet of me when the money was passed. He disappeared when the crack came on and I have never seen him since."

Ford objected to Appel's method of questioning Hood. Appel's temper flared: Ford's objections were "harassing the orderly examination" of the witness, a "contemptible" action. Ford objected to the word "contemptible" and demanded protection from the court.

Judge Hutton ordered both attorneys to calm down and to confine themselves to examination. He added that he realized "the weather is very hot and it is trying. Let us get on with the examination."

Witness for the defense: Frank Edward Dominguez,[5] attorney, a friend of Franklin's for eighteen to twenty years. Appel asked whether Franklin had told him, "I never received a dishonest dollar from Darrow. He never knew anything connected with this matter. He is too good a man to do anything of that kind; he wouldn't stand for any corruption or dirty work and he never gave me a dollar for any corrupt purposes in the world." Dominguez replied firmly, "He did."

Harry Jones, L.A. Tribune reporter:[6] Appel, after objection from the state's attorney, read into the record part of a story written by Jones in which the Tribune reporter said Franklin told newspapermen that he "intended to keep my mouth shut concerning this case until after the Superior Court acts upon it, but it is my duty to defend the good name of an innocent man. Those witnesses lied when they said I had mentioned Clarence Darrow's name to them. I wish to vindicate Darrow from any charge that may be made against him in connection with this case. I may be guilty of all I am charged with, but I am not a fool."

Each witness was part of defense strategy to discredit Franklin. From now on, for all practical purposes, the defense concentrated on the improbability that Darrow would order Franklin to bribe a juror after the McNamara guilty plea had been arranged and settled.

Wednesday, July 17, 1912. Over the state's objection, Fremont Older,[7] for seventeen years managing editor of the prolabor San Francisco Bulletin, testified. Darrow examined Older since Rogers's ailing throat prevented him from prolonged questioning. Older said he arrived in Los Angeles in immediate response to a telegram from Steffens and Darrow asking him to join them for an important conference regarding the McNamara case. They met at the Alexandria Hotel where Steffens explained that both labor and capital had to make concessions if the strife between them were ever to be ended. He had already persuaded "a number of prominent men" in the city that both sides suffered in labor wars and it was time to compromise in order to end the fighting. He had convinced them not to "demand the blood of a human being" in the *Times* building tragedy but to agree to prison terms for the defendants.

Fredericks wanted to know by whom it had been "agreed upon." Older mentioned Meyer, a Los Angeles political power, Lissner, a business leader in the city, and Otis Chandler of the *L. A. Times,* "and I think one or two others, but I do not recall them."

Older was "pretty sure" he had raised the point that if Darrow had agreed to such a compromise plea his career as a labor attorney would be over. Darrow said that was not the issue, that he had been employed to save the lives of the McNamaras and that was what he had to do. "I corroborated you," Older said to Darrow from the witness stand. By the time he left Los Angeles, Older said, he was certain the compromise would go through as planned.

"You may cross-examine," said Darrow.

"Didn't you get the idea from the conversation with Mr. Steffens and Mr. Darrow that from the standpoint of the defense that this was the best thing to do in order to save the lives of the men they were defending, whereas if they went on to trial they might be convicted and hung or hanged, whichever the proper word is?" Fredericks asked.

"Yes. I got that idea that a human life was going to be saved."

"No further cross-examination," said Fredericks.

3

July 18, 1912. Witness for the defense: Joseph Lincoln Steffens,[8] famed muckraker, who had spent seventeen years writing about politics, government, and more recently about labor and industrial problems. He was considered the star witness for the defense. He told of the weekend visit to the Scripps ranch and how the compromise idea was born and put into effect.

With Darrow's permission to attempt a compromise, Steffens appealed to Meyer Lissner to call a meeting of businessmen in order to settle the labor problems which were destroying the city. He suggested the idealistic argument of the golden rule: "Here, we've got labor down; we can hang two dynamiters who the workers think are innocent if we want to. But let's not. Let's let labor up and let their heroes go. And then have a conference of leading employers with labor leaders and see if we can't handle our labor problem in such a fashion that we can afford to make Los Angeles the best instead of the worst town in the country for labor."[9]

The argument convinced Lissner, who carried the message to other business leaders, according to Steffens. The initial proposal dictated by Lissner called for J. B. McNamara "to plead guilty and receive such sentence as the court might administer, except capital punishment, and all other prosecutions in connection with the affair to be dropped."

The businessmen and the district attorney, however, insisted that both McNamaras plead guilty, with J.B. sentenced to life imprisonment and J.J. to a prison term. Finally, the defense reluctantly agreed.

During the Darrow trial the date of this agreement loomed as the crucial factor: the prosecution contended that it had come only after, and as a result of, Franklin's arrest, while the defense insisted both sides had agreed earlier.

Steffens's performance on the stand encouraged the defense. His voice, soft and deferential, courteously deflected every jab by Fredericks. The prosecutor started, "I want to ask you a few questions which I think are a little personal, but they are to get at your view of things. As I understand it, you are an avowed anarchist."

Rogers shouted his objection, but Steffens proceeded to answer. "No, that is not true. I am a good deal worse than an avowed anarchist."

"You are a good deal worse than an avowed anarchist?" An incredulous tone penetrated the question.

"Yes sir, I believe in Christianity."

"That is worse, is it?"

"That is a good deal worse. It is more radical." Steffens explained: "Anarchism, you understand, merely believes in justice. Christianity is a doctrine, what they call love, which I interpret to be understanding mercy, and I don't believe that justice is what we want. I believe we have got to have more of a personal feeling; more mercy and more understanding."

Prepared for Fredericks's onslaught, Steffens disregarded objections of defense counsel as he expounded his views on the present social and economic situation. As Steffens spoke, Rogers lamented, "I do not seem to have any influence with this witness."

Steffens lectured: "I am trying to make a distinction between the crime that is merely done by an individual and the crime that is committed by an individual for a group which grows out of social conditions, and I think that those two lines of crime must be handled differently." Steffens assured the jury that Darrow pleaded the McNamaras guilty to save the lives of the two men after realizing that there was no defense; he had not done it to avoid any possible charges against himself.

A juror, referring to a phrase the witness had used in his testimony, wanted to know what Steffens meant by direct action by capital.

"Direct action, Mr. Juryman," said Steffens, "means, in a technical sense, the distinction between political and industrial action; for instance, a strike, in the language of labor, a strike is direct action, direct from employee to employer, as a distinction from political action, which is going to the polls to get officers or officials who will give you justice; any force that is used by anybody directly upon the man he is opposed to is, in a technical sense, direct action."

Another juror asked Steffens whether he believed in direct action.

"This experience in Los Angeles," Steffens answered, "went very far to convince me that the golden rule and the force of good will might not be sufficient, and that after all the thing would have to be fought out, but I have not finally come to that conclusion. I want to try it out a little longer."

The *L. A. Record* applauded Fredericks's cross-examination: he "did the best cross-examination of his career in an effort to break the testimony of Steffens," but was "easily frustrated by the witness' coolness and biting." That same edition of the *Record* reported, "It was the defense's biggest day." [10]

4

Thursday, July 25, 1912. Witness for the defense: LeCompte Davis,[11] a McNamara attorney.

Appel did the examining. "Do you know the witness George Behm?" he asked almost immediately after establishing Davis's credentials.

Davis had become acquainted with Behm at the beginning of the McNamara case.

"Now, you may state whether or not you or Mr. Darrow or in your presence or in the presence of each other at any time stated to George Behm to deny any fact concerning which he was to be asked or deny the truth of any fact that he might be inquired of?" in the McNamara grand jury hearing.

No, responded Davis, except that there were certain questions he might be asked at the grand jury hearing to which he had been advised to respond that "it was incompetent, irrelevant and immaterial and did not concern the case." Since Behm could not remember enough of the phraseology, Davis and Darrow suggested the succinct phrase, "That does not concern the case."

Davis, as a McNamara attorney, first became aware of the plea bargaining possibility the latter part of November. He was in Captain Fredericks's office when the district attorney suggested to him, "Why don't you come through and let those boys plead guilty and quit your horseplay?"

Certain that Fredericks's remark was made in jest, Davis responded he had not been hired to enter a guilty plea.

"You know you are going to do it, why don't you do it?" Fredericks taunted.

"I don't know anything of the kind, Captain."

To Davis's surprise, the district attorney informed him that a committee of Los Angeles businessmen was being consulted, and his office had a plea bargaining proposition before it. The next day Darrow confirmed this. "There are some negotiations on for a settlement of the case."

Davis fought the idea. He believed "the men who were paying the money for the defense" had to be consulted. To Darrow's argument that his first duty was to his clients, Davis insisted he also had a duty to himself. He warned Darrow that a guilty plea would ruin his reputation with labor and destroy his effectiveness. On the witness stand in the Darrow trial, Davis added that all the other McNamara defense attorneys who knew about the negotiations agreed with Darrow. Only Davis objected to the idea of a compromise.

Outvoted by his colleagues, Davis visited the brothers in jail on Thanksgiving Day to discuss the change of plea. "Jim first said that he would plead guilty himself, but he would never consent to John pleading guilty. I took him off to one side, and I said, 'Do you want to be hung?' and he said, 'I don't care whether I am hung or not,' he said. 'It is a matter of indifference to me, but I will never consent to my brother John taking a year.' Then I said, 'Do you want your brother hung, too?' I said, 'It looks like that to me; you want to hang your brother, too.' With that he began to cry and he finally said, 'Bring John in.'"

That evening Davis, acting as liaison, reported to Fredericks that the brothers agreed—John to get ten years and J.B. a life sentence. The district attorney promised to give his assurance the next morning at 10:00 A.M.

By morning, however, he refused to consider less than fifteen years for John, and he added, "I am not to blame," a cryptic remark which indicated "higher-ups" did not agree with the initial compromise. It took several meetings and a lot of persuading by Davis before the brothers consented to the modification in the settlement.

5

Friday, July 26, 1912, 10:00 A.M. Fredericks opened the cross-examination of Davis, plunging at once into the subject of the plea negotiations. Since the exact time would be a determining factor in deciding Darrow's guilt or innocence, he hammered away at the dates Davis talked with Darrow about in regard to the brothers' willingness to plead guilty.

Fredericks: "You remember Mr. Darrow and you coming up into my office on the afternoon of the day Franklin was arrested, and having a talk with me?"

Davis: "No, and I don't think we did. We were there the day after."

"Wednesday?"

"Yes sir."

Fredericks: "You remember that conversation?"

Davis: "We were up there to see the best terms we could get, and it was then that you said that you wouldn't let him [John J.] off unless he took a term of years, and I insisted on knowing what you meant by a term of years."

Fredericks: "Now, Mr. Davis, isn't that the very first time that the question of J.J.'s pleading guilty, or both of them pleading guilty, was ever seriously discussed between you and me?"

Rogers objected to the phrase "seriously discussed"; he insisted it called for a conclusion. The judge agreed.

"Did I ever say to you, or was there ever any discussion with you as to what difference it would make as to whether both these men pleaded guilty at the same time? Was the matter ever discussed?" Fredericks asked.

"That matter was discussed" as well as possible sentences and whether the pleas of guilty should be brought for the *Times* case, which was a murder case, or the Llewellyn bombing in which J.J. was also implicated.

Davis recalled his satisfaction that an agreement had been reached and that Fredericks would do everything he could to see that it was accepted by the judge.

XVI

Darrow Testifies for Himself

1

MONDAY, July 29, 1912. Darrow's anticipated appearance as a witness brought a crushing crowd to the courtroom. As the room filled with spectators jockeying for even standing room, more than a thousand people were turned away at the doors.

At 4:00 P.M. Clarence Seward Darrow[1] walked slowly to the witness stand in his own defense. Though he appeared calm, his face was drawn and flushed. He sat sideways in the witness chair, legs crossed, hands clasped over his knee.

"In your own way, and without taking the time to interrogate you with reference to each one, you may state the cases that you have been engaged as counsel in or as arbitrator," Rogers instructed Darrow.

As Darrow recited the litany of his legal career, it was apparent that he had acted in a wide range of cases representing both labor and management as well as arbitrating between the two.

"I have had pretty near every kind of case," Darrow continued. "I suppose nine-tenths of my practice has been civil practice and perhaps one-tenth of it criminal and about one-third of it charity for the last twenty years."

Rogers turned specifically to the McNamara case. Darrow was explaining the details of his involvement when Rogers interrupted. He wanted him to talk about Bert Franklin.

"Will you excuse me for suggesting something to you?" Darrow asked Rogers.

"Yes?"

"As to time, if I took the Behm matter, which particularly occurred in Chicago."

"As you please, Mr. Darrow."

"You want to take it up in chronological order and it might be a little easier for me so that I might carry it along."

Rogers agreed. "Do you know George Behm, the uncle of Ortie McManigal who was arrested with James B. McNamara?"

"I think I do now."

"When did you first meet Mr. Behm?"

Behm and Mrs. McManigal, Ortie's wife, came to Darrow's home in Chicago in the middle of June. Darrow had asked Harrington to be present. Mrs. McManigal complained about the manner in which Burns detectives treated her husband. One of them literally kidnapped him and J. B. McNamara from Detroit, keeping them in South Chicago for more than a week in the house of another Burns detective "without any authority at law." They had been "bulldozed and given a third degree." She complained to Darrow that Burns agents shadowed her constantly and pressured her to come to Los Angeles "to stay with her husband and help him in the position he had taken." They promised to pay her fare to Los Angeles as well as give her additional money. She refused the offer since she disbelieved the stories about her husband, but she was eager to see him. She thought he probably was crazy or had been bribed or driven into doing it. Darrow testified he told her "to get what money she could from Burns to pay her expenses, and I would give her the rest to have her come here and interview her husband, and that if her husband had made these statements, whatever they were, under threats and promises and wished to tell the truth or another story and wanted me to defend him with the rest, I would do it. But I didn't tell her or anybody else in the 35 years of my practice that I would ever win his case or clear him. That is something no lawyer ever knows."

"Did you have any conversation at that time or any other time in which you told Behm or any other person that you wanted McManigal to change his testimony or refer to it in any way?" asked Rogers.

Darrow's response flatly contradicted Behm: "I did not." McManigal had "never given any testimony and I never asked him to have it changed."

Had Darrow ever given Franklin any money to bribe a juror or jurors?

The defendant sharply denied Franklin's accusation.

Darrow made an impressive witness in his own defense. He spoke quietly and firmly, appeared at ease and self-possessed. The *L.A. Times* the next day reluctantly admitted that "some of the jurors were impressed by the words of the accused."[2]

Mrs. Darrow had moved to the chair her husband vacated when he took the witness stand. Shaking with emotion, she dabbed at her tear-filled eyes with a filmy white handkerchief. Her white dress contrasted sharply with the dark suits of the attorneys about her. Behind Ruby sat twenty-five or thirty women who had elbowed their way to the front of the courtroom proclaiming themselves "friends of the defendant." They crowded out attorneys, labor leaders, and journalists.

At one point Judge Hutton stopped the proceeding, scolding the crowd for too much levity among those inside the rail and instructing the sheriff "to sit less people" there.

2

Tuesday, July 30, 1912. Sitting in the witness seat recently occupied by his accusers, Darrow disputed their sworn statements. He spoke in slow, forceful sentences. To emphasize his remarks he used his gold-rimmed reading glasses as a baton or slapped them against his knees as he spoke.

Franklin had stressed receiving a $1000 check from Darrow on October 6, the day after they allegedly discussed bribing a juror. Darrow denied giving Franklin a check on that date, although he had given him one for $1000 to cover expenses for himself and his men two days earlier.

Then the direct question from Rogers: "Did you give him this check [dated October 4] or any other check for the purpose of paying Bain or any other juror any money whatever?" and the direct answer: "I never did." Darrow further denied ever talking with Franklin about bribing Bain or any other juror. He explained that in a case where labor and capital were involved the defense attempted to get, if possible, "as many men who were working men and whose natural sympathies would be on our side." He denied being told that Bain "had ever been opposed to unions."

Did Darrow know Franklin paid Bain to vote for an acquittal? Had he ever asked Franklin whether he thought Bain would accept a bribe to cast a not guilty vote? Rogers asked.

"No conversation of that sort ever took place between us," said Darrow.

Rogers: "Or anything like it?"

Darrow: "Nothing that Mr. Burns's detectives could not listen to if they had been around."

3

Rogers turned to the Lockwood charge. Darrow denied any conversation with Franklin about bribing Lockwood; he had not seen Job Harriman on the morning Franklin testified he got money from him for bribing jurors, nor did he ever give Harriman any money to hold at any time for such a purpose. On the morning that Franklin attempted to pass money to Lockwood, Darrow recalled, he got down to his office about half-past eight. "I had been there a little while when someone called me up and asked me if I would come over to Mr. Harriman's headquarters on some political matter. I don't remember the exact conversation; I don't know whether I would be sure, excepting from conversations and what I know about outside matters, as to who called me, although I think he gave me his name at the time. It was probably around 9 o'clock. I know it was before the session of court. I was on my way to Mr. Harriman's headquarters when I saw Mr. Franklin. I was going down on the west side of the street, and crossing over about at the Third Street crossing— there is a jog in Third Street. I presume I went across—at where Third intersects Main Street on the west, and as I went across I saw Mr. Franklin walking with a man whom I didn't know. Right behind him was Sam Browne, whom I knew very well, and had seen day after day here in court and other places, and knew he was a special detective for the district attorney's office. One or two other men were with him. I saw Browne as soon as I saw Franklin and I had no thought of any connection between the two. As I went toward him [Franklin] Mr. Browne came between us and said that he was about to arrest him and not to speak to him."

Rogers: "Just in that particular let me stop you a moment. At that time did you say to Franklin, 'They are onto you,' or anything of that kind?"

Darrow: "I said nothing of the sort. I would probably let him take his chances rather than go there, if I had known it. I said nothing to him. I said nothing whatever to him. At that time I expected this matter of the McNamara case would be closed at once. When Mr. Browne told me that he was about to arrest Franklin, of course, I was very much shocked, surprise would be rather a weak word for it. I said, 'That could not be possible. If I had ever dreamed of any such thing it could not possibly have been.' I don't know what else I might have said. I was surprised and shocked. The direct thing that came into my mind was the effect it would have on the settlement of this case for which I had been working so hard and which I looked forward to as a means of saving one man's life, if not two."

Again Darrow denied ever instructing Franklin to do an illegal act. He denied showing Harrington a roll of bills when the investigator was at the

Darrow home, or telling Harrington that he would be "ruined" if Franklin talked.

Rogers: "I call your attention now to the matter of Biddinger. Do you know a man named Guy Biddinger of Chicago?"

Darrow: "I know a Guy Biddinger; I wouldn't say I know a man by that name." This was a typical Darrow ploy—to cut down his opponent with a play on words. Biddinger "wanted to furnish me information about our case and the people connected with the organization who were giving information to Burns." Now a thrust against detectives in general: "Knowing he was a detective I had no doubt but what he would be glad to make some money. I told him I would be glad to pay him for any information he would give me. He promised to make reports. I didn't hear from him for some time. I gave him no money, I told him as the work developed if it amounted to anything I would. He said when he came here he was going to have an office next to Burns and he would keep me posted about our men who were in the confidence of Burns."

Rogers interjected: "That is, traitors to your camp?"

Darrow: "Yes, and he probably said he would give me other information from Burns's office the next time I saw him in Los Angeles. He told me again that Mr. Burns was getting all kinds of information in the central office at Indianapolis, which we had before suspected, and that he was getting information from this coast," and especially from a member of the union's executive board.

Biddinger said he was leaving for San Francisco within a few days and would be able to "give me specific information" regarding the identity of the traitors. He wanted $1000 in advance. Darrow demurred, offering $500 until he got the definite information. "I gave it to him for that purpose, which was perfectly legal, in my opinion."

Darrow said the first time he heard of the proposition that Biddinger should be jumped and evidence taken away from him was from Biddinger's testimony on the witness stand.

In response to a question from Rogers, Darrow reiterated that by November 28 there was neither necessity nor purpose for bribing any juror or talesman. "As we went on in the preparation of this case it kept growing on all of us that there was no possible chance to win; it grew on us from day to day and from week to week, the exact condition we were in and that our clients were in, which a lawyer never knows at once, the same as a doctor learns that his patient is going to die."

The defendant struggled with emotions as his eyes filled with tears. He had difficulty controlling his voice when he related Davis's insistence that the attorney had no right to settle the case without consulting organized labor, since labor had furnished the money for the defense. Furthermore, Davis had argued, the settlement would ruin Darrow with labor.

But Darrow believed that, though organized labor provided the money, it was not the client, and "nobody could possibly give us money that could in any way influence us in an action that was due to our clients; that so far as I was concerned I had no right to consider myself, or should not, and that all I had to consider was these two men."

Harriman was not consulted about the settlement because he had been deeply involved in his campaign for mayor of Los Angeles, and "we all knew that the matter would seriously involve his campaign, and that he was not in a position to advise and ought not to be asked to take any such responsibility."

"We are all tired," confessed Fredericks as the afternoon adjournment hour neared.

4

Wednesday, July 31, 1912. The court ordered the "swarm of woman partisans" excluded from inside the rail, permitting only a few persons in the coveted vantage ground.

Darrow in his testimony suggested that the jury might be interested to learn that investigating of talesmen in important cases is customary. To enlarge on this comment, Rogers asked whether Darrow ever heard of a lawsuit tried before a jury where efforts were not made to ascertain all possible information about talesmen. Darrow said he never heard of "a case where there was any great public feeling or discussion where both sides didn't do it, if they had money enough to do it, and I know it was done by the state and by us in the McNamara case."

In direct examination Darrow, on the stand for almost two days, filled more than a thousand pages of typewritten testimony before the defense rested. For the most part he seemed relaxed and in control; "objections by counsel for the state did not ruffle him," reported the *L.A. Times.*[3]

XVII
Darrow Cross-Examined

1

BEFORE Ford began the cross-examination, several jurors questioned Darrow. One wanted to know how many persons in the United States were directly interested "in your handling of the McNamara case through their contributions to the defense fund, through their affiliated unions?"

About two million, Darrow answered. When the McNamara case started, the AFL imposed a twenty-five-cent assessment on its members. About one-fourth paid, adding $200,000 to the defense coffers. Persons from all walks of life contributed, as had the Socialist organization. "Everybody in the United States took sides on that case, and were interested, actively interested," Darrow believed.

Fredericks objected. "I think that is going too far."

"Strike out the answer," ordered the judge.

2

Ford straightened his tie, brushed back his thick curly hair with both hands. As he walked toward the witness, Darrow, who had been sitting sideways in the witness chair, turned and directly faced his examiner.[1]

It was a very warm summer. The air was humid and hung heavy in the courtroom despite the ceiling fan. Ford "drank immense quantities of ice-water" as he conducted his cross-examination. "You stated on direct examination, Mr. Darrow," he said as he began a rapierlike duel with Darrow and Rogers, "that you were the author of various books." He displayed a little pamphlet.

"Yes sir. That pamphlet which you have there" is among the books, Darrow answered.

"'Crime and Criminals'?" queried Ford.

"Yes sir. That is the stenographer's copy of an address that I delivered off-hand in the county jail to prisoners" about ten years ago.

Ford explained that his purpose in introducing the pamphlet—in which Darrow declared his disbelief that "there is any sort of distinction between the real moral condition of the people in and out of jail"—was to show Darrow's attitude toward crime in general, and he wanted to know whether this was Darrow's state of mind on November 28, 1911, when Franklin was arrested on the jury bribery charge.

Rogers shouted his objection—not proper cross-examination; incompetent, irrelevant, immaterial; an author could not and should not be judged by an isolated sentence or part of a book. He was ready to stipulate, however, that Darrow's philosophy and views on general sociological and ethical subjects were matters of consideration in the trial. He offered to send in copies of all of Darrow's books "and let the jury read every book he ever wrote, at their leisure."

Though both state and defense might agree to that stipulation, members of the jury looked apprehensive. They were not ready to tackle all of Darrow's books.

Judge Hutton, sustaining Rogers's objection, said direct examination had not gone into the question of Darrow's sentiments as expressed in his writings.

The cross-examination continued: Why, if there had been a settlement of the McNamara case on Sunday, as Darrow testified, why did he do such a vigorous examination of a prospective juror on Monday and Tuesday?

"On Saturday and Sunday and Monday," Darrow responded, "I had no more doubt about the settlement than we do about affairs in life that seem settled, although nothing is settled until it is finished. On Tuesday morning, Mr. Franklin was arrested. I didn't know how it could affect the settlement. I was very much afraid on Tuesday and on Wednesday and until Thursday night that all our efforts would go for nothing and these men might be killed and there was nothing for us to do at any time except to go right along just as we had always gone in the face of the newspapers and the public and everybody concerned, until it was tried."

Ford: "As soon as you were employed to defend the McNamaras, Mr. Biddinger—you sent Mr. Harrington up to Detroit to inquire into the circumstances of the arrest of J. B. McNamara, did you not?"

Darrow: "I would rather change my name, if you don't mind. You called me Mr. Biddinger. I object to that."
Ford: "Mr. Darrow?"
Darrow: "Yes, that is better."

3

Ford reopened the controversy of the Dictograph when he asked whether Darrow met John R. Harrington in room 431 of the Hayward Hotel in Los Angeles on February 14 and had a conversation with him there from about 2:25 to 3:09 in the afternoon.

The attempted introduction of the "wiretapping" matter had aroused more arguments than any other subject during the trial. The state's attorney maintained the right to question Darrow regarding incriminating questions asked of him in the hotel conference and his replies. If Darrow admitted the replies, the matter was ended. If he denied them, however, the Dictograph records could be introduced in rebuttal.

Judge Hutton considered the premise important. He asked both state and defense lawyers to furnish him with authorities on the admissibility of Dictograph evidence which he would study before ruling. In the meantime, he suggested that counsels might want the jury to inspect the premises where detectives had hidden themselves in order to witness Franklin passing the money to Lockwood. The defense questioned whether Detective Browne could have witnessed the passing of the money if he had been positioned where he said he was.

Court recessed, convening on the corner of Third and Los Angeles Streets. The jury, attorneys, defendant, clerk of the court, newspapermen, and the court reporter were shuttled from the courthouse to the street corner, then to the nearby saloon and into the rooming house—all sites that entered into the testimony of Detective Browne.

On the street corner, Judge Hutton opened court and proceeded to point out to the jury the peculiarities of the street layout and the specific sites where Captain White and Lockwood met, where Franklin was arrested, and where Browne had been hiding.

During the tour, to the defendant's horror, spectators nudged one another as they gaped at the inspection group. "Where's Darrow?" "Can you see Darrow?" A woman holding a small child in her arms pointed a finger at him and exclaimed, "There, that's him."[2]

4

Monday, August 5, 1912. Judge Hutton disappointed the exceptionally large number of lawyers who came to hear his ruling on the competency of the Dictograph evidence when he ruled it was not an issue at this time. The only issue he acknowledged was the propriety of the prosecution asking an impeaching question of a witness who was also the defendant. "I do think counsel have a right to propound an impeaching question" was the judge's final decision. In quick response, the prosecution began a series of "impeaching" questions as they related to conversations between Darrow and Harrington.

Darrow ignored Rogers's advice that he need not reply, and under Ford's cross-examination he admitted meeting with Harrington in the Hayward Hotel, although not to discuss a bribery fund nor to converse about the money used by Bert Franklin in his attempted bribery. He maintained he never showed Harrington a roll of bills. "I never said anything about jury bribery. I remember he told me the authorities were not after me but others."

A juror wanted to know whether Darrow believed at that time that Harrington was implicated in bribery matters.

"The question had run through my head."

Ford asked whether Darrow believed at that time that Harrington was accusing him of attempting to bribe jurors.

Rogers objected: not cross-examination; calls for conclusion. Sustained, ruled the court.

But Darrow wanted to answer the question. He asked Rogers to withdraw the objection.

"Go ahead and answer it," agreed Rogers.

Darrow: "At that time Mr. Harrington told me in coming to Los Angeles he had seen in some of the papers a statement that he was going to be called as a witness against me, and he told me at no time or place had he said anything either to you [Ford] or to Mr. Lawlor or to anybody else or ever had any such intention. You will find it in your Dictograph trap, if you have got anything."

"Did you think Harrington was trying to trap you?" asked Ford.

"No. I didn't think anybody would do a thing as mean as that, the District Attorney or Harrington or anybody else, or even the Erectors' Association," replied Darrow.

With the completion of Darrow's testimony the defense virtually completed its part of the trial. The few remaining witnesses neither added nor subtracted from the defense's case.

Abruptly, late Friday afternoon, four days later, Captain Fredericks announced, "The People rest."

Rogers: "The defendant rests."

From his seat on the bench, Judge Hutton announced that each side would have two and a half days for argument. He instructed the bailiff to set aside the seats within the rail for any outside attorneys who desired to hear the summations. These seats had been used by friends of the defendant, "but the lawyers of the city have some rights in the courtroom that must be regarded," the judge said. In an expansive mood, he made available extra reserved seats for the families of the attorneys on both sides. Over the weekend, before the start of the summations, the jury was taken on an auto trip and a picnic.

XVIII

"Judas," Shouts the D.A. at Darrow

1

MONDAY, August 12, 1912. The courtroom doors remained open to permit the hundreds standing in the corridors to hear the final arguments. Admission into the courtroom was by ticket only.

Ford opened for the state [1] by characterizing Darrow as an enemy of society and recalling that traitors and bribers had existed throughout history.

The defendant leaned back in his chair, his face a study in pain, as Ford excoriated him for making "a mockery of the courts and a shame of justice by bribing both jurors and witnesses in an important murder trial."

Ford rose to heights of oratory using classical allusions. He compared Darrow with Francis Bacon, Judas, and Benedict Arnold. "Bacon's rise was magnificent, until he became lord chancellor of England. Yet, he accepted a bribe; he was bribed. Like Darrow, when he told Guy Biddinger to do his work boldly to avoid defeat, so Lord Bacon boldly accepted a bribe, pleaded guilty before the bar of the house of lords, and was deprived of his office.

"Judas was a brilliant man, a great thinker, yet he was bribed; he sold his lord for 30 pieces of silver.

"In the revolutionary days there was a brilliant young captain in Washington's army. He planned many successful attacks. He saved the whole American army at Saratoga. Yet this man, Benedict Arnold, was bribed.

"History is filled with stories of great men who have gone wrong. Previous reputation does not keep men from committing crime.

"Billy Mason testified for Darrow in this case as to Darrow's character," Ford continued. "Mason is one of the many politicians who have testified in this case. Billy Mason was Lorimer's seat mate."[2]

"I object," interrupted Darrow, the first of many objections the defense would shout during Ford's summation. "He was not. Mr. Ford misstates facts; Mason ran against Lorimer."

"It's immaterial anyway," retorted Ford as he charged that "many criminal lawyers have abused their privileges; they have taught the criminals that there is a war between them and society; they have told the criminals all they need is a smart lawyer like Clarence Darrow."

Appel, on his feet, yelled, "I object. I object to him telling the jury anything like that."

Ford stood at ease, his arms folded, his eyes riveted accusingly on Darrow. Judge Hutton instructed the jury to take Ford's statement as an argument, not as evidence.

Ford discussed the McNamaras. "Poor little J. B. McNamara, the miserable wretch when he blew up the L.A. *Times*, profited by the example of men like Darrow—"

"I object," Appel thundered, but Ford was not to be stopped. "Shortly after the McNamaras were arrested, Darrow knew that the case against them was helpless, and—"

Darrow jumped up. "There is no such evidence, Mr. Ford. I take exception."

Ford paid no attention. "Darrow has the effrontery to stand before you and tell you he has a right to employ spies in the ranks of the prosecution. By that he admits his guilt.

"The policeman has a right to shoot a criminal he is pursuing. Has the criminal a right to turn and shoot the policeman?" asked Ford rhetorically. "We have a right to employ spies. It's not a nice business employing spies, but we do it to get the criminals," the assistant district attorney argued.

Playing on maudlin sympathy, Ford now talked directly to one of the jurors who during his examination for juryman had observed that Darrow might be a victim of a frame-up. "You cannot acquit Darrow of this charge without convicting honest George Lockwood, a veteran of the civil war, of the crime of perjury."

With his closing words, Ford told the jury that "this case reeks with perjury and corruption. It will be the duty of the District Attorney to investigate some angles of this case as it did that of the McNamaras."

Appel leaped to his feet to challenge the district attorney, screaming that he would not be intimidated or submit to any threats from the district attorney's office. The judge warned Ford not to threaten the defense.

Ford changed his theme. His voice softened with compassion, he expressed his sympathies to the jury for their long and arduous duty, and explained they had been sequestered to keep them free from "any possible advances by agents of the defense."

Judge Hutton corrected Ford: seclusion of the jury was provided by law.

2

Tuesday, August 13, 1912. Horace Appel rose from the defense table.[3] His short, rotund body was a mass of nervous energy as he paced up and down before the jury box, meeting each juror's eye. "What a shame it is that Clarence Darrow whose name is inscribed in the heart of every laboring man in the country, should, when he has reached the highland of life, and is now on his path to the lowland, be pointed at as a perjurer and a criminal.

"Can you convict on suspicion only?" Appel asked, and answered his own question. "No, you cannot convict him unless you can put your hand on your heart and ask your souls if he is guilty."

Referring to Franklin's testimony, Appel sneered, "You must view the testimony of an accomplice with suspicion, because an accomplice is a convicted felon, in the eyes of God and man, when he goes on the witness stand.

"Judas Iscariot," the lawyer's voice broke with emotion, "Judas Iscariot was a better man than Franklin or John R. Harrington. He was a gentleman and hung himself after betraying his Master."

Appel charged the prosecution with trying to frame Darrow. Speaking all morning and most of the afternoon, he dismissed impatiently the idea that Darrow tried to obtain a hung jury by bribing such unlikely candidates as Bain and Lockwood, two veterans of the Grand Army of the Republic.

About three-thirty, Rogers, wearing his long, black velvet frock coat, began his summation.[4] He ridiculed Harrington's statement that Darrow, at Franklin's arrest, voiced fears he would be ruined if the investigator talked. He challenged Harrington's assertion that Darrow had shown him a roll of bills to be used for "fixing" jurors. Rogers insisted tendentiously that one could not be convicted "on that kind of stuff."

He discussed the spying in both defense and state camps during the McNamara case. "When I was employed by the Merchants and Manufacturers Association," Rogers told the jury, "I put men in every union in the city. Two hours after they held their meetings I had reports of what was said and done. Can you blame Darrow for using the same tactics that the prosecution was using? There are traitors in every camp and if Darrow saw a chance to use a Burns operative hadn't he a right to do so?"

Rogers noted he had been fighting unions all his life, and disorder and lawlessness. Yet, despite his own disagreement with the defendant's philosophy, despite the fact that men like Darrow and Steffens were "giving their lives to propagate doctrines that perhaps you and I don't believe," he charged Ford with being cruel "to try to hurt Darrow for his ideas" by claiming he was responsible for the McNamaras and other dynamiters.

If money had been given to Franklin, Rogers contended, it was given by someone "who had infinitely more necessity, and infinitely more motive to bribe a juror than Darrow."

Logic and common sense argued against using Franklin to bribe a juror. "Will you tell me how any sane, sensible man, any man who knows anything about the law business—and he [Darrow] has been in it 35 years—could make himself go to Franklin and say to him: 'Just buy all the jurors you want. I put my whole life, I put my reputation, I put my clients, I put everything I have into your hands. I trust you absolutely. I never knew you until two or three months ago, and I don't know very much about you now, but here you are, go to it.'"

Despite his courtroom accolades of Darrow as a lawyer, Rogers intimated to friends that he did not consider the Chicago attorney a great attorney but rather one who could deliver emotional appeals to juries and knew how to manipulate the press. The truth is that Rogers did not like Darrow. Ideologically conservative—purely a criminal lawyer with no social vision—he distrusted Clarence's ideas both politically and philosophically. Each man had a strong ego. Each one also lived a distinctive life-style which the other considered uninviting. They had been brought together only by the common cause of client and counsel. This was a rough case for Earl Rogers, and his disagreements with his client over trial techniques and finances created major hostilities between them.

Rogers concluded his summation at 2:20 on the afternoon of August 14 and left the room immediately. Now, it was Darrow's turn. The courtroom was already jammed beyond its limit. Chairs had been placed in the aisles, and the doors opened. When a crowd attempted to enter that afternoon, the iron doors clanged shut in the faces of about a thousand clamoring men, women, and children. And behind them were a thousand more. And more. Bailiffs with drawn clubs pushed back the solid mass of perspiring humanity.

3

Wearing the same gray suit and black string tie that he wore throughout the trial, Darrow walked haltingly to the front of the jury box carrying "a huge sheaf of paper"[5] "Gentlemen of the jury," he started. He hesitated a moment. The shuffling and whispers died away. He spoke in a low voice as the jurors strained to hear his words. "An experience like this never came to me before. I am quite sure there are very few men who are called upon by an experience of this kind, but I have felt, gentlemen, after the patience you have given this case for all these weeks, that you would be willing to listen to me. I felt that at least I ought to say something to you 12 men besides what I have already said upon the witness stand."

Darrow's eyes wandered from juror to juror. One of his great courtroom strengths was the quality of making each juror feel that he was speaking to him directly. "What am I on trial for?" Darrow asked eloquently. "I am not being tried for the bribery of Lockwood. I am here because I have stood for labor all these years and fought their prosecution by the criminal rich."

Darrow played on the feelings and emotions of the jury and courtroom spectators as a concert pianist sensitively touches the keys of his instrument, and his audience responded. There was hardly a dry eye in the room; men and women wept openly. Sometimes his voice faltered: "It cost me many friends, friends who have been slowly coming back since this thing is more generally understood.

"The McNamara case fell like a thunderclap on the world. It caused a class struggle, gentlemen, with all the hatred engendered in a class struggle, with these 2 bodies meeting in almost mortal combat. They called on me to go and defend them, and I didn't want to go.

"Gentlemen, I hate war. I love peace, and I have taught it all my life. The world is full of hate, and war, and murder, and strife, and violence. But we are going ever upward toward the sunlight where there is no more hate and war.

"I could have gone ahead with that McNamara case." Darrow's poignant words penetrated the stillness of the courtroom. Judge Hutton sat with head bowed, slowly tracing figures on his desk.

"It was a war—a war between the rich and the poor. If these men had been hanged there are thousands in the world today who would have still believed them guiltless. I could have gone on with it, and made honor, and fame, and money."

He paused. "Let me tell you something about these laboring men. They lay the rails, they man the locomotives, so that you and I may ride in peace in

Pullman cars, they take their lives in their hands, they walk on frames of buildings 10 and 12 stories above the ground, and often their mangled remains are found on the earth beneath.

"I took up their case. The *Times* disaster was a terrible moral accident. As time went on I realized that J. B. McNamara and his brother would go. I felt as does a doctor, who realizes that his patient must die.

"On one side was the Burns men and the National Erectors' association and all its money. On the other, the fund raised out of the wages of the laboring man. I couldn't consider politics, I couldn't consider persons, if I was to save the men's lives. Did I betray my client?"

From nearby St. Vibiana's Cathedral the chimes rang out in celebration of a wedding. The tones reverberated in the courtroom.

"If you 12 men send me to the penitentiary—I'll go," said Darrow, the piercing caliber of his soft tones reaching the edges of the room. "Life is like a game of whist. The unseen cards are shuffled and dealt by the hands of fate. I don't like the way the cards are shuffled, but I like the game.

"I'll play the game through the long, long nights with the cards I'm dealt until the break of day."

Again he paused, and for a moment the room was tensely quiet. Then he said, "Gentlemen, thousands of men, women and children deep down in the mines, in the stores, the shops, and on railroads, on the iron frames of skyscrapers and in the bowels of steamships are looking to you to save me and vindicate my name."

He stood in front of the jurors briefly before he turned and walked over to Ruby. She placed her hand on his arm as he sat down, the tears coursing down her cheeks. Even the district attorney appeared moved by Darrow's powerful and plaintive plea.

Judge Hutton adjourned court immediately as friends and well-wishers crowded around the defendant to shake his hand and congratulate him on one of the most masterly summations ever heard in a courtroom.

4

Thursday, August 15, 1912, 2:00 P.M. Captain Fredericks,[6] a veteran of fourteen years with the county, approached his summation in a cool, logical manner, determined to erase the effect of the defendant's impassioned plea and bring the jury back to the cold evidence. He admitted Darrow's extraordinary eloquence and reminded the jury he had warned them at the very beginning against the defendant's superb and subtle oratory. "When I asked you, or when you said at the beginning of this trial that you would not permit the oratory or personal appeal of the defendant to influence your verdict, you did not mean, and I didn't mean our hearts would not be touched, and that perhaps a tear would not dim your eye when you were confronted with the unfortunate predicament in which the defendant finds himself.

"We are all human, and Clarence Darrow is very human.

"Clarence Darrow," Fredericks continued, "told you that while he had some notions in regard to the advisability of these McNamaras escaping punishment for the crime they had committed, he would have walked from the East to the West in his bare feet to have prevented the commission of that crime.

"Gentlemen, that is not the way to prevent the commission of that crime and other similar crimes. That would be idle, sentimental and useless. The experience of the ages has taught us—yes, the handiwork of Almighty God teaches us—the way to prevent wrong and crime is by punishment.

"Mr. Darrow has told you he is being persecuted because he is a friend of organized labor. I tell you I am a better friend of that vast part of organized labor that abhors crime because I am trying to have the laws observed.

"Jury bribery should be made a dangerous calling. My heart has been tender as a woman's though I have long been in my present position. But I do not believe in the maudlin sentiment that applauds the work of dynamiters and murderers."

Darrow, Fredericks predicted, would free the McNamaras and thereby encourage more dynamiting. He reminded the jury that no bombings had occurred while the McNamaras languished in jail. "You know and I know, gentlemen, that the intelligence that was back of Franklin came from the defense, for he was working for the defense and everyone of his acts was for the defense.

"I don't care what they had agreed to about the McNamaras, they had to play out the Lockwood string. Of course, you can well imagine an ordinary man would wonder why the defense was trying to compromise on the one hand and to reach jurors on the other, but it was all a part of the plan to free the two McNamaras.

"Do you suppose Darrow didn't know what his trusted employee was doing?" Fredericks's tone left no doubt that, in his opinion, Darrow had known.

Fredericks continued: "I want to tell you, gentlemen that you have listened to one of the most marvelous addresses, orations or pleas—whichever you wish to call it—ever delivered in any court room when you listened to Mr. Darrow. Plausible, eloquent, his 35 years of training back of it, his terrified and tremendous interest in it, made it indeed a wonderful plea, but that, gentlemen, only reflects the ability of a man and has mighty little to do with his guilt or innocence.

"If your sympathy for Clarence Darrow weighs more with you than the desire to blot out this damnable thing, then let him go. But let me call your attention to the fact that history tells us that George Washington wept when he signed the death warrant of Major André.[7] But he signed it, nevertheless."

Fredericks's final words to the jury: "You cannot make any mistake when you find Clarence Darrow guilty of this crime. And if you do not, I tell you the result of that verdict will not end in your lifetime or mine."

5

After three months and two days of legal fireworks the case of the State of California versus Clarence Darrow was completed. There remained only the judge's charge to the jury, the deliberations, and then the verdict.

Judge Hutton apologized for the complexity of his instructions, blaming a combination of exhaustion and lack of adequate time to simplify them. His concluding words would become the basis of the verdict: "The court instructs the jury that an accomplice cannot corroborate himself, and that he cannot be corroborated by the evidence of another accomplice. The court instructs you that it is not the duty of the defendant to prove himself innocent, or to prove who, if anyone, furnished any money to Bert Franklin for the purpose of bribing the juror."

The jurors filed out of the room in absolute silence. Ruby broke down and cried hysterically as they left, while Clarence, hands deep in his coat pockets, began pacing the courtroom, occasionally stopping to sip water from a glass on the defense table. He was tense and ill at ease, the nonchalance he had displayed the previous day completely gone. "He was a man of the moment— hunted, nervous."[8]

Exactly thirty minutes after the jury left the courtroom, they rang for the bailiff, and at 9:55 the foreman of the jury began to read the verdict. Darrow nervously chewed on a pencil. A trembling Ruby held a handkerchief to her lips.

"Gentlemen of the jury, have you agreed on a verdict?"

"We have, your honor," replied the foreman.

"You may read it."

"Not guilty."

From the cheers and applause that erupted within the courtroom, the message went down the corridor. Darrow sighed heavily as Ruby embraced her husband.

Wild confusion reigned, an explosion of joyous pandemonium. A carpenter was sitting next to Mary Field, "and the next thing I remember after the jury gave its verdict was that he was sitting in my lap."[9]

As court adjourned, friends surged around the Darrows, shaking his hand, patting him on the back, hugging and kissing both Clarence and Ruby. "Oh, I can't talk. I am too happy," Ruby sobbed with joy. "It is wonderful." The jury held an unprecedented reception in the jury box as hundreds filed past to shake their hands. Each juryman shook Darrow's hand. [10]

Among the first to congratulate Clarence was Judge Hutton. "An extraordinary act for the court," reported the *Los Angeles Times*. More extraordinary were the words of the judge: "Now that the case is ended I consider it entirely proper for me to congratulate Mr. Darrow upon his acquittal. I know that millions of hallelujahs will go through the length and breadth of this land." [11]

Prosecutor Fredericks disagreed. "There has been a miscarriage of justice in this case. I am thoroughly satisfied in my own mind that Mr. Darrow is guilty." [12]

The verdict disgusted L.A. Chief of Detectives Browne. "Go tell Sheriff Hammel to open the jail doors and turn them all loose. The jury should never have let him go." [13]

Union officials rejoiced. From John I. Nolan, secretary of the San Francisco Labor Council: "The joy of the news almost takes me off my feet."

"There was never any doubt in the minds of laboring men that Darrow was innocent," said Ed Nockels, secretary of the Chicago Federation of Labor.

One labor leader was conspicuously absent from the enthusiasm. Samuel Gompers still felt betrayed by the McNamaras' change of plea and found it hard to forgive those involved.

Some jurors reported that only one ballot was taken; others said that there were three but that two were unofficial. The first unofficial ballot: nine to three for acquittal; the second, ten to two for acquittal; and the third, the official vote, a unanimous "not guilty."

The foreman of the jury presented Mrs. Darrow with the twelve yellow slips of paper which recorded the "not guilty" verdict. These are now part of the Darrow Collection at the Library of Congress.

6

Darrow remained in California. He reaffirmed his earlier acceptance of the invitation issued by the San Francisco labor unions to speak at the city's Labor Day rally in Shell Mound Park.

Traveling to San Francisco by the steamer *Harvard*, Darrow arrived on the Saturday morning before Labor Day to be greeted by crowds of admirers and labor leaders. Wild cheers greeted his appearance on the gangplank and followed him as he was escorted to a waiting auto.

On Labor Day, more than thirty-five thousand marched in the parade. "One figure dominated the marching hosts above all others," reported the *S.F. Daily News*. "Time and again his name rang out, flashing along the line from end to end and back again—Darrow—labor's big-hearted champion." [14]

The *San Francisco Daily Morning Call* complained that the band played "no patriotic American music, but divided its program between Socialist airs and popular tunes."[15]

Darrow, with P. H. McCarthy, president of the Building Trades Council and president of the day's celebration, and other union officials shoved and elbowed their way through the dense crowds to the platform. The brass band escorting them played the "Marseillaise," the French revolutionary anthem.[16]

McCarthy introduced Darrow as the man who did more for labor than any other, and he expressed the gratitude of organized labor to the twelve honest men who pronounced Clarence Darrow innocent. The crowd cheered for ten minutes before Darrow was able to speak. He appeared listless, a change wrought by the strenuous days of both the McNamara trial and his own trial.

His first words were facetious. This was the first time in his life he had ever participated in a parade. He did not much care for them. It made him tired to walk in the dust, and he didn't like to ride when everyone else was walking. Then he became serious, and the estimated twenty thousand people in the park fell silent under the spell of his voice.

"In the last two or three days," he said, the president of a "powerful association of manufacturers in the East has been indicted for planting dynamite in such a way that workingmen could be charged with using it— which gives some official recognition to something that workingmen have long known—that not all the dynamite found in the homes or houses of workingmen was placed there by them—but some of it was put there by people of the other side."

Darrow did not want the man punished or sent to the penitentiary. "We know that he, like J. B. McNamara and like hundreds of others on both sides, was simply caught in the great industrial machinery and was guilty of social crime, and nothing else."

He turned philosophical as he came close to advocating Socialism. "Men must work in large numbers, and all men cannot be workmen, and all men employers unless there is joint ownership of the art and the implements of production. And peace can come in no other way." His conclusion was international in scope: "Great happiness and prosperity cannot come through war but only through co-operation of man with man. Then it will not matter whether you are an American, a European, an Asiatic or a member of this union, of that union, or no union, if you are a fellow man that will be enough."[17]

This was Darrow's day. Labor's abandonment of him during the trying days in Los Angeles had broken his heart. This massive demonstration gladdened him and brought tears to his eyes. He considered it a vindication of the record of his life. The *San Francisco Herald* reported that, although the crowd showed esteem and affection for all the labor leaders who spoke, "for Darrow the demonstration was special and exceptional."[18]

While in San Francisco Darrow also delivered his famous lecture on "The Industrial Conspiracy." He would deliver a similar lecture in Portland, Oregon, several days later. "The conspiracy laws, you know, are very old. Conspiracy is the charge they always make against anybody when they 'want him,' and particularly against working men, because they want them oftener than they do anybody else." [19]

He returned to Chicago to await disposition of the second indictment.

XIX
Once Again, a Jury of His Peers

1

IT seemed unlikely that the second indictment would be brought to trial. The Lockwood bribery had been the state's strongest case. With the overwhelming confidence the jury had shown in Darrow's innocence, a dismissal of the Bain matter appeared to be in order. Fredericks, however, angry and disappointed over the acquittal, pointed out that the only justification for dismissing a grand jury indictment was lack of sufficient evidence to convict. "It is my present belief that there is sufficient evidence" to convict Darrow on the Bain bribery charge.[1]

What the future held for Darrow was indicated in a letter he received from R. F. Pettigrew, former senator from South Dakota, who said the district attorney had told him he would get Darrow to confess. Pettigrew believed they would fail to convict Darrow the next time also but that they were intent on destroying him. "It is clear persecution," he wrote to Darrow.[2]

2

No imminent action, however, was forthcoming, and for a time it seemed that the State of California would drop the second indictment. From Chicago, uncomfortable with the ever-present threat of going to trial again, Darrow asked Geisler, in Los Angeles, to find out the status of the indictment on the Bain bribery. Geisler replied that Fredericks would not commit himself other than to say it probably would never be tried.[3]

But the second indictment was not dropped. The trial opened January 20, 1913, five months after the acquittal on the Lockwood charge. Since almost everything of consequence had been brought out in the earlier trial, the Bain matter appeared to be regarded as merely a formality on the part of the state. There were, however, two basic differences between the trials. While Lockwood had been only a potential juror, Bain was one of eight already sworn in. Money was passed to Lockwood after the compromise agreement; Bain received payment before. At the same time there were also major forces involved. There is no doubt that the focus of the case—capital versus labor—did not permit dismissal of the second indictment. Proponents of the open shop wanted Darrow in prison, and reportedly the structural and steel corporations victimized by the bombing contributed heavily to the prosecution. Furthermore, Darrow's conviction would give added impetus to the open shop.

3

On the eve of the second trial, newspapers reported that Earl Rogers would not be at the defense table. Rogers's office countered that the veteran criminal attorney definitely would continue as chief counsel. The defense staff, in fact, would remain essentially the same, except that former Judge O. W. Powers of Salt Lake City replaced Horace Appel, who had another commitment.

Wheaton A. Gray, a former counsel for the Merchants and Manufacturers Association and considered one of the best lawyers in the West, had been named special prosecutor in the state's second duel with Darrow. With him was Ford.

Judge William M. Conley of Madera County presided in a courtroom smaller than the one used for the first trial. From the start, the room was entirely inadequate to house the crowds who poured through its doors. Heavy tapestries covered the windows, and portraits of long-deceased jurists stared from the walls, giving the room an air of gloom and depression. Although an effort was made to transfer the proceedings to a larger courtroom before final arguments, nothing came of it, and the forensic abilities of the attorneys remained confined to the smaller room.

From the opening day, the judge dominated the proceedings in Extra Session Four of the Superior Court. Actively participating in jury selection, he cut through the long-winded and often tiresome and repetitious questions of the attorneys. Although he kept stressing the importance of an impartial jury, he also insisted on speed in getting the trial under way.

"In 10 minutes he accomplished what it took hours to do in the previous trial," applauded the *L.A. Times.*[4] Determined to avoid the bickerings and personal asides that had plagued the first trial, the accusations and the recriminations of counsel on both sides, Judge Conley declared firmly that personality clashes between the lawyers would not be tolerated. "I mean just what I say."[5]

Darrow, rather than Rogers, did most of the questioning of the prospective jurors, and within seven court days the twelve jurors and an alternate were selected. The jury of Darrow's peers consisted this time of a butcher, an artist, three ranchers, a retired merchant, a walnut grower, a mining engineer, a lodging house proprietor, a music teacher, a building contractor, and an orange grower. The thirteenth was a retired farmer.

With the completion of the panel, Judge Conley cautioned them that they were honor-bound to abide solely by the evidence and the instructions of the court. "Do not let any previous newspaper reading influence your minds. Have no bias or prejudice against the attorneys." Then he showed an astounding lack of comprehension of human curiosity: "You will be permitted to read the daily papers but I will ask you to refrain from reading anything touching upon the case at issue until you have rendered your verdict."[6]

Late Friday afternoon, January 31, 1913, Ford opened for the prosecution by citing the charges in the indictment. When he mentioned the Lockwood matter, Rogers hurled his first objection, emphasizing that the defendant already had been found not guilty of this charge.

Judge Conley gave tacit approval to the introduction of the charges of the first trial when he said, "There is no occasion for any interruption. It is difficult to make a statement without using some positive assertions. The jury will understand that it is not evidence." Whether the judge was correct in permitting mention of the first trial is open to legal interpretation.

4

Franklin, again the star witness for the state, spent less than two days on direct and cross-examinations compared to almost a week during the first trial. Again he testified that Darrow had told him "it was time to get busy with the jurors."[7]

Rogers, scheduled to cross-examine Franklin, did not appear in the courtroom. His office associates refused to comment on his whereabouts despite rumors that he had been in a sanitarium for the past several days.

With chief counsel absent, Darrow began the cross-examination. Hands in pockets, head thrust forward, he fired at Franklin question after question which the witness cunningly parried. Whenever an opening presented itself, Franklin, flushed and sullen, hurled the word "briber" at the agitated defendant attorney. Darrow laboriously bore down on his accuser in an effort to shatter his damaging testimony, but the defiant Franklin successfully evaded the lawyer's thrusts. Darrow wanted to know about Franklin's visits to the Bain farm. "Why did you go there?"

"To bribe Robert F. Bain, at your request," answered Franklin boldly.[8]

Darrow tried to get Franklin's admission that he was responsible for keeping Bain on the McNamara jury and that Darrow, who believed Bain prejudiced against labor unions, did not want him. Franklin steadfastly denied this.

5

Earl Rogers appeared in court Friday morning accompanied by a nurse and a doctor. Ill and weak, he sat in a swivel chair opposite the witness stand. His doctors advised him to retire from the case, but he refused, determined to grill Lockwood, the next witness. "I wish to finish questioning Lockwood and when I am through with him I shall decide whether I can appear again or not," he insisted.[9]

Rogers's questions went over practically the same ground covered in the first trial and also suggested the possibility that Lockwood and Franklin had teamed up to "get" Darrow.

His vigorous cross-examination of Lockwood soon exhausted Rogers. After calling the noon recess, Judge Conley joined the attorney and his physicians at the defense table. "I had a talk with Dr. Brainerd," said the judge, "and he told me that you have got to quit this case, and if you don't you're liable to die as a result."

"I can't, Judge. I have to stay with the case, and I'm going to do it if it kills me. What the doctors say is true, and I know it, but I'm not going to retire from the case."

"Well, if you won't of your own free will, I'll have to figure out some way to make you," Judge Conley threatened. "Give me a chance and I will put you in jail for contempt, and I am going to figure out some way whereby I can commit you to the hospital in this case."

Rogers did not return to the courtroom after the recess, capitulating to his physician and two nerve specialists who agreed that "he might lose his mind and possibly risk his life if he tried to continue the case."[10]

"I deeply regret the fact that I am forced to lose Rogers as counsel in the case," Darrow told reporters as he entered the courtroom to complete the cross-examination of Lockwood. "It means much to me at this time, but I know his physical condition."[11]

There is no doubt, however, that Darrow was relieved when his chief counsel stepped down. Rogers's drinking and courtroom absences had become burdensome as the trial proceeded. There was another reason, too. It was difficult for Clarence to take second place in the conduct of a trial, even his own. He chafed to take the reins into his own hands. Without Rogers, Darrow, the defendant, became his own chief counsel.

6

February 10, 1913. Prosecution witnesses, too, generally were the same as in the first trial. Ortie E. McManigal, however, the self-confessed dynamiter and principal witness against the McNamaras, appeared for the first time. He related the pressures exerted upon him by his wife and his uncle. His wife threatened never to come to the jail again unless he would "talk" to Darrow, but, he said, he refused to change his "true" confession and told his wife, "I am going to stick to it." [12]

The state presented its case in seven days.

Darrow opened for the defense in a three-hour statement [13] which closely resembled a summation: "Gentlemen of the jury. I feel somewhat handicapped, and it is somewhat unfortunate that I should have to defend myself and take so much part in this case.

"All the evidence the State has produced against me, as we will show, was submitted to a jury of twelve men of this country, and after three long months of testimony that jury immediately pronounced me not guilty.

"If a tribe of savages had compelled a man to run the gauntlet once, they would have been satisfied and would not have compelled him to run it the second time."

Powers, cocounsel with Darrow, offered the same forty depositions from Chicagoans testifying to Darrow's reputation as had been introduced in the first trial. Judge Conley saw no need for reading these. Assistant District Attorney Ford stipulated that "the defendant's previous reputation was good." Since Darrow insisted the depositions be read, the judge admitted the reading of five.

The defense witnesses, too, were the same as in the first trial, and they all repeated the testimony they had given earlier. Ruby Darrow, however, was called this time in a surprise move to impeach John Harrington's testimony that her husband had brazenly flourished money and bragged that it would "reach" some of the McNamara jurors.

Ruby, more accustomed to being in the background, was obviously uncomfortable in the bright glare of the courtroom with every eye fastened on her. Her determination to impress the jury with Clarence's innocence did not falter. Her voice was clear and confident as she described how Harrington had come to the Darrow home in Los Angeles shortly before Christmas. "He said it seemed too bad to be away from home at the holiday season, but was glad he could be with us. He told me that he did not know of any reason for being subpoened before the Federal grand jury and said that there was nothing against Mr. Darrow that could get him into trouble." She and Harrington's daughter were in sight and hearing of Darrow and Harrington in the Darrow home at 803 Bonnie Brae Street, near Echo Park, and there was no discussion regarding possible bribery and no show of money, she said.[14]

After an absence of two weeks, Earl Rogers reappeared briefly in court only to examine Clarence Darrow. He looked well; apparently the rest had restored his legal fire and brilliance, though his health would not permit him to remain on the case through its completion. Flinging his hat and overcoat into a corner, he plunged into his questioning of Darrow.

"Why did you accept Robert Bain as a McNamara juror?"

"Because Bert Franklin's reports on him indicated that he was a desirable man."[15]

"When was Franklin directed to cease working for the defense?" asked Ford.

"He was never directed to stop."

"Well, when did he stop working?"

"I don't know whether he ever began."

"Were you suspicious of Franklin's loyalty?"

"I was suspicious of his loyalty. I knew the interests in this town which were anxious to strike at me, and I didn't think that Franklin was strong enough to hold up against the forces that would be brought to bear on him to get the man that was wanted—and that was me."[16]

After the defense completed its case and the state offered rebuttal witnesses, Judge Conley announced that each side would have eight hours for final arguments.

7

March 4, 1913. Special Prosecutor Gray spoke first. "Moral idiot," he yelled, pointing his finger at Darrow, "the greatest power for evil in the United States today." He discussed Darrow's role in the bribery scheme and accused him of receiving "for purposes of corruption" at least $200,000 of the projected $800,000 expected to swell the McNamara defense fund. "How could so much money have been spent legitimately?" Gray asked. "The very size of the fund denotes corruption.

"What motive had Franklin in God's world for the bribery of this juror except in the interest of his principal? It is nonsense to suppose for a minute that he would have bribed this man without instructions from Darrow. Darrow had a motive in that he wanted to win his case," Gray declared.[17]

The special prosecutor went on to tell the jury, "If you want to please dynamiters, murderers and the criminals of the world, acquit this man. But if you want to do your duty to society, then convict him. It should be made impossible for jury bribery to exist in this city, but if Darrow is acquitted, then you can never find a lawyer guilty who passes a bribe by an agent." [18]

8

Judge Powers, who had replaced Horace Appel on the defense team, saw it differently as he told the jury that "there is nothing to base even a suspicion that Darrow was guilty.

"The prosecution witnesses in this case have been, without exception, traitors, detectives, spies, immunity hunters, informers and self-confessed criminals, like those mental Siamese twins, Franklin and Harrington. These two characters are the only ones who directly charged Darrow with anything, and this whole nauseating collection of witnesses is rightly headed by them," he said.

Powers suggested that he had as much evidence to show that Franklin got the money from the National Erectors' Association as the prosecution had that he got it from Darrow. "What strong hand has the district attorney by the throat to make him pursue Darrow this way? There is every indication that this is a frame-up. The war cry is 'Convict Darrow or break him.'" [19]

9

Darrow closed for the defense. [20] The day before he had sat with bowed head and stooped shoulders as Gray hurled accusations against him. Now, speaking to a packed courtroom as he had during his first trial, he seemed eager and determined. The second summation outdid his earlier oratorical efforts in his own behalf. He rose to heights of eloquence and descended to simple denunciation of his accusers. Mobs of people had battled unsuccessfully to get in. Steffens was there as were several of the jurors from the first trial who had been loyal attendants throughout this one. Darrow, still smarting from Gray's vilification of him, spoke first to the prosecuting staff. "I wish the attorneys on the other side would be kind enough to send for Gray," he said. "I have some things to say to him, and I would rather that he be here to hear them."

Then he began softly, "Gentlemen of the jury, it is not an easy task that I have to perform. I have stood before juries a great many times, with more or less success, and in a great many kinds of cases; but never but once before have I had occasion to talk to a jury for myself."

He looked to see if Gray had come into the courtroom. He hadn't. Clarence turned back to the jury: "Gentlemen, I've told all this story before to 12 jurors. They have heard all this. They went to their room and pronounced me not guilty, and it should have ended there. But here I am again. I have grown weary and tired of it and I'm ready for that last sleep that comes to all of us.

"I've done my duty as the infinite being gave me light. Your verdict must content me. I know what it will be. But if, by any chance, this jury should consign me to prison—I could still work even there. I don't want to go. For my family, I don't want to. For the millions of friends who have come 'round me in this tribulation, I don't want to. I'd rather go to the penitentiary with the commendation of the poor than live in a palace with the price of dishonor."

Gray did not appear. Clarence preferred to say his piece directly to Gray, but if the special prosecutor would not come to the courtroom, well, he would say it anyway. He challenged Gray's comment that all honest people wanted Darrow convicted.

"He lied!" Darrow roared. "If I cannot go out in this community where I have been less than two years and get ten friends to Gray's one I will go down to the Venice pier and jump into the ocean.

"Gray has stood before this jury vilifying me for four hours. He said nothing about the case except that he wanted to get me; to get me because the interests that he represents have considered me their enemy."

Then came the argument that Rogers had feared. Without his chief counsel to restrain him as he had earlier, Darrow proceeded to explain the social implications of the *Times* bombing, and provoked a storm of criticism for what many considered a glorification of the bomb. Darrow, however, believed that the McNamara trial had been political, part of the struggle between labor and capital, and he would not hesitate to explain it in terms of the class struggle.

"Here is J. B. McNamara," he said. "If there is no other man on earth who will raise his voice to do justice to him, I will do it, even if I am pleading for myself.

"Was J. B. McNamara personally interested in the placing of dynamite in the *Times* building?" Darrow asked. "You know he was not. He was a fanatical trade unionist. He believed in force. I do not. I believe the law of love is the only law that can conquer in the end, but he believed in force. He did not do that for himself.

"I would give a great portion of my life to have these two boys understood as they will one day be understood; and I want to say to this jury, even if it costs me my liberty, that the placing of dynamite in the *Times* alley was not 'the crime of the century'; it was not even a crime, as crimes are understood. I want to make myself plain upon that, if it costs me the vote of every man in this jury box: I was sorry then, and I am sorry today for those boys. I took my life in my hands to help them save their lives, because they were my clients, and I understood them. And I will take my life in my hands again to have them brought back to society, as I think some time they will be."

Throughout his speech he insisted that "somebody" wanted to get him. Unleashing torrents of oratory, he said, "Gentlemen of the jury, there is nothing in this case—nothing. But I have enemies—strong, powerful, influential—who are seeking to encompass my ruin." He reiterated a thought he had used in previous labor cases, this time in his own behalf: "I know that today where men are working and where women are toiling there are prayers going up in my behalf.

"I know where sewing girls are bending over their tasks a tear will be dropped and sewn into the garments of the rich. I can live wherever you say, but I choose to be vindicated again, as I have been before."

Pacing up and down before the jury box, his thumbs thrust in his vest armholes, he turned on his adversaries. The accused became the accuser. "I'm not asking for mercy! I don't have to ask for mercy! I can fight! I'd die before I'd ask for mercy from this gang of brigands! I haven't asked quarter, and I will not. I've been treated by this district attorney as no man was ever treated before. I've been hunted by a treacherous band of brigands who want my life blood, and I'll fight them as long as they come!"

He was growing old and weary of the fight, he confessed. "If my enemies had a sense either of pity or decency it wouldn't have happened—but they have neither." He quoted the poet Swinburne:

> I am tired of tears and laughter,
>   And men who laugh and weep;
> Of what may come hereafter
>   For men that sow to reap:
> I am weary of days and hours,
> Blown buds of barren flowers,
> Desires and dreams and powers
>   And everything but sleep
>
> From too much love of living,
>   From hope and fear set free,
> We thank with brief thanksgiving
>   Whatever Gods may be,
> That no life lives forever;
> That dead men rise up never;
> That even the weariest river
>   Winds somewhere safe to sea.
>
> Then star nor sun shall waken,
>   Nor any change of light,
> Nor sound of waters shaken,
>   Nor any sound or sight:
> Nor wintry leaves nor vernal,

> Nor days nor things diurnal;
> Only the sleep eternal
> In an eternal night.

"I am ready for that sleep."

He concluded, "Gentlemen, after my long career, after my hard fight, after all the bitterness and hatred of the past, I come to you worn and weary and tired, and submit my fate, the fate of my family, and the hopes and the fears and the prayers of my friends—to you."

He wept as he finished his four-hour attack on the charges against him. He had mustered all his strength for the final refutation and was on the verge of collapse. He had run the whole gamut of emotion. "At one minute he was like a child; the next a powerful man defying all who dared to asperse his name," reported the *L.A. Examiner*.

10

At the evening session, Assistant District Attorney Ford followed in a plea[21] which many court observers described as "his most powerful jury argument" since he had joined the prosecutor's office. "I do not wish to indulge in invective, but I tell you gentlemen, that organized society must be protected against such crimes as jury bribery. We can have no justice and no law if jurors can be corrupted with immunity.

"I pity this defendant," said Ford. "I appreciate the tremendous self-control he has shown during this and the former trial and the suffering, guilty or innocent, he has undergone. I appreciate all that, and, further, what a verdict will mean to his faithful wife who has stood by him in all his trouble. I also appreciate his feeling of contempt for Franklin and Harrington, who have come here to testify against him. But most of all, I pity him that a man with such an intellect, a man of such endowments, would stoop to such a crime."

Ford asked the jury to disregard the verdict of the first trial and to render their decision "solely according to the evidence and the law. Convict Clarence Darrow," he shouted in a dramatic conclusion, pointing his finger at the defendant, "just as you would an ordinary sneak-thief who had been proven guilty. If we cannot get a verdict of guilty on the evidence submitted here, then this community is against law and order, and I will never prosecute this case again."

In a courtroom crowded almost to suffocation, Judge Conley ended his forty-minute instructions to the jury at 9:06 P.M. They were similar in content to those given by Judge Hutton. The jury retired, too exhausted to take a ballot until the next morning. "We can't keep awake any longer, your honor," one juror had complained.[22]

On March 8, after thirty-eight hours of deliberation, the jurors reported a hopeless deadlock—eight to four for conviction. Although they had moved from the first ballot of six to six, four of the six who stood for acquittal from the start refused to change. Judge Conley thanked the jury for their efforts and dismissed them. In sharp contrast to the first trial, the jury left quickly and quietly after disclosing the results of the balloting.

The hung jury was a crushing disappointment to both Darrow and the prosecution. Immediately, however, the role of lawyer replaced that of defendant as Darrow took the initiative in setting a date for a third trial.

11

Many theories have been advanced to explain Franklin's attempt at bribery. There is the straightforward assertion, despite the findings of the first jury, that Darrow furnished the money in an effort to win the McNamara case, that he was discouraged by the realization that the men were guilty, and that he was under pressure from labor to get them off to save its reputation; also, that he felt acquittal of the McNamaras would enhance his own prestige.

This, however, is totally at variance with Darrow's character and all of his actions up to that time and afterward. Darrow was a shrewd lawyer who understood personalities and, had he contemplated bribery, would have moved carefully and meticulously. Certainly he would not have chosen Franklin, whom he had only met just prior to the McNamara trial, to carry off a bribery mission. Certainly he would not have arranged for $1000 bills—difficult to exchange and easily traced—to be used for the payoff. Certainly there was no reason to go ahead with the Lockwood payoff after the McNamara compromise had been worked out. Franklin caricatured the act of bribery by choosing the most improbable actors with whom to enact the illegal passage. Darrow would never have allowed such unlikely individuals as the fanatically antiunion Bain and the reluctant, righteous Lockwood to be approached. The McNamara case was very important to him—but many of his other cases were equally so. Clarence had practiced many years; he understood full well that a lawyer's final reputation is the sum of his work and not the winning or losing of one case. He had too much pride in his accomplishments to risk the loss of the reputation he had built. An act of bribery could only degrade and hurt him and the union movement he represented.

During the organizing drives of the CIO in the 1930s, a labor attorney recalls, one of the top union organizers told him, "There are certain things we do that we do not ever tell our lawyers." So it is possible that some of the labor people, too, either on their own or at Franklin's suggestion, were not above purchasing jury votes. This could easily have been done without Darrow's knowledge. They did not realize, as Darrow would have, how easy detection would be. When caught, Franklin could save himself only by adopting the prosecution's goal of "getting" Darrow.

It is possible, also, that Franklin, whose services were always available for a fee, was serving antilabor forces at the same time that he was on the McNamara payroll. This would account for his insistence that Bain be accepted on the jury, and his overtures to Lockwood and to several other talesmen.

12

More than six decades later, Darrow's guilt or innocence is still being debated, nor is it known from whom Franklin obtained the bribe money. Attacks on and praise of Darrow's actions in the McNamara trial continue.

Rogers's daughter, Adela Rogers St. Johns, in her 1962 biography of her father, insisted that her "stomach," which had been relied upon as "an oracle" by lawyers in her father's office, "howled warnings. But they didn't listen. . . . Never in my whole life had it been as sure of anything as it was that Darrow was Guilty."[23]

W. W. Robinson of the California Bar, in a fifty-two-page pamphlet titled *Bombs and Bribery* published fifty-six years later, wrote that he was "unable to find a lawyer or anyone else directly connected with, or an observer of, the McNamara and Darrow trials who believed in Darrow's innocence."[24]

Jerry Geisler, however, who "contracted a case of hero worship" for Darrow during his defense of Haywood and Moyer, believed that since Clarence's death "it has been fashionable to think of him as having been pure of mind. I believed that of him before it became fashionable."[25] And LeCompte Davis, a principal defense lawyer in the McNamara case and one who did much of the negotiating with Fredericks in the McNamara plea bargaining, called Darrow "a good decent lawyer. I had faith in him. I liked him." Darrow, said Davis flatly, "didn't bribe anyone."[26]

In 1974, former L.A. Judge Isaac Pacht, reflecting on the Los Angeles events, said he had always considered the prosecution of Darrow part of the emotional climate resulting from the bombing of the *Times* building. "I am and have always been of the definite opinion that CD was completely innocent of the jury bribery charges brought against him as an outgrowth of the McNamara prosecution."[27]

Some of Darrow's friends, however, have suggested that he would not have been immune to bribery. Though none made a direct accusation, Victor Yarros, a law associate of Darrow for more than eleven years, wrote in 1950 that Darrow often suggested, "Do not the rich and powerful bribe jurors, intimidate and coerce judges as well as juries? Do they shrink from any weapon? Why this threatened indignation against alleged or actual jury tampering on behalf of 'lawless' strikers or other unfortunate victims of ruthless capitalism?"[28]

Darrow, reflecting on his own trial, is ambiguous. His words lack the eloquent disclaimers one might expect. "Whatever the facts might be, there had been no sordid or selfish motive connected with the affair. They would know that if the charge was true it was because of my devotion to a cause and my anxiety and concern over the fate of some one else."[29] Perhaps he was feeling responsible for not recognizing at the time hints, mannerisms, even snatches of talk between Franklin and himself which, looked back on, could be interpreted as having had his tacit approval.

13

An analysis of the two trials raises the question: Why did the first one, admittedly the stronger, result in acquittal, while the second jury, with almost the same evidence and witnesses, could not reach a verdict?

The loss of Rogers and Appel as his attorneys played a decisive role in the outcome of a hung jury. Without them to restrain him, he engaged in acts of self-indulgence in both his animus toward Special Prosecutor Gray and in his defense of labor's use of dynamite. To the jury of his peers in the second trial, all of them exposed to the earlier newspaper accounts of the tragic labor bombings, he appeared to be "whitewashing" a "horrible murder" as a "social crime." This was a deciding factor in the eight "guilty" votes, those jurors told newspaper reporters. They believed that this philosophy would enable him to resort to any means to keep his clients from being punished.

Yet, some of the same oratory captured the sympathy of the jury in the first trial. Then he said the *Times* bombing grew "out of a condition of society for which McNamara was in no wise responsible. He had nothing to gain. He believed in a cause, and he risked his life in that cause."[30]

If the eight members of the second jury voted guilty because of Darrow's summation, then they had forsaken their vows to pass only on the evidence submitted in the trial. An attorney's plea is not evidence.

Furthermore, the Indianapolis trial in which officers of the Structural Iron Workers Union were charged with conspiracy to destroy property had been held during the period between the two Darrow legal battles. McManigal had been a principal witness in that trial, an outgrowth of the *Times* bombing. The Indianapolis trial was a widely and sensationally publicized case, and thirty-eight of the forty defendants, including the union president, were found guilty, which undoubtedly affected the second Darrow trial. Judge Conley had injudiciously permitted jurors to read the newspapers, requesting them only "to refrain from reading anything touching upon the case at issue." Judge Hutton, in the first trial, had banned newspapers.

14

On Friday evening, March 14, 1913, a few days after the second trial ended, a hundred representatives of organized labor and their wives gathered in Los Angeles to honor Darrow and Mary Field, who under Darrow's tutelage had achieved a reputation as a labor writer.

In response to the ovation, Darrow was his old militant self. In his address he decried the few men on Wall Street who can "in the twinkling of an eye take away all labor's gains by raising the prices on all commodities." He talked of a general strike, the theme of the radical Industrial Workers of the World. "If all of the laborers could be induced to cease work for one day, they would accomplish something. If they would cease for a week or a month, they could control the world," Darrow asserted.[31]

A week later he spoke to a capacity audience under the auspices of the California Single Tax League at the Temple Auditorium, the largest theater in Los Angeles. He announced jovially that the topic for his address was "On Land and Labor." "As I never had much land or did much work, I ought to be fitted to talk upon the subject." He concluded on a serious note: "Men still dream of a time when greed will disappear, when there will be no rich and no poor, no master and no slave, no rags and no luxury, no black and no white— when each human being who lives upon the earth will find his greatest happiness in the good of all."[32]

He was in fine spirits. Earlier in the day he had received a telegram from Frederick D. Gardner, a wealthy stranger from St. Louis who in a few years would be elected governor of Missouri. Gardner offered him "all the money you need for the case. Am now sending draft for one thousand dollars." Included in the envelope was another draft for $200 from Mrs. Gardner.

15

Three myths have been perpetuated about the McNamara case and subsequent cases tried by Darrow.

Myth 1: In his book *Dynamite*, Louis Adamic, popular historian of labor violence, says that the McNamara affair "took the militant spirit" out of the American Federation of Labor.[33]

Rebuttal: The respected labor historians Professors Selig Perlman and Philip Taft, commenting on Adamic's assertion, point out that "if by militancy is meant a defense by labor of its claimed rights by force of arms, the author has evidently overlooked the significance of the West Virginia and Colorado coal strikes of 1912 and 1913. . . . The embattled miners fought the deputy sheriffs and the state militia, unmoved by the fear of being outlawed by the public."[34]

The McNamara confessions did hurt the labor movement, but in a relatively short time labor redeemed itself, and within the next few years the nation witnessed important political successes by the AFL in Congress: for example, the Colorado atrocities, widely reported in hearings before the U.S. Commission on Industrial Relations, helped to erase the Los Angeles episode from the public's memory.

Workers responded to union organization. After the virtual cessation of growth during the years 1905 to 1910, membership of the American Federation of Labor rose from 1,562,000 in 1910 to 1,996,000 in 1913, an increase of 434,000. Specifically, the iron workers union, which was directly involved in the McNamara affair, grew from 10,928 in 1911–12 to 13,189 in 1913–14.[35]

Myth 2: Socialists claimed the McNamara confession was responsible for the defeat of the Socialist mayoralty candidate in the Los Angeles election.

Rebuttal: The Socialist ticket was not defeated in Los Angeles exclusively because of the McNamara confession. Undoubtedly, it would have lost even if the confessions had never been made. There was no difference between what the victorious Good Government party in Los Angeles offered in that campaign and what successful Socialist party candidates had promised in Schenectady, Milwaukee, and other places where Socialists had been on the ballot. And the Good Government party was more appealing to many more since it did not carry the stigma of a Socialist label. The combination of votes cast by the opposition parties for mayor was more than enough to defeat the Socialists. Once they joined forces against the Socialist candidate, his election was lost.

Myth 3: "Darrow," said Adela Rogers St. Johns, "went down in history almost entirely for cases he tried after his escape from the jury bribery charges in Los Angeles and, to pin it down, *few* of them had much to do with the poor, the weak and the helpless."[36]

Rebuttal: Not true. Darrow's fame does not rest entirely on the cases he tried after the Los Angeles events. Certainly his 1902 presentation on behalf of the anthracite miners before the Federal Commission is a classic in labor-capital arbitration and a victory for labor. Surely the Kidd case and the Haywood, Moyer, and Pettibone cases are remembered vividly, and—with the Debs trials—are not only a part of labor history but of the greater panorama of U.S. history. Darrow's cases after his acquittal in Los Angeles continued in the same way: in defense of the poor, the helpless, the dissident; occasionally the strong, but never the strong against the weak.

16

The nightmare almost behind him, Darrow returned to Chicago to await word of a possible third trial. Friends welcomed him at a massive meeting in Riverview Park, where a crowd of fifty thousand greeted the veteran attorney.

He was also honored with a banquet [37] where the president of the Lawyers Association of Illinois, Edward Maher, set the tone of the tribute: "We are gathered with the idea of expressing our confidence and respect for a man who has been a member of this Bar for a quarter of a century."

A boyhood companion, the Reverend Dr. John B. Brushingham, told the dinner guests he had refused to officiate at a wedding ceremony that evening. "I told the family to get some other clergyman, as I might possibly some future day have another wedding, but I could not everyday attend a banquet in honor of Clarence Darrow."

Henry J. Toner, a fellow lawyer, said, "Every lawyer at the Chicago Bar knows Clarence Darrow never caused a tear to be shed; that no dirty dollar ever soiled his pocket; that he never betrayed a trust; nor did he ever turn his back on friend or foe!"

Darrow's response was uncharacteristically brief. The Los Angeles experience, it was apparent, had hurt him deeply. He thanked the guests for their warmth and their kind reception. "I have not so very long ago heard considerable objections to myself, not as flattering as I have been listening to tonight. I have a suspicion that neither my enemies nor my friends have told the truth. And still a stronger suspicion that I shall not tell it either, at least not all of it."

It was nine months before Fredericks decided to drop the second charge.

17

The pain of the trials left its mark, and despite the friendship that had been extended to him he never got over the ache of abandonment, the blow to his vanity by those who had believed him guilty. He was hurt by the infidelity of many he had trusted. He kept his personal hurt hidden, but his letters to Mary Field reflect some of the agony. She was in San Francisco, and he had been promising to come there to visit her and Fremont Older. She had apparently chided him for not keeping his promise. His response, dated March 31, is anguished:

"Ever since I came back I have been trying to go to Cal. but always the old horror of it all comes on me and keeps me here. It is so hard to go back to the scene of all the indignities, insults and humiliations I suffered which I was helpless to prevent. Of course I want to go . . . the friends are so many and dear but when I think of it a black cloud comes over the sky . . . have been thinking it would wear away, but with the thought of going comes the dread of the memories of everything. Is it because I am weak and cowardly or sensitive?" he asked.[38]

Again, on December 15 (no year): "I would like to go out to Cal. long to go, but with the longing comes the horrible revulsion—wish I was not built that way. I am so weak, but when the time comes I will overcome it."

Over the years he continued to talk about how he "would really like to come" to California. But he never went back, except to pass through briefly in 1933 on his way home from the Honolulu Massie case.

XX

"You Must Not Leave the Law"

1

THE fee Darrow had earned in the McNamara case amounted to only a small fraction of the debts he had accumulated in his own defense. He returned to Chicago discouraged and nearly penniless, vowing to leave the practice of law and to devote the rest of his years to lecturing, debating, and writing.

His acceptance of the McNamara defense had exacerbated the problem-ridden relationship with Masters, and by the time he returned the partnership had been dissolved. Darrow's prolonged absence had dissipated his law practice—the fear of "guilt by association," because of his own jury bribery indictment, drove away clients, both corporations and individuals, and no new ones clamored for his services.

Many years earlier, at the Socialist meetings he enjoyed attending, he met a law student, a Russian Jewish immigrant named Peter Sissman. Tremendously impressed by the young man's abilities and sense of humanity, Darrow brought him into his law firm in 1894 when Peter finished his studies. There he remained until he opened his own law firm two years later.

Sissman came to see Darrow shortly after the older man's return from Los Angeles. "You must not, you cannot leave the law," he pleaded—and invited Darrow to join in a law partnership. Clarence resisted, Sissman persevered, and finally the fifty-six-year-old Clarence agreed.[1]

Slowly his practice grew: individuals charged with crimes, labor unions in need of negotiations and arbitrations with employers, divorce suits.

A group of blacks came to see him. They had no money, but his friendly relationship with the National Association for the Advancement of Colored People was well known, and did not Darrow "help people, Negroes particularly"? His visitors asked him to defend their friend, Isaac Bond, a black indicted for the particularly brutal murder of a white nurse. She had last been seen walking down a country road with a tall black man. Her watch and several items of jewelry, apparently taken during the crime, turned up in a pawnshop in a black neighborhood, and two pawnshop men identified Bond through mug shots of ex-convicts in the police files.

"Shall we take the case?" Clarence asked Victor Yarros, who had recently come to work for him as a law assistant. "I am for taking it," he added. Then, almost as if he were trying to talk himself out of the defense, "We may even have to pay court costs ourselves. There's not a cent in it for us." [2] But the lure of defending an underdog proved too strong. They took the case.

At the trial, one of the pawnshop men made a definite identification; the other was hesitant. Many of Bond's friends refused to testify in his behalf because they feared reprisals from the police; those who did placed the defendant in a cheap saloon in nearby Gary, Indiana, on the day of the murder.

Yarros had his "doubts about the veracity of the witnesses. Darrow never alluded to that angle of the case." The presiding judge—an admirer of Darrow—sent the jury out of the room and pointed out to the defense that "there is a whole lot of clumsy perjury in this testimony, and while I don't attach any blame to you gentlemen, I must, I feel, warn you to bear that in mind." Darrow, however, objected to the warning as "improper and ill-advised." [3]

The state demanded the death penalty.

Members of the jury debated all night, but the racial issue and the brutality of the crime were too strong. Although they rejected the state's demand for the gallows, they found Bond guilty and the judge sentenced him to life imprisonment, a "substantial victory" for the defense. Several years later, when Clarence brought the case before the Pardon Board, the plea for commutation of sentence was denied. One member of the board who wanted to see Bond paroled said that the board "dare not touch" the case unless proof "was complete as to who committed the act." [4] Within ten years Bond died, a victim of tuberculosis, denying his guilt to the end.

2

"It is hell to be the Genl Counsel to the poor," Clarence wrote to Mary Field. "Yesterday I was down to the penitentiary pleading with the prison board . . . generally go down every month—and the board seem[s] to like to have me talk and to listen to my queer ideas, that they are no better than the fellows inside."[5]

Despite the Los Angeles contretemps, labor still considered Darrow its spokesman. Although he never held an official position with a union, he had spoken on labor's behalf so often that he was accepted as its voice. When he lectured in Cedar Rapids, Iowa, on November 20, 1913, the mayor introduced him as a man with "the courage of his convictions." Darrow spoke on "The Labor Problem" to an audience wholeheartedly in sympathy with his views.

Labor and capital—he reiterated a theme which led many to insist that Clarence "is getting more and more anarchistic"[6]—"are not friends, they are industrial enemies, each trying to get the best of each other." His scars from Los Angeles, the citadel of the open shop, were still raw.[7]

In Ottumwa, Iowa, urging a "closed shop," Darrow declared that if businesses were run according to the golden rule, there would be no need for labor unions. However, "the law of business is the law of the jungle; every one goes in and grabs what he can get, runs away with it and holds it if he can. He is entitled to what he gets. If the working man can get more, then he is entitled to more" and the "'closed shop' will help him get more."[8]

He expressed the same thoughts two years later in his testimony before the U.S. Commission investigating labor unrest centered around the recent Colorado mine outrages. Among the witnesses were John D. Rockefeller, Jr., the major shareholder in Colorado's largest coal company, labor leader John Mitchell, and Clarence Darrow. The day Darrow testified, Rockefeller sat in the hearing room "with as much patience as he could muster."[9] With him was Ivy Lee, his adviser and the man who created the profession of public relations when he responded to early criticism of Rockefeller by publicizing replies to the charges, something that big business had never done before.

During his testimony,[10] Darrow was asked whether labor could not attain its purposes sooner through legislation than the use of force.

"No," he replied without hesitation.

"What is to hinder their getting what they want through the will of the people expressed by the ballot?" Commissioner Weinstock asked.

Darrow responded sardonically, "Oh, the Congress, the Senate, the President of the United States and finally the Supreme Court." The sympathetic labor audience laughed and applauded. Rockefeller's face betrayed no emotion.

Commissioner Weinstock wanted to know about Darrow's fees in the Haywood, Moyer, and Pettibone cases and the McNamara cases. Darrow sat up straight, ran his hand along the side of his face. He was silent a moment. Then he said, "Three-fourths of the labor cases I have taken I have handled for nothing. In the coal strike case, I spent four months as chief attorney, and we got an award of $10,000,000 to $15,000,000 and back pay to the amount of $500,000. I charged them ten thousand dollars. Corporation lawyers would have got ten or fifteen times as much. It was the only case in which I ever made anything." Although the Haywood case paid him $35,000, his illness and the loss of clients during that period ate up most of the fee. He spent the $48,000 McNamara fee, and more, defending himself against the bribery charge.

Another commissioner, Mrs. J. Borden Harriman, wanted to know what he meant by the term "a fair social system." He had his answer: a system in which private ownership of mines, railroads, and the land is abolished; prisons as punishment are abolished, and in place of jails are hospitals to detain the so-called criminal class until "cured."

For the first time in American history a government agency forced business to defend itself in the glare of public opinion. The hearings became avenues of propaganda for the unions. As a result, the American labor union movement assumed a more forceful position on the national scene.

3

Over a period of time, Darrow, the independent Democrat who talked like a radical Socialist, defended a series of Republican officeholders charged with graft and corruption. In some of these cases he was associated with Charles Erbstein, a successful criminal attorney in Chicago who, unlike Clarence, was not burdened with a sense of social responsibility and social vision.

Darrow won the acquittal of Assistant State's Attorney Bernard J. Mahoney, accused of fraudulently marking ballots. The prosecutor asked the jury to convict and send Mahoney to the penitentiary "as a warning that the sanctity of the ballot must be protected."[11] The jury did not convict, and the "sanctity of the ballot" continues to be challenged not because of lack of conviction but because the system encourages temptation.

Darrow agreed with his friend Lincoln Steffens. Asked by a minister during the question period at one of his lectures who he believed created the system of corruption, Steffens responded that most people blamed Adam; Adam said no, it was Eve, the woman. Eve said no, it was the serpent. But, said Steffens, "I'm here trying to show you that it was, it is, the apple"—the system of privilege.

In 1915, Republican William Hale Thompson began the first of two consecutive terms as mayor of Chicago. He would serve a third term after a four-year hiatus during which a Democratic chief executive headed the city. The Thompson administrations exploded with graft exposures and partisan battles.

Oscar DePriest, black alderman of the second ward of Chicago, was a loyal supporter of Thompson. Completing his first term, DePriest announced he would not run again. He had been indicted on a conspiracy charge "to protect" gambling houses and houses of ill repute in his ward. The Municipal Voters League, a watchdog organization, approved the alderman's decision. "No alderman piled up a more notorious record in so short a time," said the league.[12]

Darrow, however, considered DePriest's indictment politically motivated, and he agreed to defend the alderman.

During the week-long trial, witnesses called DePriest a "faithful guardian of a flock of gambling resorts" and charged him with "tipping-off" houses for pay. One witness described himself as a "general utility man" for the alderman and said that on at least two occasions DePriest sent him to gambling clubs "to tell them a raid was coming that night."

In his summation to the jury, Darrow first warned against the danger of racial prejudice in their verdict. "Gambling is a horrible crime," said the lawyer who loved his poker games. "Why doesn't our industrious state's attorney attack it in the women's clubs, where they play bridge whist for money and prizes? That is gambling. Why doesn't he pull down my house and yours when we play cards? If this defendant has gambled he would be liable to a $200 fine. But if he conspired to permit gambling by others he may be sent to the penitentiary for five years. It is not fair." The all-white jury found the black alderman not guilty.

DePriest, with a loyal following, would in 1928 be the first black elected to Congress in twenty-seven years. His seat from Chicago's First Congressional District has been held ever since by black representatives.

4

Clarence's antagonism to Thompson did not prevent him from defending the mayor's aging police chief charged with graft conspiracy, associating with underworld characters, and being part of a corrupt political machine. Co-defendants with Chief Healy were a detective sergeant, and Billy Skidmore, characterized as an "influential politician" who had been a gambler and was now a $5-a-day bartender.

"This is not a prosecution against vice and gambling," shouted the district attorney, "but a prosecution against men who have preyed on vice and realized money from its protection." He pointed out that Healy, as a witness, had taken refuge behind the answer "I don't remember" 217 times during his examination.

As he usually did, Darrow in his summation placed the state's witnesses on trial. They were crooks and criminals, he said, who had turned state's witness to save themselves. Admittedly, his client made a poor witness, but "in this trial I have seen vice, corruption and infamy paid for and rewarded at the expense of my client. I ask you to deal with him as you wish others to deal with you at the grave and serious times of your life."

Earlier Darrow had admitted that if he were mayor and knew Healy as Thompson undoubtedly did, he would not have appointed him chief of police. "It takes a clever man to be chief of police and keep out of jail." Healy "is the child in the hands of the criminals who had testified against him. My client is old, weary, feeble and broken physically and mentally." [13]

Ben Hecht said that Darrow in his "poor man's suit" and "baggy pants . . . sang his songs of humanity to the jurors" who already had listened to witnesses for eight weeks. [14] They voted the three defendants not guilty "to the surprise of the town and the disgust of the good," Darrow said. [15]

He further described the trial in a letter: "I wish you could have heard the case with its short witnesses and its long one, with its detectives and dictagraphs and tapped telephone wires, with its stool pidgeons and informers swearing for immunity. . . . The list of witnesses would make you laugh. We had Mike the Pike, Nick the Goose, Mary Ann the Gun, Jew Florence . . . and a lot more." As an attorney, Darrow believed he was legally and morally justified in taking full advantage of all the technicalities and maneuvers that the law allowed. Contrary to the criticisms often swirling around him for this conduct, he did not consider his behavior cunning and shrewd. He had a definite philosophy concerning crime and its causes. Like Leo Tolstoy, he did not believe that punishment prevented crime, but that circumstances caused crime, and changing those, not punishment, would remove it.

As he usually did, Clarence supplemented his concentrations on trial work with the stimulus of lectures and debates in his free time. During the Healy trial, Clarence had debated George Burnham Foster, theologian and professor at the University of Chicago, on the topic "Is There a Law of Progress in the World?" As usual, he took the negative side. The following day the *Chicago Tribune* [16] published some "Darrowisms" from the debate, which included such one-liners as:

"The human being who has the least intelligence has the most faith."

"There's been no progress in law. We've made more statutes, more ways of sending people to jail, but nothing to make people happier."

"The people of today are more than half ruled by the heritage of the past. If the other half of their lives is going to be ruled by their duty to the future I don't know what is to become of the present."

"The higher criticism has destroyed hell, so now we haven't even that consolation."

"Evolution as popularly conceived is in itself a religion."

5

In 1917 a cabdriver in Chicago had not been too careful with the company's money. "You know—some of the fares went into my own pocket." The company caught up with him; he was indicted and sent to jail.

"I was in a cell with two or three other guys, no lawyer, no money for bail, nothing. I was pretty low. . . . I was just a kid . . . it looked as if my future was screwed up for good. . . . I figured [the company] was out to make an example of me because some of the other drivers had been doing the same thing. Well . . . about the third day one of the fellows who was in there with me poked me and said, 'Hey, why don't you talk to that guy?' I looked out through the bars and saw this big fellow, who looked like a bum himself, walking down the corridor. . . .

"So this guy with me tells me it was a man by the name of Clarence Darrow and that he was a lawyer and that he helped guys who'd had tough breaks. Well, I figured there was nothing to lose so I called out to him, 'Hey, Mr. Darrow, could I talk to you for a minute?' You can imagine my surprise when he ambled over and sort of leaned up against the bars and said 'You want to talk to me?' Well, I told him the story and when I got through he said 'Alright, Harry, I'll drop by again tomorrow.' Well of course I figured that I'd never see him again, but he did turn up the next day and he had it all fixed to be my lawyer. . . . From then on he spent as much time with me as he would have spent with one of the big boys themselves. My case went to trial and he took on those smart company lawyers as if they were babies. When it came time for him to make his talk to the jury, he kept telling them what a kid I was and how the money I had taken didn't really mean much to the company and how he was sure that if the Judge and the Jury would just be human about it I'd probably never do anything like that again. . . .

"They let me off. . . .

"I've been driving a cab for almost 40 years now—for the same company, mind you—and I've never taken a nickel since then that didn't belong to me." [17]

6

Six years after Clarence's defense of Thompson machine politicians, he again became the lawyer for a Thompson partisan. Fred Lundin, a longtime boss of the Thompson-Lundin political machine, was the mastermind of a ring of alleged conspirators who plundered the Chicago Board of Education treasury. The prosecution charged they obtained key positions in the board's offices from where they manipulated school board purchases of coal, boilers, insurance, doors, plumbing, printing supplies, light bulbs, books.

Jacob Loeb, a former president of the school board, testified that on his first day as president Lundin told him, "We want fellows" who have been faithful to the political organization and "who will vote the way we want them to. We don't want highbrows on the school board." The school engineer told the jury that the board paid $7500 for boilers worth $4000; the director of special schools said buses for crippled children were rented at $28.50 a day from a Lundin-sponsored firm instead of the usual $12.50 per day; an insurance broker said he wrote all the school system's insurance through Lundin and Lundin's nephew, one of the other defendants, and they took 30 percent of his 40 percent commission.

The prosecution painted Lundin as a corruptor of his fellowmen, ruthless, egotistical, and immoral, but Darrow saw the Lundin case as a conspiracy engineered by enemies of the Thompson-Lundin machine, a matter of "political persecution." Giving benefits to political friends, he argued, has always been done, in all administrations.[18] He introduced witnesses who lauded Lundin as a public servant interested only in the good of the city. Mayor Thompson interrupted his Hawaiian vacation to swear that Lundin was innocent and "against politics in the police and on the school board."

Darrow strode back and forth before the jury. "If Fred Lundin or any other man in this case could be convicted on this evidence, made up of suspicions and cobwebs, then I want to retire to a cannibal island and be safe! This is an infamous conspiracy against the liberties of man!" He insisted that the entire charge was the result of two political factions fighting for power and lamented the prosecution's apparent hatred for the defendants, their suspicion of privilege. "We all do it. I am too honest to tell you that I am not dishonest."[19] Clarence's demeanor was humility and sympathy as he expounded on a favorite theme: no man is all good or all bad. Who is to judge? Each has his detractors, each his admirers.

The jury listened for twelve weeks. Four hours after they received the case they returned to the courtroom with a verdict of not guilty.

In the aftermath of the Lundin trial, the *Bloomington* (Ill.) *Daily Bulletin* editorialized, "Only last week [Darrow] cleared Lundin and his group in Chicago, who were charged with glutting the school funds. His argument was a poetic blending of philosophy and law. 'There is only one Darrow,' is the compliment that ran through the courtroom and corridors. It was the highest tribute that could be paid genius."[20]

During the course of the trial, Darrow was visited by a friend who accused him of using his talents to defend grafters. "Why?" she asked.

His answer to her was similar to the one he had given twenty-seven years earlier to another friend in social work: he did it "for the money" and because he "hated jails and good people." He "had fought for many things that her people believed in," but had never seen one of them send him a case that offered a fee: they had sent him many poor no one else would look after, he said, but "if one had money they sent him to a respectable lawyer. . . . Any how it never occurs to me that I should refuse to defend any one."[21]

7

The Faherty-Detwiler case in Chicago made local headlines at the same time the nation was reading about the Teapot Dome scandal in which certain oil interests were adjudged to have bribed members of President Warren Harding's administration.[22]

In the Chicago case the corruption involved Michael Faherty, president of the Board of Local Improvements under the Thompson-Lundin City Hall administration, and Herbert B. Detwiler, an official of the White Paving Co. Darrow represented Faherty.

The charge against Faherty was that he had used bribery during the construction of the Michigan Boulevard bridge in Chicago. The defense argued that Faherty spent the money to get the link bridge finished by a certain date. "There is no politics in the prosecution," the district attorney insisted. "Faherty is being prosecuted for a crime against the state, not because of politics."[23] The sum in question amounted to $28,000.

Faherty admitted he had paid "a lot of extras and bonuses to the men and concerns working on the Michigan Blvd. link bridge. I spent more money than the contracts called for, but I got the bridge completed two years before the specified time. That's good business and in the end it saved the city a lot of money."[24]

Darrow referred to the bridge as "a great improvement" which would be "the pride of Chicago" long after the prosecution was forgotten, and Faherty would be remembered as "a man of vision and imagination to sketch a plan in his mind in which he could see real buildings, real viaducts, real boulevards, and a noble Chicago."

Darrow disdained the charge of bribery. He turned the early completion date and the money passed out to accomplish it into an act of heroism as he told the Faherty jury: "Some time they build monuments to men who have done great deeds. Sometimes they indict them, and sometimes even send them to jail. I want to say this as a matter of prophecy that the day will come when Chicago will recognize the force, intellect, genius and imagination of Michael Faherty. . . . When Chicago has more or less realized his dreams they will know his worth, . . . they will build him a monument."[25]

In his summation, Darrow glorified the issue by repeating a theme he often used for weightier cases. He said it in the Kidd case in Oshkosh, Wisconsin; he repeated

it in the 1920 Communist case: "I want to say to you that all through the ages the
blood of the martyrs stains the pathway of the human race . . . monuments have
been built to them." [26]

Within five hours the verdict was reached: not guilty. New generations of
Chicagoans know nothing of Michael Faherty, and, contrary to Darrow's
courtroom forensics, no monument has been erected to Faherty's memory.
The Michigan Avenue bridge, however, is one of the city's most traveled, and
Faherty's name is duly inscribed on plaques affixed to the bridge as well as to
other "public improvements" in the city.

8

Clarence had an insatiable curiosity about an amazing range of subjects.
Despite the pressures of his law practice and his activities in debating,
lecturing, and writing, there was always time for more discussion. For almost
a decade a group of some forty men, calling themselves the Biology Club, had
been gathering once a week to hear lectures on a variety of topics—among
them biology, psychology, anthropology, geology, astronomy, and biblical
history. At first they met at the Darrow home on the Midway, only a few
blocks from the University of Chicago. Many of the members were university
faculty, others were businessmen and professional men. "We've been guessing
all our lives," said Clarence. "It would be a darn good thing to find out the
facts." The lecturers brought the facts as the members listened. It was a male
world which met during the fall and winter months. Women were not invited
because, the men reasoned, "it would only distract from the seriousness of the
evening." [27]

Clarence described the club in a letter: "We have organized a biology class
meeting once a week. Prof. Foster and a good number of other philosophers
and near philosophers belong and we have an expert talk to us and it is very
interesting. I feel that I am finding out some real things that shed a little ray of
light here and there. Anyhow the evenings are interesting and as life is flying
fast this is the main thing." [28]

9

As many fathers do, Clarence had hoped that after graduation from
Dartmouth his son Paul would study law, eventually joining him in a father-
son law practice, but Paul was much more attracted to the business world.
The summer he worked in the Darrow law offices he fell in love with Lillian

Anderson, a beautiful dark-haired secretary. After they were married, they moved to Estes Park, Colorado. Here Paul managed the Greeley gas works in which both he and Clarence held a financial interest.

It was the summer of 1914, and Clarence was visiting Paul and his family— three little granddaughters who "are growing fine, and getting older and more interesting every time I come."[29]

"There is no joy like a child," he wrote to Mary Field, who was expecting her own child. ". . . the last thirty years nothing has brought me the consolation that Paul has brought. . . . It is the order of nature to bring forth and it must be done and it satisfies one of the strongest instincts and emotions."[30]

While he was in Colorado, war broke out in Europe. He devoured the news as Austria-Hungary moved against Serbia and as Germany intensified her war effort against Russia, France, and England. He deplored the inhumanity of war but avoided pointing an accusing finger at one side or the other. As the months passed, he continued in public to maintain his stance of pacifism, but privately he began to struggle with the opposing concepts of the conflict and his lifelong philosophy of nonviolence. "I wonder what I really do beleive [sic] anyhow and how long I will beleive [sic] it," he wrote in confusion.[31]

"The whole world has failed in its ideas of civilization," he lamented. "We had supposed—at least a large number of people in the world had supposed— that wars were over; that they belonged to the barbarism of the past . . . yet, almost out of a clear sky, without any apparent cause—certainly without any sufficient cause, the greatest war in the history of the world has come upon us. We find that all the theories have failed; religion, socialism, trades-unionism, capitalism, education—every theory has been swept away by war, and it is worth while to find out the cause, if we can."[32]

Socialists especially disappointed him. Many were eager to get into the war. In the United States a chasm developed among party members as to whether or not the country should join the conflict alongside the Allies. In Europe many of the leaders and followers of Socialism, who had always proclaimed "international solidarity," now became defenders of their respective father-lands, and "international brotherhood" became an empty slogan as German Socialists and British Socialists killed each other on the battlefield.

In the early fall of 1914 he spoke before the Chicago Society of Rationalism at the Germania Theatre in Chicago. He told them that, although the Christians believed Christianity would stop war, "the Christian German is praying to his God to help him kill the Christian Russian and the Christian Russian is asking the same God to help him kill the Christian German, and He seems to be helping both of them." President Wilson, a Presbyterian, proclaimed a day of prayer in the neutral United States and asked the Lord "to stop the war." "It seems to take the Lord longer to mobilize than it does the

Russian Army," Clarence quipped, noting that four weeks later the war was still accelerating.[33]

He thought he knew the answer: "The people who do not condemn, who do not judge, who really love, are the ones who will solve this question. There are many of them, but there are not yet enough to stop war. This is a religious feeling in so far as it is an appeal to the higher instincts and sentiments of man; . . . when these higher feelings reach out beyond themselves to their fellowmen, to the world, then wars will be over, and we will develop some strong emotion that will fill the lives of men, and make for the real happiness of the world."[34]

Though his immediate sympathies were with England and France, he insisted that the United States remain neutral as he campaigned for the reelection of President Wilson. "Few men in high places have ever been moved by such sympathies as Wilson," he said.[35]

He was still the pacifist, the Socialist agitator, the philosophical anarchist. Fourteen years earlier he had written that the doctrine of nonresistance need not "only be held by dreamers and theorists" but could have a "place in daily life. Every government on earth," he charged then, "is the personification of violence and force," but "the instinct" for "non-resistance is as old as life upon the earth" and we must "conform to the highest reason and judgment of man."[36] As a follower of the Russian philosopher and writer Tolstoy, he quoted Matthew 5:38.39 on the frontice page of *Resist Not Evil:* "Ye have heard that it hath been said: An Eye for an Eye, and a tooth for a tooth. But I say unto you, that ye resist not evil, but whosoever shall smite thee on thy right cheek, turn to him the other also."

Then the Germans invaded neutral Belgium.

What does a pacifist do who believes that an innocent nation is being ravaged, that a militarist country is determined to conquer its neighbor? What does a pacifist do when he hears about mutilated Belgian children, their hands severed; about women with breasts cut off? How does a pacifist reconcile his nonviolence with such bestiality?

For Darrow the answer was obvious. When "Germany sent her great army into Belgium . . . I recovered from my pacifism in the twinkling of an eye." He explained: "I discovered that pacifism is probably a good doctrine in time of peace, but of no value in war time."[37]

In a letter to Mary Field he tried to explain his ideological change and to defend his new doctrine. "Here was Germany preparing for years to destroy civilization . . . to make the world Prussian they trampled Belgium under foot violating their written word. They invaded France and Poland. They ran their submarines under ships and destroyed them without warning. The world had to submit to Germany and to go back to barbarism or fight for what they had. There can be no peace while Prussian militarism lives and I want to see it destroyed because I don't believe war is ideal. Unless the Allies can lick

Germany there can be no peace on earth, and I want to see them licked if it takes the whole world to do it." [38]

In that same letter he wrote, "When an orthodox socialist . . . finds that his theory runs up against a fact he says to hell with the fact. I try to be right and I know I can't change a fact so I modify my theory."

XXI
Ex-Pacifist Defends War Objectors

1

ONCE America declared war on April 16, 1917, the country went wild with war euphoria. Many Socialists joined the patriotic throng. Such important names in the party as Charles Edward Russell, A. M. Simmons, William English Walling, and Upton Sinclair became supporters of the war. Clarence, too, joined the forces beating the drum of patriotism. He helped to sell Liberty Bonds, he spoke at rallies and lectured on the war. The principles he espoused in *Resist Not Evil* were still valid, he said, but "my error then, as I see it now, was the belief that you could make a general rule of life that would cover every case. This, I believe, is the fundamental error of the pacifist. If the theory of non-resistance is absolutely true, then it must apply to the insane as well as to the sane, to animals as well as to man. You must be willing to say that if an insane man should attack you or some one dear to you who is utterly defenseless and the only way you can save your life or your friend's life is to kill the man, you would not do it."[1] The pacifist, Darrow said, would not take a life under these circumstances.

This is an old argument which antagonists of nonresistance have propounded for many, many years. The wonder is that it took a war for Darrow to discover it. On October 21, 1917, he told a cheering audience at the

Auditorium Theater in Chicago that "our American pacifists sat neutral while Belgium was invaded, while France was invaded, while the submarines were killing their victims upon the German ocean. . . .

"We waited patiently and the pacifists protested that we had no right to ride on what they termed munition ships, munition ships that were the vessels of Commerce and trade of American citizens and that all nonbelligerents had the right to use before the German Kaiser told us to stay off the seas."

"Chicago was a new city today after the tonic of patriotism it took yesterday," reported the *Chicago Daily News.*[2] "The high pitch of enthusiasm was reached in the Auditorium when Attorney Clarence S. Darrow spoke. Mr. Darrow now styles himself an 'ex-pacifist.' His indictment of Germany and of disloyal Americans and his appeal for wholehearted support of the government until Germany is beaten to her knees or until the country's war leaders believe a satisfactory peace can be obtained brought the thousands to their feet time after time."

Carl Sandburg, in an article in the *Chicago Daily News,* noted a "tightening of feeling" against free speech. "Darrow, for instance, has always been a stickler for the right of free speech. Yet he is now making addresses in which he says that the pacifists' free speeches are working overtime in a way that helps nobody as much as the Kaiser, and he, Darrow, has his doubts as to whether free speech in the service of autocracy is any good for a nation warring for democracy."[3]

Darrow had no doubt that the United States should be in the war, "first, because every feeling in me is for Belgium and France and Poland and Serbia, as against Germany and Austria. . . . I am thoroughly convinced that not only was it the right of America to enter this war, but was her duty, if she recognizes duty, and that had she stayed out she would have been so cowardly that she would have received and deserved the contempt of all the right-thinking people of the world."

Like the repentant atheist who becomes a religious fanatic, Darrow vigorously denounced his pacifism: "I believe that neither in logic, philosophy, law or, what is more, the commonest instincts of humanity, have the pacifists a chance to make a case. I respect them as I respect every one who stands for his honest convictions, but in this I believe they are wrong—woefully wrong; and that while they are professing to believe in democracy, they are giving all the strength of their character and their mind to autocracy, force, violence and war."[4]

"I can stand for disagreements with my friends," he wrote, "although I can't see why you don't believe as I do. Still . . . many people are obsessed of a theory and non resistance is nothing but a theory and a fool one at that. In spite of Jesus and Tolstoi and Darrow."[5]

He used all his energies to defend U.S. participation in the war. He labeled the German attack on the *Lusitania* and other ships of commerce "murder and piracy on the high seas" and compared the war with prizefighters who must abide by the marquess of Queensberry rules. "If one sees that in a fair fight he must lose, it gives him no excuse to strike below the belt, and if he does, every non-combatant looking on will see that he does not win.

"A neutral world looked at Germany as over and over again she struck below the belt. It knew that civilization could not tolerate such a power, and so the world united to put her down."

He attacked Socialist propaganda which insisted "that this is a rich man's war; that we have joined with the allies against Germany to make dollars for Wall Street. I have no love for Wall Street, and no desire to defend her selfishness and greed, but the statement that this is a Wall Street war is a slander which has no foundation in the truth."[6]

Earlier in the war he had written, "I can't see why human beings don't hate the Kaiser don't greive [sic] for Belgium and France don't want the German Barbarians driven back to the Fatherland—even though it doesn't make the world safe for Democracy 'which it doesn't.' Even if it did we would need another war to 'make the world safe *from* Democracy.' . . . I simply want Germany beaten. Of course I find myself with some new and strange company . . . but such is the way of life."[7]

2

In San Francisco, Tom Mooney and Warren K. Billings, militant labor men closely associated with the anarchists, were arrested and framed on the charge of tossing a bomb into the city's prepreparedness parade. Not until thirty years later was Mooney unconditionally pardoned and Billings paroled. Police raided IWW halls and offices across the country and arrested the radical organization's officers and members. In Chicago, more than a hundred members, including Big Bill Haywood, were convicted of impeding the war effort. Criminal syndicalism laws were passed in many states. Anarchists Emma Goldman and Alexander Berkman were deported to Russia as undesirable aliens, as were hundreds of other dissidents.

Darrow undertook to defend a few conscientious objectors. The IWW wanted him as their attorney, but he advised them he was "engaged in 'war work.'" He did offer them, however, "the use of his investigating agency, second to none in the city," according to Ralph Chaplin, one of the IWW defendants. According to Chaplin, years later Clarence expressed regret that he had not defended the Wobblies (IWW).[8]

Eugene Victor Debs was another to remain antiwar and to be arrested, tried, and convicted of sedition. Clarence wrote him a letter which can be interpreted as an offer to serve as his attorney. "I'm sorry for your indictment," he wrote, "and that you now as always have my deepest love and sympathy and that if I can ever be of any assistance to you, I will give all the aid in my power. I know you always follow the right as you see and no one can do more."[9] But Debs, disapproving Clarence's prowar activities, did not invite him to become his legal counsel.

3

January 1918. Chicago was buried under high drifts of snow. Darrow was lonely, "lonelier all the time." Even if he now traveled in a crowd, still they were not his true companions. He found the city "cold and hard and inhuman. It makes one think that the warmth of the crematory would be welcome." He did not dissemble in his letters to Mary. They were the outlet for his loneliness and his depression. He longed to see her and Fremont Older. The refrain appears in many of his letters throughout the years. "How I wish I could see you and Older, somewhere in a spot where all the world was not shouting and looking and spying and talking about business and labor unions, and making the world safe for Democracy and spying and cheating and lying and killing and sending to jail—how I do like to cheet [*sic*] the jail and that at least I have a chance to do now and then."[10]

He ends this letter with the poignant words, "I am always the same as you knew me with my dreams and my loves and hates . . . and many many of these are connected with the thought of you."

4

On April 18, 1918, with the war raging in Europe, 135 friends of Clarence celebrated his sixty-first birthday in the Auditorium Hotel Parlor on Michigan Boulevard. War differences were laid aside as the "eulogies" ran on, lauding Clarence as a "defender of the defenseless," "a humanitarian," "a philosopher," "a philanthropist," "an orator," "a friend," "a comrade." Carl Sandburg told the assembled guests, "A big point about Clarence Darrow is, he is not exclusive. You can go up to his office there, and as you watch the procession, you will find that he is 'inconclusive.'" Clarence's partner, Peter Sissman, spoke: Darrow "is willing, not only to deal in wholesale generalities, but, when it is necessary, to make a fight for the freedom of one man, he will make the sacrifice and make the fight. . . . He is a philanthropist in the sense of real living."

When the tributes were over, Clarence rose to cheers. "If I had known just what I was to run into here," he stated, "I would have worn a gas mask."

Then, pensively, "A man is never painted as he is. One is either better or worse than the picture is drawn. This is the first time that I have felt I was worse."

He had only a gentle reminder of his age, he said—an occasional twinge of rheumatism. "Of course I know that my intellect is just as good as it was; I am sure of that." As for looking young: "I had my hair cut about a month ago; a friend remarked, 'It makes you look ten years younger,' so I had it cut again."

He promised not to follow Leo Tolstoy's example who, when he had passed sixty-one, turned "good" and began "to moralize," a silly occupation. "I trust I shall die before I begin moralizing."

He assured his friends "that age does not bring wisdom." Sometimes "caution, but not always that" either.[11]

5

Despite his strong defense of the government's war effort, Clarence believed "the courts had gone mad" in punishing antiwar advocates "and were heartless in their horrible sentences that would shame savages for their severity; perhaps I should have said: should shame civilized people."[12]

From time to time he appeared at government offices in Chicago to speak for antiwar dissidents accused of disloyalty. He even traveled to Washington where he met with the president and the attorney general. He urged them "to be more lenient and humane to those who if they had the power would be as cruel as the rest," but he held no hopes that his words would be heeded. "Whether they remember what I said after the next visitor arrives I don't know—probably they will not."[13]

The war propaganda machine continued to issue reports of German atrocities in Belgium and, coming closer to home, of "mutilated Belgian children" living in Chicago. Stirrings of doubt touched Darrow as he reflected that "the liars' brigade" is always mobilized by governments in time of war to play on the emotions of the public. He made offers of $100 to anyone who would bring such a child to his office. There was never a response.[14]

In the summer of 1918 he was one of a group asked by the United States government to visit France and England to tell the people there "the truth about America" and its war policies.

The invitation pleased him for more than the importance of the mission. He needed to get away from Ruby's solicitations and ministrations, which were overwhelming him; he needed room for himself without her hovering over his shoulders, telling him what to eat, what to wear. The trip afforded a plausible opportunity to be without her.

As the years passed, the Darrow marriage had settled into a pattern. Once Lincoln Steffens asked Clarence how he was getting along with Ruby. Darrow answered, "Fine, because Ruby and me, we both like Darrow."[15] Ruby learned to accept Clarence's vagaries, his eye for women and his attractiveness to them, the fact that his was an independent spirit and that she could not hope to enter all the departments of his complex being. There would always be areas off limits to her. She accepted that reality—but never made her peace with it. Jealous of his women friends, she carried on her antagonism to them long after his death. Some of her letters written to Irving Stone, when he was writing his Darrow biography, are filled with righteous tirades against the women who, she believed, had tried to entice her husband. She loved him deeply and completely. The ultimate caretaker, she saw that he ate properly and even cut up his food on his plate. She was cook, valet, laundress, an oversolicitous and overwatchful wife. He chafed, then he learned to tolerate it. Usually he made no fuss, but quietly and stubbornly went his own way. He played the role of a man under the influence of his wife, but actually he did exactly as he pleased.

In New York before the boat sailed for Europe, newspaper reporters wanted to know what he would talk about to the British and the French. He said he would tell them that, though America had gotten into the war slowly, many Americans had urged a declaration of war long before. "We have the greatest resources of any nation, I shall tell them. We have twice as many men of fighting age as the Germans have after four years of war. Our people are more than casually intelligent, believe in a democratic form of government and hate autocracy.

"I shall tell them that we have always had a traditional love for France, and that the great bulk of us are of English stock. Americans feel almost as strong for the French and English, to say nothing of the others, as for themselves. They are resolute, determined, and never leave a job unfinished. And no matter how long it takes, this country will never stop until Prussian militarism has been destroyed."[16]

6

Clarence especially loved the English. In a series of articles on this visit which he wrote for the *Chicago Daily Journal,* he noted the changes in London since his previous visit. "Most of the loafers, the down-and-outs, the derelicts, have been banished from the streets. They have been taken up by war and industry. Many of these were only discouraged and disconsolate. The war has given them a purpose and ambition and they are working like the rest."[17]

Again he justified Allied entry into the war. "Only a very small handful of hopeless pacifists believe that England could have kept out of the war. These are the theorists who take no account of facts; the sleep-walkers who dream on though the world is crashing around them."[18]

He responded to the criticisms of Allied bombing of German cities by reminding the critics "that the bombardment of open towns, the destruction of noncombatants, the violation of all rules of the game was begun by Germany; and the Allies slowly and reluctantly followed in their footsteps when all appeals had failed. Now when the supremacy of the allies in the air has been made plain, the enemy is protesting." [19]

In France he visited with Brand Whitlock, who was now U.S. ambassador to Belgium but living in Le Havre since Belgium had been invaded by the Germans. Whitlock found his old friend "slightly older, fatter, and more wrinkled" but "delightful in his witty and agreeable pessimism, full of humorous and true observations, and on the war, wholly right. Much disillusionment, of course; as to labour unions, for instance, down on the leaders." [20]

The disillusionment Whitlock had noted from Darrow's conversation had already been voiced to Fremont Older: "What you say of the labor fellows is true and that hurts the most," Clarence wrote in a particularly moving letter. "Still it couldn't be otherwise. The fact is that you and I have both overplayed the labor question, placed it clear out of its proportion to all the rest of life. I am for the poor and shall always be but there are other things in life." [21]

The doubts he had begun to feel about his justification of the war coalesced during his European trip, and he was plagued by uncertainty and guilt over the fervor of his prowar activities. Ever driven by a deep sense of compassion for the war victims and by outrage and indignation at the injustice that created them, Darrow responded no differently to the plight of the war sufferers than to those crushed by poverty and crime. In Europe he was overwhelmed by the total horror of the war's destructiveness—the ravaged cities, the maimed, the rows upon rows of crosses crowding the cemeteries. It seemed to him that the American public had been emotionally played upon to obtain its support, that the acts of the enemy, however bestial, had perhaps been exaggerated, that maybe he had been carried away by war propaganda. He returned from Europe not nearly as sure of the rightness of Wilson's war policy as he had been on his arrival there.

Fortunately he was spared the necessity for a public about-face as the war ended shortly after he returned from his mission.

7

The next decade was probably the most active of his career, with America entering a political maelstrom and Darrow actively engaged in resisting the reactionary forces that attempted to impose themselves on the country. He crusaded—in his trial work, in lectures and debates—against capital punishment, prohibition, immigrant restrictions, censorship, racial discrimination.

Charles Edward Russell, whose position on the war had been identical to Clarence's, complained that after the war was over "Parlor Pinkdom" pardoned all Darrow's offenses but declined "the least amnesty for mine, which only (and humbly) duplicated his."[22]

Debs's imprisonment was particularly disturbing to Clarence. He traveled to Washington, D.C., to urge that Debs be released, but Attorney General Alexander Mitchell Palmer refused to act. Darrow appealed to President Wilson:[23] "I earnestly petition the Government for the release of Eugene Victor Debs." He wrote that he was doing this as a friend of Debs for more than twenty-five years and "after full consultation with him in prison." He said he was aware that Debs violated the Espionage Act and that Debs admitted this in his address to the jury hearing his case.

"I know that Mr. Debs," Darrow continued, "like many other sincere men and women, did not believe in war and that he could not bring himself to think that the United States was justified in entering the conflict."

Darrow reminded President Wilson that he had urged U.S. entry into the war from the time Belgium was invaded and "I gave my time and energy without reserve to support the Allies cause.

"But the war is over and it is right to examine the motives of men; and to keep imprisoned one who felt it his duty to disagree, after the need has passed, would not be self-defense but a punishment undeserved."

President Wilson, too, refused to act. "It was left for President Harding and Harry Daugherty [attorney general under President Harding] to pardon Debs. Although I was never a disciple or follower of either Mr. Harding or Mr. Daughtery, I always remember them with kindness when I think of Gene. . . . They pardoned Debs!"[24]

8

The Red Scare following World War I equaled in intensity and injury to democracy the "red hysteria" exploited by Senator Joseph McCarthy in the 1950s when he attacked "liberals," "fellow travelers," and Communists in a sensationalist effort to purge the country of dissenters.

Many events combined to create the anti-red lunacy which pervaded the United States in 1920: foremost among them, the Russian Revolution of 1917 and a series of strikes in 1919—steel, coal, the police in Boston, the Seattle general strike. The country was terrorized. It saw revolution lurking everywhere, a "red" threat to the "American way of life." Attorney General Palmer initiated a series of raids and arrested radicals of all persuasions: anarchists, Socialists, Communists, IWWs. The case of Sacco and Vanzetti, anarchists charged with murder but in reality ultimately executed for their anarchism, was an outgrowth of this atmosphere of political hysteria; as were

Henry Ford's anti-Semitic campaign, the Ku Klux Klan successes in Indiana, the Immigration Acts of 1921 and 1924.

During the 1920 Red Scare, nearly half of the states passed statutes against sedition, anarchy, and criminal syndicalism—legislation that in effect outlawed free political and economic discussion.

Darrow was heartsick over the frenzied fear enveloping the country. He believed wholeheartedly that even a wrong idea had a right to be heard, that free expression was the basis of democracy, that intellectual growth proceeded from discussion. Palmer's words chilled him: "Like a prairie-fire, the blaze of revolution . . . sweeping over every American institution of law and order. . . ," said Palmer, "eating its way into the homes of the American workman, its sharp tongues of revolutionary heat were licking the altars of the churches, leaping into the belfry of the school bell, crawling into the sacred corners of American homes, seeking to replace marriage vows with libertine laws, burning up the foundations of society.

"Robbery, not war, is the ideal of communism . . ." Palmer cried. "The American government must prevent crime . . . there could be no nice distinctions drawn between the theoretical ideals of the radicals and their actual violation of our national laws."[25]

Benjamin Gitlow, a Communist party leader, was one of the first to be tried in a series of the cases in the immediate post–World War I era in which Darrow defended Communists and their right to freedom of expression. Gitlow, however, had not been indicted under the recently passed criminal syndicalism laws but rather under the Criminal Anarchy Law enacted in 1902 as an aftermath of the assassination of President McKinley. The law made it a criminal offense to advocate or advise either in spoken word or in writing the overthrow of organized government by force or violence. Gitlow had written a pamphlet in pure Marxian jargon analyzing capitalism, the demands of the Communists, and the Russian Revolution. He urged the overthrow of the capitalist government in the United States and the establishment of a proletarian government similar to that set up in Russia as a result of the revolution in 1917.

So dedicated was Darrow in these postwar years to the rights of free speech, whether he agreed with the protagonist or not, that he undertook the defense of the Gitlow case without even meeting the defendant. The first time they saw each other was on the eve of the trial in January 1920. "Oh, I know you are innocent," he assured his client then, "but they have the country steamed up. Everybody is against the Reds."[26]

The defense in the New York courtroom called no witnesses, nor did Gitlow take the stand. Instead, he addressed the jury on his own behalf. "Well, I suppose a revolutionist must have his say in court even if it kills him," said Darrow.[27]

Detectives filled the courtroom. The prosecutor was especially hostile, and the judge did not hide his prejudice.

Gitlow told the court that "in the eyes of the present day society I am a revolutionist" and proud of it.

He wanted Darrow to defend the right of revolution in his summation, an order that Clarence had no difficulty fulfilling[28] since he had done so many times on public platforms and in the courtroom. "For a man to be afraid of revolution in America," Darrow told the Gitlow jury, "would be to be ashamed of your mother. Nothing else. Revolution? There is not a drop of honest blood in a single man that does not look back to some revolution for which he would thank his God that those who revolted won."

If George Washington had not won, he would have been hanged; if there had not been a revolution in France, absolute despotism would have prevailed in Europe. Clarence quoted Abraham Lincoln's interpretation of the American Revolution in his first presidential inaugural address: "This country, with its institutions, belongs to the people who inhabit it. Whenever they shall grow weary of the existing government, they can exercise their constitutional right to amend it, or their revolutionary right to dismember or overthrow it." As far as Clarence was concerned, if Lincoln were alive to utter those words during the Palmer era, the attorney general "would send his night-riders to invade his office and the privacy of his home and send him to jail."

The advocate of freedom of speech and of the press would want "no fetters on thought and actions and dreams and ideals of men, even the most despised of them. Whatever I may think of their prudence, what I may think of their judgment, I am for the dreamers," said Darrow. With a flourish he added melodramatically, "I would rather that every practical man shall die if the dreamer be saved."

The manifesto was a record of Gitlow's dream, Darrow told the jury. "It is pointing out something that will some day happen. The Communists believe they have seen the truth, that they have a vision of this day when there shall be real equality. . . .

"Some time perhaps we will reach a plane above the commercial age," he said. "Some time in the realm of ideas, in the realm of good emotions, in the realm of kindness and brotherly feeling, we may find truth that is higher than men, and, gentlemen, no one has the right to stand in the way of finding it."

But the jury was not swayed by Darrow's eloquence. It brought in a verdict of guilty. The judge fined and sentenced Gitlow after praising the jury for the "intelligence" of the verdict. He reflected the country's fear of Communism as he said, "There must be a right in organized society to protect itself. Its citizens who accept the benefits of organized government, who have the opportunity of employment because of the protection given by organized government to the conduct of business, if they do not recognize that the government that fosters them, and which is created by law and based upon law should only be overthrown by lawful methods, then it is difficult to see where civilization can be maintained and the benefits that come from civilization can be preserved."

Darrow did not participate in the Gitlow appeal to the U.S. Supreme Court, which sustained the lower court. Justice Edward T. Sanford wrote for the majority in ruling that the words employed by Gitlow were "the language of direct incitement." Justices Holmes and Brandeis were the only dissenters. "Every idea is an incitement," Holmes said in his opinion. "It offers itself for belief and if believed it is acted on unless some other belief outweighs it or some failure of energy stifles the movement at its birth. The only difference between the expression of opinion and an incitement in the narrower sense is the speaker's enthusiasm for the results."

Gitlow went to jail. On his release he became involved in "factional party squabbles." From a Marxist idealist he became a government informer. In 1930 he renounced his Communist sympathies and subsequently identified his former comrades before congressional committees as well as in local investigations of subversive activities. He died of a heart attack at age seventy-three in 1965.

9

Rockford, Illinois, in the spring of 1920. Clarence and Ruby visited with their friend Fay Lewis as Clarence prepared to defend Arthur Person, charged with joining an organization which called for the violent overthrow of the government. The Swedish-born Person had come to Rockford about twenty years earlier. He "spent a lifetime knitting stockings and beveling glass" to support his ailing wife and three children. The family doctor, a veteran Socialist, urged the poorly educated Person to join the Communist party, and Person began to attend meetings in the doctor's office less out of conviction than in respect for the man who brought him there. In time Person became secretary of the group. One day government agents arrested him and confiscated the secretarial notebook. Questioned in the state's attorney general's office, he confessed that he voted the Socialist ticket and believed in a government of, for, and by the workers.

Darrow could not understand the "malign and deadly influence" that would cause the district attorney to bring such a case into court. On April 24, 1920, he told the Person jury,[29] "If you want to get rid of every Socialist, of every Communist, of every trade unionist, of every agitator, there is one way to do it, and there is only one way to do it, and that is to cure the ills of society. You can't do it by building jails, you can't make jails big enough or penalties hard enough to cure discontent by strangling it to death. No revolution is possible, no great discontent is possible, unless down below it all is some underlying cause of this discontent; men are naturally obedient, too almighty obedient. They are naturally lazy. They are willing to go along. They don't like to resist, and it takes the gravest discontent and the bitterest cause before this can come."

As Darrow saw it, "Those who are trying to send men to jail for their opinion are the ones who are hastening a collapse of civilization, and we must save them from themselves." He had fought the battle against the power of greed for many years in his own way. He had tried to do it in kindly fashion and had never condemned the individual man. The captains of industry were made of the same stuff as he, and he understood that "this mad fever has possession of them and they brook nothing that stands between them and their gold. I know that they would destroy liberty that property would live. It isn't the poor and despised alone but here and there all through the ages men of clear vision and strong intellect and fine imagination have raised their voices to this cause for which I speak today."

He accused the prosecution of engaging in the "common occupation of seeing red. This world at its best is a sad mix up where everyone is trying to get all he can. I don't know that love of humanity is a part of the make-up of the captains of industry. I don't know of any reason why I should object if the working man tries to get more than he has. Of course, I can get along all right as it is. I fancy if the Communist notion of property should come into vogue in America here, and all the tools of production and distribution, the lands and the mines and the factories were owned by people in common, I fancy I wouldn't get as much as I am getting now.

"I can play this game and live, but I wouldn't stand in the way of people who believe the other way, even though I cannot get as much.

"I believe that since the world began the men who do the work have had much less than they should have, and I am glad to see an effort amongst the common people to get more and in trying to get it. I don't imagine they will all be wise. They haven't had a chance to be as wise as we lawyers are, and we disagree a lot. But I wouldn't want to take the hope and inspiration from them, because when you take that away a man is dead."

He discussed the law under which Person had been indicted. "It came from the people who would strangle criticism; and if we give them their way in this world, every man, if he would be safe, should wear a padlock on his lips and only take it off to feed himself and lock it up after he gets through."

His final words to the jury: "Gentlemen, Arthur Person is a common man; an ignorant man in the language of the world, but one of that class upon whom the foundation of society rests. Every captain of industry may die and the world at least will be no worse. Every worshiper of gold may go his way and people will survive; but the foundation of civilization and the security of the state and the welfare of man is built upon the bodies and souls of men like Person."

Jury deliberation was short: the verdict, "not guilty."

10

Darrow had defended Gitlow as one of the founders of the Communist Labor party, a man educated in its intrigues and manipulations, one whose whole life "has been dedicated to the movement." In the Person trial Clarence represented a "man who never did anything in his life but work." Now only a few months after Person's acquittal, Clarence was in the Criminal Courts of Cook County in Chicago defending intellectuals and theoreticians of the Communist movement, including the "millionaire Communist" William Bross Lloyd, the son of his old friend, Henry Demarest Lloyd, who had written *Wealth Against Commonwealth*.

William Lloyd and nineteen others, arrested during one of Palmer's raids, were indicted on a charge of advocating the forceful overthrow of the government. More than fifteen hundred veniremen were examined before a jury was impaneled sixty days later. In his opening statement, the prosecutor claimed that the defendants intended to tear down the "stars and stripes, raise the Red flag, as a national emblem, annihilate the American government and establish a dictatorship of the proletariat." The Communist Labor party platform, he said, "urges the unskilled laborer to start a revolution; that its aim is to stir up the passions and hatred of that class, that it tells the laboring man he should hate his government because capitalism and democracy are the same and all that is done for him is to coerce and suppress him and that it tells the laborer to hate and destroy his employer because he is a murderous master." [30] The district attorney denounced the prowar Darrow for defending this case.

Darrow answered [31] quietly that he was doing so for two reasons: when he entered law practice, he had vowed that there would never be a case, however unpopular, that he would refuse to defend, and he had "seldom seen a case where I believed so heartily that I am right as this.

"I believed in the war," Darrow admitted. "I believed in it to make the world freer and fairer and better for all mankind; I believed that Europe would be freer; I believed that America would be freer, and I did the best I could. But there is something that I believe in more than I do in my country, and that is human freedom.

"I have loved America first of all because she stood for this. Make us a nation of slaves, and I shall love it no more."

He repeated a theme from Justice Holmes's dissenting opinion in the Gitlow case: "If in the long run the beliefs expressed in proletarian dictatorship are destined to be accepted by the dominant forces of the community, the only meaning of free speech is that they should be given their chance and have their way."

Darrow pleaded, "If there can ever come a time when the workingman can rule . . . , I will say he ought to have that chance to see what he can do; and yet to tell you that is to believe in the 'dictatorship of the proletariat'—well, why not?"

He ended with the prophecy, "The proletariat may lose their idealism as they get a better chance in the world. That often happens, too."

For ten weeks the jury listened to witnesses and to lawyers' arguments and pleas in the Communist 20 case, but it took them only a few hours to return a verdict of guilty. The sentences ranged from one to five years in prison plus fines. Robert Morss Lovett reported in the *Nation* a juror's comment after the verdict: "Although no evidence of overt acts was presented in this case, we were certain that had the defendants carried their revolutionary program to its logical conclusion, or had it run its course, a state of anarchy would have been brought about . . . The defendants would have disrupted the labor organizations."[32]

The case was appealed to the Illinois Supreme Court which affirmed the decision of the lower court. But, as in the Haywood case, one justice—Chief Justice Orrin Carter—dissented; he believed that the act under which the defendants were convicted had been "drafted for the purpose of forbidding any person who held opinions distasteful to the majority of our citizens to express these opinions."

Two years later, on November 29, 1922, quoting from Justice Carter's dissent, Governor Len Small of Illinois pardoned the men while they were still out on appeal.

Lloyd retired from political life and disavowed Communism. He died in Boston on June 30, 1946, at the age of seventy-two.

Darrow's own disillusionment with the Soviet experiment is indicated in his membership on the International Committee for Political Prisoners. One of the pieces of literature published by the committee is a book entitled *Letters from Russian Prisons* which carries an introduction by Clarence's friend, Roger Baldwin, longtime director of the American Civil Liberties Union and more recently a United Nations consultant on human rights. "Russia," Baldwin wrote, "presents the unique spectacle of a revolutionary government based on working-class and peasant power imprisoning and exiling its political opponents in other revolutionary parties. . . . The Bolsheviks in power send again to a new exile and prison their former comrades in suffering under the Tsar."[33]

11

During these postwar years, with America looking for scapegoats to allay her fears, a depressed and weary Darrow was convinced that civilization was a failure. "Chicago is now in a mad hunt for criminals, the big ones are after the little ones as usual except worse. People are getting more cruel all the time more insistent that they shall have their way. I wish I was either younger or older. If I was younger I would go to the South Seas or somewhere East of Suez. If I were older I shouldn't care so much, anyhow it wouldn't have the same personal meaning for one. I have grown quite convinced that the happiest time of the human race was in Barbarism and likewise convinced that we are going back to it." [34]

To Fremont Older he wrote he was disappointed that he had not seen him during the year but would not let another year go by without doing so. "We are both getting too old. My health in the main is pretty good, but I find myself out of gear quite often and not coming back as I once did. I don't think I could stand as hard a jolt as I once could, and the truth is, I don't want to. Of course I would be sorry to have you think that all of this means self-pity. I believe I have conquered this form of egoism, and that when I look things over as an intellectual process I am quite sure I have had as much as anyone else and would not change places with those who seem to have the most." [35]

Later he would ask Older whether his will to live "grows stronger or weaker as you grow older?" Darrow thought his "weakens" but was "not quite certain." [36]

XXII

"All Life Is Worth Saving"

1

MANY vicious and senseless crimes of violence have been committed since the summer of 1924 when two scions of Chicago millionaires attempted to commit the "perfect crime." No murder case, however, has had a comparable mix of ingredients to capture the imagination of the public—the wealth and brilliance of the defendants and the savagery and heartlessness of the crime. Through the years, much has been written about the case: newspaper features, magazine articles, books both fiction and nonfiction, as well as theater and film productions. It has become a milestone in criminal justice as the obvious punishment—the death penalty—was thwarted. Psychiatric evidence for the first time formed the major basis of a defense.

Chicago, May 21, 1924. Fourteen-year-old Robert Franks left the Harvard School for Boys, a private school on the South Side of Chicago, after his last class. When he had not returned home by the dinner hour, Jacob Franks, a prominent Chicago industrialist highly respected in the community, checked with some of his son's friends. Together with school authorities, they searched the nearby school building and the surrounding neighborhood.

The search was fruitless. That evening Franks received a telephone call confirming his fears that Robert had been kidnapped. He was instructed not to notify the police but to wait for further instructions.

A special-delivery letter received the next morning spelled out the kidnapper's demand: $10,000 to be made up of $2000 in $20 bills and $8000 in $50 bills. "The money must be old. Any attempt to include new or marked bills will render the entire venture futile."

While Franks prepared to meet the kidnapper, a relative followed a newspaper reporter's suggestion that he view the body of a young boy just brought into the morgue. The body had been found, naked and with a crushed skull, in a culvert under a railroad crossing on the Far South Side of Chicago. It was the missing Robert Franks. The coroner's report said death had probably occurred before the family received the telephone call notifying them of the kidnapping.

Reacting to the prestige of the victim's family and to increasing public criticism, police within the next few days made arrests indiscriminately, often using force in their questioning. In the end, however, there was nothing to tie any of the suspects to the crime.

A week after the murder, *The New York Times* editorialized that the police had so far "accomplished nothing except to bring suspicion of the most terrible sort on persons against whom they can have no real evidence."[1]

During a continuing search of the area where the body was discovered, police found a pair of horn-rimmed eyeglasses and traced them to Nathan Leopold, Jr., eighteen-year-old University of Chicago graduate, the son of a wealthy box manufacturer. He was taken to the LaSalle Hotel in Chicago's downtown and questioned by Assistant State's Attorney Joseph P. Savage.

Leopold admitted being familiar with the area where the body was found. As a birdlife expert, he had been there many times studying birds. But not on May 21, the murder date. On that day, he said, he had been in Lincoln Park bird watching with his friend Dick Loeb, a distant relative of the murder victim. In the evening they had gone for an automobile ride around Jackson Park.

At age seventeen Richard Loeb was an honors graduate of the University of Michigan. The son of a vice-president of Sears, Roebuck & Co., he was related to several of Chicago's prestigious families. During the investigations he had shown an unusual interest in the crime, offering suggestions to police and reporters whom he frequently accompanied in their search for evidence. Loeb was questioned about his activities on the day of the crime.

Within twenty-four hours, both he and Leopold confessed to the kidnapping of Bobby Franks "for the sake of a thrill." Each accused the other of wielding the death weapon.

"I have a hanging case," announced State's Attorney Robert E. Crowe. "The state is ready to go to trial immediately."

Informed of the confession, the distraught families rushed to Darrow's home. "Save our boys," they pleaded, begging Clarence to join their family attorneys. "Only you can save them from being hanged."

He hesitated. At sixty-seven he had looked forward to retiring. His excuse as almost always for the past decade: he wanted to write, to read and relax. Yet, even as the family pleaded with him he knew he would agree to undertake the defense. The poor might be punished with a life sentence, Darrow reasoned, but "in a terrible crisis there is only one element more helpless than the poor, and that is the rich."[2] The combined wealth of the Loeb-Leopold families was estimated at $15 million, an astronomical figure in 1924. No judge could overlook the overwhelming public clamor for the death penalty.

Newspaper headlines at once shouted, "Millions to defend killers," while the prosecutor's office issued a statement that the case came down to "millions versus the death penalty."

Darrow, however, saw something bigger than a "million-dollar defense." The trial would provide him with a courtroom platform from which to espouse his lifelong crusade against capital punishment.

Many accused Darrow of "selling out" for a fee. The "millionaire murderers" would cheat the gallows, rose the cry. Clarence noted that he "never saw so much enthusiasm for the death penalty," which was being "discussed as a holiday, like a day at the races."

Shortly after being retained as counsel, he read to the press a statement on the families' behalf: "The families the accused boys desire to say that they have lived in Chicago for more than 50 years and the public can judge whether they have conducted themselves in their relations with this community in such a way as to earn a standing as truthful, decent, upright, law-abiding citizens, conscious of their duties and responsibilities to the community in which they live. . . .

"There will be no large sums of money spent either for legal or medical talent. The fees to be paid to the medical experts will be only such fees as are ordinary and usual for similar tests.

"The lawyers representing the accused boys have agreed that the amount of their fees shall be determined by a committee composed of the officers of the Chicago Bar Association.

"In no event will the families of the accused boys use money in an attempt to defeat justice."

2

Almost immediately after the arrest the state obtained the services of the leading alienists[3] in Chicago to examine the defendants. These included Dr. Hugh T. Patrick, professor of nervous and mental diseases at Chicago Polyclinic and neurologist at various Chicago hospitals, and Dr. William O. Krohn, a specialist in mental and nervous diseases. Also working for the state were Dr. Archibald Church, head of the Department of Mental and Nervous

Diseases at Northwestern University, and Dr. Harold D. Singer, a graduate of the University of London.

With the most prominent Chicago psychiatrists already employed by the state, the defense recruited its medical experts outside the city. Walter Bachrach, a lawyer for the defense, visited the annual convention of the National Association of Psychiatrists in session at the time in Atlantic City. Three doctors agreed to examine the boys: William Alanson White, president of the American Psychiatric Association and superintendent of St. Elizabeth's Hospital in Washington, D.C., the government mental institution; Dr. William Healy, graduate of Harvard and of Rush Medical School, psychiatrist for the Baker Foundation of Boston; and Dr. Bernard Glueck, head of the psychopathic clinic at Sing Sing prison and a former president of the Society of Medical Jurisprudence. The defense also employed several other psychiatrists, including Dr. Carl M. Bowman, of Boston, who joined Harold S. Hulbert, of Chicago; both were specialists in mental and nervous disorders.

Chicago's newspapers had a heyday. The *Tribune* offered to broadcast the trial over its own radio station; the *Evening American* mocked the *Tribune's* suggestion with one of its own—that the White Sox baseball park be used as an open-air courtroom. Neither idea was attempted, of course, but both the *Tribune* and Hearst's *American,* sensing circulation possibilities, approached Sigmund Freud, the father of psychoanalysis. Hearst offered Freud any fee he wanted to study the boys. Learning that the doctor was ill, Hearst was ready to charter a special liner so that Freud could travel undisturbed by other passengers. Colonel Robert McCormick of the *Tribune* instructed a staff member to offer Freud $25,000 or any sum he named to come to Chicago to psychoanalyze the defendants.

Freud turned down both proposals. He told the *Tribune* that he "cannot be supposed to be prepared to provide an expert opinion about persons and a deed when I have only newspaper reports to go on and have no opportunity to make a personal examination. An invitation from the Hearst Press to come to New York for the duration of the trial I have had to decline for reasons of health."[4]

For days, for weeks, hour after hour, first the state and then the defense alienists probed the minds of the two boys; family members were interrogated, governesses and friends questioned. Never before had there been so much attention devoted to the workings of the mind, the psychic motivation of men charged with murder. Every indication pointed to an insanity plea. "Were Leopold and Loeb mentally capable of knowing the difference between right and wrong?" "Did they know they were doing wrong?" These were the questions around which the trial would be centered. It would be a battle of alienists, the courtroom resounding with such Freudian terminology as "split personality," "fantasies," "the subconscious." The trial, helped by sensational reporting, popularized Freud and made him a household word in the United

States. There would be no attempt to get an acquittal, Darrow reiterated. "The question of insanity alone is involved."

In mid-June, Darrow summoned his two clients to the lawyers' room in the jail. "Boys," he said, "we're going to ask you to do something that may strike you as very strange. But you must trust us. Your lawyers have arrived at this very difficult decision after much discussion. We're going to ask permission of the court to withdraw our pleas of not guilty. We're going to plead you guilty." He explained the reasoning behind the move. "Mr. Crowe, not satisfied with what he calls his 'perfect hanging case,' wanted two bites at the apple, not one. He had you indicted both for murder and, separately, for kidnapping for ransom," Darrow told them. "We plead not guilty. All right. He'd try you on one charge, say the murder. If he got less than a hanging verdict, he'd turn around and try you on the other charge. He'd have two chances for the price of one!

"There is only one way to deprive him of that second chance: to plead guilty to both charges before he realizes what is happening and has the opportunity to withdraw one of them. That's why the element of surprise is absolutely necessary. And surprise depends upon absolute silence. He mustn't know until we actually make the motion in court that we have in mind changing our plea."[5] Darrow had expected an argument, but the defendants nodded in agreement.

3

Chicago's Criminal Courts building on the northwest corner of Dearborn and Hubbard streets, north of the downtown section of the city, stands like a fortress, its massive gray-stone blocks blackened by an accumulation of years of city soot. The county jail was the next building north. On Monday morning, July 23, 1924, at 9:30, the trial of Nathan Leopold and Richard Loeb for the murder of Robert Franks opened.

Security was tight. Police surrounded the outside of the old building in an effort to control the mobs trying to get in. Credentials were carefully examined; only those with passes or on official business were permitted to enter.

Darrow, wearing his usual baggy gray suit, his tie slightly askew, came into the courtroom followed by Nathan Leopold, Sr., and cocounsel Benjamin C. Bachrach, who accompanied the Loebs. State's Attorney Robert E. Crowe walked in briskly. At exactly ten o'clock, the sixty-three-year-old Judge John R. Caverly ascended the bench. The two defendants, dressed in dark suits and white shirts, were escorted into the courtroom.

"You may proceed," said the judge.

"Your Honor, I only want a few minutes' preliminary indulgence in this matter."[6] Darrow hooked his thumbs into his galluses, his jacket fell open. His voice was soft. "Of course, it is unnecessary to say that this case has given us many perplexities and sleepless nights. Nobody is more aware than we are of what this means and the responsibility that is upon us.

"Of course, this case has attracted very unusual attention on account of the weird, uncanny, and terrible nature of the homicide. There is in the public mind a feeling that in some manner the lawyers might succeed in getting these two defendants into an asylum and having them released.

"We want to state frankly here that no one in this case believes that these defendants should be released. We believe they should be permanently isolated from society."

What trick was Darrow up to? Reporters glanced at one another as they frantically scribbled down his words. "We know, your honor, the facts in this case are substantially as have been published in the newspapers and what purports to be their confession, and we can see we have no duty to the defendants, or their families, or society, except to see that they are safely and permanently excluded from the public.

"Of course, after that is done, we want to do the best we can for them within those limits."

Then, to the astonishment of the court, he said, "After long reflection and thorough discussion, we have determined to make a motion in this court for each of the defendants in each of the cases to withdraw our plea of not guilty and enter a plea of guilty."

Leopold, Sr., cried "like a child." Jacob Loeb, Dick's uncle, sobbed.[7]

The strategy depended on the law that provides that evidence may be offered in mitigation of the punishment when a defendant pleads guilty. In such a case the judge has discretion as to the sentence.

In the courtroom, Darrow solemnly told Judge Caverly that he realized the "seriousness and gravity" of throwing this burden upon the court, but "a court can no more shirk responsibilities than attorneys. And, while we wish it could be otherwise, we feel that it must be as we have chosen." The defense asked the judge for permission to present evidence of the defendants' mental condition and degree of responsibility for their acts, and with this evidence to consider mitigation of the punishment.

"The fact that the two murderers have thrown themselves on the mercy of the court does not in any way alleviate the enormity of the crime they committed," was the prosecution's immediate response.[8]

Judge Caverly accepted the change of plea.

4

In his 292-page book on *Crime: Its Causes and Treatment,* Clarence summarized his philosophy. He contended that "the laws that control human behavior are as fixed and certain as those that control the physical world." He admitted the book might be considered "a plea or apology for the criminal. To hold him morally blameless could be nothing else. Still if a man's actions are governed by natural law, the sooner it is recognized and understood, the sooner will sane treatment be adopted in dealing with crime. The sooner too will sensible and humane remedies be found for the treatment and cure of this most perplexing and painful manifestation of human behavior."[9]

The book had a limited distribution; not many people knew of it, and fewer read it. With the Leopold and Loeb case in the headlines, however, the international press focused on Darrow's views on crime. Despite the fact that the defense and the prosecution were both using psychiatric experts, Darrow believed that the expert "takes the case of the side that employs him, and does the best he can. The expert is an every-day frequenter of the courts; he makes his living by testifying for contesting litigants. Of course scientific men do not need to be told that the receipt of or expectation of a fee is not conducive to arriving at scientific results. Every psychologist knows that, as a rule, men believe what they wish to believe and that the hope of reward is an excellent reason for wanting to believe."[10]

Lest he be accused of trying to "belittle scientific knowledge or to criticize experts," he explained that his comments were not "beyond such general statements as will apply to all men."

5

July 23, the opening day of the trial, was hot. By afternoon the temperature rose to the high eighties. A heavy fan stood to the right of Judge Caverly's bench. Several others were on ledges attached to the courtroom pillars.

Judge Caverly was already on the bench when the defendants entered. At the prosecutor's table with State's Attorney Crowe were his four assistants— Joseph P. Savage, John Sbarbaro, Thomas Marshall, and Milton Smith. For the defense, in addition to Darrow, were the Loeb and Leopold family counsels, the brothers Benjamin and Walter Bachrach.

Crowe approached the bench. He spoke for an hour and forty-five minutes in his opening statement.[11] Both the defendants, he said, were "sons of highly respected and prominent citizens of this community; that their parents gave them every advantage wealth and indulgence could give to boys. They have attended the best schools in the community and have, from time to time, had private tutors. These young men behaved as a majority of young men in their social set behaved, with the exception that they developed a desire to gamble, and gambled, for large stakes, the size of the stakes being such that even their wealthy companions could not sit with them."

He clearly stated the state's theory: that the boys committed the crime for money and for nothing else. He continued: "The evidence will further show that along in October or November of last year these two defendants entered into a conspiracy, the purpose of which was to gain money, and in order to gain it they were ready and willing to commit a cold-blooded murder.

"The state will show to your honor by facts and circumstances, by witnesses, by exhibits, by documents, that these *men*"—he emphasized the word—"that these men are guilty of the most cruel, cowardly, dastardly, murder ever committed in the annals of American jurisprudence."

Crowe paused. Again, as he would many times during his preliminary statement, he pulled a handkerchief from his pocket and wiped his glasses. "In the name of the womanhood, the fatherhood, and the children of the State of Illinois, we are going to demand the death penalty for both of these cruel and vicious murderers." He slowly walked back to his table.

Judge Caverly nodded to Darrow, who rose from his chair and began speaking even as he walked toward the bench. "A death in any situation is horrible but when it comes to the question of murder, it is doubly horrible." He slipped his thumbs into his galluses. "But there are degrees perhaps of atrocity." Anybody with any experience of a murder trial, Darrow said, expected the prosecution to accuse the defendant of having committed "the greatest, the most important and atrocious killing" in the history of the state or the nation.

Crowe objected, his shouts permeating to the farthest corners of the courtroom. "Argumentative." "Improper." "No time for speech making."

"Your honor," Darrow interjected, "it comes with poor grace from counsel after for more than an hour he sought to stir up feelings in this community." Darrow admitted awareness that his remarks may not have been proper, but he nevertheless felt impelled to make them as he was "outraged at the whole statement that has been made in this case. That accounts for it."

The spectators leaned forward, straining to catch every word. His tousled graying hair falling over his forehead, Darrow looked tired as he explained that the state's evidence had been "added to statements already made publicly and have no bearing on this case whatever with pleas of guilty in it." No one on the defense team denied the conspiracy, or the murder, or the certainty that it had been committed by the two defendants.

"We shall insist in this case," Darrow stressed, "that, terrible as this is, terrible as any killing is, it would be without precedent if two boys of this age should be hanged by the neck until dead, and it would in no way bring back

Robert Franks or add to the peace and security of this community. I insist that it would be without precedent, as we learned, if on a plea of guilty this should be done."

Since the defense admitted all the state's charges, Darrow had hoped the prosecution would forgo exposing the details of the boys' lives and concentrate only on the experts' testimony. Crowe and his associates, however, had their own ideas. They called to the stand more than eighty witnesses to tell all they knew of the defendants. Darrow cross-examined only a few because he wanted to avoid a repeat of the damaging testimony they might offer. He concentrated his cross-examination on the experts.

6

The defense began its presentation of evidence in mitigation on July 30. The first alienist called, Dr. White, described both boys as having an emotional maturity of six to seven years of age. "Their personalities are split by over development of intellect and retarded emotional growth."

The next day an alienist for the state told newspapers that "these circumstances do not condone the crime. Any criminal has an unbalanced nature." [12]

Crowe cross-examined Dr. White. "And did Richard Loeb on the 31st day of May, 1924, know the difference between right and wrong?" he asked.

The doctor answered, "He knew intellectually, for example, in my opinion, that murder was proscribed by the law; but I conceive that the knowledge of right and wrong which the average person possesses—and—"

Crowe: "I am talking about Richard Loeb."

Dr. White: "He knew intellectually that it was against the law."

Crowe: "Did he know it was morally wrong?"

Dr. White: "He had not adequate feeling toward its moral wrongfulness."

Crowe persisted: "But did he have sufficient capacity to refrain from killing?"

Dr. White: "I don't know."

Crowe: "Is Richard Loeb, in your opinion, insane?"

Walter Bachrach objected to the question. The court sustained the objection. Crowe shifted his approach. "What distinction, Doctor," he asked, "is there between mental illness and insanity?"

Dr. White: "Well, mental illness is sickness of the mind. Insanity is something you gentlemen know about. I don't. It is purely a legal and sociological term. It is not a medical term at all."

The alienist for the defense said he had been asked to come to Chicago to examine the boys so that the defendants' attorneys "might more intelligently conduct the defense."

Alienist Healy stripped the boys of "their moral and mental underpinnings," reported the *Chicago Daily News*[13] of the next defense witness, who called Loeb "untruthful, unscrupulous, disloyal even to his friends" and impelled to murder for the sake of a new experience. As for Leopold, Dr. Healy described him as the "superman" who had discarded conscience and belief in God when a child. He contemplated murder "the same as he would decide whether to have pie for supper."

Dr. Hulbert testified that Leopold's "king and slave" fantasy was the focus of his attachment to Loeb, whom he saw as the dream king. Whatever Loeb ordered, Leopold would obey. Therefore, when Loeb wanted to commit the "perfect crime," Leopold, the dream slave, joined his king without protest.

The alienists for the state had completely different opinions. Dr. Patrick found no evidence of mental disease in either of the two boys "unless you assume that any person who commits such cold-blooded crime is by that fact alone shown to be mentally diseased."

Dr. Singer saw evidence "of clear thinking and normal emotional reactions but no evidence of mental disease."

On Monday morning, August 18, the state called its final witness to the stand. Like the others who testified for the prosecution, Dr. Krohn, considered a key witness, found no evidence of mental disease. He had examined the defendants under the ideal conditions, he believed, with no posing, no pretense, no defense reactions on their part. Loeb, he said, "was not suffering from any mental disease when I examined him."

Darrow objected to Dr. Krohn's speechmaking instead of answering questions "without any introductory of hot air."

The doctor fumed, "What did you say about hot air?" Judge Caverly cut off the impending argument by ordering Krohn, "Go ahead, Doctor." Crowe, however, couldn't resist. "Mr. Darrow is an authority on hot air," he exclaimed to the amusement of the spectators.

Years later, Leopold recalled Darrow's manner of cross-examination: He rose in a leisurely way, said Leopold, shambled over to the witness stand, and hovering over the witness, spoke in a "friendly, conversational, intimate tone of voice. But . . . suddenly he straightened up from his habitual stoop. His right forefinger shot out in the direction of the witness. The questions came as if from a Thompson sub-machine gun."[14]

7

Opening summation for the prosecution was made by Assistant State's Attorney Thomas Marshall, who stressed that there "is but one penalty that is proportionate to the turpitude of this crime"—the death penalty. Marshall insisted that, just as the Haymarket anarchists were hanged in 1887 for murder, Leopold and Loeb should be sent to the gallows for killing Bobby Franks, and the superman philosophy should not excuse them any more than the anarchist philosophy had excused the Haymarket defendants.

Assistant State's Attorney Savage followed.[15] His deep voice was "the outraged law itself" as he charged, "You have before you one of the most cold-blooded, cruel, cowardly, dastardly murders that was ever tried in the history of any court." Turning to the defense's plea for mercy, he questioned the "mercy" Leopold and Loeb had shown "little Bobby Franks. . . . It is an insult in a case of this kind to come before the bar of justice and beg for mercy! I know your honor will be just as merciful to these two defendants sitting here as they were to Bobby Franks.

"If we do not hang these two most brutal murderers, we might just as well abolish capital punishment, because it will mean nothing in the law. And I want to say to your honor that the men who have reached the gallows prior to this time have been unjustly treated if these two do not follow!

"Hang them! Hang these heartless supermen!" Savage cried.

Jacob Franks, father of the young victim, tears streaming down his face, whispered to the woman sitting next to him, "I can't stand it any more," and left the courtroom.[16]

Savage's denunciation was thorough and damning. For the first time during the trial spectators shed tears for Bobby Franks, the young victim.

8

A few days before Darrow made his plea to Judge Caverly, several newspapermen confronted him in the corridor of the courtroom. "Tell us, Mr. Darrow," asked one, "why does a famous lawyer like you dress so carelessly?"

Darrow looked at his baggy trousers and wrinkled coat. "Well, I'll tell you. I spend as much for my clothes as any of you boys do. See this suit—it was tailored in London—finest Scotch tweeds, but—I guess you fellers don't sleep in your clothes."

Mrs. Darrow was annoyed when she heard about the interview. She contacted one of the reporters and asked him to talk to her husband again. In front of the reporter, Ruby asked Clarence, "Did you tell this young man that you slept in your clothes?"

Clarence looked at the young man. "Well, I guess you'll have to change that. You write in your story, young man, that I don't sleep in them—I sleep on them."[17]

Suave, calm Benjamin Bachrach delivered the first of the final defense summations. He barely touched on Savage's argument in his twenty-minute plea for tolerance. "Judge them," he urged, "as a father would judge his children."[18]

It was the afternoon of August 22 when Darrow began his final summation.[19] Many in the legal profession suggest that Darrow was no great lawyer, merely a brilliant pleader who could move juries. In the Leopold and Loeb case, Darrow faced no jury; he argued before a scholarly judge, who listened attentively, chin cupped in his right hand. Standing before the bench, Darrow had to raise his voice to be heard over the turmoil in the courtroom and in the corridor. "Our anxiety over this case," he told Judge Caverly, "has not been due to the facts that are connected with this most unfortunate affair, but to the almost unheard-of publicity it has received. And when the public is interested and demands a punishment, no matter what the offense, great or small, it thinks of only one punishment, and that is death." He talked about the rumors of a million-dollar defense. "We announced to the public that no excessive use of money would be made in this case, neither for lawyers nor for psychiatrists, nor in any other way. We have faithfully kept that promise."

Darrow always used a foil in a trial—in the Kidd case it was Paine; in the Haywood trial, Orchard. Now it was Savage and Krohn. He called Dr. Krohn a "professional perjurer," who for sixteen years had been "going in and out of the courtrooms in this building and other buildings, trailing victims without regard to the name or sex or age or surroundings. But he had a motive, and his motive was cash."

As for Savage, Darrow wondered whether he had been "picked for his name or his ability or his learning?—because my friend Mr. Savage, in as cruel a speech as he knew how to make, said to this court that we pleaded guilty because we were afraid to do anything else. Your Honor, that is true."

Surprisingly enough, he did not mention Marshall's comparison with the Haymarket defendants who had been exonerated and pardoned by Governor Altgeld.

Darrow, his scant hair flying, his tie hanging limp, held forth against capital punishment: "If these two boys die on the scaffold—which I can never bring myself to imagine—if they do die on the scaffold, the details of this will be spread over the world. Every newspaper in the United States will carry a full account. Every newspaper of Chicago will be filled with the gruesome details. It will enter every home and every family.

"Will it make men better or make men worse? I would like to put that to the intelligence of man, at least such intelligence as they have."

Then he pictured the execution scene. The boys are awakened in the "gray light of morning, furnished a suit of clothes by the state, led to the scaffold, their feet tied, black caps drawn over their heads, stood on a trap door, the hangman pressing a spring, so that it gives way under them; I can see them fall through space and stopped by the rope around their necks."

There was not much in Darrow's plea to cheer the defendants. "Sympathy, yes," said the *Los Angeles Times*, "but sympathy with their humanness, not with their deed. Darrow damned them heartily enough; denied them in their own name, the right ever to be at liberty again. . . . Loeb dug his fists into hs eyes like a child, and Leopold blinked back tears."[20]

While Darrow was talking, Leopold sat spellbound. "He carried me along with the grandiose sweep of his thought. Even I was convinced that I should not be hanged," said Leopold many years later. "I hadn't wept at any time through all the horrible preceding three months. If I didn't weep while Mr. Darrow was speaking, I certainly had to blow my nose suspiciously often. He made even me feel with him that terrific tenderness of his for the whole undeserving human race."[21]

Clarence lamented that the boys had nothing to look forward to, yet he hoped that "sometime, when life and age have changed their bodies, as it does, and has changed their emotions, as it does—that they may once more return to life."

Brand Whitlock had once given Clarence a copy of A. E. Housman's book of poetry, A Shropshire Lad. As he had with Omar Khayyám, Clarence found a simpatico with Housman, and he memorized many of the verses and recited them frequently both in and out of court.

Now, he quoted to Judge Caverly from Housman:

> Now hallow fires burn out to black,
>   And lights are fluttering low:
> Square your shoulders, lift your pack
>   And leave your friends and go.
>
> O Never fear, lads, naught's to dread,
>   Look not left nor right:
> In all the endless road you tread
>   There's nothing but the night.[22]

Darrow softly read the poet's soliloquy of a boy about to be hanged, words Leopold and Loeb could well have spoken.

> The night my father got me
> His mind was not on me
> He did not plague his fancy
> To muse if I should be
> The son you see.[23]

Later, Housman would banter that Darrow made use of his poems "so often . . . to rescue his client from the electric chair. Loeb and Leopold owe their life sentence partly to me." Clarence gave a copy of his plea to Housman, who complained humorously that "two of my pieces are misquoted."[24]

Clarence stood silently before Judge Caverly for a moment. "You may hang these boys," he said, "you may hang them by their neck until they are dead. But in doing it you will turn your face toward the past. In doing it you are making it harder for every other boy who, in ignorance and darkness, must grope his way through the mazes which only childhood knows. In doing it you will make it harder for unborn children." His unusual plea asked for humanity from the bench as opposed to what the law demanded. "You may save them and make it easier for every child that sometime may stand where these two boys stand. You will make it easier for every human being with an aspiration and a vision and a hope and a fate."

For two court days Darrow spoke, his final words a quotation from Omar Khayyám, with whom Clarence felt a special kinship. Like the poet, Darrow believed that man was not essentially bad, only weak and without inner strength to overcome his inherent human faults. The Persian poet, said Darrow, "saw the heavy hand of destiny, ever guiding and controlling, ever moving its creatures forward to the inevitable fate that all the centuries had placed in store for the hopeless captive, marching shackled to the block." [25]

> So I be written in the Book of Love,
> I do not care about that Book above;
> Erase my name or write it as you will,
> So I be written in the Book of Love. [26]

Tears streamed down the judge's face. Hardly a breath of air moved in the courtroom. The lines on Darrow's face were deeper. It was difficult to tell where his voice stopped and the silence took over.

"When I closed I had exhausted all the strength I could summon," Darrow admitted. "From that day I have never gone through as protracted a strain, and could never do it again, even if I should try." [27]

9

State's Attorney Crowe had the last word. Emotional, passionate, "his voice stayed up above the pitch of wrath, until his face purpled with the strain of it and the veins in his neck stood out." Darrow, he said, wanted the golden rule. "But we're not yet ready for that." [28]

Crowe [29] said he had heard so much about "the milk of human kindness" that he was somewhat surprised to know that Darrow had "so much poison in his system. Is it wrong, if your honor please, for the state's attorney and his two assistants to refer to these two perverts, these two atheists, these two murderers, in language they can understand?"

The prosecutor called Darrow an "anarchistic advocate" whose real defense of Leopold and Loeb was his own "dangerous philosophy of life." He produced a story from the *Chicago Herald-Examiner* of June 10, 1924, before the case had been assigned. The article attributed to Leopold a comment that he desired to plead guilty before a "friendly judge." Everybody connected with the defense except for Nathan Leopold's father "have laughed and sneered and jeered and if the defendant, Leopold, did not say that he would plead before a friendly judge, his actions demonstrated that he thinks he has got one."

Darrow jumped to his feet. Objection. Judge Caverly, however, waved him aside; he wanted the court stenographer to record the prosecutor's words.

The state's attorney concluded that only the death penalty would fit the crime. Judge Caverly[30] glanced at him as he ordered stricken from the record "the closing remarks of the state's attorney as being a cowardly and dastardly assault upon the integrity of the court."

"It was not so intended, your honor," apologized Crowe. "If your honor please, the state had no such intention."

Judge Caverly did not listen. That statement "could not be used for any other purpose except to incite a mob and to try to intimidate this court. It will be stricken from the record. This court will not be intimidated by anybody at any time or place as long as he occupies this position."

10

September 10, 1924. Judge Caverly entered the courtroom promptly at nine thirty. Crowe, Marshall, Savage, and other members of the prosecution were already there as were Darrow and several relatives of the defendants. Loeb's mother was not there, nor had she been at most court sessions. The bailiff rapped his gavel three times, the judge nodded to his clerk, who in turn called for Leopold and Loeb.

Asked whether they had anything to say before sentence was pronounced, each said no. Judge Caverly read his decision in a low voice.[31] "In view of the profound and unusual interest that this case has aroused not only in this community but in the entire country and even beyond its boundaries, the court feels it his duty to state the reasons which have led to the determination he has reached."

There was no indication of his decision. "It is not an uncommon thing that pleas of guilty are entered in criminal cases, but almost without exception in the past such pleas have been the result of a virtual agreement between the defendants and the State's attorney whereby in consideration of the plea the State's attorney consents to recommend to the court a sentence deemed appropriate by him, and, in the absence of special reasons to the contrary, it is the practice of the court to follow such recommendations."

This case is different, said the judge, pointing out that the guilty plea was entered without the knowledge and to the surprise of the prosecution. The state already had a confession from both defendants.

"By pleading guilty," Judge Caverly continued, "the defendants have admitted legal responsibility for their acts; the testimony has satisfied the court that the case is not one in which it would have been possible to set up successfully the defense of insanity as insanity is defined and understood by the established law of this state for the purpose of the administration of criminal justice."

Neither Leopold nor Loeb showed any sign of emotion as the judge noted the testimony revealed "a crime of singular atrocity," executed with "every feature of callousness and cruelty."

The defendants, said Judge Caverly, "have been shown in essential respects to be abnormal; had they been normal they would not have committed the crime. It is beyond the province of this court, as it is beyond the capacity of humankind in its present state of development, to predict ultimate responsibility for human acts."

Clarence smiled. The philosophy of free will had been one he had long debated, always arguing that man was not a free agent. His address to the prisoners in Cook County jail at the turn of the century had shocked the inmates. They were astonished to be told that they were in jail simply because of circumstances for which they were in no way responsible.

Continuing, Judge Caverly said that "the court is willing to recognize that the careful analysis made of the life history of the defendants and of their present mental, emotional and ethical condition has been of extreme interest and is a valuable contribution to criminology. And yet the court feels strongly that similar analysis made of other persons accused of crime will probably reveal similar or different abnormalities."

The judge discussed the law and the proscribed penalties for the crimes: the penalty for kidnapping is death or imprisonment "for life, or for any term not less than five years," for murder, death or "imprisonment in the penitentiary for his natural life or for a term of not less than fourteen years. If the accused is found guilty by a jury they shall fix the punishment by their verdict; upon a plea of guilty, the punishment shall be fixed by the court."

Judge Caverly was willing to meet his responsibilities. Of course imposing the death penalty would be the path of least resistance. "In choosing imprisonment instead of death, the court," he said, "is moved chiefly by the consideration of the age of the defendants, boys of eighteen and nineteen years."

Before passing sentences of life plus ninety-nine years on each defendant— life for the murder, ninety-nine years for the kidnapping—the judge felt he had to comment on the effect of the parole law for them. "In the case of such atrocious crimes it is entirely within the discretion of the department of public welfare, never to admit these defendants to parole. To such a policy the court urges them strictly to adhere."

The prison doors closed behind the "thrill killers."

With the trial ended, the newspapers began to report its cost. The state estimated it had spent $60,000; Drs. Singer and Krohn, testifying for the state, each received $6000 as they had been present every day during the trial; Church and Patrick were each paid $1000.

Defense expenses were estimated at $50,000, excluding attorney fees. The defense alienists each received $250 per day.

The families ignored Darrow's bills. Eventually, they sent representatives to Darrow's office to discuss the fee. Clarence's suggestion of $200,000 as reasonable was turned down.

"When representatives of these families with an aggregate wealth of ten million dollars, came to me pleading for me to take the case, and when I pointed out to them the difficulties involved and the danger of the boys' being hanged—nobody fainted then," an annoyed Darrow said.[32] He reminded the families that they had agreed at the beginning to allow the Bar Association to settle the fee. They rejected the idea. Their spokesmen said it would not be to their advantage since both Darrow and the arbitrators were lawyers. They refused to pay more than $100,000, from which they deducted Darrow's $10,000 retainer fee. The $90,000 was divided equally among Darrow and the Bachrach brothers—a far cry from the million-dollar defense newspapers had headlined when he was first retained.

Soon afterward, Clarence left his partnership with Sissman to become associated with a firm of successful criminal attorneys who had been courting him for some time.

Loeb was slashed to death in the Joliet prison in 1936 by a fellow inmate for alleged sexual misconduct.

It was twenty-nine years before Leopold appealed for a parole hearing. He had been advised not to apply until 1965, but he appealed in 1955 and, again, in 1956. Denied both times, he requested a board hearing for executive clemency in July 1957. Though the governor denied clemency, he suggested that the parole board reconsider the Leopold petition.

Each time newspapers reported a move toward parole, they quoted Judge Caverly's advice against it and also noted that Darrow had indicated the prisoners should never be at liberty again. Yet, few ever cited Darrow's words, in that same plea, when he said, "I know that these boys are not fit to be at large. I believe they will not be until they pass through the next stage of life, at forty-five or fifty."

Or a letter Darrow wrote to Leopold in 1928: "I don't know how anybody else feels about it, but I shall always cling to the idea that sometimes you will be out but it will not be very near, still, at that, you have a longer time to live outside than I have."[33]

Probably the first indication of a new climate of opinion to make parole possible for Leopold came at a meeting of the Headline Club [34] where the program celebrated the centenary of Darrow's birth. The moderator asked Circuit Judge Sbarbaro, who had been one of the assistant state's attorneys in the Leopold trial, whether he believed Leopold should be paroled. The former assistant prosecutor said, "It is my contention that Nathan Leopold should be released. He should be paroled."

At the parole hearing, Chicago attorney Elmer Gertz represented Leopold. Hans Mattick, prominent criminologist at the University of Chicago and former assistant warden of the Cook County jail, was one of the witnesses urging parole. Looking back at the crime in a search for cause and motives, Mattick suggested to the Parole Board that Leopold, emotionally immature, had been greatly affected by the death of his mother when he was seventeen, and by his father's attitude toward him. The senior Leopold, sensing an arrogance in his son, attempted to temper it by a relative lack of enthusiasm for his accomplishments. "Intellectually well-endowed," wrote Mattick, "he had demonstrated fitness for manhood by high intellectual achievements which had brought only a moderate response from the father who, by his lack of enthusiastic acceptance, barred the way to Leopold's impatient pursuit of the adult role he so much desired to assume."

Mattick believed Leopold needed to "prove" himself both to his father and to Loeb. When, therefore, Loeb suggested "the perfect crime," Leopold looked upon it as a challenge.

Mattick, in 1958, agreed with Darrow that the crime was perhaps a mere accident caused by "strange and unfortunate circumstances that might not occur again in a thousand years." [35]

On the day of the final hearing, Leopold wrote Gertz a grateful letter thanking him for his efforts. "It is you who, if we are successful, will have given meaning to what Mr. Darrow did so many years ago."

The board in a split decision announced on February 20, 1958, that Leopold could be freed under a five-year parole agreement. At ten o'clock on the morning of March 13, 1958, the twentieth anniversary of Darrow's death, as a wreath was being tossed into the Jackson Park lagoon where his ashes had been strewn, Nathan Leopold, accompanied by Gertz, walked out of the Joliet penitentiary. He was discharged from parole five years later.

11

Thirteen days after Judge Caverly had rendered his decision, Judge Alfred J. Talley, of the Court of General Sessions in New York, complained that "it is not the criminals, actual or potential, that need a neuropathic hospital. It is

the people who slobber over them in an effort to find excuses for their crime."
He challenged Darrow to a debate on the subject of capital punishment.

They met at the Manhattan Opera House on October 26, 1924, to debate
"Is Capital Punishment a Wise Policy?" Tickets sold for $1.65 to $4.40.

Judge Talley opened. "In the heart of every man is written the law: 'Thou
shalt not kill.'"

Darrow fended off the opening statement with humor. "I think every man's
heart desires killing. Personally, I never killed anybody that I know of. But
I've had a great deal of satisfaction now and then reading obituary notices." [36]

Darrow carried his campaign against capital punishment from city to city.
In Bloomington, Illinois, he spoke to a thousand people on the topic "Crime
and Criminals." Adlai Stevenson, who would become a governor of Illinois and
twice a Democratic presidential nominee, was an usher at the meeting. The
heart of Darrow's theme: "Man is a creature of circumstance of birth and
environment and his work is laid out for him. What society can do is improve
the environment. We must treat crime scientifically. If we try human charity,
human love, we will find it cheaper to serve and be humane than to destroy." [37]

In a debate in New Orleans, his opponent declared that "the Bible is good
enough for me" and argued that capital punishment is the only safeguard for
womanhood and family life. If the "fear of God" were instilled in the hearts of
the criminal, crime would decrease. Darrow called his opponent's argument
"antiquated and absurd." He said that nine out of ten of the laws of Moses
demand death as punishment and dared society to "go ahead, enforce them." [38]

Testifying before the Judiciary Subcommittee of the House District
Committee in support of a bill to abolish capital punishment in Washington,
D.C., Clarence reasoned that if an execution by the state "keeps some other
man straight, as advocates of capital punishment claim it does, then hanging
should be public. Why not show hangings in the movies and then everyone
would be good? If there is anything at all in this theory that punishment stops
crime, then the punishment should be given all the publicity that ingenuity
can devise." [39]

12

In those years it was not only the death penalty that Darrow labored to
abolish. Prohibition—the Volstead Act—was another target of his scorn.

He had predicted as early as 1909, almost ten years before the Volstead Act
and its resultant bootlegging, that prohibition would not interfere with the
rich, because any man who had the price would be able to obtain liquor. "Of
course, the poor man would be shut off now and then; but why not? What
business is there for a poor man to drink; it is his business to work," he said. [40]

On December 23, 1924, Clarence returned to New York City to debate prohibition with the liberal pastor of the Community Church, his friend Dr. John Haynes Holmes. Again the debate took place in the packed auditorium of the Manhattan Opera House. What kind of a poem, Darrow asked Holmes, "do you think you can get out of a glass of ice water? Take out of this world the men who have drunk, down through the past, you take away all the poetry and literature, practically all the work of genius that the world has produced.

"If you could gradually kill off every body who had ever drunk, or wanted to, and leave the world to prohibitionists—my God, would any of us want to live in it."[41] Clarence, in his debates and lectures on prohibition, often allowed himself a flippancy which he banished from his writings on the subject.

"We always had whiskey in our home," Paul Darrow recalled. "Mother believed she needed it for medicinal purposes, though I never saw anyone drink it. But when prohibition came father was darned mad, and he took to drinking anytime anyone would offer him a drink. He never drank to excess, but he drank frequently. It was his way of protesting against prohibition"[42]

XXIII

Tennessee versus Scopes

1

THE name of the man responsible for the antievolution law in Tennessee is virtually forgotten—John Washington Butler, a Primitive Baptist by faith, a farmer and schoolteacher elected to the Tennessee state legislature in 1922. The previous year a visiting preacher told Butler about a young woman who had been exposed to the theory of evolution at a university and returned to her hometown a nonbeliever. To his surprise, Butler learned that evolution was being taught in Tennessee public schools despite the boast among Tennesseans that religious revivals were a part of the daily life of the citizenry. Butler worried about the effects the teaching of evolution would have upon his children and those of his neighbors.

An antievolution law introduced by a fellow legislator during Butler's freshman term had died in the rush for adjournment. Butler's own bill, introduced in his second term, was passed on March 21, 1925, by a Fundamentalist-dominated legislature, and Tennessee became one of the first states to prohibit the teaching of evolution in tax-supported schools: "Be it enacted—that it shall be unlawful for any teacher in any of the universities, normals, and all other public schools of the state which are supported in whole or in part by the public school funds of the state, to teach any theory that denies the story of the Divine Creation of man as taught in the Bible, and to teach instead that man has described from a lower order of animals."

William Jennings Bryan, former U.S. secretary of state and a three-time presidential candidate, predicted that more states would soon follow Tennessee's lead. At sixty-five an energetic, opinionated politician and statesman, Bryan was also a fervent evangelist who traveled throughout the South urging the enactment of antievolution laws. The American Civil Liberties Union, guardian of the First Amendment and of the separation of state and church, was apprehensive that Bryan's prediction would come true and offered to support a test case of the constitutionality of the Tennessee law.

Not long thereafter, George Rappelyea and a group of his friends were in the ice-cream parlor of Robinson's Drug Store in Dayton, Tennessee, a town where most of the inhabitants still professed belief in the literal interpretation of the Bible and in all the myths and miracles described in the Book. The Rappelyea group, opposed to the antievolution law, recognized an opportunity to test the law and at the same time to capture newspaper headlines for Dayton.

All agreed that John T. Scopes, the unmarried, twenty-four-year-old substitute biology teacher in the local high school who also opposed the law, would be the logical defendant. When Scopes joined the group, Rappelyea asked him whether biology could be taught without evolution. Scopes snapped, "Impossible."

The plan to test the constitutionality of the antievolution law was hatched when Scopes agreed to be the defendant. F. E. Robinson, proprietor of the drugstore and chairman of the Dayton school board, called the *Chattanooga News:* "We've just arrested a man for teaching evolution." A wire to the ACLU asking for assistance brought the Dayton insurgents an immediate reply: "We will co-operate Scopes case with financial help, legal advice and publicity."

William Jennings Bryan volunteered to represent the state. Because Darrow always held Bryan responsible for the passage of the antievolution law, he and Dudley Field Malone, a New York attorney, wired the local attorney representing Scopes: "We are certain you need no assistance in your defense of Professor Scopes, who is to be prosecuted for teaching evolution, but we have read the report that Mr. William Jennings Bryan has volunteered to aid the prosecution." With Bryan's real-estate dealings and lecture-circuit activity in mind, Darrow and Malone went on to say, "In view of the fact that scientists are so much interested in the pursuit of knowledge that they can not make the money that lecturers and Florida real estate agents command, in case you should need us, we are willing, without fees or expense, to help the defense of Professor Scopes in any way you may suggest or direct."[1]

Scopes, Rappelyea, and John Neal, a Dayton lawyer, traveled to New York City to meet with the ACLU executive committee. According to Roger

Baldwin, then the ACLU director, the committee was divided. "Should we enlist conservative constitutional lawyers and make it a top issue of separation of church and state, freedom of teaching the truth as laid down by the very textbook which Scopes taught, approved by the state? Or should we make it a contest between religion and the unreasonable restraint on science imposed by the laws? Should we attempt to get into the federal courts with an injunction against enforcing a state law violative of the First Amendment guarantee?"[2]

If a vote had been taken during the Executive Committee's first forty-five minutes of discussion, the Darrow-Malone offer would have been rejected. Most of the argument was directed against Darrow: too radical, a headline seeker, not skilled enough as a lawyer. Darrow would turn the trial into a circus, and the issues in the case would be lost. Felix Frankfurter, Harvard professor and future U.S. Supreme Court justice, was vehemently opposed to Darrow. He believed the attorney should be conservative and a traditionalist in religion, preferably a Protestant.

At one point an Executive Committee member suggested that the ACLU accept only Malone, but Malone objected: Darrow *and* Malone, or neither.

As chairman, Baldwin interrupted the discussion to suggest that the defendant be heard. Young Scopes stood up. Darrow or no Darrow, the circus was already in Dayton, Scopes said; it had been there ever since Bryan joined the prosecution. The town was already filled with "screwballs, con men, and characters. It's going to be a gouging, roughhouse battle," and, "If it's going to be a gutter fight, I'd rather have a good gutter fighter." He would welcome any additional lawyers the ACLU might suggest, but he insisted on Darrow and Malone. The committee acceded.[3]

In late June, Darrow visited Dayton to assess the situation. He came into town properly wearing his jacket, but the extreme heat and his usual disregard for clothing soon found the jacket slung over his arm. That weekend, Darrow, Scopes, and Neal were invited to be the guests of Edward J. Meeman, editor of the *Knoxville News*. En route to Knoxville, they learned that the county court was in session. Darrow was eager to see a Tennessee mountain court in operation, and the three took the side trip. The trial involved a rape charge against a "half-witted young fellow who wasn't sure what was going on"; the plaintiff was "a young woman who seemed to know too well what was going on." Scopes described her as "a sophisticated bitch" and the trial as a "travesty on decent court procedure; in the name of justice, a poor imbecile or moron was being railroaded to the pen."

Darrow watched the proceedings quietly, then announced to his friends, "I'm going to defend that boy." They remonstrated that the intervention of an outsider could only hurt the defendant, but Darrow persisted until Neal and Scopes each grabbed one of his arms and propelled him to the door.[4]

2

Dayton, the seat of Rhea County, lies thirty-eight miles northeast of Chattanooga at the junction of Routes U.S. 27 and Tennessee 30; the Georgia line is thirty-six miles away. In 1925, with a population of 1800, Dayton voted Democratic, although Rhea County voted Republican. While the church set the atmosphere and the standards, only half of the townspeople attended regularly. The iconoclastic "writing fellow," H. L. Mencken of the *Baltimore Evening Sun,* liked referring to the citizens of Dayton as "yokels."

The "yokels" prepared for the Scopes trial. Huge signs—"Sweetheart, Come to Jesus," "God is Love," "Read Your Bible"—greeted visitors. Hot dog and lemonade vendors welcomed them. For a trial which would remain known as "the Monkey Trial," monkey motifs decorated the town. Pins were sold bearing the inscription "Your Old Man's a Monkey." Not only newspapermen flocked there, spectators did, too—lawyers, Fundamentalists, atheists, poets, artists, Socialists, anarchists, IWWs, freethinkers. The *New York Post* reported, "Greenwich Village is on its way to Rhea County."[5]

When the Bryans arrived in Dayton, the Progressive Club honored them at a dinner in the Hotel Aqua. Short speeches paid tribute to the Great Commoner. In reply he harangued against evolution. "The contest between evolution and Christianity is a duel to the death," he said. "If evolution wins in Dayton, Christianity goes—not suddenly, of course, but gradually—for the two cannot stand together."[6]

The crowd that met Clarence and Ruby at the railroad station two days later was about the same in size and enthusiasm as the crowd that had greeted the Bryans. The defense headquarters was set up a mile outside of town in an old Southern home known to the community as "The Mansion"—but soon to be dubbed "The Monkey House."

The Progressive Club, determined to show its impartiality, honored Darrow at a dinner as it had Bryan. Darrow's response was much gentler than Bryan's. He was informally and whimsically autobiographical and made no reference to the issue that had brought him to Dayton. He said he came from an even smaller town, that he went to school for a while and then quit school and "started my education. I was one of the town loafers and got to like the tinsmith. He was reading law, but he didn't have time to read much because he was too busy working. So, since I was the town loafer I found time to read law to him while he worked.

"I started practicing law. For a while I was playing poker on the side and practicing law, and I almost starved. But then I started playing poker and practicing law on the side, and I made enough money to go to Chicago and open an office."[7] But Clarence, even at his folksiest, could not break through the townspeople's reserve and their distrust of his iconoclasm.

3

The trial of the State of Tennessee versus John T. Scopes opened Friday, July 10, 1925, in the Eighteenth Tennessee Circuit Court. John T. Raulston, who called himself "jest a reg'lar mountin'er jedge," presided. Once the leading lawyers of both the state and the defense came on the scene, Scopes became merely a prop in the legal battle. At the prosecution table with Bryan sat his son as well as Circuit Attorney General E. T. Stewart, father and son Ben and J. Gordon McKenzie, and local lawyers Sue and Herbert Hicks. Representing the defense were, besides Darrow, Arthur Garfield Hays and Dudley Field Malone, both of New York; W. O. Thompson, Darrow's law partner from Chicago; and John Randolph Neal, a former Tennessee judge and dean of the University of Tennessee Law School.

The jury included six Baptists, four Methodists, one Disciple of Christ, and one who "didn't go to church as often as he should." Scopes knew them all, "by sight if not by name."

Mencken wired his newspapers that "it was obvious after a few rounds that the jury would be unanimously hot for Genesis."[8]

A cool breeze offered some relief to the hot July morning when court convened on the following Monday.[9] By afternoon, as the sun beat into the courtroom, Darrow, Bryan, and the other attorneys sat in their shirt-sleeves. The jury was excused so the lawyers could argue the indictment and the constitutionality of the antievolution law. Defense Lawyer Neal claimed the indictment was too vague; Stewart, for the state, disagreed: "This indictment says that John Scopes on such and such a date, taught a theory denying the divinity of Christ and that man is descended from a lower order of animals. . . . What is there vague and indefinite and uncertain about that?" he asked.

Darrow cited cases to build his argument. The state, by its constitution, was committed to the doctrine of education. It was committed to teaching the truth. His words were sarcastic, biting. He admitted he found it difficult to put his mind "back into the 16th century," a condition encouraged by the indictment. Without question the statute was unconstitutional. "If today," he started to say, when Judge Raulston interrupted to call adjournment. Darrow insisted on five more minutes. "Proceed tomorrow," the judge cut him off. Darrow paid no attention. "I shall not talk long, your honor. I will tell you that—" Judge Raulston sat uneasy, the crowd squirmed as Darrow repeated, "If today you can take a thing like evolution and make it a crime to teach it in the public school, tomorrow you can make it a crime to teach it in the private schools, and the next year you can make it a crime to teach it to the hustings or in the church. At the next session you may ban books and newspapers. Soon you may set Catholic against Protestant and Protestant against Protestant, and try to foist your own religion upon the minds of men. If you can do one you can do the other. Ignorance and fanaticism is ever busy and needs feeding." He was off on another favored platform—freedom in education.

As he talked, energetically moving his arms for emphasis, his sleeve ripped. He was unaware of the tear, but Ruby noticed it immediately. After he closed his argument she rushed up to him. "Clarence, don't you think you had better put on another shirt?" His mind still on the argument he had just completed, Clarence smiled indulgently. "Well, Rube, don't you think it's too hot today for two shirts?" She shrugged helplessly.[10]

Mencken wired his paper that night: "The net effect of Clarence Darrow's great speech yesterday seems to be precisely the same as if he had bawled it up to a rainspout in the interior of Afghanistan. . . . You have but a dim notion of it who have only read it. It was not designed for reading, but for hearing. The clangtint of it was as important as the logic. It rose like a wind and ended like a flourish of bugles. The very judge on the bench, toward the end of it, began to look uneasy. But the morons in the audience, when it was over, simply hissed it."[11]

Judge Raulston opened each session with a prayer. On the third day of the trial, before the jury came into the courtroom, Darrow rose to object to the public prayer. Spectators sneered. Judge Raulston wasted no time. "Objection overruled." He banged his gavel. The jury filed in, and Dr. Stribling led the prayer: "We ask that thou will enlighten our minds and lead us to understand and know truth in all its every phase, we ask it in the name of our blessed Redeemer, Jesus Christ, amen."

4

On the afternoon of the fourth day, with the jury present, the state began to build its case: Howard Morgan, fourteen years old, had been in Scopes's general science class. How did Scopes teach his class? the prosecutor asked. "Well, sometimes he would ask us questions and then he would lecture to us on different subjects in the book." Scopes had said that "the earth was once a hot molten mass, too hot for plant or animal life to exist upon it; in the sea the earth cooled off; there was a little germ of one cell organism formed, and this organism kept evolving until it got to be a pretty good sized animal, and then came on to be a land animal, and it kept on evolving, and from this was man." The book the class read classified "man along with cats and dogs, cows, horses, monkeys, lions, and horses" as mammals.

In his cross-examination, Darrow's last question to Howard was whether learning about evolution had hurt him in any way.

"No, sir," he responded.

Harry Shelton, a seventeen-year-old high-school student, also studied biology with "Professor" Scopes, who taught evolution to his class. Again Darrow's cross-examination was brief.

Q. "Are you a church member?"

A. "Yes, sir."

Q. "Do you still belong?"

A. "Yes, sir."

Q. "You didn't leave the church when [Scopes] told you all forms of life began with a single cell?"

A. "No, sir."

Darrow: "That is all."

The state rested.

5

The defense had brought to Dayton prominent scientists and Bible scholars "to show first what evolution is, and secondly, that any interpretation of the Bible that intelligent men could possibly make is not in conflict with any story of creation, while the Bible, in many ways, is in conflict with every known science, and there isn't a human being on earth believes it literally." Judge Raulston ruled against the introduction of these expert witnesses, although he agreed to allow their affidavits to be entered for appeal purposes.

Bryan demanded the right to cross-examine the experts. The judge said that, if he changed his mind and allowed them on the stand, Bryan could cross-examine. An exchange between the judge and Darrow followed which culminated in Darrow's complaint that he did not understand why "every request of the state and every suggestion of the prosecution should meet with an endless waste of time, and a bare suggestion of anything that is perfectly competent on our part should be immediately over-ruled."

"I hope you do not mean to reflect upon the court," an indignant Judge Raulston replied.

"Well," said Darrow, "your honor has the right to hope."

Court: "I have the right to do something else, perhaps."

Darrow: "All right, all right."

Darrow had baited the judge in a moment of frustration and exasperation. To the surprise of the press which expected the attorney to be held in contempt, Raulston took no action.

Since the judge had denied the defense's plan to put experts on the witness stand, the reporters considered the trial to be over, and they began to desert

Dayton. Mencken filed his last dispatch on the sixth day of the trial: "All that remains of the great case of the State of Tennessee against the infidel Scopes is the formal business of bumping off the defendant. There may be some legal joustling on Monday and some gaudy oratory on Tuesday, but the main battle is over, with Genesis completely triumphant." [12]

But Mencken was wrong. He and others of the press corps who had left with him did not anticipate the newsbreaks that came Monday morning with lightning speed: Darrow cited for contempt, his bond set at $5000; Darrow's apology; Bryan called as a witness for the defense.

Judge Raulston accepted the apology but only after delivering a Fundamentalist sermon concluding that he and the people of Tennessee forgave Darrow and would "commend him to go back home and learn in his heart the words of the Man who said, 'If you thirst come unto Me and I will give thee Life.'" The people of Tennessee applauded. Because the blistering July heat did not let up, Judge Raulston moved sessions to the courtyard.

Defense lawyers objected to the sign Read Your Bible clearly visible to the jury. They requested its removal. Request granted.

6

"Hell is going to pop now," said Malone to his client as Associate Counsel Hays addressed the court. "The defense desires to call Mr. Bryan as a witness."

Attorneys for the state jumped to their feet, objecting. Stunned, Raulston waited for the bailiffs to bring the court to order. Would the judge rule against the defense again? Bryan, however, agreed to testify if the defense lawyers would also be put on the stand.

What followed is perhaps one of the most unique and dramatic scenes ever enacted in a courtroom. Darrow started out casual and conversational in his questioning, then became irritated, angry, disgusted. The shrug of his shoulder was more expressive than his words. Bryan, seated at a table, a glass of water near his elbow, fanned himself vigorously. He qualified some of his answers, determined to win the duel with the man who had supported him twice for the presidency of the United States and whom he now considered his foe.

There was no indication at the start that the two hours that followed would take the form of an intellectual inquisition, with the mood at times so tense that the protagonists would shake their fists at each other.

"You have given considerable study to the Bible, haven't you, Mr. Bryan?" asked Darrow.

Bryan: "Yes, sir, I have tried to."

Darrow: "Then you have made a general study of it?"

Bryan: "Yes, I have studied the Bible for about fifty years, or sometime more than that, but, of course, I have studied it more as I have become older than when I was but a boy."

Darrow: "Do you claim that everything in the Bible should be literally interpreted?"

Bryan: "I believe everything in the Bible should be accepted as it is given there; some of the Bible is given illustratively. For instance 'Ye are the salt of the earth.' I would not insist that man was actually salt, but it is used in the sense of salt as saving God's people."

Darrow: "But when you read that Jonah swallowed the whale—or that the whale swallowed Jonah—excuse me please—how do you literally interpret that?"

Bryan: "When I read that a big fish swallowed Jonah—it does not say whale."

Darrow: "Doesn't it? Are you sure?"

Bryan: "That is my recollection of it. A big fish, and I believe it, and I believe in a God who can make a whale and can make a man and make both do what He pleases.

Darrow: "Now, you say, the big fish swallowed Jonah, and he there remained how long—three days—and then he spewed him upon the land. You believe that the big fish was made to swallow Jonah?"

Bryan: "I am not prepared to say that; the Bible merely says it was done."

Darrow: "You don't know whether it was the ordinary run of fish, or made for that purpose?"

Bryan: "You may guess; you evolutionists guess."

Darrow: "You don't know whether that fish was made especially to swallow a man or not?"

Bryan: "The Bible doesn't say, so I am not prepared to say."

Darrow: "But do you believe He made them—that He made such a fish and that it was big enough to swallow Jonah?"

Bryan: "Yes, sir. Let me add: One miracle is just as easy to believe as another."

Darrow: "It is for you."

Bryan: "It is for me."

Darrow: "Just as hard?"

Bryan: "It is hard to believe for you, but not for me. A miracle is a thing performed beyond what man can perform. When you get beyond what man can do, you get within the realm of miracles; and it is just as easy to believe the miracle of Jonah as any other miracle in the Bible."

Darrow: "Perfectly easy to believe that Jonah swallowed the whale?"

Bryan: "If the Bible said so; the Bible doesn't make as extreme statements as you evolutionists do."

Darrow: "Do you consider the story of Jonah and the whale a miracle?"

Bryan: "I think it is."

Darrow: "Do you believe Joshua made the sun stand still?"

Bryan: "I believe what the Bible says. I suppose you mean that the earth stood still?"

Darrow: "I don't know. I am talking about the Bible now."

Bryan: "I accept the Bible absolutely."

Darrow: "Mr. Bryan, do you believe that the first woman was Eve?"

Bryan: "Yes."

Darrow: "Do you believe she was literally made out of Adam's rib?"

Bryan: "I do."

Darrow: "Did you ever discover where Cain got his wife?"

Bryan: "No, sir; I leave the agnostics to hunt for her."

Darrow read from the Bible. "'And the Lord God said unto the serpent, because thou hast done this, thou art cursed above all cattle, and above every beast of the field; upon thy belly shalt thou go and dust shalt thou eat all the days of thy life.'

"Do you think that is why the serpent is compelled to crawl upon its belly?"

Bryan: "I believe that."

Darrow: "Have you any idea how the snake went before that time?"

"No, sir."

"Do you know whether he walked on his tail or not?"

"No, sir. I have no way to know."

Laughter from those of the press corps who had not left with Mencken. They were joined by some of the spectators.

As Darrow continued with his questions, Bryan grew impatient. He turned to Judge Raulston. "Your honor, I think I can shorten this testimony. The only purpose Mr. Darrow has is to slur at the Bible, but I will answer his question. I will answer it all at once, and I have no objection in the world, I want the world to know that this man, who does not believe in a God, is trying to use a court in Tennessee—"

Darrow jumped to his feet. "I object to that."

Bryan's evangelistic momentum did not lose its fervor as he continued to shout, "—to slur at it, and while it would require time, I am willing to take it."

"I object," Darrow interrupted, "to your statement. I am examining you on your fool ideas that no intelligent Christian on earth believes." Darrow and Bryan glared at each other.

Judge Raulston had the last word: "Court is adjourned until nine o'clock tomorrow morning."

7

The experience with Bryan left Clarence with a feeling of great sadness as he recalled the man for whom he had campaigned for president in 1896 and 1900; his sense of humor, his statesmanship, the pleasing smile. "He did not grow old gracefully," Clarence thought.[13]

The next morning, Tuesday, July 21, court again opened with a prayer. The judge ordered Bryan's testimony expunged from the record.

Darrow asked that the jury be brought into the courtroom and that the court "instruct the jury to find the defendant guilty." Darrow told the jury that and the other defense lawyers had come to Dayton "to offer evidence in this case and the court has held under the law that the evidence we had is not admissible, so all we can do is to take an exception and carry it to a higher court to see whether the evidence is admissible or not." The jury listened. As expected, their verdict: "guilty."

Judge Raulston began to pass sentence on Scopes when one of the defense attorneys reminded him that he had not given the defendant an opportunity to state why punishment should not be imposed.

For the first time during the eight days of trial, Scopes spoke officially in the courtroom. "Your honor, I feel that I have been convicted of violating an unjust statute. I will continue in the future, as I have in the past, to oppose this law in any way I can. Any other action would be in violation of my ideal of academic freedom—that is, to teach the truth as guaranteed in our constitution, of personal and religious freedom. I think the fine is unjust."

Mencken's *Baltimore Evening Sun* furnished the $100 fine imposed, and Scopes was released.

8

Immediately after the trial Bryan left for Chattanooga. He spent some time revising a speech he had planned to deliver in the courtroom but did not. He went for a routine physical examination, met Mrs. Bryan, and both drove to Winchester where they lunched with the Raulstons. On Sunday the Bryans returned to Dayton where he ate a heavy meal and lay down for a nap before speaking at evening services. He died in his sleep.

Newspapers began to report that many of Bryan's friends believed his death was hastened by Darrow's onslaught during the trial.

Clarence heard of Bryan's death while relaxing in the Great Smoky Mountains. An Associated Press reporter asked him for a statement. "I am pained to hear of the death of William Jennings Bryan. I have known Mr.

Bryan since 1896, have supported him twice for the presidency. He was a man of strong convictions and always espoused his causes with ability and courage. I differed with him on many questions, but always respected his sincerity and devotion." [14]

One Darrow biographer wrote that, after delivering this eulogy, Clarence said to friends: "Now, wasn't that man a God damned fool?" [15] Another biographer said that in response to the suggestion that Bryan died of a broken heart, Darrow murmured, "Broken heart nothing. He died of a busted belly." [16]

Darrow would write to Mencken that he was sorry Mencken had missed "my examination of Bryan. I made up my mind to show the country what an ignoramus he was and I succeeded." [17]

Appeal of the Dayton decision came a year after the trial. Disharmony again prevailed at the American Civil Liberties Union, some of whose leaders opposed Darrow's appointment as the attorney to handle the appeal as they had when his name first came up as the attorney for Scopes. They believed that a more conservative lawyer would be more effective. There was, furthermore, a great deal of antagonism because he had not consulted with them during the trial. Clarence, however, resisted all pressures to resign. He and Arthur Garfield Hays went to Nashville where they argued the appeal before five judges of the Supreme Court of Tennessee. One of the judges died before the decision was rendered; the four others, however, were unanimous in reversing the lower court on a technicality: the jury, not the judge, should have fixed the fine.

"I'm still proud," said Morris Ernst, "that I rejected the advice of friends who asked me to request Darrow's withdrawal from the Scopes case. . . . Some members of the committee supporting and financing the Scopes defense had been persuaded that Darrow was associated with too many minority causes, too many unpopular clients. They had then rationalized their stand against Darrow by pleading—untruthfully—that he was good only before a jury. He was not an appellate-type lawyer, they said, hence he should not handle the Scopes appeal. . . . I watched my friends try to give the great old man his discharge. Happily, the words stuck in their throats." [18]

Dayton returned to its small-town obscurity. The circus left; there were no more hot dog stands and lemonade vendors; no more "foreign newspapermen." Life resumed its idyllic, casual pace.

9

The Scopes trial has captured the imagination of the public more than any other Darrow case, except perhaps the Leopold and Loeb case. Jerome Lawrence and Robert E. Lee's play *Inherit the Wind,* based on the Scopes trial, was first successfully produced in 1955 on Broadway. It toured the country for a long time and later was made into a movie. Scopes himself wrote a book about the trial, the court transcript was digested into book form, and there have been several other books written about the case.

It was not until April 1967 that the Tennessee House of Representatives and the State Senate repealed the antievolution law. A year later the constitutionality of the antievolution law of Arkansas was tested in the U.S. Supreme Court. In his majority decision, Justice Abe Fortas—also a Tennessean—said, "There can be no doubt that Arkansas has sought to prevent its teachers from discussing the theory of evolution because it is contrary to the belief of some that the Book of Genesis must be the exclusive source of doctrine as to the origin of man. . . . The law's effort was confined to an attempt to blot out a particular theory because of its supposed conflict with the biblical account, literally read. Plainly the law is contrary to the mandate of the First, and in violation of the Fourteenth, Amendment to the Constitution.[19]

XXIV

"I Speak for a Million Blacks"

1

CLARENCE was a popular attraction on the lecture platform. People were eager to hear the man who had saved the lives of Leopold and Loeb, who debated evolution and championed the freedom to teach. They liked what he said and how he said it, and he enjoyed speaking. At sixty-eight, the lines in his face were deeper and his movements slower, but he remained mentally quick and sure. When a judge censured him for attempting to prejudice a jury in his opening remarks, he asked the judge, "What do you think I'm here for? It's my business as a lawyer to prejudice the jury." [1]

2

When he returned from the Scopes trial, Clarence was determined not to take another case that required such intensive work. In addition to the novel he wanted to write and the book on evolution, there were books he wanted to read, books that had been set aside over the years. Books were everywhere in his large apartment—books on philosophy, on psychology, on religion, on sociology. These were the areas in which he wanted to concentrate.

Too long he had stood up against the majority, spoken for the unpopular. Now he wanted to abdicate that responsibility for peace and contemplation—to travel, to see Southern Italy, the French Riviera, to write.

He would write for a variety of national magazines, including H. L. Mencken's *American Mercury* in which he wrote on such subjects as prohibition, "How to Be a Salesman," and "The Eugenics Cult." He told Mencken after his first article had been accepted that if the magazine had a "who's who" he did not want to be listed as a "labor lawyer. You can say I am a lawyer. If necessary, that I am well known and live in Chicago. If more is needed—I have written several books. The last was *Crime: Its Causes and Treatment*. Also, that I have given many addresses on political, economic, and other subjects. Please don't say I am a criminal lawyer—although I am both. . . ." [2]

But in 1926 the attorney for whom "the cause was worthwhile" was easily lured back to the courtroom by a cause perhaps more important to him than any of his other trials—the People versus Sweet et al. In Detroit, Michigan, Dr. Ossian Sweet, a successful black physician, and ten other blacks were charged with the murder of a white man, the outgrowth of mob harassment when the doctor and his family moved into a white neighborhood. Although the case missed the national attention that many of his others received, Clarence considered it the most important case in which he had ever participated. [3]

3

Darrow came to the Sweet case naturally. His interest in the black man stemmed from his early childhood. Many times when he spoke in black churches, he talked about his family's support of the Underground Railroad and about his own desire to help blacks: "Ever since I can remember I have been possessed of the feeling of injustice that has been visited upon the Negro race—assuming you are a race. All races and colors are mixed with us and why you are classified is because you are persons of chance. I have always thought the same ever since I have had any intellect or feeling on the subject." [4]

He defended blacks in court. He defended them in robbery and rape and murder trials. In the Sweet case, though the charge was murder, he saw it differently: he saw it simply as the inherent right of a man to defend his home. "If the Negro is a man, then all people, high and low alike, should demand for him all the privileges and rights of every other citizen; should judge him for what he is, and not on the color of his skin," Darrow had written in August 1908 during the race riots in Springfield, Illinois. [5]

To Clarence, no man was either black or white, only freckled; and each had the right to freedom. In the Sweet case Darrow exposed for the first time in a courtroom the virulence of racial segregation. The underlying question: Do blacks have a right to live in the urban North in a desegregated neighborhood? The Detroit events in 1925 would be the dress rehearsal for the civil rights movement of the 1960s.

Like other Northern cities, Detroit saw a large migration of blacks from the South. Its black population had exploded since 1910 from 6000 to approximately 70,000, with most of the increase taking place during World War I when the auto industry enjoyed record production. Both the poorer Southern whites and the blacks had been lured by jobs in the automobile plants. While there was room for blacks in the factories, no provision had been made for expanded housing, with the result that, as the black ghetto swelled, its families spilled over into white neighborhoods. With racial prejudices deeply ingrained in the whites, the Ku Klux Klan found a receptive audience and much encouragement to organize under the guise of various improvement associations and neighborhood clubs.

4

Dr. Sweet was caught in Detroit's postwar housing shortage. In the summer of 1924, he and his wife Gladys and their baby returned from Europe where he had studied gynecology and pediatrics in Vienna, and radiology under Madame Curie in France. The thirty-year-old doctor reestablished his practice while they lived with Gladys Sweet's well-to-do parents in a white neighborhood. The following spring, with Ossian Sweet's practice flourishing, they began looking for a house. A white real-estate agent showed them one for sale but advised them to purchase it in the name of a white friend in order to avoid trouble. Ossian indignantly refused. He subsequently negotiated for a two-story bungalow at 2905 Garland Avenue in a lower-middle-class white neighborhood in Detroit. Since it was owned by a white woman married to a black, he did not expect his move to arouse white hostility. He was unaware, however, that the community did not know of the mixed marriage.

Dr. Sweet was fully aware of the racial tensions plaguing the city; he knew of other blacks who had moved into white areas and been harassed until they retreated to the ghetto. When he moved into his house on September 8, 1925, Ossian brought a supply of guns and ammunition along with his furniture. The baby had been left with her grandmother. Helping them move were the doctor's two brothers—Otis, a dentist, and Henry, a law student—and seven friends. They were in the house when the trouble started.

The first night a crowd gathered in front of the house, but remained relatively peaceful. The second night the crowd was larger and more belligerent. Taunting shouts: "Niggers!" "Niggers!" "Get the damn niggers."

A staccatolike shower of stones and rocks hit the house, breaking a few windows. Inside there was pandemonium. In the midst of the bedlam, shots were fired from several windows on the second floor, killing Leon Breiner, a white man standing across the street, and wounding another. Police immediately arrested the eleven blacks in the house and charged them with first-degree murder.

The black community held racial discrimination and racist policies responsible. The National Association for the Advancement of Colored People viewed the attack on the house as an attempt at segregation by mob violence. They believed Dr. Sweet had exerted his fundamental rights of "self-defense" and of "ownership and occupancy of residential property by Negroes." They sent Walter White, the association's assistant secretary, to Detroit to assess the situation and obtain proper legal defense, which in this case particularly meant an attorney who had a reputation for undertaking what he considered a just cause rather than an attorney notorious for getting the guilty freed. They believed, too, that since the case had national implications, it was essential that a white attorney of eminent reputation head the defense.

White's efforts to find such an attorney in Detroit met with no success. The lawyers he contacted did not want to become embroiled in a racial case that had already strained relations in their city and caused much bitterness.

The NAACP then wired Darrow in Chicago asking him to head the Sweet defense. Darrow accepted, providing it was satisfactory to the defendants and to the black lawyers already retained by some of the defendants.

"Although Darrow was at that time at the very peak of his considerable fame as a lawyer and a champion of human liberty," recalled Walter White, NAACP national secretary, "it was characteristically modest of him to believe that there might possibly be some objection to his appearing as chief counsel for the defense."[6]

The defendants and their lawyers wholeheartedly approved the choice of Darrow. He met with White to discuss the case. "Did the defendants shoot into that mob?" he asked.

"I am not sure." White hesitated, afraid that Darrow might reconsider and drop out of the case if he admitted that the defendants, too, had fired shots.

Darrow shook his head in annoyance. "Don't try to hedge. I know you were not there. But do you *believe* the defendants fired?"

A direct answer could not be avoided. "I believe they did fire." White started to explain, to justify the act, when Clarence interrupted, "Then I'll take the case. If they had not had the courage to shoot back in defense of their own lives, I wouldn't think they were worth defending."[7]

Seen in the context of Darrow the pacifist, the believer in nonresistance, these remarks appear contradictory. Darrow, however, was also the defender of Big Bill Haywood who proclaimed class war in labor's struggle for a better life, the defender of the McNamaras who believed in dynamite as a means to soften capital in order to effect labor unionization, the protagonist for World War I because of German atrocities, the orator lauding John Brown's militant—and military—espousal of the abolitionist cause. Darrow, who longed for peace and brotherhood, nevertheless understood the basic hungers that drove men to hurt one another. He could defend Haywood and McNamara for the sake of labor; he could defend U.S. entry into World War I as a means to halt Prussianism; he could say of John Brown: "Of all the foolish questions asked by idle tongues, the most childish is to ask if a great work should not have been done some other way."[8]

On his return to Chicago from New York after accepting the defense, Darrow stopped off in Detroit to learn more about the case. Except for Gladys Sweet who had been admitted to bail, his clients were in a dingy city jail. Clarence's appearance in the jail cheered the prisoners, but they remained "not hopeful."

In his initial interviews with them, Clarence warned against evasive answers; he wanted the truth, the whole truth. Their stories conflicted. One defendant maintained he had been taking a bath during the excitement. Another took pride in what had happened: at long last those whites had learned a lesson; now they knew Negroes would fight back. Each of the defendants maintained ignorance of the others' activities during the time of the shooting. Slowly, building their confidence as he spoke, Darrow convinced his clients that in the truth "lay the only hope of their defense."[9]

5

In the late fall of 1925, in an atmosphere tense with racial antagonisms, the rigors of premayoral election campaigning, and KKK influence, the Sweet case came to trial in the Recorders' Court, City of Detroit. Thirty-five-year-old Judge Frank Murphy, elected two years earlier on a nonpartisan ticket, presided. Murphy later became a governor of Michigan, and then an associate justice of the U.S. Supreme Court.

According to the state, the defendants "premeditatedly, and with malice of forethought" banded together and armed themselves and conspired that one or more of them would kill if there was "threatened or actual trespass" of the Sweet house, or any threat to anyone in the house.

The defense, on the other hand, denied such a conspiracy. It concentrated on the "attitude of mind" of the defendants at the time of the shooting: Did they think they were in danger? Were they frightened? "They had become heroes in the eyes of their race. Not all of them cared to admit they had been scared."[10]

With Darrow and Hays for the defense were three black Detroit lawyers: Cecil O. Rowlette, Charles H. Mahoney, Julian W. Perry, and one white attorney, Walter M. Nelson. Herbert J. Friedman joined the team from Chicago. At the prosecutor's table sat Robert M. Toms, state's attorney, with assistants Lester S. Moll and Edward J. Kennedy.

The antiblack hysteria in Detroit made jury selection difficult. Prejudice was pervasive among the talesmen, yet few admitted that bias would affect their judgment to render an impartial verdict in a murder case involving black defendants. About 150 men and women were interviewed before a jury of twelve white men was selected.

The prosecution based its case on the contentions that the "few" people who were around the Sweet house on the night of the killing were there out of "curiosity," and that on both September 8 when the Sweets moved in and on September 9 when the trouble took place police were there to protect the Sweets and their property.

Darrow slouched in his seat working a crossword puzzle as the prosecutor examined his witnesses. At times he gazed out of the window or affected catnaps, appearing as if his mind was on other affairs, but his incisive questioning of witnesses indicated otherwise. He was determined to dignify his clients before the all-white jury, and hence his dress in Detroit was more formal than it had been in Dayton; his hair was neatly brushed. No hint of the famous galluses appeared behind the unaccustomed well-pressed jacket.[11]

The trial proceeded.[12] Witnesses for the state who lived in the Sweet neighborhood admitted that the Water Works Improvement Association was formed when they learned Negroes intended to move into the home on Garland and Charlevoix.

Shocked by the righteous attitudes of the association members, Darrow read into the record the "proposed objects of the Association," all seemingly innocuous until point f: "Co-operating in the enforcement of the present property restrictions and ordinances; and organizing and supporting other restrictions which may be deemed necessary to conserve this particular locality that it remain a desirable community and property owners may continue to dwell in peace, security and harmony."

Under Darrow's cross-examination a state's witness testified he had joined the association as a property owner "to keep the neighborhood in the same high standard as it always has been," and that meant keeping the blacks out.

Mrs. Florence Ware,[13] whose husband "doesn't mingle" but "is a great reader," walked to the Sweet house out of "curiosity" to see "the crowd of people—police on our corners."

Darrow: "Now, you first said 'crowd of people,' and you changed."
Witness: "I meant policemen."
Darrow: "You didn't mean people?"
Witness: "No, sir."

William Goad, property owner,[14] hesitated. "There didn't seem to be anything happening, very much. Everybody seemed to be jolly; mostly women and children there; I suppose they were there the same as I was, out of curiosity."

"What kind of curiosity did you have to take you up there?"

"It is a curiosity to see a policeman around that neighborhood."

"You are a member of that Association?"

"Yes, sir."

"And you joined it with the idea that it might help keep colored people out of the district, didn't you?"

"I joined it for the good of the neighborhood."

"Well, now, do you object to answering my question? Did you join it—"

"Well, I suppose that was primary, one of the reasons."

As the trial progressed, Dr. Sweet confessed to a friend that he "wouldn't have taken that house as a gift" had he anticipated such trouble. "But after I bought it, I felt that I could never again respect myself if I allowed a group of hoodlums to keep me out of it." [15]

Eber A. Draper, tool salesman. [16] "Do you belong to the Water Works Improvement Association?"

"Yes, sir."

"When did you join?"

"I don't know. When it first started."

"When did it start?"

"I don't know."

"Well, now, don't you think you could tell us if you tried?"

"No, I don't think I could."

"Well, about when did you join it?"

"It must have been back in the middle of the summer."

"The middle of last summer?"

"Something like that."

"When did you hear Dr. Sweet was going to move into that neighborhood?"

"That was a long time ago too."

"You joined the club at the time you heard it, didn't you?"

"I think it was afterwards."

"Why, you know, don't you?"

"No."

"You don't know whether you joined the club at the time you heard it or not?"

"No."

"Well, you think it was after you heard it that you joined the club?"

"I think it was."

"Did that have anything to do with your joining the club?"

"It possibly did."

"Oh, tell us now, don't you know? Is there any reason why you should not tell us if you know?"

"No."

"Well, did it?"

"Yes."

"And you joined the club so as to do what you could do—I am not saying you did right or wrong—but to do what you could do to keeping that a white district?"

Draper said, "Yes."

Slowly the defense, through cross-examination, built its case. It exposed the purpose of the association: to keep blacks out of the neighborhood; and it showed that the neighborhood around the house the night of the killing was neither peaceful nor quiet.

George Suppus, thirteen, took the stand.[17] "Do you know about when it was that you heard that these colored people were coming into the neighborhood?" Darrow asked him.

"Oh, just about a month before they moved in."

"You heard it from the people around there?"

"I heard it from a few of the boys over there."

Urlic Arthur, thirteen, offered testimony that gave the defense the opening it sought.[18] "Did you see anybody throw stones?"

"Well, there was four or five kids between the houses, they were throwing stones."

"Where were they throwing them?"

"They were throwing them at the house where the colored people moved in."

Seventeen-year-old Dwight Hubbard[19] added another break.

Darrow: "When you first started to answer the question as to what you saw, you started to say a great crowd there, didn't you?"

Witness: "Yes, sir."

Darrow: "Then you modified to say a large crowd, didn't you?"

Witness: "Yes, sir."

Darrow: "Then you said a few people after that?"

Witness: "Yes, sir."

Darrow: "Do you know how you happened to change your mind so quick?"

Witness: "No, sir."

Darrow: "Any officers talk with you about it?"

Witness: "No, sir."

Darrow: "What?"

Witness: "Lieutenant Johnson, if you consider him an officer."

Darrow: "When is the last time he talked with you about it?"

Witness: "I think it was yesterday morning."

Darrow: "When you started to answer the question, you forgot to say a few people, instead of a great many?"

Witness: "Yes, sir."

The courtroom audience roared with laughter.

The state presented about seventy witnesses, all of whom testified that only a few people were around the Sweet house. Darrow, through cross-examination, created a contrary scene. Fear pervaded the neighborhood—fear of the unknown, fear that the value of property would fall, fear that the wrong people would move in—and the wrong people were black.

Hays opened for the defense with a statement to the jury that became the theme of the defense witnesses: "The defense in this case faces and admits facts which are sometimes subject to equivocation and avoidance. We are not ashamed of our clients and we shall not apologize for them. We are American citizens; you men of the jury are American citizens; they are American citizens. Each juryman said that he conceded equal rights to all Americans. On the basis of the legal rights of the defendants we make our defense. We say this with the full realization of the sacredness of human life and having quite as much sympathy for the bereaved family of the deceased as has the prosecution."[20]

Hays reminded the jury that they had heard only one side—the white side outside the house. They would learn now how the eleven blacks inside, with their history of racial brutality and bigotry, viewed the events. "In other words, we shall show not only what happened in the house, but we shall attempt a far more difficult task—that of reproducing in the cool atmosphere of the courtroom, a state of mind—the state of mind of these defendants, worried, distrustful, tortured and apparently trapped—a state of mind induced by what has happened to others of their race not only in the South where their ancestors were slaves, but even in the North in the States which once fought for their freedom."[21]

The contrast between the witnesses for each side was sharp. Unlike those for the state, most who testified for the defense were black, college graduates and professionals, cultured and refined.

Phillip A. Adler, a newspaperman, was one of the few whites to appear for the defendants. He had been driving south on St. Clair Avenue. "As I was about to turn into Charlevoix I saw a considerable mob near the school house."

The prosecutor objected to "considerable mob." Darrow asked Adler to be more specific.

"Well, I first noticed it as I slowed down. My estimate as I drove up Charlevoix was that there were between 400 and 500 persons. The street was somewhat congested with cars. I noticed a lot of people around Garland and Charlevoix and I wanted to drive out on Garland, but the traffic officer made me go straight ahead."

Parking his car nearby, he walked toward the crowd. He heard a man threaten to remove the Sweets forcibly. Shouts of "There goes a nigger!" "Catch him!" "Stop him!" "Lynch him!" rent the air every time the mob caught sight of a Negro, testified Adler.[22]

Shortly before noon on Thursday, November 18, Hays called Dr. Ossian Sweet to the witness stand. Guided by Hays, he related his background. He had been born in Orlando, Florida, one of six children, his father a minister and "a poor farmer." At the age of fourteen he had received a scholarship from Wilberforce University in Wilberforce, Ohio, only to learn, when he got there, that there was only $10 left in the fund. He worked his way through college as a janitor and later as a part-time chemistry instructor. During the summers he worked in Detroit as a bellhop on the D & A boats. He studied medicine at Howard University, in Washington, D.C., waiting tables at night. In 1921 he passed the Michigan state medical examinations and opened his office in the rear of a drugstore at 1405 St. Aubin Avenue. A year later he married.

Dr. Sweet related the events which had led to the shooting. "When my wife and I arrived home on the afternoon of September 9, my wife received a telephone call. It was from a girl acquaintance who had been at our house all of the night before and who said she had heard a conversation on a streetcar and that we ought to know about it. She told of a white woman who told the motorman of the streetcar that the crowd around my house the night before was there because a colored family had moved in. She said we wouldn't be there after that night." [23]

The doctor said he then asked Joe Mack, who was in the house with him, to get some of their friends. When the friends came in, Sweet "showed them through the house. While doing so we came to the closet where the guns were. I told them the guns were there as a matter of protection.

"After that we played cards. I played some of the time.

"Something hit the house. Some one went to the window and looked out. Then I remember this remark—'The people, the people—we've got to get out of here; something's going to happen pretty soon.'

"I ran out to the kitchen to where my wife was. Everybody left what they were doing and some of the fellows went upstairs. I went to see if the side door was locked. It was unlocked. I opened it. I could see people but they couldn't see me. Then I heard someone say 'Go to the front and raise hell, I'm going to the back.'"

Hays asked, "Did you have a firearm in your hands then?"

"No, I didn't."

"What then?"

"I went to the closet and got a gun. I lay across the bed. Stones kept coming against the house. The intervals became shorter. After fifteen to twenty minutes a stone crashed through the glass and some of it hit me. I made a dozen trips up and down the stairs. It was a general uproar.

"Then I heard someone say 'Someone is coming. Don't open the door.' I went to the door myself. It was my brother, Otis, and William Davis. I heard someone in the mob say 'They're niggers, get them.'

"Just as they ran in the mob gave a surge 10 or 15 feet forward. It looked like a human sea. Davis said 'What shall we do? What shall we do? I . . .' The stones were getting thicker and coming faster.

"Then I heard glass breaking upstairs.

"Almost immediately I heard one shot. Then there were eight or ten more in rapid succession. By this time it seemed to me stones were hitting the house on all sides, mostly the roof.

"Somebody knocked at the door. It was Inspector Norton Schuknecht. 'What in hell are you shooting at?' he asked. I said 'They are destroying my home and my life is in imminent danger.' Then I took him up to the room where the window was broken. He dropped his head and said 'I didn't know they were throwing stones and breaking your house. I will drive them away and there will be no more stones thrown.'

"Shortly after that more police officers came. They raised the blinds, turned on the lights and handcuffed us in clear view of the mob."

"State your frame of mind at the time of the shooting," Hays said.

The question unleashed an outpouring of memories from Dr. Sweet. He recounted the tragic story of blacks in the United States, the lynchings, burnings, the assaults on black women, the horrors of race riots, the frenzied mob. "When I opened the door and saw that mob, I realized in a way that I was facing that same mob that had hounded my people through its entire history. I realized my back was against the wall and I was filled with a peculiar type of fear—the fear of one who knows the history of my race."

Prosecutor Toms was merciless in his cross-examination. He asked several times whether Sweet had felt threatened, to which the witness answered that he did not understand what he meant by "threatened."

"That's a good Anglo-Saxon word. You ought to know what it means," Toms taunted.

Darrow interjected, "The witness isn't Anglo-Saxon."

6

In each of his cases, Darrow represented his clients as universal symbols. In the Kidd case: "I do not appeal for him. That cause is too narrow for me." [24] *In the Communist trial in Chicago: "My clients are my last concern; I ask you to do your part in the great cause of human freedom, for which men have ever fought and died." In Leopold and Loeb: "I am pleading for the future. I am pleading for a time when hatred and cruelty will not control the hearts of man."* [25]

And now in Sweet:[26] "To me this case is a cross section of human history. This case also involves the future and the hope of some of us that the future shall be better than the past."

Clarence began quietly: "It is not an easy matter to talk or to listen to a case of this sort. It has taken much of your time, but the end is in view. You know how important it is. In the first place 11 people are on trial for something that might imprison them for life.

"Back of it is the everlasting problem of color and race. If I thought you had an opinion against their race, I would not worry.

"You can change a man's opinion but not his prejudices. If it had been a white man defending his home from a member of a negro mob, no one would have been arrested nor put on trial."

Darrow paused. He hooked his thumbs in the armholes of his vest, turned sideways to the jury as he told them, "These witnesses that the state has put on here are liars and I will show you why. They are owners of small homes and in ordinary things of life are honest and decent, but in a case like this, surrounded by such circumstances, they deliberately lied.

"Every police officer that took this stand is guilty of murder and to shield themselves they deliberately perjured themselves when they testified here."

With sarcasm and irony he exposed the charter of the Water Works Improvement Association: it was nothing but a mob organized for the sole purpose of driving the Sweets from their home in violation of the law. From the defense table he picked up a copy of the association's charter and read a bylaw that called for the enforcement of traffic laws, particularly for the safety of the children. "To protect the children if they are white children," he interjected.

He read another clause that promised that each member would cooperate with the police to maintain law and order. "And they did co-operate, gentlemen," said Darrow; "never did any criminal conspirators co-operate better with the police than they did."

"Did I say the state's witnesses lied. I repeat, they did. Even the little children, thought they were taught to lie. Men and women and children had been schooled to lie on this witness stand. Ordinarily those persons are honest. In another case under different circumstances they would tell the truth. I don't place the blame on them. I can understand why they did not want Dr. Sweet. But they are not to blame for their prejudices.

"I want to close this just as I began. I am anxious only about one thing, and that is your prejudices," said Darrow.

"I speak for a race which will go on and on to heights never reached before. I speak for a million blacks who have some hope and faith remaining in the institutions of this land. I speak to you in behalf of those whose ancestors were brought here in chains. I speak in behalf of the faces, those black faces, which have haunted this courtroom since this trial began. I ask you in behalf of yourselves, our race, to see that no harm comes to them. I ask you in the name of the future to do justice in this case."

Darrow sat down. A palpable silence seemed to hang over the courtroom. He wiped the tears from his eyes.

7

Only five minutes intervened between the time Clarence completed his summation and Toms began his closing plea.[27] "I shall not attempt in any way to settle the race problem," Toms said. Nor did he believe the outcome of this trial would do so. He rejected the defense's contention that sociological problems were an integral part of the trial, and vehemently objected to their turning the trial into a sociological and psychological proceeding.

The case had taught him, he admitted, that there was no solution to prejudice. "I do not think there is any panacea that you can apply to this situation. Maybe it is to be done by a process of mutual forbearance. Maybe it is to be done some other way. I do not know. Nobody else knows. I do not know whether anybody ever will know how this thing is to be settled.

"I am willing to grant Sweet the right to live where he chooses, but why was not Breiner equally entitled to a right to merely live. Breiner has been allowed to lapse into an insignificant figure here, while the defense has taken us on a tour of 'Darkest Africa' and the American cities where they say riots occurred that bred fear in Sweet.

"I concede the right under the law of any man, black or white, to live where he likes or wherever he can afford to live, but we all have many civil rights which we voluntarily waive in the name of public peace, comfort and security, and because we are ashamed to insist upon them.

"I have a right to be a domineering, arrogant martinet to my subordinates; I have a right to remain seated in a street car while an elderly woman or a mother carrying a child stands; I have a right to keep my hat on in church or in the theater; I have a right to play the piano or honk my automobile horn when a woman next door is tossing on a sick bed—all these and many more civil rights which I may insist upon. But I would be ashamed to insist upon them, and so would you. But there is one civil right, more precious than all the others, which no man surrenders, except at the command of his God or his country, and that is the right to live."

Toms, who had the last word, launched into an attack on Darrow's plea against prejudices: "He himself is victim of one of the worst possible prejudices, that police officers and prosecutors are liars and twisters of facts. He has made liars out of the police wherever he has tried cases." Toms concluded, "It is not so important to us that Dr. Sweet was once an excellent waiter or that he could apparently cure lockjaw. This is all a smoke-screen, gentlemen, thrown out to hide the real question to be decided.

"And that is: Who is responsible for the killing of Leon Breiner?

"Back of all your sophistry and transparent political philosophy, gentlemen of the defense, back of all your prating of civil rights, back of your psychology and theory of race hatred, lies the stark dead body of Leon Breiner with a bullet hole in his back."

Toms looked at Clarence. "All your specious arguments, Mr. Darrow, all your artful ingenuity born of many years' experience—all of your social theories, Mr. Hays, all your cleverly conceived psychology, can never dethrone justice in this case. Leon Breiner, peaceably chatting with his neighbor at his doorstep, enjoying his God-given and inalienable right to live, is shot through the back from ambush. And you can't make anything out of those facts, gentlemen of the defense, but cold-blooded murder."

Judge Murphy delivered his instructions the day before Thanksgiving. After dismissing the conspiracy charge, he listed the four verdicts from which the jury could choose: guilty of murder in the first degree, guilty of murder in the second degree, guilty of manslaughter, and not guilty.

The jury retired. Angry shouts erupted from the jury room from time to time. One outcry was clearly distinguishable in the adjoining courtroom: "I'm younger than any of you fellows and I'll sit here forever before I condemn those niggers."[28]

Rumors continued to fly throughout the court building: 11 to 1 for acquittal; 10 to 2 for a murder conviction. On the third day the jury reported it could not reach a verdict. Judge Murphy declared a mistrial. The final count behind the locked door of the jury room had been 7 to 5 for conviction on manslaughter.

Darrow immediately petitioned that the defendants be released on bail, a request Judge Murphy quickly granted.

8

The second trial opened five months later, in April 1926. The scene almost repeated itself as Toms and Moll again sat at the state's table and Judge Murphy presided. In place of Hays, who had a previous commitment, the defense employed Thomas Chawke, a prominent black attorney whom Dr. Sweet had wanted before the involvement of the NAACP. Chawke joined Darrow and Julian Perry, who had also been in the earlier trial.

Chawke had asked for $10,000 for his role in the defense, but settled for $7500. The NAACP feared Darrow would be unhappy if Chawke received more than he did. Disturbed that they felt this way, Darrow wrote to the association,[29] "You need not worry any on the basis that he gets more than I do. I am interested in the matter. He probably has no such feeling as I have, but I am sure that he would be very valuable in the case."

At Chawke's suggestion, it was decided to request that each defendant be tried separately.[30] For the first defendant the state selected the doctor's brother Henry, who in the confusion of the arrest had admitted firing the shot.

It took five and a half days for the selection of the jury, which was then immediately sequestered. Chawke realized during the questioning of the talesmen that Darrow would not be an easy man to work with. The complaints of Masters and Rogers, and of Richardson in the Haywood trial, had had some basis in fact. Clarence refused to take a secondary role. With Chawke now prominently in the case, the restless Darrow constantly interrupted Chawke's questioning of prospective jurors to offer suggestions.[31]

In many ways it seemed that the second trial might be easier: much of the hatred had spent itself and left only a simmering of the violent prejudice which had marked the first trial. The election in which race had been an issue was over, the influence of the Klan had receded, and it seemed that race relations had calmed down, for the time being at least.

Toms's opening statement[32] was similar to what he had said in the first trial: "The defendants in the house were there for the purpose of shooting whether it became necessary or not. I will state frankly that I am not able to show who fired the shots. There is no way to find out. Either Henry Sweet did or he aided and abetted the man who did. We will show that Henry Sweet fired shots in the general direction of where Leon Breiner stood. Regardless of whether his shot killed Breiner, his act was the act of 10 other persons in that house and their act was his."

Darrow, as in the first trial, laid the responsibility for Breiner's death on the Water Works Improvement Association. This time, however, the defense drew from Alfred H. Andrews, a state's witness the second time around, that "action" had been advocated at the association meeting held soon after the Sweets moved in. They had been urged on by the representative of another neighborhood improvement association who had come to the meeting to give them a "pep talk." Darrow smiled. Unwittingly he had been given a new line of attack.

Referring to the "pep talk" given at the meeting, Darrow asked Andrews, "Did he tell you about any race riot trouble they had in his neighborhood?"

"Yes, he told us about a Negro named Dr. Turner who had bought a house on Spokane Avenue."

Darrow: "Did he say his organization made Turner leave?"

Andrews: "Yes. He said his organization wouldn't have Negroes in their neighborhood and that they would cooperate with us in keeping them out of ours."

"Did the crowd applaud him?"

"Yes."

"Did you applaud?"

"Yes."

"You feel that way now?"[33]

"Yes, I haven't changed."

"Did the speaker talk of legal means?"

Andrews: "No, he was a radical. I myself do not believe in violence."

"Did anybody in that audience of five hundred or more people protest against the speaker's advocacy of violence?"

"I don't know."[34]

Toms objected. Sustained. Darrow relaxed: "That's all."

In cross-examination Patrolman Schaldenbrand, an officer on duty that night, made the sweeping statement that policemen are not supposed to think. Darrow had been questioning him about the size of the crowd in the vicinity of the Sweet home when he began, "I didn't think—"

Darrow interrupted: "What do you mean, you didn't think? Don't policemen think?"

"No, a policeman is not supposed to think," the confused Schaldenbrand replied.

The state concluded its case after the testimony of its sixty-four witnesses—all of them white.

9

On Wednesday, May 5, the defense began to call its witnesses, ten of them character witnesses for Henry. Darrow and Chawke did not believe it was necessary to put Henry on the stand. Again Dr. Sweet was the main witness for the defense; again, through the doctor's testimony, Darrow introduced into the court record the history of various race riots. He tried to prove that Ossian Sweet and the friends who were in the house with him on the night of the killing were victims of psychological fear. According to the *Detroit Free Press*, Darrow used Sweet as "a rosetta stone with which to unlock the hereditary hieroglyphics of the Negro racial mind." He wanted the jury to feel Henry Sweet's fear, his remembrance of other blacks victimized by mobs, as he watched the frenzied mob throwing stones and rocks at the house.

Moll, in a three-hour summary[35] for the state, called Dr. Sweet a "quasi-intelligent" shifting and evasive witness "who is passing as a second Lincoln. The defense would have you believe that there was a menacing mob outside the house and that an attack was made. I challenge anyone to find, anywhere in the record of this trial, any evidence that would show the home of Dr. Sweet was damaged beyond the smashing of one small window. For the breaking of a window are we to trade the life of Leon Breiner?" he asked.

Chawke opened for the defense.[36] He regretted that he had to say "the officers of the law were in sympathy with the crowd and that is clearly demonstrated by the evidence. If the police officers stationed around the home had done their duty, and had dispersed that mob before there was any hostile move against the Sweet home, Leon Breiner would not be dead today."

Darrow followed Chawke. "The prosecutor," said Darrow,[37] "insists that this isn't a race question, that this is a murder case and that race and color have nothing to do with it.

"I insist that there is nothing but prejudice in this case," he said emphatically; "that if it was reversed and eleven white men had shot and killed a black while protecting their home and their lives against a mob of blacks, nobody would have dreamed of having them indicted. I know what I am talking about, and so do you. They would have been given medals instead.

"Here were eleven colored men," Darrow continued, "penned up in the house. Put yourselves in their place. Make yourselves colored for a little while. It won't hurt, you can wash it off. They can't, but you can; just make yourself black for a little while; long enough, gentlemen, to judge them, and before any of you would want to be judged, you would want your juror to put himself in your place. That is all I ask in this case, gentlemen. They were black, and they knew the history of the black."

As Darrow talked, the vision of slave ships with human cargo moving from Africa to America was brought before the eyes of the jury. "Gentlemen, I feel deeply on this subject; I cannot help it. Let us take a little glance at the history of the Negro race. It only needs a minute. It seems to me that the story would melt hearts of stone. I was born in America. I could have left it if I wanted to go away. Some other men, reading about this land of freedom that we brag about on the Fourth of July, came voluntarily to America. These men, the defendants, are here because they could not help it. Their ancestors were captured in the jungles and on the plains of Africa, captured as you capture wild beasts, torn from their homes and their kindred; loaded into slave ships, packed like sardines in a box, half of them dying on the ocean passage; some jumping into the sea in their frenzy, when they had a chance to choose death in place of slavery. They were captured and brought here. They could not help it. They were bought and sold as slaves, to work without pay, because they were black. They were subjected to all of this for generations, until finally they were given their liberty, so far as the law goes—and that is only a little way, because, after all, every human being's life in this world is inevitably mixed with every other life and, no matter what laws we pass, no matter what precautions we take, unless the people we meet are kindly and decent and human and liberty-loving, then there is no liberty. Freedom comes from human beings, rather than from laws and institutions."

Almost ready to conclude, Darrow had another thought. "Now, gentlemen, just one more word, and I am through. I am the last one to come here to stir up race hatred, or any other hatred. I do not believe in the law of hate. I may not be true to my ideals always, but I believe in the law of love, and I believe you can do nothing with hatred. I would like to see a time when man loves his fellow-man, and forgets his color or his creed. We will never be civilized until that time comes. I know the Negro race has a long road to go. I believe the life of the Negro race has been a life of tragedy, of injustice, of oppression.

"Gentlemen, what do you think is your duty in this case? I have watched day after day, these black, tense faces that have crowded this court. These black faces that now are looking to you twelve whites, feeling that the hopes and fears of a race are in your keeping.

"Their fate is in the hands of twelve whites. Their eyes are fixed on you, their hearts go out to you, and their hopes hang on your verdict."

Darrow concluded his plea and sat down heavily, pale and tense. His plea had lasted seven hours.

10

Toms spoke for the prosecution.[38] He took Darrow to task for characterizing most of the state's witnesses as "liars and cowardly curs. . . . We rather thought we had pretty decent people here in Detroit, but it took a Chicago lawyer to come here and tell us that the people of a whole neighborhood of our city are liars and cowardly curs."

He asked the jury not to get "switched off" into philosophical speculations. "Let's not be persuaded into solving the Negro problem," he said. "It is not our place to decide if the Negro's ancestors have been rightly treated. We are here to learn why one man was killed, and for no other reason.

"When Mr. Darrow says the Negro is in the hands of the enemy when he is in the hands of the police he isn't helping to solve the race problem. That doesn't fit his theory that man's love for his fellowman is the basis for the solution.

"I do know we have got to occupy the same land together; we have got to be citizens of this land together. It's got to be done by mutual charity and forebearance, and by giving the colored man a chance by education to learn law.

"I can't compete with this emotionalist from Chicago, neither verbally nor emotionally, but if you stick to the facts I have no fear of the outcome.

"It takes more than Darrow's enunciation to make liars out of the whole neighborhood. Because people do not agree it does not mean they are testifying falsely. When 71 people, months after an event, cannot agree on every detail are they forever to be branded as liars?" Toms asked.

"Remember, I admit that Dr. Sweet had a right to buy that house, where the trouble occurred. I grant he had the right to defend it against attack. But I also claim the right of people in the neighborhood to sit on their porches. I claim that citizens may exercise their rights without being shot at while doing so."

Three hours and thirty-five minutes after the jury began deliberations, they reached a verdict. Toms's face flushed as the jury filed into the courtoom. Darrow gripped the arms of his chair. The foreman read, "Not guilty."

11

To Judge Murphy, hearing Darrow's final summation was "the greatest experience" in his life. Although the judge saw his role in the Sweet case as merely "enforcing legal equality," Darrow felt that "it was the first time in all my career where a judge really tried to help, and displayed a sympathetic interest in saving poor devils from the extreme forces of the law, rather than otherwise."[39]

Clarence "never mouths Christianity but always practices it," commented Judge Murphy.[40]

The cost to the NAACP of both trials totaled $37,849. The organization published the complete text of Darrow's plea in the second trial because "of its historical, legal, and humanitarian value."

For more than a year the possibility of another trial haunted the defense. Finally, on July 21, 1927, the prosecutor moved to dismiss all charges against all defendants. The eleven blacks were free at last.

The Sweets never went back together to their home at Garland and Charlevoix. Tragedy stalked them the remainder of their years. Gladys and the child both died of tuberculosis within two years of Henry's acquittal. Fourteen years later Henry also fell victim to the disease. Ossian, twice married and twice divorced after Gladys's death, did move back to the house in 1930 and remained there for twenty-one years. In 1934 he ran as a Republican candidate for the State Senate, and in 1950 as a Democratic candidate for the U.S. Congress. He was defeated both times. He had two more court experiences: first, when he was fined for selling cigarettes without a license in a pharmacy he owned; later, to fight a paternity suit. Suffering intense pain from arthritis, Ossian fatally shot himself on March 19, 1960.

12

There was a short-lived utopia following Murphy's dismissal of the other charges. The badly bruised relationship between the whites and blacks seemed to have been mollified by the verdict, and for a time incidents between the two races decreased. Toms believed that whites would now be more inclined to recognize the inherent right of blacks to live where they chose.

Darrow said, "Prejudices have to be reckoned with as much as facts. And the whites cannot be held responsible for their prejudices for all of us are products of environment. . . ." He cautioned blacks to "remember that it takes a long time to overcome habits and prejudices. Their progress is bound to be slow, but I feel that it will be sure. It will come by mutual understandings and consideration rather than legislation. I believe that the outcome of this case will be a benefit to the whites and the black men alike."

The optimism expressed by Darrow, Toms, and the judge was premature. The bitter riots of 1943 and 1967 in Detroit opened old wounds and created new ones. Darrow's concluding words in the second Sweet trial were ironic— and prophetic—commentaries.

The law has made the Negro equal, Darrow said then, "but man has not. And after all, the last analysis is, what has man done?—and not what has the law done? I know there is a long road ahead of him, before he can take the place which I believe he should take. I know that before him there is suffering, sorrow, tribulation and death among the blacks, and perhaps the whites. I am sorry. I would do what I could to avert it. I would advise patience; I would advise toleration; I would advise understanding; I would advise all of those things which are necessary for men who live together."[41]

XXV
Itinerant Debater

1

OVER the years attempts had been made to obtain paroles for the McNamara brothers. Almost immediately after his return from California, Clarence wrote to Fremont Older about helping them. Still, he was uncertain of the best way to go about it. It might be too early to ask for release, he thought. Perhaps it would be best first to get labor solidly behind any move, "which I think can be done with work and patience." [1]

John J. McNamara, however, was not paroled from prison until after serving ten years of his fifteen-year sentence.

In 1926, James B. McNamara, who had been sentenced to life for the *Los Angeles Times* bombing, discussed with Older the possibility of regaining his freedom if he would assert that he had taken no part in the bombing. Older asked for Darrow's opinion. Clarence adamantly rejected such an approach. "Remember," he told Older, "he pleaded guilty. He was fully advised by his lawyers Davis, Scott and myself." Not only had J. B. pleaded guilty, "but he made a written statement telling how it was done. . . . It is absolutely out of the question to succeed on that line." Darrow reminded Older that J.B. "never intended killing anyone. His statement shows that it was only for a scare. He has been there long enough. . . . There has never been a time and never will

350

be where I won't help but it must be on lines that have a chance of success."[2]

Darrow suggested that Older press McNamara to wait until Steffens returned from Europe to use his influence in trying to obtain a parole. McNamara agreed to wait, but the attempt at parole failed. He died in prison.

2

Darrow's office at 140 North Dearborn Street continued to be a Mecca for the lowly and the famous—the worker seeking legal advice, the intelligentsia looking for intellectual stimulation, the literati passing through Chicago, the prisoner just released from jail, the indicted facing trial, the lone black seeking help, the representative of a black organization asking the attorney to speak at a fund raising. And Clarence found it difficult to turn anyone away.

"In the outside office is always a stream of people waiting," Clarence lamented to Mary Field, "and I am tired before I can get away. I don't want them to come but I can't help it. I go somewhere else for relief and there they are the same crowd forever and forever. The mail is full of letters that I don't want to read and can't answer. . . . Good bye dear girl. I always think of you and love you."[3]

He was a strong advocate of First Amendment rights even for those with whom he disagreed and did not admire, whether politically or on a personal level. Frank Harris, author of *My Life and Loves,* which had been banned in the United States but was being illegally distributed, wanted to know whether Darrow would defend him if he returned from England and the U.S. government decided to prosecute him once he was again on his native soil. Harris asked Elmer Gertz, then a University of Chicago undergraduate with whom he had been corresponding, to find out. Clarence promised Gertz that if Harris came to America and needed his services he would do everything he could to help him. Harris did come but was not harassed, so Clarence was not called upon.

Assuming that Darrow admired Harris, Gertz invited him to speak at a memorial meeting for Harris. The response from Clarence was immediate—and unexpected. "I would not want to speak at a memorial for Harris or to help raise funds. In fact, I never admired him."[4]

3

The Biology Club arranged a testimonial for Darrow's seventieth birthday anniversary. Twelve hundred people came "in the sacred name of friendship, to acknowledge what as yet we can do very little consciously to produce—Nature's supreme achievement in creating a man," said Professor T. V. Smith of the University of Chicago, toastmaster for the evening. He added that Clarence was as much a Chicago institution as the Wrigley Building and the Municipal Pier (now called Navy Pier).

It was one of the most extraordinary gatherings ever held in the history of Chicago—diverse political views were represented; men and women of wide social and economic background were there: industrialists and labor union leaders, professors and tailors, political dissidents, judges and former clients. Scopes came, and Lincoln Steffens. Will Rogers, a political satirist, telegraphed, "Darrow is the only free-thinker America has ever allowed to reach 70."[5]

Chicago Judge Harry M. Fisher, one of the speakers, debunked the charge that Darrow ever encouraged disrespect for the law. No man had done so much to promote it. "His issues are the living, throbbing and pulsating human problems which try men's souls."

Donald Richberg, a Chicago attorney, said Clarence "never defends a case but that he puts the universe itself on trial before the case is over; and he never has a defendant for whom he is not also an advocate."

The Reverend John Haynes Holmes, of New York City, had earlier summed up the thinking of Darrow's friends: despite Clarence's agnosticism, if Jesus came to Chicago today He would find one difference from His experience in Jerusalem. "In Jerusalem Jesus had no defender; in Chicago He would have a defender—Clarence Darrow."[6]

"Ladies and Gentlemen," announced the toastmaster, "Clarence Darrow."

Clarence shrugged his large shoulders as he approached the podium. "I am the fellow that all the talk has been about! And I am glad it is over. I always suspected I was a hell of a fellow but never thought I was like this. Anyhow, whether I am like it or unlike it—and I suppose I know less about it than some of my friends—whether it is deserved or not deserved, I will confess that I have liked to hear it. I don't believe that all of these wonderful addresses would have been possible unless there had been a worthy subject!

"I am moved by the more than kind words of those dear friends who have spoken tonight. There is a wonderful discrepancy of notions between them and some other things I have heard at times."

Clarence turned philosophical as he confessed he sometimes wondered what kind of person he really was. Brave? He wouldn't want his friends to know how much he feared doing some of the things he couldn't help doing. "It has been no more brave for me oftentimes to speak what is in me than it has been for the automaton to be in a place of danger because something put it there. . . .

"Much as I hated and feared and suffered for what I did, I would have suffered more had I failed to do that which I thought I ought to. Everyone is the product of his machine and his environment and that is all."

He claimed never to have courted danger; he was hurt by abuse, and many times criticism from those whose opinions are not worth anything have "cut me to the quick."

In token of the evening Clarence was presented with a bust of himself sculptured by Kathleen Wheeler. He lampooned the gift and the evening. The bust, he said, was "not the only thing that gives it somewhat the character of a funereal occasion. First, there is a long list of honorary pall-bearers on here, and then there is seventy years, and here is the monument."[7]

4

"Does Man Have Free Will?" "Can the Individual Control His Own Conduct?" "Is Man a Free Agent?" Darrow debated the subject of man's free will with philosophers, theologicians, anthropologists. In Detroit, in May 1927, one year after Will Durant's classic *The Story of Philosophy* was published, he debated "Is Man a Machine?" with Durant.[8] Introducing Judge Frank Murphy as moderator, Aaron Drouk, past president of Pisgah Lodge, B'nai B'rith, sponsor of the event, announced that the purpose of such programs was to foster discussion and to educate the public. A cynical Darrow opened by saying that had he known he was to educate the public he would not have agreed to participate. "It simply can't be done. I hope nobody thinks I am that foolish."

His task in the debate, Clarence said, was to tell what is known about man; Durant would tell them what is not known. "And then you will have it all." As far as he was concerned, man was a piece of mechanism built on the lever principle. "His legs are levers with which he walks. His back is a lever, by which he is able to lift things, through the contraction of the muscles. His arms are levers which he uses in all the activities of life. There is nothing about him that anybody can find—and of course I can't talk about anything I can't find—which isn't mechanical."[9]

Clarence characteristically hooked his thumbs in the armholes of his vest, shrugged his massive body, and relinquished the podium to his opponent.

Durant glanced at Darrow. Three decades younger and vibrant with enthusiasm, he noted that Darrow's life was his "first and most fundamental argument against" Darrow's theory. "I don't believe what Clarence Darrow says; I believe what he does. He has not regarded men as irresponsible, helpless tools, cogs, levers and wheels; he has regarded them as suffering, growing, dying organisms. The very fact that a thing can die is proof that it is not mechanical. How could a machine die?" He accused Clarence of adopting "the mechanistic theory as a protest against all forms of obscurantism and superstition."[10]

As with all of their debates, neither changed the other's tightly held opinions. Durant believed Darrow overcame him by "brilliance of wit and sheer force of personality." Afterward they would "dunk doughnuts" together in a nearby coffee shop. When Darrow lectured at a synogogue in Flatbush, New York, near the Durant home, he spent the night with the Durants and kept Will and Ariel Durant entranced for an hour "as he sat on the bed in his night dress, reading . . . Housman's *Shropshire Lad.* He was especially fond of Mrs. Durant, who loved him this side of adultery. Doubtless he had his faults," but the Durants "never found them."[11]

5

For two weeks during the fall of 1927 Clarence and Ruby traveled in Europe—Italy, Germany, the French Riviera. As the S.S. *Majestic* sailed across the Atlantic, Clarence relaxed by playing deck horseshoes and poker. The first to greet him when they disembarked in France were newspapermen who questioned him about the Sacco-Vanzetti case, in which two Italian anarchists had been tried and sentenced to death for the murder of a paymaster and a guard in South Braintree, Massachusetts. Many believed they had not been given a fair trial. For seven years agitation continued against the planned execution of the "good shoemaker and poor fish peddler." "The least the State of Massachusetts can do in the case of Sacco and Vanzetti is to commute their sentence to life imprisonment. There has long been grave doubt as to their guilt," Darrow told reporters in Paris. "The great masses of the people do not believe that the men are guilty. Moreover, if this doubt had not existed in the minds of the Massachusetts judiciary, why did it continue to grant stays of judgment for all of seven years when the officials claimed they were so sure the men were guilty?" he asked.

He derided claims that the agitation was due to Red propaganda. "The fact that the world's best minds, the minds of men who definitely have no connection with radicalism, have come to the conclusion, after careful study of the case, that Sacco and Vanzetti have not had a just trial, disproves that contention."[12]

The protests were in vain. Sacco and Vanzetti were electrocuted in Boston the night of August 22, 1927.

The case of the two anarchists had all the elements to lure Darrow to the courtroom. Many questioned his absence. In his biography of Darrow, Charles Yale Harrison explained that Clarence had not undertaken the role of defense attorney because he was not "called upon to do so until long after their conviction, and when the appeals were being made," he felt the case was being handled in "an efficient, capable manner."[13]

In 1977, on the fiftieth anniversary of the execution, Massachusetts Governor Michael S. Dukakis signed a proclamation which cited abuses by the Sacco and Vanzetti prosecution and stated, "There are substantial, indeed compelling grounds for believing that the Sacco and Vanzetti legal proceedings were permeated with unfairness." [14]

6

The Darrows were in Europe in 1927 when the initial battle was waged by Chicago Mayor Thompson in his bloodless war against the city's public library. He instigated an investigation of the library as a harbinger of anti-American books, and he ordered pro-British books removed from the shelves or he would burn them, a precedent to Hitler's book-burning extravaganzas. A long-standing antagonism to Great Britain had led to the mayor's infamous threat to "crack" King George of England "in the snout" if he ever came to Chicago. [15]

On his return to New York City, Darrow labeled the mayor's attempt at book censorship "probably the most infinitely stupid thing ever suggested." Darrow believed that despite American emphasis on democracy there was more freedom in England than in the United States. "It is a sane country, and to ban all books which put George Bernard Shaw in a favorable light is like a person being prejudiced against his own mother." [16]

Two days later, in the library of his Chicago home, surrounded by books on every conceivable topic, Clarence talked to a reporter of the *Chicago Journal*. The library fiasco is "the craziest thing I ever heard of," he said. "How far does Mayor Thompson propose to go? When he gets through throwing out English books, or books written with a bias in favor of England, he can start with an endless chain favoring France, Germany, even the Turk and any other country you can name. In the end he will have nothing left but fairy tales." [17]

7

That same year, two Fascists dressed in full regalia—black shirts, military riding breeches, tassled caps—on their way to march in a Memorial Day parade were stabbed to death as they approached a subway station in the Bronx, New York City. The double murder on May 30, 1927, created little furor in a city inured to violence. But when the Italian ambassador made a special trip from Washington, D.C., to New York to attend the funeral, and when in Rome Mussolini and his ministers paid tribute to the martyrs, Fascists in the United States and abroad clamored for vengeance.

Within six weeks, New York police arrested fourteen persons, including Calogero Greco and Donato Carillo, two workers known to be active anti-Fascists. Their sympathizers, suspecting they had been arrested only because of their anti-Fascist activities, feared the consequence of a second Sacco and

Vanzetti case. The anti-Fascists of New York, headed by the colorful Italian-American anarchist editor, Carlo Tresco, spearheaded the formation of a defense committee.

Arthur Garfield Hays, Darrow's friend and cocounsel at the Scopes and Sweet trials, had come into the case at Tresco's request. He wanted Darrow as chief counsel. Clarence, in New York on a lecture engagement, was visited in his hotel room by a committee, including Hays and Greco's brother.[18]

"You know, Clarence," said Hays, "these men are innocent."

A long silence. Then Clarence gave what had become his standard excuse before he finally accepted a case: "I'm afraid I can't take it. I'm tired, I want to rest, I'm past seventy. You can handle it, Arthur. You don't need me."

In a corner of the room Greco's brother began to cry softly. Darrow protested, "All right—all right—I'll take the case. For God's sake, stop crying."

The two-week trial opened in the Bronx County courtroom of Judge Albert Cohn. Much of the testimony by both state and defense witnesses was given in broken and imperfect English or in translation from Italian to English. A prosecution witness hesitated when given an opportunity to identify the defendants as the murderers. Suddenly he was unsure. Under direct examination by the prosecution, he said, "If you want me to say it's him I'll say it's him and I'll go away, but I am not sure why should I send an innocent man to jail for nothing when I'm not sure." The prosecutor asked him if he had changed his testimony because he was afraid. The witness responded, "I am not afraid of no one. I am going to die just the same. I am a Catholic."[19]

In his summation, Darrow used sarcasm to lash the state's methods of "making" evidence. "Everybody knows the difficulty of identification, of remembering even the people you know, much less a man whom you had never seen before."

His left hand thrust deep in his coat pocket, his right arm extended, he turned propagandist as he concluded softly, "I ask you, gentlemen, to take this case as you find it—these children of Italy who came here to better their condition, who have lived honest lives, who have worked for their families, worked at plain, manual toil, who bore the bullets of the enemy in defense of America and in defense of Italy, who loved freedom and hated despotism, and, therefore, hate Mussolini, because the name Mussolini is only another name for despotism—I ask you for their sake, gentlemen, for a verdict of 'not guilty.'"

The jury returned a "not guilty" verdict on Christmas Eve.

8

The previous June Darrow had delivered a lecture on capital punishment at Dartmouth College, Paul's alma mater. When he finished, an elderly cleaning woman at the school shoved a brittle, yellowed sheet of paper into his hand and challenged him to fulfill the promise his son had made to her twenty-three years ago. Paul, a student at the college in 1904, had been riding in a horse-drawn carriage when his horse bolted at the screech of a train and fatally injured a four-year-old child. Grieving over the accident which he had been unable to prevent, Paul gave the child's mother a note promising that if ever a member of the Darrow family could be of help to her or her family, she need only ask and "the service will be rendered."

The woman told Clarence of her nephew, John O. Winter, found guilty of the brutal murder of a young woman in Windsor, Vermont, and sentenced to the electric chair. "I know he is innocent, and I know you are probably the one man sufficiently skilled in the law to save him. Will you do it?" she asked Darrow.

Clarence, who knew of the promise, replied, "Of course I'll do it."

In January 1928 he made a special trip to Vermont to appeal the decision of the lower court before the Vermont Supreme Court. The lawyers in the courtroom were favorably impressed with "the scholarly and resourceful way" in which the seventy-year-old Clarence worked.[20]

The New York Times reported, "Although handicapped by lack of familiarity with the courts of the state and by his late entrance into the case, Mr. Darrow won admiration by the manner in which he handled the exceptions taken by counsel at the time of the trial."[21]

In the initial trial, Darrow insisted, the court erred in excluding the offer by the defense to present certain testimony as it pertained to blood on the defendant's clothing. In a short sentence he voiced his personal credo of the law: "Law is not a system of tricks, it is a system of getting justice." Citing the lower court's error, he explained, "Blood is an important factor in a murder case. I don't know what the jury would have done with the evidence, but it had a right to it."[22]

"It is important to punish murder, but still more important that all the safeguards surrounding a trial should be given in each case," he stressed.

Winter's sentence was commuted to life imprisonment. Twenty-two years later, in 1949, the governor of Vermont paroled him.

With this case completed, Clarence officially announced his retirement—once again.

9

He had been receiving many letters from blacks in various cities—Philadelphia, Boston, New York, Washington, Baltimore, Kansas City, Akron, Ohio—asking him to speak. As he told James Weldon Johnson, secretary of the National Association for the Advancement of Colored People, he would like to accept the invitations but did not want to profit from the lectures, nor did he feel his services should be free. He resolved his quandary by suggesting that, after his expenses had been deducted, three-quarters of the fee should go to the NAACP and one-quarter to the John Brown Memorial. "I know perfectly well that it is better to look after the living than the dead," he admitted, "but there is a little more than that involved in the question and I think it would do the negroes good if they erected a suitable monument" to Brown.[23]

He would accept only a limited number of engagements, but they had to be in major cities. Large cities would be expected to guarantee a fee of $1000. From smaller cities $500 would be acceptable.

The itinerary arranged, Darrow began his tour, speaking to large audiences in black churches and in halls, always to warm receptions. While in Florida, however, he learned that a group of black ministers in Washington, D.C., where he was scheduled to speak, refused to allow their churches to be used for that purpose.

W. E. B. Du Bois, a notable civil rights agitator and educator, was outraged and lashed out at the black ministers in his column in the *Crisis.* "There is not a Negro church in the United States that ought not throw wide open its door to Clarence Darrow and beg him to come in. He will criticize those churches, and they ought to be criticized. He says frankly and openly what their own members say namely: they are spending too much money for church edifices and not enough for the social uplift which Christianity stands for, if it stands for anything."[24]

Even if some black ministers did not want Clarence to speak in their churches, Noval H. Thomas, local president of the NAACP in Washington, D.C., urged him to come. Darrow, he said, was more popular and beloved among Negro audiences than many presidents of the United States.

Perhaps some of the black ministers were reacting to Darrow's complaint about "having some damn fool preacher start . . . off with a prayer and close with a benediction" whenever he spoke in a hall.

"I don't have this even among white christians *[sic]* who are bad enough, if I am speaking in their churches. I can see some point in conforming and should not raise the question, but I wish you would tell them that when I speak in a hall I don't want them to do it. I am not interested in God and he is not interested in the colored people. I don't believe in their forcing themselves on a fellow like me and shall be apt to say something about it in my remarks if it is done."[25]

Clarence attracted large crowds whenever he was announced as the speaker. As the iconoclast, the debunker, he decried sham and pretense. Once, at a gathering of labor men, the chairman introduced him as a friend of the worker. Clarence retorted he'd rather be a friend of the worker than a worker.

The chairman at a convention of the American Society of Newspaper

Editors introduced Clarence: "We have a number of friends of doubtful value who are always willing to tell us what wonderful work we are doing, what great supports of democracy we are. We have few friends who are frank enough to tell us our faults.

"Mr. Darrow will talk to us on the subject 'This Is What I Don't Like about the Newspapers.'"

The topic was a surprise to Clarence, but he rose to the occasion. It wasn't a question of how many readers a newspaper can get, he told the assembled editors, but "what kind of advertising you get. Readers are all right incidentally, because, if you didn't have readers, they couldn't get swindled on the advertising the next day and therefore you couldn't get higher advertising rates." At the turn of the century he had advised the inmates in the Cook County jail to find a legal way of picking pockets. Now Clarence told the editors that "the advertisers get the cleverest ad writers there are to help pick peoples' pockets, to write up alluring and false statements to induce some person to buy something that he doesn't need and can't afford, and the newspapers have to publish them."[26]

10

During the 1928 Hoover-Smith presidential race, Clarence spoke nearly every night for six weeks campaigning for Alfred E. Smith, governor of New York. There were two major issues to which he addressed himself: In a country dedicated to separation of church and state, the question of Smith's Catholicism aroused fears that the Church might become too powerful if he became chief of state. "Why be afraid of a Catholic president?" Clarence asked. He wasn't, and he stressed that there were Catholics on the U.S. Supreme Court, in the U.S. Congress, and in the armed forces. "We have never refused to let them die for us although we have refused them the right to be president." The agnostic lawyer added that he was no more suspicious of a Catholic president than one of any other religion.[27]

Smith was against prohibition, and Darrow liked him for that. Clarence charged, "Prohibition has built up a nation of informers, spies, crooks and murderers who go about killing for the benefit of the prohibitionists, who approve of it.

"I am against prohibition. I don't like it. I hate it. And I'm going to tell you why. The first reason is because I like to take a drink. I wouldn't compel a prohibitionist to drink if he didn't want to, but I object to him telling me I can't."[28]

He employed satire and cynicism in his denunciation of Hoover, "the Harding gang," prohibition, and the Anti-Saloon League. He lauded Smith as standing "as high above Hoover as the heavens above the earth." If Hoover is elected, "he'll do one thing almost incomprehensible to the human mind. He'll make a great man of Coolidge." [29] Coolidge, he told thirty thousand men and women jammed into the Krueger Auditorium in Newark, New Jersey, "was successful in doing something that I did not think was possible for a human being to do. He made a statesman out of Harding—by comparison." [30]

"If America votes as it drinks, Smith will be elected almost unanimously. If Hoover is elected it will be by the vote of hypocrites." [31]

In New York City he lashed out at Hoover again. "All my life I have been trying to get away from efficiency experts, and now comes the High Priest of efficiency seeking the presidency. What is efficiency? Well, I'll tell you; efficiency makes one job grow where two bloomed before," a prophetic remark in view of the Depression which followed soon after Hoover's election.

Stumping for Smith, he found himself one night in Gary, Indiana, before an all-black audience. [32] He would not have come had he known they were Negro, he told them. All his life he had refused to talk politics to blacks. "There was never any party of white men who treated Negroes decently. I do not want any friend of mine, with a black face, to ever vote any ticket because I do. You do not owe anything to the Democratic party or to the Republican party or anybody who is white. I know what I would do if I was colored." The once professed pacifist again allowed his emotions to sidetrack the philosophy of love: "I know I would feel like killing every white person, just as you do. But I would not do it, just as you do not."

Over and over he stressed that blacks owed nothing to the Democrats, and whatever they owed to the Republicans because of Lincoln they had paid for "a hundred times over."

He said his father had been a friend of John Brown and the family had been brought up to think colored people not only equal to whites but better. "I have got over that. I do not think anybody is better than anyone else in this world, that is, as a race or a people." He had only one piece of advice to give black people which he had given over and over again in time of elections: don't let them take your vote for granted.

Darrow never believed it was the "wet" or "dry" issue which defeated Smith, nor was it the "bigoted people" who refused to vote for a Catholic. It was, rather, the nation's prosperity; voters had seen no reason to change political parties. If Coolidge was okay, so was Hoover. Almost everybody bought stock—Clarence did too—and everybody believed the market would continue to go up.

11

When he was seventy-two years old, Clarence wrote his life's credo for *The Saturday Evening Post;* [33] he regretted little about his own life. Though he argued that life was not worth living, few men, he agreed, had lived a more interesting, intense, lusty life than he.

"I well remember the time when I imagined that no pleasure would be left for me when I should be too old to play baseball," but he found that urges and emotions still persisted as they had in his teens, only now they were softer—and duller—to fit the later years. As a youth he had been very active in the outdoors. Now "a park bench furnishes every opportunity to see the trees and grass, and feel the fresh, invigorating air that blows from the lake, bringing the same sensation that it did long years ago."

He never judged or condemned anyone. He stood with the minority on almost every important question that divided men. "I also know that the truth is many-sided and relative and shifting, and yet it seldom occurs to me that any of my opinions can be wrong. . . . As a propagandist I realize the work that I shall always find to do. No matter how long I live, I shall still be seeking to convert a blind and credulous people to abandon their idols and join the thin ranks of the minority and help bear its soiled and tattered banner to ultimate victory. Still, I know that I shall fail. I know that, if perchance the majority could be ranged on my side, it would be as intolerant and senseless as majorities have always been."

He recalled his prowar stand during World War I, the rare time he held a majority viewpoint, but even then he soon found himself again in a minority role. "The only reason why I do not join the pack is because my human structure is not adjusted to the easier way of life. To me, the easiest way is the hardest way."

The man who always argued that "life was not worth living" contradicted himself in his life's summation: "I see no chance to grow weary of life. I am interested in too many questions that concern the existence and activity of the human race."

As he had in his younger years, Clarence still loved to travel, and the year his article appeared in *The Saturday Evening Post* he and Ruby went back to Europe—to England, Scotland, Wales, France, Switzerland. They visited old friends—writers, artists, economists, sculptors, statesmen—H. G. Wells, Brand Whitlock, Jo Davidson, John A. Hobson, William R. Kellogg, T. P. O'Connor.

For years Clarence had resisted suggestions that he write the story of his life. He likened the genre of autobiography to a cry for attention; it was like standing on a street corner shouting, "For God's sake, look at me for a minute!"[34]

In Montreux, however, on the shores of Lake Geneva, where "not an ugly spot or blot or prohibitionist marred the summer nights," Ruby rented a typewriter "and typed and revised" as Clarence "spun . . . reveries into form." Across the garden, in another wing of the Beau Rivage Hotel, was the muckraker and Socialist Charles Edward Russell, and his wife Theresa, who inspired and goaded Clarence to keep on writing, while Russell worked on his massive *Life of Charlemagne*. Together the four friends "watched the changing colors of the waters, the mountains, the trees, and skies as the sun went down, all of the beauty heightened and mellowed by wonderful wines of that little land." [35]

The Story of My Life, more the essence of his philosophy and his longings than the story of his activities, was published in February 1932 and quickly reached the number 9 spot on the nonfiction best-seller list that year. The most successful of his books, it has an air of humility, almost an apology for the use of the first-person pronoun.

The critic in *The New Republic* wrote, "Sitting down to write of himself, he cannot separate himself from his cause and quickly forgets himself in its favor." [36]

"His book," according to the *Yale Law Journal* reviewer, "is a combination of an absorbing narrative with philosophical excursions into the nature of crime, the nature of the human end, and the nature of life itself." [37]

12

Paul and his family had moved back to Chicago from Colorado while Clarence and Ruby were in Europe. Clarence wrote regularly to his adored granddaughters, letters that showed an impish sense of humor:

"Dear kids, [38]

"Eye take mi penn in hand two let U no that Eye am wel and hop UR the sam. . . .

"Eye have bin thinking how lucky it waz that Eye got U to kum to Chicago so I woodent be so far away from U when U kum. Eye diden't think about kumming to Europe but now I am 4 thozand miles aweigh but if U haddent kame to Chicago Eye wood now bee 5 thousand miles awa and what wood we have dun then. You kan see for yourself."

From Cannes, he wrote to the "kids": [39] ". . . I havent time to write you a real letter for I am too busy doing nothing. It takes up every minute of the day. Sumething funny happened to me last week. I was away over Sunday and forgot my watch. When I got back I found that it had stopped seeing I had went and nobody was watching my watch. Well sir it had stopped at one oclock, and had run down. I started to set it and then, I couldn't make up my mind whether it had stoped at one oclock in the afternoon or one oclock in the morning. And so I figured on that some more, I didnt know whether it had stoped on Saturday or Sunday or Monday so if I started it going I couldnt tell whether it was day or night. Then I couldnt tell weather it was last week or this week or next (necks weak) so I might just as well let it stand still since I wouldnt know whether it was rite if I set it; I went to the watchmaker and told him about it but he didnt seem to understand me cause I spoke English and he spoke French and I couldnt understand him and I didn't have any interrupter to translate the stuff out of French and into English and I really dont know where I am or when or who.

"I have been intending to sail for Chicago on the 8th of March on the Saturnia, an Eyetalian ship that leave from here but I dont see how I can do it for if I got down to the dock I might find that it was night time instead of day time, and that the bote had already went, or I might find that it was last week and I would have to wait on the wharf til next weak or that it *was* next week and the bote had sailed last week and so I dont no what in the devil to do. You can see yourself. I thank you——

C.S.D."

13

Clarence and Ruby returned to the states in mid-March 1930. The "Big Bull Market," which had collapsed less than eight months after Hoover took his presidential oath of office, caused Clarence grave financial losses. To alleviate economic anxiety, he began a series of four-way debates on religion, similar to those in which he had participated earlier. Notable for their ecumenical format, they always featured a rabbi, a Protestant minister, a lay Catholic, since the Church at that time frowned upon clerical participation, and Clarence, who spoke as an agnostic. He generally received $500 for such debates plus $50 expenses. Each speaker had thirty minutes to state why he believed—or disbelieved. The order of speakers was determined by lot.

In Columbus, Ohio, in 1929, 4257 people had assembled in an auditorium which had a capacity of 3661.[40] They filled the stage, stood at the back and down the sides of the hall. Bishop Edwin Holt Hughes championed Protestantism. "I am a Protestant," he said, "because all my study of individual and national life convinces me that the free evangelical faith is the producer of democratic education. . . . In the Protestant fold I have found freedom, faith, peace, hope, redemption; I confidently expect at the last to pass my soul up to God and Father of our Lord Jesus Christ, amid the cheering assurances of my fellow-confessors, but without the mediation of an ecclesiastical monarchy."

"As I see it," said Rabbi Jacob Tarshish of Columbus, "this is an experiment in intellectual brotherhood. I am a Jew because I believe the teachings of the Jewish religion and because I am proud of the contributions of the Jewish people. . . . The Jewish people have given the world the monotheistic idea of God, and the Old Testament, including the Ten Commandments."

Darrow opened with the flat statement, "An agnostic is a doubter. . . . I am an agnostic as to the question of God. I think that it is impossible for the human mind to believe in an object, or thing unless it can form a mental picture of such object or thing."

The Catholic layman, Judge John P. McGoorty, of the Superior Court of Chicago, said, "Christ's Church must be somewhere on earth today. It can only be that church which possesses the classic and essential features—that is to say—that it is One, Holy, Catholic or Universal and Apostolic. That Church is the Catholic Church."

In Nashville, Tennessee, in 1931, a crowd of about 3500 listened to the arguments.[41] Rabbi Julius Marks: "I am a Jew because wherever there is suffering, the heart of my people weeps, and wherever there is despair, the heart of my people hope. I am a Jew because I regard it more important to help create a heaven on earth than to chaperone souls into Heaven. I am a Jew because I am not interested in converting anybody to my beliefs, but I am most decidedly concerned with helping in the task of conveying mankind to righteousness, justice, love and peace."

Quinn O'Brien: "We do not have to lay our hands on things to be able to believe them. Justice, love, electric currents and the like we have never seen, but we know that they are there."

Darrow: "I wish these fellows would caucus on their Bible anyway. I say it is just like any other book. They say it is different, but they never agree on just how it is different. The truth of the matter is that they believe as I do. They don't believe all those gags about Noah and the ark and Jonah and the whale."

Bishop H. M. DuBose, member of the Episcopal College of the M.E. Church, South: "Why I Am a Protestant? Its answer does not come of sectarian promptings, but is humanistic and of essence of universal Christian consciousness."

When Clarence debated in Houston, 3500 were in the audience.[42] The next day the *Houston Press* published an applause score tallied for the four speakers:

	Interruptions for Applause	Time
Darrow	34	2 minutes
Rabbi	4	40 seconds
Catholic	12	26 seconds
Protestant	1	23 seconds

In describing the audience, the *Press* noted that "in 30 minutes of ridicule, irony, impiety and materialism, the 74-year-old freethinker—who makes his home in the machine gun center of America [referring to the gang wars terrorizing Chicago]—was not interrupted once by anyone who might be in disagreement of what he was saying.

"And when he had concluded, with the remark that if you rather would live a lie than the truth, you can keep your religion, the applause was so persistent that he was obliged to lift his tall, angular form from the chair and take a bow.

"He took it with that slow, engaging smile of his (which on a little boy's face would be impish) and slouched back into his seat with his broad shoulders hunched up around his neck."

14

Clarence could win juries into a courtroom, he could win lecture and debate audiences, but he could not sway those committed to a particular view of history. In 1931 a national radio network presented a series of corporation-sponsored mock trials of historic figures. A "considerable fee" was offered to Clarence to defend Benedict Arnold. The idea was "to ask for clemency on account of former devotion and service, and my opposition to capital punishment. . . . I did not think about the feeling of the public against Arnold anymore than I had not ever thought of such matters."[43] He admitted Arnold's guilt and granted the sinfulness of his act, but, he concluded in his plea, as he usually did in the courtroom, "So far as is given man to understand the meaning of justice, my client deserves consideration and clemency at the hands of this jury; and I ask you to recommend it to the Court."[44] Clarence failed to persuade the twelve nationally prominent men and women who acted as the jury that Arnold deserved mercy.

In 1931 he also starred in a movie on evolution with Professor H. M. Parshley of Smith College. The full-length film presented a brief history of evolution, from amoeba to man, noting the similarities. Dr. Parshley explained the scientific facts, and Clarence commented on them "with the whimsical, pessimistic remarks for which he is known." When, for example, Parshley explained the difference between man and beast, Darrow countered, "Yes, we think—some of us—some of the time, and occasionally correctly."[45]

The movie was favorably reviewed and popularly received. Clarence was already planning another movie to show the causes and treatment of crime. The project never reached fruition. In the few years of his life that remained, he became involved in other cases and causes, and then was plagued by ill health.

XXVI

A Folk Hero in His Time

1

ONLY once in his long career as a lawyer did Clarence withdraw from a case. In April 1931 nine black youths aged twelve to nineteen years were convicted for raping two white women on a moving freight train and sentenced to the electric chair in Scottsboro, Alabama. Both the International Labor Defense, an arm of the Communist party, and the NAACP watched the case with special interest, each for their own motives. The *Daily Worker*, official organ of the Communist party, considered it a "capitalist atrocity." The paper saw a similarity to the way Sacco and Vanzetti had been railroaded and believed that, if properly publicized, the story would dramatically illustrate the plight of the black man in the South.

The NAACP, concerned that the constitutional rights of the boys were being abridged, employed Darrow and Arthur Garfield Hays to appeal the conviction before the Alabama Supreme Court. The day the two lawyers arrived in Birmingham, they received a telegram signed by the nine defendants in prison in Montgomery, Alabama. The telegram was blunt. Unless the two attorneys withdrew from the NAACP and appeared for the International Labor Defense, the boys did not want their services. They wanted only attorneys from the ILD to represent them.

Both Hays and Darrow were well aware of the NAACP's long and untiring devotion to defend black men and women in trouble, and neither of them would forsake the organization. "I am sure that we could have done nothing else than take this stand," Darrow said.[1] As he left Alabama, he explained he did not object to anybody's politics, but "you can't mix politics with law." This was a criticism of the ILD who wanted to turn the Scottsboro case into a political trial. The case, he emphasized, had to be won in Alabama and "not in Russia or New York."

2

In 1932, four decades after he defended Eugene Victor Debs, his first labor client, on a conspiracy charge, Darrow spoke at a meeting at the University of Chicago on behalf of forty-three Kentucky miners charged with conspiracy to murder during a strike in Harlan County, Kentucky.[2] The use of conspiracy laws against labor unions had not eased since the day he resigned as Chicago & Northwestern Railway counsel to defend Debs.

Comparing the conspiracy laws with the once infamous Star Chamber of England, he said, "Whenever the powers that be wanted to get somebody out of the way, they took him into the Star Chamber, and he never came back. Most of the world condemned England, America more than the rest, and when the Constitution of America was written all such methods were strictly forbidden. That constitution is in existence now, but it is not working. You can have all the constitutions in the world but they do no good unless the people are interested.

"I am not surprised at the cases in Kentucky," Darrow said. He had "seen them, watched them and read of such everywhere in America. There is no place so far away, no people so powerful, but may be caught in the same trap of unconstitutional prosecution." Darrow's pessimism was as strong, at age seventy-five, as at any time during his life: "Most people are not interested in what happens to others, they are only interested in getting rich. They do not care who goes to jail unless they go themselves—and then it is too late." England, he told his university audience, had abolished her conspiracy laws 150 years earlier, but conspiracy laws in the United States which "were imported from the old, outlawed tyrannical laws of England" remained part of the law of the land.

3

Darrow was officially retired. He had not been in a courtroom for four years. He had even closed his office in the Chicago Temple Building at 77

West Washington Street, though the firm name of Darrow, Smith & Carlin remained on the building directory for almost two decades afterward. He liked the idea of not having to get up at the sound of an alarm clock and rush off to his office. It felt good not to have the responsibility of getting to the courtroom on time. He wanted no obligations—just to spend his twilight years doing what he wanted when he wanted. Time to read, write, to visit his friends, time to think.

And then he was asked to head the Massie defense.

The trial grew out of the rape of the twenty-year-old wife of Navy Lieutenant Thomas Massie in the Waikiki Beach section of Honolulu on September 21, 1932. Five island youths charged with the crime awaited a second trial after the first ended in a jury disagreement. Joseph Kahahawai, the leader of the group, had just left his probation officer to whom he reported regularly under his bail provisions, when he was kidnapped by three white men, Lieutenant Massie among them, brought to the home of Mrs. Fortescue, mother of the alleged rape victim, and killed there.

Rushing to dispose of the body, Mrs. Fortescue and two of the murderers were stopped for speeding. The body was discovered, and they were charged with murder. Lieutenant Massie, left behind at his mother-in-law's home, was also arrested and charged with murder.

Clarence was asked to represent the defendants in the Massie-Fortescue case. He accepted, then was burdened with doubts. There were rumors that the question of "race conflict" would be brought into the trial. He did not want to be "in a position" where he would "be compelled to take a position, even in a case, at variance with what I felt *and* had stood for."[3]

He advised the defendants that he would not take the case if it revolved around the race issue. "After a day or two," Clarence wrote to Harry Elmer Barnes,[4] "they wrote me that they thought I was right in my position on the race question, and they wanted that attitude maintained in court, and all would be as I wished. Which left nothing for me to do but go."

Always sensitive to the feelings of his friends, Clarence explained to Barnes that, since the case would not be fought on a race basis, he saw no "impropriety" in taking it, "assuming that I stick by my convictions in the trial of the case, which I shall do; of course I have occasionally in the past represented people of wealth," and he cited Leopold and Loeb.

Then his oft-repeated reason for taking a case his friends thought he should not: it was a question of income. "I don't know what I should have done if now and then a fairly well-to-do client had not come my way."

Clarence reiterated to Barnes that he was sorry that his acceptance of the Massie defense "pains" Barnes, "as you know that my affection for you is genuine and deep." He suggested that Barnes follow the events and see "if you can criticize anything I do in the matter. And I do want you to keep your faith in me."

Despite his efforts, however, the case remained embroiled in racial antagonisms. Almost fifty years later both the Massie case and Darrow are recalled with hostility by many of the inhabitants.

Now came the question of Darrow's health. At seventy-five, his age bore heavily on him. He was not well, and his physicians would allow him to go to Honolulu only if he secured an associate to help with the details of the case. George Leisure, a Wall Street attorney, was recommended as an associate. Clarence invited Leisure to join him and New York Mayor James Walker at the Colony Restaurant in New York. After lunch the mayor suggested that the three attend a performance of George Gershwin's *Of Thee I Sing.* In the theater, word spread that Darrow was sitting in the front row. Autograph seekers and admirers beseeched him for his signature, while the popular mayor of New York City was virtually overlooked. All through the play, to the annoyance of those sitting nearby, Darrow talked to Leisure sotto voce about the Massie case. [5]

Leisure became his associate counsel for the Hawaiian trial. Mr. and Mrs. Leisure joined Clarence and Ruby in Chicago, and together they traveled to Honolulu. At each stop en route to the West Coast, newspapermen boarded the train and plied Clarence with questions. He refused to talk about the case, always changing the subject to prohibition. In Omaha a reporter interviewed him about prohibition. In his best Socratic manner, Darrow asked the newsman whether he had ever taken a drink. Reluctantly, the young reporter admitted he had. "Well," drawled Clarence, "then what is the matter? Don't you want anybody else to have any fun?" [6]

In Hawaii, the attorneys found fear and racial bitterness: U.S. sailors clashed with the natives; white women were being molested; other women, reliving in their fantasies the alleged experience of Thalia Massie, feared to be alone.

The trial opened in early April. Theon Wright of the *Honolulu Advertiser* described Darrow: "A strange, half-sleeping colossus, his body grown weary in the evening of life but his eyes still sharp with the fire of a brilliant mind. The instant you come into contact with this man, you are impressed with one thing that overshadows everything else—his intense and loveable humanism. You are filled with an inescapable belief that Clarence Darrow does not hate anyone . . . and does not resent anyone." [7]

The judge, Charles S. Davis, was a native New Englander who had come to Honolulu as a child. During jury selection Darrow faced for the first time in his life the "fantasy of many races, alien thoughts and strange tongues, unique to Hawaii," and he had to mesh his own thoughts and background with the complex psychology of the various races resident on the island.

It took four days to select a jury made up of five men of American descent, one Dane, one German, one Portuguese, three Chinese, and one a combination of Irish, Hawaiian, Scottish, Tahitian, and French ancestry.

John C. Kelly, prosecutor, opened for the state. The jammed courtroom remained silent as for almost an hour he wove a web of circumstantial evidence. Although he never indicated who might have fired the shot that killed Kahahawai, he described vividly the scene of the murder.

The Honolulu newspapers carried details of the direct and cross-examination of the witnesses. In reply to the prosecutor's insistent questions about who fired the shot that killed Kahahawai, Lieutenant Massie implied he had fired the fatal shot when Kahahawai admitted his participation in the assault. "The last thing I remember," his voice broke with emotion, "was the picture of my wife, praying for mercy . . . and he answered her with a blow that broke her jaw. That's all I remember." [8]

4

The strain of the trial showed on Clarence. His thinning shock of hair fell about his forehead as, gray and gaunt, he leaned over the jury box. His plea was without oratory or verbal pyrotechnics. He stepped up to the jury box, shoved his hands into the drooping coat pockets of his gray suit which looked "as though they had too long carried the burden of his fists." He began to speak. [9]

"This case illustrates the mysterious working of human destiny more than any other case I have handled. It illustrates the effect of grief and sorrow and mishap on human minds and lives. It shows us how weak and powerless human beings are in the hands of relentless powers. As always, the question of free will."

For four hours Darrow spoke. "I have looked at this Island, which is a new country to me. I've never had any prejudice against any race on earth. I didn't learn it, and I defy anyone to find any word of mine to contradict what I say. To me these questions of race must be solved by understanding—not by force." It was fundamentally a question of "causes and motives." He concluded, "I have put this case without appeal to the nationality or race of any juror, asking them to pass on it as a human case. . . . You are a people to heal, not to destroy. I place this in your hands asking you to be kind and considerate both to the living and to the dead."

Clarence walked back to his seat.

Kelly rose from the prosecutor's table and approached the jury box. [10] Where Clarence preached human pity and mercy and "the mysterious working of human destiny," Kelley preached a sermon on law: "I stand here before you for the law—opposed to those who have violated the law and those who ask you to violate the law.

"Are you going to decide this case on the plea of a man who for fifty years has stood before the bar of justice which he belittles today, or are you going to decide this case on the law?

"Let us suppose, for the time being that this defense they offer is an honest defense.

"If Lt. Massie went into one of these trances the doctors give such funny names to, where were the officers of the submarine base? Did they bring them here to tell you what his condition was? They were conspicuous by their absence.

"If Kahahawai had said 'yes, we done it,' which no Hawaiian would have said, a Hawaiian would have said: 'yes, we been do it,' Did you hear of a dying statement? No matter how good or bad you think that boy was, he had a right to his life just as you and I have."

Judge Davis's instructions to the jury stressed that no one has the right to take the law into his or her own hands. Thus given no choice, the jury returned a verdict of "guilty of manslaughter" with a recommendation for leniency. A disappointed Darrow had expected an acquittal or, at the very least, a hung jury. The judge sentenced each defendant to ten years at hard labor.

Within an hour the governor of the island commuted the sentences to time served.

The prosecution paid tribute to Clarence's forensic abilities by offering him a fee to help prosecute Mrs. Massie's assailants, but he turned them down. He had never been a prosecutor; it was a role he never wanted.

For Clarence the case was finished. He advised Mrs. Massie to leave the island and to drop the idea of another prosecution of her rapists as it would only add more turmoil and dissension in Honolulu and would mean reliving the horrors of her experience—an advice she heeded.

5

Clarence's acceptance of the Massie defense, despite his need for the money, puzzled those who knew him. Everything about the case was at variance with what he believed. It was not a defense of the poor, a political dissident, or labor. It was neither a cause nor a crusade. His clients this time were part of the military establishment, and both the Massie and the Fortescue families were socially prominent on the Mainland. That the defendants committed the murder was never denied—but there were rumors which questioned whether Thalia Massie had been raped. It appeared that Clarence was on the wrong side. Leisure believed Darrow considered only the tragedy that had befallen the Massies and desired to help fellow human beings. This, however, is at variance with the Darrow of old who certainly would have been more moved by the plight of the islanders who may have been innocent.

Darrow himself had difficulty explaining his motives. He said he accepted the defense because the case involved psychology, philosophy, and sociology.

In the 1934 edition of his autobiography he added a chapter on the Massie case and attempted to explain his involvement. "I was not sure then, and am not sure now. I had never been to that part of the Pacific . . . the more I thought of those islands in the Pacific . . . and the more I investigated the strange and puzzling case, the more I felt that I had better go. . . . Then, too, the so-called 'depression' had swept away practically all the savings that I thought I had for keeping me comfortable to the end, and I needed the fee. This was not at all large, but it was sufficient. I do not know the relative importance of these motives, but I know that these reasons, and others, took me to Honolulu."[11] He had been promised $30,000 plus expenses.

Part of the Darrow legend is that he never defended a case in which he was not interested in the principle. Asked by the press on his arrival in Honolulu why he took the case, he answered, "My job is to defend people. That is the principle in every case where a man or woman is brought before the bar of justice. This case interests me; that is why I took it." Then a reference to his need for money: "A lawyer would not get along very well who barred clients who could pay their bills. I do not remember having told anyone I didn't accept fees for my work."[12] Again he explained that only in this way could he handle the half of his schedule for which he received no fee.

The final word on the Massie-Fortescue case and Darrow's involvement in it should come from Theon Wright who covered the trial for the *Honolulu Advertiser*. Writing in 1966 in his book *Rape in Paradise*, Wright said that Darrow came to Honolulu "believing his personal presence and his known tolerance and understanding of human suffering would help smooth over any racial problem that might exist. When he left the Island two months later the racial issues were more deeply graven than ever.

"There were many who blamed CD for the outcome of the Massie-Fortescue trial, which in itself was a paradox. He had always hated injustice and arrogance; he had nearly always aligned himself with the downtrodden people of his day, the unprotected victims of a hostile society. Yet in Honolulu he found himself ranged on the other side, fighting for those things he despised; arrogance and ruthlessness of economic overlords, the failure of man-made justice to protect the weak and disenfranchised."

Wright recalled a conversation his father had with Darrow after the Massie trial ended but before Clarence left for the Mainland. Editor of the Japanese-English newspaper, the *Hawaii Hochi*, the elder Wright pointed out to Darrow that the islanders resented "a concept of justice that would throw five boys of mixed Hawaiian and other racial origins into prison, as hoodlums and gangsters—even though there had been no real proof of their guilt; and at the same time it would allow four mainland *haoles* [whites, originally strangers] to go free, after they admitted killing Joseph Kahahawai." [13]

Darrow thought deeply. The accusation troubled him. He had intended the opposite. "I suppose," he sighed, "that's the reason for the verdict. I tried to keep the race question out of it—I'd like to see them all go free. It's bad enough just being in this world, without being hounded and persecuted by law." [14]

While waiting for the judge to pass sentence, Clarence appeared as a dinner speaker in Honolulu at the Representative Club. Much of his talk was about crime and criminals. "If we can get people to stop hating and to understand each other, if we stop punishing and try to cure, we will get where we want to go.

"Cure poverty and you will cure most of the crime," he told 150 members of the club. [15] *His theme was similar to what he had told the inmates of the Cook County jail thirty years earlier. "If every man and woman and child in the world had a chance to make a decent, fair, honest living," he had said then, "there would be no jails and no lawyers and no courts." [16]*

6

Clarence leaned against the rail of the S.S. *Malolo* as it docked at San Francisco on Friday, May 13. At his side stood Lieutenant Massie. Clarence talked about the "unwritten law," much discussed during the trial: "What, through innumerable murder trials has come to be known as the unwritten law does not exist because it is written," he said. "It is written when the circumstances leading up to a murder are so bad, so terrible, that the jury will refuse to convict." [17]

This would be his first and only time in California since his own trials, but he still could not bring himself to visit Los Angeles. Clarence and Ruby remained in the Bay area only a few days before returning to Chicago, long enough for him to speak at the monthly luncheon of the San Francisco Bar Association and at a meeting of the Alameda County Bar Association. At the San Francisco bar luncheon he was surely thinking of the Massie trial when he said, "Individuals do not control themselves but are, themselves, controlled by circumstances." He urged proper child care and education and elimination of poverty as the surest ways to eradicate crime, a thesis criminologists continue to discuss. [18]

"Since I have not had time to prepare a speech," he told attorneys in Oakland at the Bar Association of Alameda County the next evening, "I thought I had better talk about myself." He concluded, "If I've done anything worthwhile, I am not to blame for it. I believe I am an object of chance or destiny—whatever you wish to call it. I am the result of the accident that happened to my father and mother. I was a victim at birth and a victim in life."

He could not resist, however, a dig at lawyers in civil practice. "I would not go back to civil practice, it deals with dead things, money.

"Criminal law deals with men and women, emotions, life and death, pain and sorrow. Back of every act is a cause, and back of that cause another, and so on. There is no free will."

Again he repeated the theme of his 1902 talk at the Cook County jail: "Men are in jail because they have no place else to go. Life is hard; men are unfortunate. Jails are for the poor."

And again the plea for love and understanding: "There should be more human sympathy, more love instead of hate. When that time comes, there will be no more prisons to cast their gloom over life." [19]

7

Clarence had become a folk hero during his lifetime, his name a household word. Dr. John Haynes Holmes teased him about having acolytes eager "to sit at your feet." Editors sent reporters to his home for interviews; magazines asked for articles. He made pilgrimages to governors and parole boards and judges to plead for clemency and against executions.

As in the Prendergast case earlier in his career, Darrow became attorney for seventeen-year-old Russell McWilliams after the young man's conviction and death sentence. Twice McWilliams had been tried and twice sentenced to death for the murder of a streetcar motorman in Rockford, Illinois. In October 1932 Darrow represented him in his second appeal to the Illinois Supreme Court and argued that in McWilliams's earlier trial the judge had erred in refusing to grant a change of venue after the case had been sent back to him by the Supreme Court.

The case became front-page news across the country, a cause célèbre in the fight against capital punishment. The law-and-order advocates who believed the death penalty prevented crime were pitted against the "do-gooders" who found capital punishment repugnant and ineffective as a deterrent.

The Illinois high court remanded the case for a rehearing and ordered a change of venue. When the case went to trial for the third time, Darrow defended the convicted grade-school dropout who admitted being drunk when he killed the conductor. "Drunk on the cheap stuff that came with prohibition," Darrow proclaimed, striking a blow at another of his bêtes noires.

For the first time in his three trials, the young prisoner went on the stand. He described his background in a mining camp, the harshness of the drab and weary life, its abject poverty. Again, Darrow's lifelong philosophy that man has no free will dominated his plea. McWilliams, he contended, was only the product of his environment, the determining factor of his conduct. "No books, no pictures, no chance. He killed a man. Why did he do it? He said he wanted to get some money to have some fun. Isn't that an honest answer? That was his motive and that's the motive of life."

Darrow turned to the judge as he had in the Leopold and Loeb case almost ten years earlier: "Nobody in this world knows what justice is, and nobody can know. Man loves vengeance and he calls vengeance justice. There is only one object of punishment and that is hate. No man can take away another's life or liberty unless he hates him."[20]

Unlike Judge Caverly, however, the Rockford judge was not moved to mercy, and again McWilliams was sentenced to die. Using the final resource, Darrow traveled to Springfield, the Illinois capital, to plead before the State Board of Pardons and Parole to recommend clemency to Governor Henry Horner.

The veteran attorney waived all legal technicalities as he stood before the board and simply stated his thesis: "It is not the policy of this state to kill children." He told the ten-man board, "One of the first concerns of the state is to protect the young. There was no protection in this case. It couldn't have been worse the way the two judges who tried the case three times handled it. The mind of the child is not the mind of the man. The child does not have the experience that alone can guide in life. The civil laws recognize this. Why should not the criminal laws recognize it," the aging Darrow asked rhetorically.[21]

"Clarence Darrow cried today," reported the *Chicago American*. "The once deep rumble of thunder in the voice that cried in the world 76 years ago next Tuesday was muted; there was a sob in his throat, tears in his eyes as he pleaded—as a child might ask for something and not be able to understand why it should be denied to him—for the life of a 'boy who never had a chance.'"[22]

A week after the board hearing, Governor Horner commuted McWilliams's death sentence to ninety-nine years imprisonment. "The ancient theme of 'an eye for an eye and a life for a life' is not the inflexible rule of modern criminology," Horner declared.[23] He announced his verdict on April 18, Darrow's seventy-sixth birthday anniversary. "No greater birthday present could have been tendered to me," an elated Clarence said when he received the news.[24]

McWilliams would write to Darrow on the attorney's seventy-eighth birthday, "I haven't heard from you for a long time, Mr. Darrow but I remember that Thursday is your birthday. Whatever you may be doing you are thinking of unfortunate people and sympathizing with them and helping them."[25]

Darrow's lean fingers trembled as he held the greeting. "You know," he said, "no man ever killed anyone without a real or fancied reason. But capital punishment is deliberate and cruel. Why can't we have more tolerance in the world?" he sighed. [26]

In 1950, seventeen years after the crime, McWilliams was paroled.

8

When Bruno Richard Hauptmann, the kidnapper and murderer of the Charles Lindbergh baby, was sentenced to the electric chair in 1936, many people questioned whether he had had a fair and impartial trial. The United Press wanted to know Darrow's opinion.

"The Lindberghs, the prosecuting attorney and the public should prefer that no stone be left unturned in their attempt to prove definitely his connection with the crime," he said. [27] He believed the fear surrounding the case created a hysteria for a hasty execution and recommended that Hauptmann be tried again in a cooler climate of opinion.

9

He appeared before a subcommittee of the Illinois State Parole Board to plead for the release of Jessie Binga, seventy-one, a black ex-banker serving a ten-year prison sentence. Binga, president of the defunct Binga State Bank, had been convicted in 1933 of embezzling $32,000 of the bank's funds. The ex-banker had already served eleven months of his term. "I have known Binga for 30 years," Clarence said, "and he is a man of fine character. He lost his fortune trying to keep his bank open." The bank could have survived, he pointed out, if the Clearing House had given aid. Again—his client had been the victim of a stronger force. [28]

Even in his retirement there was never enough time. *Scribner's* invited him to write an article on "Who Knows Justice?"; for the *Forum* he wrote "The Futility of the Death Penalty"; and in *Rotarian Magazine* he discussed "Capital Punishment."

Esquire asked him to explain his modus operandi in selecting a jury. The article, titled "Attorney for the Defense," appeared in the May 1936 issue. He advised against accepting Presbyterians, Baptists, Lutherans, prohibitionists, and wealthy men. He suggested that Englishmen and Germans, and "Unitarians, Universalists, Congregationalists, Jews and other [sic] agnostics" be accepted. As for Christian Scientists, he "never experimented" with them; and he had his doubts about the compassion of women jurors.

The *Chicago Times* asked his ideas on Christmas. Scroogelike, he replied, "It is humbug!" Stores utilize Christmas "to get money out of people. They sell the customers goods they don't want or need to give to people who don't like the gifts at exorbitant prices, until the rush is over, then dump what's left—bargains—to lure shoppers a second time. . . . Christmas is a source of profound sorrow for fathers and mothers who cannot afford to fill up their children's stockings with gifts."[29]

Sixteen years earlier, in a letter to Fremont Older written on Christmas Day, he had said, "I gave no presents to anyone and wished no one a Merry Christmas. This is one kind of bunk I cut out long ago. I am as fast as possible cutting out all bunk."[30]

10

The year 1933 suffered the worst depression the United States had ever experienced as twelve to fourteen million men and women lost their jobs, factories closed, and families doubled up in homes. Evictions, mortgage foreclosures, farm bankruptcies, both large and small fortunes lost in bank failures, breadlines, discontent, and desperation haunted the nation as Franklin Delano Roosevelt was inaugurated in March of that year for the first of four terms as president of the United States. Clarence considered Roosevelt "a man of culture, a student, and a scholar. In political life he has made good. I have long respected his courage and devotion. I like him for his open and frank discussion of political questions, for the clarity of his ideas and his honest sympathy with the fortunes and fate of his fellow men."[31]

In his acceptance speech at the Democratic party convention on July 2, 1932, in Chicago, Roosevelt said the nation's economy must be reconstructed. "I pledge you, I pledge myself to a new deal for the American people." The New Deal became the epithet that would identify his administrations.

Millions of Americans congregated around their radios on Inauguration Day, March 4, 1933, as the new president encouraged a despairing nation: "Let me assert my firm belief that the only thing we have to fear is fear itself." He promised "action now." In his first hundred days he prevailed on Congress to enact such legislation as the Emergency Banking Act; he was responsible for the Civilian Conservation Corps, the Federal Emergency Relief Act, and the Emergency Farm Act which provided for refinancing farm mortgages, as well as the National Recovery Administration, designed to regenerate industry and put men to work. Severe criticism soon attacked the NRA. Instead of helping small businesses as was its professed intention, the various codes it created made it an instrument of monopoly.

The critique resulted in the formation of the National Recovery Review Board. At the suggestion of Senator Gerald P. Nye of North Dakota, one of the NRA's most vocal critics, General Hugh S. Johnson, the NRA administrator, asked Darrow to head the Review Board. Clarence responded that he was no longer young and his health "not altogether reliable but am inclined to accept your invitation."[32]

Ruby and Clarence moved to the Willard Hotel in Washington, D.C., for the duration of the review. On their arrival, Clarence paid a courtesy visit to the president and came away satisfied that the opinions of the Review Board were to be made independent of political considerations. The Review Board would begin to work as soon as offices were allocated.

Much to Clarence's distress, however, General Johnson had arranged for office space "next or close" to the administrator. Clarence protested. He believed it unwise for board members to be located so close to the agency they were reviewing. He also made it very plain that his intentions were to report directly to the president, not to the administrator. The board was provided with a meeting room in the Willard Hotel.

A few days after the hearing began, Clarence participated at the first NRA Code Authority conference. Called on for a statement,[33] he smiled and said he had discovered, after listening to the previous speakers who represented management, that "the rich love the poor. They should do so. They have lived off them for many years." He compared the "fervor of many of those who protested most loudly their belief in the NRA with the religious revival meetings he attended as a boy" and his comprehension "that the worst boys always got religion, but they always get over it as soon as the meeting was out." He didn't know whether the Review Board could accomplish anything, but he promised it would try. If NRA has "worked toward monopoly we will tell the president."

"It is easier," a cynical Clarence said, "to find fault than to tell what to do" to correct the situation. He added capriciously, "This is why I always find fault," referring to his negative positions in debate.

Clarence and the other members of the Review Board, and the staff headed by Lowell B. Mason, worked day and night. Mason was a former Illinois state senator and at this time a Washington, D.C., lawyer. He would be named a member of the Federal Trade Commission in 1945.

One sunny afternoon, Clarence visited the White House again. "Mr. Darrow," said President Roosevelt, "you are doing a wonderful job." Protocol called for Darrow to be humble and merely murmur, "Thank you, Mr. President. You are so kind." Clarence, however, had never been bound by conventions. He responded, "Do you really think so, Mr. President?"[34]

The Review Board held 60 public hearings, examined 34 codes, studied 3375 complaints, and prepared 3 reports, the first of which was sent to the White House. It set the tone for the following reports.

The New York Times headline of May 21, 1934, summarized the report and the reaction of the administration.

Darrow Board Find NRA
Tends Toward Monopoly:
Johnson Condemns The Report

Johnson raged that he had never seen "a more superficial, intemperate and inaccurate document." The Review Board "is not in good faith," he said. "It assumes, after a few hours of cavalier inquiry and prejudiced and one-sided testimony, to pass on codes upon which we spent days and weeks on inquiry and negotiations."[35]

Testifying before a congressional committee investigating the NRA, Darrow contradicted Johnson. His board had obtained the "best of evidence . . . in the quickest way," in response to the administration's repeated requests for "the necessity of speed." To Darrow it appeared that the NRA insidiously sought to help big business even if it meant taking "the business away from the small fellows."[36] When Clarence was a guest at the Port Washington, New York, home of Arthur Garfield Hays a few months later, however, he commented that despite his criticism of the Roosevelt plan he did not know "of anything to take its place."[37]

One of the few who understood Darrow's political iconoclasm was the English historian and Fabian Socialist H. G. Wells, whose book *The Outline of History* remains a classic. He saw Clarence's insurgence as a "fine" flower of "American insurrectionism." Clarence, he said, believed "superstitiously in the individual unorganized free common man, that is to say he is a sentimental anarchist. He is for an imaginary 'little man'—against monopoly, against rule, against law, any law."[38]

Eventually, the United States Supreme Court ruled the NRA unconstitutional.

11

Arthur Garfield Hays held a party for Darrow in New York. Mary Field Parton came with her husband. Many literary people were there. Darrow seemed to Mary "broken, bent, shrunken. Beside the younger men, he looked small." Thomas Wolfe was there, "a huge creature who could swallow Darrow in one gulp." The lights were turned low, and conversation rippled in subdued tones. Darrow sat on a couch. People came, conversed with him quietly, then "swam like silent fish about the room, drank highballs . . . or sat high and dry on the sofa."[39]

Mary had not seen Clarence for almost three years and was shocked at the change in him. She and her husband left the party early, "feet aching horribly in my party shoes . . . heart aching horribly at the sign of death upon my old friend."

The next day Mary came to his hotel to take him to lunch, but "it wasn't Darrow who went. It was his shadow—physically, mentally. God what a tragedy! He was utterly indifferent to me. I mean nothing to him now. Well, it is better to mean something to a person when his mind and heart function than when they no longer do. Lunch at Charles. Darrow forgets, didn't remember so important a historical fact as Reichstag fire—walked back and he said 'Don't come in with me I'm going to lie down.' His face is shrunken, cheeks hollow, eyes cavernous."

Some things about her old friend Mary found the same: "His smile and shoulder shrug, characteristics, are the same. His point of view, professional pessimism, same. His mind runs over that old track with the ease of accustomed routing of thought. He is old fashioned. A preacher of doom as was Cotton Mather in his day, only without idea of punishment. I felt so depressed with his 'passing.'"[40]

12

For many years Clarence made annual nostalgic vistis to Kinsman. The town in which he spent his youth was always respectful in its welcome, but underneath was a subtle agreement that, native to Farmdale and Kinsman though he was, Clarence had always been and still remained an "alien" in their midst.

Soon after *The Story of My Life* appeared, the librarian of the Kinsman Free Public Library asked Clarence for a library copy. He sent a copy, but could not resist telling her he wished some of the townspeople would have wanted to purchase the book. "Anyhow," he added in his letter, "I have a warm feeling toward Kinsman and no animosities against anyone who lives there or ever did." Capriciously, he warned her to be "very careful" to whom the book was lent. "No one under sixty should be permitted to read it, for while it is very religious in spots, in fact all through, it is not orthodox in anything—and I know Kinsman. I can hear the old Presbyterian bell ring now as I write this letter and expect to hear it amongst the last sounds that ever reach my ears."[41]

At the age of seventy-nine Clarence made his last sentimental journey to Kinsman and its environs. He visited nearby Farmdale, the hamlet in which he had been born, and Andover, ten miles north where he had begun his law practice. He still remembered the humiliation and resentment he felt when an older opposing counsel referred to him as "Bub." He visited the burned-out site of the No. 3 School House where he had taught. There were visits with the few remaining old friends in Kinsman. He was delighted when the librarian of the Kinsman Library told him that his autobiography "hasn't been in the library over night since the day we got it." He kept away from the cemetery where his mother had been interred sixty-five years earlier, the only time he had passed through its gates. As he left the memories of the day behind, Clarence hummed a hymn he had learned in his boyhood, the words of which he professed to disbelieve: "In the Sweet By and By, We Shall Meet on That Beautiful Shore."[42]

13

As he neared his eightieth birthday the infirmities of age forced him to spend more and more time in bed. He became perceptibly weaker, yet he left a sickbed to argue before the Michigan State Legislature against the reestablishment of capital punishment in the state where no judge or jury for ninety years had imposed the death penalty. The bill was defeated.

The only public observance to honor his eightieth birthday came in the publication of answers to written questions submitted to him by the Associated Press. [43] He said he was "fairly well satisfied" with his life and his actions; his "efforts in behalf of unfortunates" had brought him "the greatest and most lasting gratification"; his most difficult task had been "to help overcome the cruelties of the world. Worst of all, the horrible punishments, tortures and injustices inflicted; like lynching, the rankest vengeance; capital punishment, which does not deter others." He admitted society was "burdened with many abnormal and misfit humans, who are the victims of their own conduct, nevertheless they deserve to be treated as patients in institutions instead of imprisoned and punished." He would "like to see a crop of lawyers developed . . . with more genuine, humane ambition to benefit the poor and unfortunate clients, rather than mainly themselves."

He had not changed his attitude toward religion. "I feel as I always have, that the Earth is the home, and the only home, of man, and I am convinced that whatever he is to get out of his existence he must get while he is here."

He rarely left his apartment now except for a short walk along the Midway or to visit Paul and his family who lived a block away. Many times during his last illness, Clarence would walk to the bay window of the large Midway apartment and look toward the Museum of Science and Industry and the Wooded Island in Jackson Park. When he had a visitor, he might point to the site and comment, "That is the prettiest view on earth."[44]

14

Since the NRA days he had been failing in health. Ruby hovered over him, tenderly cared for him, aware that his days were numbered. The last seven months of his life she hired around-the-clock nurses to help her. His memory was failing, he spoke little, dozed much of the time. Occasionally, the nurses would prop him up in a chair for short intervals. But the old warrior of courtroom battles became progressively weaker. He died on Sunday afternoon, March 13, 1938. At his bedside were Ruby, Paul, and his sister Jenny Moore.[45]

His body lay in state at the Skeeles-Biddle Funeral parlor on East Sixty-third Street. Morning, noon, and night, men and women, old and young, passed by the solid mahogany casket, a gift in his memory from a friend. The weak and the meek, the professor and the bum, the prostitute and the teacher, judges and thieves, plumbers, mechanics, bricklayers, steelworkers, store-keepers and clothing workers, lawyers and doctors, all came. A clothing worker who had walked the picket line in the 1910 strike at Hart, Schaffner & Marx turned to his wife as they passed the coffin: "He was our lawyer during the strike. What he did—it can't be measured."[46]

"No, I didn't know him personally, exactly—just what he'd done for us— the ironworkers' union—you know."[47]

"There ought to be more like him," said a black man.[48]

On Tuesday afternoon the body was moved to Bond Chapel on the University of Chicago campus. Darrow lay dressed in an Oxford gray suit; the galluses so much his trademark now formally hidden by the jacket; the black string tie lay neatly over a white shirt.

Clarence and his friend William H. Holly, a former law partner and now a federal judge, had promised each other that the "last man" would officiate at the other's memorial services. Judge Holly in his eulogy[49] reminded the mourners that "while this is a time of sorrow, is it not better to think for a while of the great fact that he did live, that we did hear his voice, that we did grasp his hand, that we knew his big loving heart.

"It is a magnificent thing that he lived. The colored race will long remember him with grateful hearts for his heroic battles in their behalf. The man who toils with his hands, the poor and unfortunate whom society hunted down, found him ever ready to devote his extraordinary talents in their behalf. He gave up a brilliant legal career that could have made him one of the rich men of the country to espouse the cause of labor."

Slowly the mourners filed out of Bond Chapel. Darrow had requested that he be cremated just as his father had been. George Whitehead, his friend and his lecture manager, and the three male nurses who had attended Clarence followed the hearse to the cemetery and watched the cremation. That same evening the four men returned with the ashes to the Midway apartment. Paul joined them there and they drove to the bridge over the Jackson Park lagoon. Facing the Museum of Science and Industry, they opened the container and the ashes flew off with the sharp March breeze.

15

The American Federation of Labor set aside its bitterness against him because of the McNamara affair. William Green, AFL president, said, "Organized labour mourns the passing of a true friend in the death of Clarence Darrow. He was America's pioneer labor attorney during a period when few lawyers dared to champion labor's cause. His devotion to progressive ideals, his fearless and independent thinking and his outspoken advocacy of the rights of the downrodden make him a notable figure in American history." [50]

Tom Mooney, a labor leader serving a life prison sentence on a framed-up charge of tossing a bomb in a prepreparedness parade in San Francisco in 1916, and who would be unconditionally pardoned in 1939, said he had studied Darrow's life and work. "He was a champion of labor and the underdog. He will always be remembered by them as the highest type of counsellor." [51]

NAACP's James Weldon Johnson called Darrow "one of the greatest of Americans . . . members of my race, feel gratitude for his courage and willingness to stand always as the champion of fair play and justice for the Negro. And I loved him for all his high and true qualities as a friend." [52]

In New York, Mary Field Parton wrote in her diary: "12:30. Darrow died today at this hour. Goodbye, dear friend. We spoke the same language—the inarticulate language of the heart. You who never knew a moment free from heartache over man's travail, now are free . . . yet death ending consciousness, you do not know you are free. Oh grave where is thy sting? I know. It is in life itself, for such as Darrow. Farewell. Good night." [53]

Epilogue

Even after death Darrow remained an outsider to Kinsman natives. Anthony Weitzel, writing in the *Akron Times Press* from Kinsman two days after Clarence died, reported the attorney's "home town slid his memory into a lonely niche of legend beside the folk-effigy of his father, Kinsman village infidel. Kinsman never did quite figure out old Amirus Darrow, the haywire undertaker who roosted his chickens on his rickety hearse . . . the godless unbeliever who paid a dollar a year for a cut-rate pew in the Presbyterian Church."[1]

In 1960 when the consolidated high school in Kinsman for Hartford, Vernon, and Gustavus merged, the citizens voted down the suggestion that it be named in memory of Clarence. His agnosticism lost him the honor, which went to Joseph Badger, a famed circuit rider.

The first memorial in Trumbull County, Ohio, to Darrow, one of its native sons, came in October 1975 when a fifty-acre park was named the Clarence Darrow Park. About the same time, the Darrow house in Kinsman was placed on the National Register of Historic Places.

In Chicago, the bridge in Jackson Park from which his ashes were strewn carries Darrow's name, as does a community settlement house in a black housing project. And in 1979, a new library in the Cook County jail was dedicated as the Clarence Darrow Library.

384

The centenary of Darrow's death saw a daylong celebration in Chicago honoring the "attorney for the damned." Sponsored by the Clarence Darrow Centennial Committee—whose members included the presidents of the American, Illinois, and Chicago Bar Associations—together with the Adult Education Council of Greater Chicago, the event opened with the dedication of the Clarence Darrow Memorial Bridge in Jackson Park.

During the day, associates and friends and Darrow admirers gathered at Chicago's historic Sherman House in organized seminars and meetings to reflect on the Darrow they knew and the legacy he left. A Darrow exhibit was on display for a month at the Newberry Library. In the evening the grand ballroom of the Sherman House overflowed as more than twelve hundred people came to celebrate the life of Clarence Darrow. Actor Melvyn Douglas read excerpts of Darrow pleas.

Joseph N. Welch, prominent Boston lawyer and attorney for the U.S. Army during the Army-McCarthy hearings of 1954, concluded the evening. Clarence was "so brave and so fearless that he never seemed to realize he was either." Perhaps now, said Welch, he is "in some Nirvana where there is . . . only endless sleep" or where there are "books to read, a group to sit and listen at his feet, a handful of cases to try and unpopular causes to defend." [2]

Notes

Introduction (pp. 9–14)

1. Darrow, *The Story of My Life* (1932), pp. 223–24.
2. Eastman (1948), pp. 424–25.
3. In re Anastaplo 366 U.S. 82 at 115 (1961).
4. William Kunstler letter to authors, July 7, 1977.
5. Charles Morgan, Jr., in conversation with AW, January 1979.
6. Mitgang (1968), p. 545.
7. Elmer Gertz in conversations with authors.
8. Robert S. Whitehead letter to authors, August 8, 1979.

Chapter I: "Who Is This Man Darrow?" (pp. 15–29)

1. *Los Angeles Times,* October 2, 1910; cited in Stimson (1955), p. 368.
2. Ibid.
3. Gompers (1911), p. 3.
4. Ibid., pp. 3, 4.
5. "Who Is This Man Darrow?" *Current Literature* 43 (August 1907): 159, 157.
6. Darrow, *The Story of My Life* (1932), p. 60.
7. From the proceedings of the Fifth Biennial Convention of the Amalgamated Clothing Workers of America, Chicago, 1922; cited in Weinberg (1963), p. 104.

8. Darrow, *The Story of My Life* (1932), p. 13.
9. Ibid., p. 1
10. Darrow, *The Story of My Life* (1932), p. 2; *Chicago Daily News,* April 29, 1932.
11. Darrow family records, Kinsman Free Public Library, Kinsman, Ohio; census records, Newberry Library, Chicago.
12. Darrow, *The Story of My Life* (1932), p. 8.
13. Clarence spells his father's given name as "Amirus" and we have used that spelling. According to the Chicago census records, however, it was spelled "Ammirus." Amirus lived the last years of his life in Chicago.
14. Darrow ms., Darrow Collection, Library of Congress.
15. Darrow, *The Story of My Life* (1932), p. 14.
16. Darrow ms., Darrow Collection, Library of Congress.
17. Ibid.
18. Darrow, *The Story of My Life* (1932), p. 14.
19. Ibid., p. 11.
20. George G. Whitehead, *Cleveland Plain Dealer,* April 18, 1937.
21. Description of the Farmdale house is found in Darrow's *Farmington* (1932), pp. 20–22, as well as from the authors' visit to the home in May 1977. Additional description is from the *Cleveland Plain Dealer,* October 4, 1964.
22. Description of the Kinsman house is consolidated from the authors' two visits to Kinsman—in July 1968 and in May 1977.
23. Darrow, *The Story of My Life* (1932), p. 19.
24. *Chicago Daily News,* May 20, 1925.
25. Ibid.
26. Darrow, *Farmington* (1932), pp. 202, 203.
27. Darrow, *The Story of My Life* (1932), pp. 17–18.
28. Darrow, *Farmington* (1932), p. 195.
29. Paul Darrow in conversation with AW, 1956.
30. *Boston Globe,* March 17, 1927.
31. Darrow, *Farmington* (1932), p. 41.
32. *Chicago Daily News,* May 20, 1925.
33. Quotations of Darrow's remembrance of his mother appear in his *Story of My Life* (1932), p. 16.
34. "Ladies-in-waiting" was a term Ruby Darrow used in the letters she wrote to Irving Stone during the time Stone was writing Darrow's biography. The term was intended to describe women she believed were romantically interested in Clarence. Ruby's letters are in the Darrow Collection, Library of Congress.
35. *Cleveland Plain Dealer,* April 18, 1937.
36. Ibid.
37. Darrow, *The Story of My Life* (1932), p. 381.

38. Norman Thomas speaking at the symposium on "Freedom Under Law" at the Darrow Centennial Celebration, Chicago, May 1, 1957; also in conversation with authors, May 1, 1957.
39. Harrison (1931), pp. 292–93.
40. Thomas S. St. Antoine, dean, University of Michigan Law School, letter to authors re tuition fees.
41. Newspaper clipping (n.d.), Labadie Collection, University of Michigan.
42. *Hawaiian Advertiser,* May 3, 1932.
43. Darrow, *The Story of My Life* (1932), p. 29.
44. Proceedings, Illinois State Bar Association (June 1–2, 1922), p. 308.
45. Darrow letter to Ralph Johnson, secretary of the Chamber of Commerce, McPherson, Kansas, January 30, 1932; letter cited in Weinberg (1963), p. 22.
46. Mayor Richard J. Daley of Chicago speaking at the dinner which concluded the daylong Darrow Centennial Celebration in Chicago, May 1, 1957.
47. Belli (1976), p. 73n.
48. Darrow ms., Darrow Collection, Library of Congress.

Chapter II: In Search of Intellectual Stimuli (pp. 30–40)

1. *The Autobiography of Mother Jones* (1925), p. 17.
2. Carter Harrison scrapbook, Newberry Library, Chicago.
3. The words "I command you, . . ." have been immortalized on a statue dedicated to the Haymarket policemen by the City of Chicago. Over the years, the statue has been moved to various public sites in Chicago and currently stands in the lobby of the city's police training center.
4. Darrow, *The Story of My Life* (1932), p. 98.
5. A monument to the Haymarket labor men stands over their graves in Forest Home Cemetery (formerly German Waldheim Cemetery) near Chicago. It was erected in 1894 with money collected from labor unions and various radical groups. On the base of the monument are carved the last words of August Spies, one of the defendants: "There will come a time when our silence will be more powerful than the voices you are throttling today." Attached to the back of the monument is a plaque engraved with part of Governor Altgeld's pardon message.
6. Barnard (1938), p. 184.
7. Darrow, *The Story of My Life* (1932), p. 102.
8. Ibid., p. 42.
9. Darrow, "On Single Tax," *Everyman,* August–September 1914.
10. Darrow letter to Henry Demarest Lloyd, Lloyd Collection, University of Wisconsin, March 19, [1903].
11. *The New York Times,* April 18, 1937.
12. Darrow, *The Story of My Life* (1932), p. 53.

13. *Chicago Herald*, April 26, 1891; quoted in *Echoes of the Sunset Club* (1891).
14. Ibid.
15. Ibid.
16. Minutes of the Sunset Club, November 5, 1891.
17. Darrow, "Attorney for the Defense," *Esquire*, May 1936; also in Weinberg (1963), p. 320.
18. Darrow, "Liberty, Equality, Fraternity," *Vanity Fair*, December 1926.
19. Darrow letter to Fremont Older, December 25, 1920.
20. Darrow, *The Story of My Life* (1932), p. 54.
21. Ibid., p. 45.
22. Ibid., pp. 46–48.
23. *Hawaiian Advertiser*, May 3, 1932.
24. *Echoes of the Sunset Club* (1891).
25. *Chicago Tribune* (n.d.), *Tribune* morgue.

Chapter III: "I Can't Stand to Have a Client Executed" (pp. 41–48)

1. Minutes of the Sunset Club, October 22, 1891, p. 21.
2. Ibid., December 29, 1892, p. 79.
3. Quoted in Weinberg (1957), pp. 187–88.
4. *Chicago Tribune*, October 29, 1893.
5. *Chicago Herald*, October 29, 1893.
6. Kraus (1925), p. 76.
7. *Chicago Herald*, October 29, 1893.
8. *Chicago Times*, October 29, 1893.
9. *Chicago Tribune*, December 6, 1936.
10. Cited in Kogan (1974), p. 76.
11. All Prendergast material is from newspaper clippings in the Carter Harrison scrapbook, Newberry Library, Chicago.
12. Darrow, *The Story of My Life* (1932), p. 361.
13. Ibid., p. 336.
14. Darrow summation in Prendergast trial is in Darrow Collection, Library of Congress.
15. Quoted in Weinberg (1957), p. 24.
16. Ibid., p. 86.
17. Ibid., p. 58.
18. Whitlock (1914), p. 83.
19. Crunden (1969), pp. 85, 107.

Chapter IV: "I Must Resign" (pp. 49–65)

1. U.S. Strike Commission, *Report on the Chicago Strike of June–July 1894* (1895), p. 529.

2. Ibid.
3. Ibid., p. 531.
4. Lindsey (1967), p. 46.
5. Quoted in the *Chicago Sun Times,* July 30, 1974.
6. *Chicago Journal,* April 23, 1894.
7. *Chicago Daily News,* May 10, 1894.
8. *Chicago Evening Post,* May 10, 1894.
9. Ibid., May 11, 1894.
10. *Chicago Inter-Ocean,* May 12, 1894.
11. Beer (1929), p. 133.
12. Pullman scrapbook, Newberry Library, Chicago.
13. Debs (1948), p. 437.
14. Darrow, *The Story of My Life* (1932), p. 68.
15. Debs (1948), p. 243.
16. Harrison (1931), p. 65.
17. U.S. Strike Commission, *Report on the Chicago Strike of June–July 1894* (1895), p. 131.
18. Ibid., p. 177.
19. *The New York Times,* July 5, 1894.
20. Darrow, *The Story of My Life* (1932), p. 61.
21. Governor John Altgeld to President Grover Cleveland, July 5, 1894.
22. President Cleveland to Governor Altgeld, July 5, 1894.
23. Governor Altgeld to President Cleveland, July 6, 1894.
24. *The New York Times,* July 3, 1894.
25. Darrow, *The Story of My Life* (1932), pp. 60–61.
26. Ibid., p. 58.
27. In his autobiography Darrow incorrectly spells the name of the Chicago & Northwestern Railroad president as Hewitt instead of Hughitt.
28. U.S. Strike Commission, *Report on the Chicago Strike of June–July 1894* (1895), pp. 278–79.
29. Darrow, *The Story of My Life* (1932), pp. 61–62.
30. Ibid., p. 68.
31. Ibid., p. 66.
32. *Chicago Times,* September 6, 1894.
33. Ibid.
34. *Chicago Herald,* September 26, 1894.
35. Ibid., September 27, 1894.
36. *Chicago Tribune,* September 27, 1894.
37. *Chicago Herald,* September 27, 1894.
38. In re Debs, U.S. Supreme Court, October term 1894, argued March 25–26, 1895, p. 95.
39. Ibid., p. 96.
40. Warne (1955); also Willard L. King in conversation with AW, October 7, 1976.

41. *The New York Times,* July 3, 1894.
42. George R. Peck letter to Richard Olney, May 27, 1875 (Richard Olney Papers); quoted in Lindsey (1967), p. 298.
43. Darrow, *The Story of My Life* (1932), p. 67.
44. U.S. Strike Commission, *Report on the Chicago Strike of June–July 1894* (1895), p. 3.
45. Ibid., p. 162.
46. Ibid., p. 554.
47. Ibid., p. xxxiv.
48. Ibid., p. 554.
49. Ibid., pp. xlv–xlvi.
50. Ibid., p. xlii.
51. Ibid., pp. xxx–xxxi.
52. Ibid., p. liv.
53. *Chicago Evening Post,* January 26, 1895.
54. Ibid.
55. Quoted in Weinberg (1957), pp. 153–54.
56. *Chicago Tribune,* February 8, 1895; cited in Harrison (1931), p. 76; and in Stone (1941), p. 63.
57. *Chicago Dispatch,* February 8, 1895.
58. *Chicago Evening Post,* February 13, 1895.
59. Darrow, *The Story of My Life* (1932), p. 59.

Chapter V: Out of the Political Arena (pp. 66–73)

1. *Chicago Record,* November 5, 1896.
2. Koenig (1971), p. 178.
3. Darrow, *The Story of My Life* (1932), p. 92; Barnard (1938), p. 370.
4. Ibid., p. 93.
5. Darrow, "Walt Whitman," in *A Persian Pearl and Other Essays* (1899), p. 44.
6. Ibid., p. 43.
7. Darrow, "Robert Burns," in *A Persian Pearl and Other Essays* (1899), p. 103.
8. Ibid., p. 86.
9. Darrow, *Resist Not Evil* (1925), p. 5.
10. Paul Darrow in conversation with AW, 1956.
11. Darrow letter to Paul Darrow, January 7, 1891. Original letter in possession of Darrow granddaughters.
12. Darrow, *The Story of My Life* (1932), p. 33.
13. Blanche Chase, Clarence's granddaughter, in conversations with AW.
14. Stone (1941), pp. 84–85.
15. Darrow vs. Darrow, Circuit Court of Cook County, Ill. No. 7141/168056, dated March 12, 1897.

16. Stone (1941), p. 103.
17. *London Daily Express,* October 4, 1927.
18. *London Sunday Express,* September 25, 1926.
19. Darrow, "The Divorce Problem," *Vanity Fair,* August 1927.
20. Goldman (1911), p. 233.
21. Ibid., p. 237.
22. Rosa M. Perdue letter to Dr. Richard T. Ely, January 23, 1903, State Historical Society of Wisconsin, Archives, Ely Collection, Madison, Wisconsin.

Chapter VI: The Robin Hood of the Courtroom (pp. 74–88)

1. Darrow, "Capital Punishment—No," *Rotarian Magazine,* November 1933, p. 61.
2. Darrow letter to a Miss S., who is probably Ellen Gates Starr. Although the letter is not dated, it was written eight years after he came to Chicago (Darrow Collection, Library of Congress).
3. Darrow, *The Story of My Life* (1932), p. 425.
4. *Chicago Daily News,* May 9, 1899.
5. Ibid., May 8, 1899.
6. Ibid., May 11, 1899.
7. Ibid., May 13, 1899.
8. Quoted in Weinberg (1957), p. 286.
9. Ibid., p. 287.
10. Ibid.
11. *Milwaukee Statesman,* November 18, 1898.
12. *Milwaukee Sentinel,* November 18, 1898.
13. Darrow's summation in Kidd case appears in Weinberg (1957), pp. 269–326.
14. Quoted in Weinberg (1957), p. 495.
15. Swing (1935), pp. 134–52.
16. *Chicago Daily News,* November 7, 1901.
17. Ibid., November 12, 1901.
18. Ibid.
19. Francis X. Busch in a luncheon address at the Darrow Centennial Celebration, Chicago, May 1, 1957; also in conversation with authors, May 1, 1957.
20. Ibid.
21. *Chicago Evening American,* December 4, 1901.
22. Quoted in Weinberg (1957), pp. 325–26.
23. Ibid., pp. 467–68.
24. *Chicago Evening American,* December 4, 1901.
25. Dunne, text of the decision, December 7, 1901, pp. 5–17.

26. Busch (1942), p. 79; also in conversation with authors, May 1, 1957.
27. *Leaves from the Garden of St. Bernard*, July–August 1963.
28. Busch (1942), p. 133.
29. Barnard (1938), pp. 434 ff.
30. Darrow's funeral eulogy of Altgeld appears on pp. 485--87 in the 1934 reprint edition of his autobiography, *The Story of My Life*.
31. Weinberg (1963), p. 75.
32. Weinberg (1957), p. 262.
33. Drinnon (1961), p. 70.
34. Darrow letter to Jane Addams, September 11, 1901 (Swarthmore College Library, microfilm).
35. Darrow speech to the inmates in the Cook County jail in Weinberg (1957), pp. 3–15.
36. Stone (1941), p. 170.

Chapter VII: "Steadfast Champion of People's Rights" (pp. 89–112)

1. Harry Barnard in conversations with authors.
2. Darrow, *The Story of My Life* (1932), p. 113.
3. *Chicago Daily News*, November 6, 1902.
4. *Documents Relating to the Anthracite Strike of 1902*, p. 1 (Darrow's own copy with his notations is in the possession of the authors).
5. The Baer letter appears in ibid., pp. 3–5.
6. The Truesdale letter appears in ibid., pp. 6–7.
7. The Thomas letter appears in ibid., pp. 7–10.
8. The Baer statement appears in ibid., pp. 30 ff.
9. The Markle statement appears in ibid., pp. 95 ff.
10. Ibid., p. 13.
11. Cornell (1957), p. 145.
12. *The Outlook* 72 (October 6, 1902): 763.
13. President Roosevelt's wire to Mitchell appears in *Documents Relating to the Anthracite Strike of 1902*, p. 104.
14. President Roosevelt's statement to the union-management conference appears in ibid., pp. 105–6.
15. Baer's response to President Roosevelt appears in ibid., pp. 107–9.
16. Markle's statement to President Roosevelt appears in ibid., pp. 111–12.
17. Truesdale's statement to President Roosevelt appears in ibid., pp. 113–16.
18. Mitchell's second statement to President Roosevelt appears in ibid., pp. 119–20.
19. Ibid., p. 127.
20. Ibid., p. 129.
21. *Chicago Daily News*, November 14, 1902.

22. Lloyd (1912), 2: 481.
23. *Literary Digest* 25 (December 27, 1902): 862.
24. *Documents Relating to the Anthracite Strike of 1902*, pp. 92–94.
25. *Literary Digest* 25 (November 29, 1902): 695.
26. Ibid.
27. Urofsky and Levy (1971), p. 211.
28. *Philadelphia North American*, January 6, 1903.
29. Ibid., January 7, 1903.
30. Ibid.
31. Ibid.
32. Ibid., January 8, 1903.
33. Ibid., January 31, 1903.
34. *Chicago Daily News*, February 13, 1903.
35. *Chicago Inter-Ocean*, February 13, 1903.
36. *Chicago Daily News*, February 14, 1903.
37. Ibid., February 12, 1903.
38. Ibid., February 13, 1903.
39. Lloyd (1912), 2:233.
40. *Philadelphia North American*, February 13, 1903.
41. Weinberg (1957), p. 468.
42. Ibid., p. 337.
43. *Chicago Inter-Ocean*, February 13, 1903.
44. Weinberg (1957), p. 407.
45. Cited in Stone (1941), p. 58.
46. Lloyd (1912), 2:233.
47. *Philadelphia North American*, February 13, 1903.
48. *Chicago Daily News*, February 14, 1903.
49. Anthracite Coal Strike Commission, *Report to the President* (1903), p. 56.
50. Ibid., p. 61.
51. Lloyd (1912), 2:237.
52. Darrow, "Realism in Literature and Art," in *A Persian Pearl and Other Essays* (1899), pp. 134–35; also in Weinberg (1963), p. 372.
53. Darrow, "Tolstoy," *The Rubric*, January 1902; also in Weinberg (1963), p. 186.
54. Harrison (1931), p. 105.
55. *Chicago Tribune*, November 6, 1902.
56. A. M. Simons letter to Darrow, November 8, 1902 (Lloyd file).
57. Lloyd (1909), pp. 253–54.
58. Darrow and Mitchell speeches reported in the *Chicago Daily News*, February 17, 1903.
59. *Chicago Inter-Ocean*, February 17, 1903.
60. *Chicago Daily News*, February 25, 1903.
61. Darrow, *The Story of My Life* (1932), p. 119.

62. Ibid., p. 120.
63. Darrow letter to Henry Demarest Lloyd, March 19, [1903].
64. Alexander Rovinsky, "Russia and the Jews," *The Arena* 30 (July 1903): 123.
65. *Chicago Tribune,* May 19, 1903.
66. *Chicago Record-Herald,* May 19, 1903.
67. Darrow–Stephen S. Wise debate, "Is Zionism a Progressive Policy for Israel and America?" Sinai Temple, Chicago, October 24, 1927.
68. Symposium, "What I Think of Nazi Germany," Washington Boulevard Temple, Chicago, December 7, 1933. The other participants were Dr. Preston Bradley of the Peoples Church of Chicago and Dr. Louis L. Mann of Sinai Temple, Chicago.

Chapter VIII: "I Cannot Find Time to Write" (pp. 113–126)

1. Darrow, *A Persian Pearl and Other Essays* (1899), pp. 14–15.
2. Ibid., p. 19.
3. Ibid., pp. 37–39.
4. Ruby Darrow letter to Stone, n.d., in Darrow Collection, Library of Congress.
5. Darrow, *Farmington* (1932), p. 255.
6. Ravitz (1962), p. 100.
7. Cargill (1941), p. 127.
8. Darrow, *Farmington* (1932), p. 267.
9. "Capital Punishment," *Success,* 1924.
10. *Dial* 37, October 16, 1904, p. 238.
11. Dr. Preston Bradley speaking at the symposium on "Freedom Under Law" at the Darrow Centennial Celebration, Chicago, May 1, 1957.
12. Stone (1941), p. 160.
13. Garland (1931), p. 322.
14. *Chicago Tribune,* January 11, 1914.
15. Darrow, *An Eye for an Eye* [1905].
16. Stone (1941), p. 177.
17. Darrow letter to Fanny Butcher, literary critic, columnist, and editor, *Chicago Tribune,* 1925 (*Chicago Tribune* file).
18. *The Bookman* 22 (February 1906): 629; also quoted in Weinberg (1963), p. 32.
19. Ravitz (1962), p. 85.
20. *The Pilgrim* (1903); also in Weinberg (1963), pp. 383–92.
21. Ravitz (1962), p. 64.
22. Dr. Preston Bradley in conversation with authors, 1975.
23. Masters (1936), p. 270.
24. Ibid., pp. 270–71.

25. Ibid., pp. 272, 274.
26. Darrow reminiscing to Charles Eugene Banks during the Massie trial in Honolulu (*Honolulu Advertiser,* April 10, 1932).
27. Abram Adelman in conversation with AW, 1967.
28. Originally published in *Rockford* (Ill.) *Republic,* October 11, 1922; the poem first received national attention when *The New Republic* published it on May 27, 1957.
29. John Turner, "The Protest of an Anarchist," *The Independent* 55 (December 24, 1903): 3052.
30. *The Independent* 55 (December 10, 1903): 2940. (Italics in original.)
31. Turner plea, brief, and argument, p. 30.
32. *Current Literature* 37 (July 1904): 5.
33. Darrow's argument in the defense of Communists, 1920, appears in Weinberg (1957), pp. 171–72.

Chapter IX: "I Speak for the Poor, for the Weak" (pp. 127–152)

1. Quoted in Ravitz and Primm (1960), pp. 75–76.
2. Ibid., p. 82.
3. Ibid., p. 113.
4. Haywood (1929), p. 193.
5. Ibid.
6. Supreme Court of the U.S., No. 249, October term, 1906, George A. Pettibone, Appellant vs. J. Jasper C. Nichols, Sheriff, December 3, 1906.
7. *Mother Earth* 2 (July 1907): 211.
8. Darrow, *The Story of My Life* (1932), p. 134.
9. *Idaho Statesman,* February 17, 1907.
10. Ibid., February 21, 1907.
11. Ibid., February 27, 1907.
12. Ibid., March 5, 1907.
13. Darrow's summation in the Adams case was initially printed in *Wayland's Monthly,* October 1907; also in Weinberg (1957), pp. 415–16.
14. *Idaho Statesman,* March 6, 1907.
15. Darrow, *The Story of My Life* (1932), p. 143.
16. Darrow letter to Haywood, Moyer, and Pettibone, in Darrow Collection, Library of Congress.
17. *Current Literature* 42 (June 1907): 590.
18. *Mother Earth* 2 (June 1907): 177.
19. *New York Tribune,* April 3, 1907; also see Scheinberg (1960), p. 12.
20. Scheinberg, Fall 1960, p. 15.
21. *Current Literature* 42 (June 1907): 593.
22. Haywood (1929), p. 207.
23. Darrow, *The Story of My Life* (1932), p. 68.

24. *Idaho Statesman,* April 28, 1907.
25. Quoted in Haywood (1929), p. 208.
26. *Idaho Statesman,* May 17, 1907.
27. Ibid.
28. Ibid. Hawley's opening statement was made on June 5, 1907.
29. Orchard's testimony was reported in *The New York Times,* June 6–16, 1907; also reported during the trial daily in the *Idaho Statesman.*
30. Orchard's autobiography was serialized in the August, September, and October 1907 issues of *McClure's Magazine.*
31. Darrow, *The Story of My Life* (1932), p. 151.
32. *The New York Times,* June 25, 1907; also see Grover (1964), p. 3.
33. Letter and copy of Johnson's ms. sent to authors March 25, 1958.
34. *Idaho Statesman,* July 12, 1907.
35. *Rocky Mountain News,* July 13, 1907.
36. *Collier's,* July 27, 1907; see also Grover (1964), p. 14.
37. *Idaho Statesman,* July 21, 1907.
38. Ibid., July 20, 1907.
39. Ibid., July 21, 1907.
40. Ibid., July 24, 1907.
41. Darrow's summation in the Haywood trial appears in Weinberg (1957), pp. 443–87.
42. Weinberg (1957), p. 87.
43. *Idaho Statesman,* July 26, 1907.
44. *Rocky Mountain News,* July 27, 1907; see also Haywood (1929), p. 214.
45. *Rocky Mountain News,* July 27, 1907.
46. Ravitz and Primm (1960), pp. 192–93.
47. Haywood (1929), p. 206; Harrison (1931), p. 125.
48. President Roosevelt to Whitelaw Reid, July 29, 1907, quoted in *Idaho Yesterdays* 4 (Fall 1960): 15.
49. *New York World* (July 30, 1907); Ravitz and Primm (1960), p. 203.
50. *New York Press* (July 30, 1907). Only thirteen years later, however, hysteria burst through Boston's noted restraint, decidedly not in a "triumph for the American law," as a flagrantly prejudiced judge conducted the trial of the anarchists Sacco and Vanzetti and sentenced them to death. They were executed August 22, 1927. In July of 1977, Massachusetts Governor Michael S. Dukakis declared that Sacco and Vanzetti had been the victims of an unfair trial.
51. Quoted Grover (1964), p. 291.
52. *Idaho Statesman,* August 2, 1907.
53. *The New York Times,* August 5, 1907.
54. Darrow, *The Story of My Life* (1932), p. 158.
55. The story of Darrow's illness is in Darrow's *Story of My Life* (1932), pp. 157–71; also see Stone (1941), pp. 243 ff.

56. *Idaho Statesman,* November 13, 1907.
57. Ibid., November 24, 1907.
58. Ibid., November 25, 1907.
59. Darrow, *The Story of My Life* (1932), p. 165.
60. Ibid., p. 170.
61. Wood (1931), p. 361.
62. *The New York Times,* May 19, 1915.
63. Darrow, *The Story of My Life* (1932), p. 171.

Chapter X: At Home in Hyde Park (pp. 153–161)

1. Haldeman-Julius (1936), p. 18.
2. Garland (1931), p. 322.
3. Eastman (1948), p. 342.
4. Margaret Parton letter to LW, April 23, 1975; also in conversation with authors, January 22, 1976, describing her conversation with her Aunt Sara, Mary Field's sister.
5. Margaret Parton letter to LW, April 23, 1975.
6. Ibid.; also in conversation with authors, January 22, 1976.
7. Margaret Parton's unpublished biography of her mother, Mary Field.
8. Ibid.
9. Darrow letter to Mary Field, March 5, 1910.
10. Margaret Parton's unpublished biography of Mary Field.
11. Darrow letter to Fremont Older, July 26, [1910].
12. Margaret Parton's unpublished biography of Mary Field. Mary Field edited *The Autobiography of Mother Jones* (1925), for which Darrow wrote the introduction.
13. Yarros (1950), p. 7.
14. Darrow letter to Mary Field, December 6, 1915.
15. Ibid., March 15, 1921.
16. Ibid., June 17, 1928.
17. Ruby Darrow letter to Stone, n.d., Darrow Collection, Library of Congress.
18. Margaret Parton's unpublished biography of Mary Field.
19. Entry in Mary Field's diary, February 8, 1928.
20. Margaret Parton in conversation with authors, January 22, 1976.
21. Parton (1973), pp. 24–25; also in conversation with authors, January 22, 1976.
22. Ibid.
23. Judge McKay in conversation with AW, February 15, 1979.
24. Ruby Darrow letter to Stone, n.d., Darrow Collection, Library of

Congress; Margaret Parton in conversation with authors, January 22, 1976.

25. Haldeman-Julius (1936), p. 17.
26. Nathan (1932), p. 84.
27. Dr. Preston Bradley in conversation with authors, 1976.
28. Addams (1910), p. 287.
29. *Chicago Evening American,* November 27, 1908.
30. *Chicago Daily News,* December 15, 1908.
31. Before the Department of State in the matter of the demand of the imperial Russian government for the extradition of Christian Rudovitz, statement and argument, p. 68.
32. Jessup (1938), p. 67.
33. *Chicago Daily News,* January 26, 1909.
34. Addams (1910), p. 288.

Chapter XI: Dynamite! (pp. 162–180)

1. Four years after the signing of the agreement between Hart, Schaffner & Marx and the United Garment Workers Union, a rebel group split from the union to form the Amalgamated Clothing Workers of America, now the Amalgamated Clothing and Textile Workers Union of America.
2. Adamic (1931), p. 198.
3. *International Socialist Review* 11 (November 1910): 264.
4. Quoted in Adamic (1931), p. 152.
5. Stimson (1955), p. 36.
6. "Otistown of Open Shop," *Hampton's* 26 (January 1911): 31; see also Stimson (1955), p. 368.
7. Stimson (1955), p. 37.
8. Ibid., p. 441, n. 17.
9. Connolly in *Collier's;* quoted in *Current Literature* 51 (November 1911): 468.
10. Stimson (1955), p. 378.
11. *Los Angeles Herald,* April 28, 1911.
12. Ibid., October 9, 1911.
13. Margaret Parton letter to LW, April 23, 1975.
14. *Los Angeles Herald,* November 14, 1911.
15. *Current Literature* 51 (November 1911): 467.
16. Steffens (1931), p. 661.
17. Ibid., p. 663.
18. Ibid., p. 663.
19. Ibid.

20. While use of the term "plea bargaining" is relatively recent, negotiations for lesser sentences, or compromises on a guilty plea, go back to the early days of court procedures.
21. *Los Angeles Herald,* December 4, 1911.
22. Cochran (1933), p. 149.
23. *Los Angeles Herald,* December 4, 1911.
24. Ibid., December 1, 1911.
25. Ibid., December 11, 1911.
26. *Los Angeles Times,* December 2, 1911.
27. Harrison (1931), p. 171.
28. *Los Angeles Herald,* December 1, 1911.
29. Darrow, *The Story of My Life* (1932), p. 185.
30. *Los Angeles Herald,* December 4, 1911.
31. Ibid., December 1, 1911.
32. *Los Angeles Times,* December 2, 1911.
33. Ibid., December 1, 1911.
34. Ibid., December 6, 1911.
35. *Los Angeles Herald,* December 4, 1911.
36. Ibid., December 5, 1911.
37. Ibid.
38. Ibid., December 2, 1911.
39. Theodore Roosevelt, "Murder Is Murder," *The Outlook* 99 (December 16, 1911): 902.
40. "Larger Bearings of the McNamara Case," *The Survey* 27 (December 30, 1911): 1428.
41. Ibid., p. 1418.
42. Grant (1915), p. 8.
43. Ibid., p. 139.
44. *Los Angeles Herald,* January 13, 1912.
45. Ibid., December 5, 1911.
46. Steffens (1931), p. 688.
47. *Los Angeles Herald,* December 6, 1911.
48. Margaret Parton's unpublished biography of Mary Field.
49. Ibid.
50. *Los Angeles Herald,* December 5, 1911.
51. Steffens (1931), p. 681.
52. *Los Angeles Herald,* December 5, 1911.

Chapter XII: Darrow Needs a Lawyer (pp. 181–192)

1. Cohn and Chisholm (1964), p. 197.
2. Bailey (1975), p. 358.

3. Sam Gompers letter to Darrow, March 16, 1912, quoted in Taft (1957), p. 284.

4. Darrow letter to Meyers, February 24, 1912, in Darrow collection, Library of Congress.

5. Darrow letter to Eugene V. Debs, February 12, 1912. Original letter is at Cunningham Library, Indiana State University, Terre Haute.

6. Eugene V. Debs letter to Darrow, February 19, 1912. Original letter is at Cunningham Library, Indiana State University, Terre Haute.

7. Mary Field unpublished notebooks, in possession of Margaret Parton.

8. *Los Angeles Examiner,* May 16, 1912.

9. Steffens (1931), pp. 664–66.

10. Statements of attorneys, examination and cross-examination of witnesses, judge's ruling, and remarks are from the sixteen-volume transcript of The People of California, plaintiff, vs. Clarence Darrow, defendant, No. 7373, in the Superior Court in and for the County of Los Angeles, Dept. No. 11. These are reproduced verbatim; only inaccurate spelling and punctuation have been corrected. Descriptions of the general atmosphere in the courtroom, not footnoted, come from the various Los Angeles newspapers of that period.

11. *Los Angeles Times,* May 25, 1912.

12. Lockwood's testimony appears in the Darrow trial transcript, pp. 126–350.

Chapter XIII: The State's Star Witness (pp. 193–204)

1. Franklin's testimony appears in the Darrow trial transcript, pp. 351–908 and 1012–1369.

2. The figures mentioned throughout the testimony are from the court transcript. The contradictions in the sums of money are puzzling, unless the error is in the court record. Why did Franklin offer $2500 when he said he was authorized to pay $4000? Why did he give Bain $400 when he had promised him $500 for the down payment? It is strange that Bain made no objection, and stranger still that the defense did not question the discrepancies.

3. *Los Angeles Examiner,* June 1, 1912.

4. Ibid.

5. Ibid., June 4, 1912.

6. *Los Angeles Record,* June 4, 1912.

7. Flather's testimony appears in the Darrow trial transcript, pp. 908–1011.

8. Darrow, *The Story of My Life* (1932), pp. 192–202.

Chapter XIV: More Witnesses Against Darrow (pp. 205–221)

1. Dickelman's testimony appears in the Darrow trial transcript, pp. 1540–86.
2. White's testimony appears in ibid., pp. 1597–1633.
3. Browne's testimony appears in ibid., pp. 1634–1710.
4. Baillie (1959), p. 17.
5. Cohn and Chisholm (1964), p. 209.
6. Stone (1941), p. 325.
7. St. Johns (1962), p. 384.
8. Behm's testimony appears in the Darrow trial transcript, pp. 2252–2514.
9. Harrington's testimony appears in ibid., pp. 2667–3193.
10. The episode outside the courtroom between Ford and Rogers appeared in Reporter Timmons's story in the *Los Angeles Examiner*, June 22, 1912.
11. *Los Angeles Examiner*, June 25, 1912.
12. Ibid.
13. Biddinger's testimony appears in the Darrow trial transcript, pp. 3269–3466.
14. *Los Angeles Times*, July 3, 1912.
15. Burns's testimony appears in the Darrow trial transcript, pp. 3467–3574.
16. Cohn and Chisholm (1964), p. 203.
17. *Los Angeles Times*, July 3, 1912.
18. *Los Angeles Herald*, July 2, 1912.
19. Bain's testimony appears in the Darrow trial transcript, pp. 3815–78.

Chapter XV: Witnesses for the Defense (pp. 222–229)

1. Harriman's testimony appears in the Darrow trial transcript, pp. 4110–4245.
2. Johnston's testimony appears in ibid., pp. 4650–4735.
3. Pirotte's testimony appears in ibid., pp. 4750–4854.
4. Hood's testimony appears in ibid., pp. 4855–64.
5. Dominguez's testimony appears in ibid., pp. 4864–88.
6. Jones's testimony appears in ibid., pp. 4889–4901.
7. Older's testimony appears in ibid., pp. 5010–5149.
8. Steffens's testimony appears in ibid., pp. 5221–5428.
9. Steffens (1931), p. 672.
10. *Los Angeles Record*, July 20, 1912.
11. Davis's testimony appears in the Darrow trial transcript, pp. 5509–5733.

Chapter XVI: Darrow Testifies for Himself (pp. 230–235)

1. Darrow's direct testimony appears in the Darrow trial transcript, pp. 5884–6066.
2. *Los Angeles Times*, July 30, 1912.
3. Ibid., August 1, 1912.

Chapter XVII: Darrow Cross-Examined (pp. 236–240)

1. Cross-examination of Darrow appears in the Darrow trial transcript, pp. 6067–6655; redirect, pp. 6655–87.
2. *Los Angeles Examiner*, August 4, 1912.

Chapter XVIII: "Judas," Shouts the D.A. at Darrow (pp. 241–251)

1. Ford's plea was reported in the *Los Angeles Record*, August 12, 1912; *Los Angeles Times*, August 13; *Los Angeles Examiner*, August 13.
2. William Lorimer was a political fixer, an unsavory character in Chicago politics.
3. Appel's plea was reported in the *Los Angeles Record*, August 13, 1912; *Los Angeles Times*, August 14.
4. Rogers's summation was reported in the *Los Angeles Times*, August 14–15, 1912; *Los Angeles Examiner*, August 14–15.
5. Darrow's summation was reported in the *Los Angeles Record*, August 14–15, 1912; *Los Angeles Times*, August 15; *Los Angeles Examiner*, August 15; also reprinted in Weinberg (1957), pp. 494–530.
6. Fredericks's summation was reported in the *Los Angeles Times*, August 16–17, 1912; *Los Angeles Record*, August 16; *Los Angeles Examiner*, August 16–17.
7. John André was a British adjutant general who was caught negotiating with Benedict Arnold for the surrender of West Point. He was hanged as a spy.
8. *Los Angeles Record*, August 17, 1912.
9. Margaret Parton's unpublished biography of Mary Field.
10. *Los Angeles Record*, August 17, 1912.
11. *Los Angeles Times*, August 18, 1912.
12. *Los Angeles Examiner*, August 18, 1912.
13. *Los Angeles Record*, August 17, 1912.
14. *San Francisco Daily News*, September 2, 1912.
15. *San Francisco Morning Call*, September 3, 1912.
16. *San Francisco Chronicle*, September 3, 1912.
17. *Everyman*, January–February 1919.

18. *San Francisco Herald,* September 3, 1912.
19. *Everyman,* November–December 1913.

Chapter XIX: Once Again, a Jury of His Peers (pp. 252–268)

1. *Los Angeles Examiner,* August 18, 1912.
2. R. F. Pettigrew letter to Darrow, August 29, 1912, in Darrow Collection, Library of Congress.
3. Jerry Geisler letter to Darrow, September 21, 1912, in Darrow Collection, Library of Congress.
4. *Los Angeles Times,* January 21, 1913.
5. Ibid., January 22, 1913.
6. Ibid., January 31, 1913.
7. Ibid., February 5, 1913.
8. Ibid.
9. Cohn and Chisholm (1964), p. 208.
10. *Los Angeles Examiner,* February 8, 1913.
11. Ibid.
12. Ibid., February 11, 1913.
13. Darrow's opening statement was reported in the *Los Angeles Record,* February 13, 1913; *Los Angeles Times,* February 14; *Los Angeles Examiner,* February 14.
14. *Los Angeles Times,* February 27, 1913.
15. *Los Angeles Record,* February 27, 1913.
16. *Los Angeles Examiner,* March 2, 1913.
17. Ibid., March 5, 1913.
18. *Los Angeles Times,* March 5, 1913.
19. *Los Angeles Record,* March 5, 1913.
20. Darrow's plea in his own defense is taken from the *Los Angeles Examiner,* March 6, 1913; *Los Angeles Record,* March 6; *Los Angeles Times,* March 7; also *Everyman,* May 1913.
21. Ford's plea is taken from the *Los Angeles Examiner,* March 7, 1913; *Los Angeles Times,* March 7; *Los Angeles Record,* March 6.
22. Juror Silas Setchell's statement was reported in the *Los Angeles Record,* March 7, 1913.
23. St. Johns (1962), p. 405.
24. Robinson (1969), p. 45.
25. Geisler (1960), p. 6.
26. Davis quoted in *Los Angeles Free Press,* April 18, 1957, on the Centennial Celebration of Darrow's birth.
27. Judge Isaac Pacht letter to authors, December 12, 1974.
28. Yarros (1950), p. 9.
29. Darrow, *The Story of My Life* (1932), pp. 203–4.

30. Weinberg (1957), p. 512.
31. *Los Angeles Record,* March 15, 1913.
32. *Everyman,* June 1913.
33. Adamic (1931), p. 239.
34. Perlman and Taft (1935), 4:324–25.
35. Grant (1915), p. 126.
36. St. Johns (1962), p. 458.
37. Transcript of dinner remarks in Darrow Collection, Library of Congress.
38. Darrow letter to Mary Field, March 31, [1914].

Chapter XX: "You Must Not Leave the Law" (pp. 269–281)

1. Stone (1941), pp. 346–47.
2. Yarros (1950), p. 4.
3. Ibid.
4. Darrow, *The Story of My Life* (1932), p. 207.
5. Darrow letter to Mary Field, April 27, 1915.
6. Garland (1931), p. 22.
7. *Cedar Rapids Tribune,* November 21, 1913.
8. *Ottumwa* (Iowa) *Courier,* October 10, 1913.
9. *The New York Times,* May 19, 1915.
10. Ibid.
11. *Chicago Daily News,* April 15, 1914.
12. Ibid., February 13, 1917.
13. *Chicago Tribune,* January 12, 1918.
14. Hecht (1955), p. 142.
15. Darrow letter to Mary Field, January 29, 1918.
16. *Chicago Tribune,* December 24, 1917.
17. Forty years later, in Chicago in 1956, when actor Melvyn Douglas was touring the country portraying a lawyer resembling Darrow in *Inherit the Wind,* a play based on the Scopes trial (see pp. 328–329), the cabdriver told him the story as he drove Douglas from the theater to the hotel. Douglas repeated it to the authors during the Darrow Centennial Celebration in 1957. He also described the incident in an article entitled "Discovering Darrow," *The New Republic* 136 (May 27, 1957): 14–15.
18. *Chicago Tribune,* June 6, 1923.
19. Wendt and Kogan (1953), p. 213.
20. *Bloomington* (Ill.) *Daily Bulletin,* July 1, 1923.
21. Darrow letter to Mary Field, February 1, 1923.
22. Albert B. Fall (1861–1944), U.S. secretary of the interior, was convicted of bribery, and oil operator Harry F. Sinclair with contempt of the U.S. Senate.
23. *Chicago Daily News,* March 6, 1924.

24. *Chicago Tribune*, March 1, 1924.
25. Pp. 82–83 of Darrow's plea in the Faherty trial. Copy of plea in authors' possession.
26. Weinberg (1957), p. 171.
27. *Chicago Daily News* clipping (n.d.) in Darrow Collection, Library of Congress.
28. Darrow letter to Mary Field, December 6, [1915].
29. Ibid., September 10, [1914].
30. Ibid., May 29, 1915.
31. Ibid., November 14, [1914].
32. Darrow lecture, "The War in Europe," before the Chicago Society of Rationalism at the Germania Theatre, Fall 1914.
33. Ibid.
34. Ibid., pp. 30–31.
35. *Labor Leader* (Dubuque, Iowa), October 1, 1916.
36. Darrow, *Resist Not Evil* (1925), pp. 11–12.
37. Darrow, *The Story of My Life* (1932), p. 210.
38. Darrow letter to Mary Field, April 27, 1915.

Chapter XXI: Ex-Pacifist Defends War Objectors (pp. 282–296)

1. Darrow letter to a socialist friend, Daniel Kiefer, "Brief for the War," *Liberal Review* 2 (July 1917): 9; the entire letter is also reproduced in Weinberg (1963), pp. 335–46.
2. *Chicago Daily News*, October 22, 1917.
3. Ibid., September 12, 1917.
4. Darrow letter to Daniel Kiefer, "Brief for the War."
5. Darrow letter to Mary Field, January 29, 1918.
6. Darrow address under auspices of the National Security League, Chicago, November 1, 1917.
7. Darrow letter to Mary Field, January 29, 1918.
8. Chaplin (1948), pp. 225–26.
9. Darrow letter to Debs, July 20, 1918.
10. Darrow letter to Mary Field, January 29, 1918.
11. *Kessinger's Midwest Review*, n.d.
12. Darrow, *The Story of My Life* (1932), p. 69.
13. Darrow letter to Mary Field, January 29, 1918.
14. Darrow, *The Story of My Life* (1932), p. 213.
15. Steffens (1938), p. 459.
16. *The New York Times*, July 22, 1918.
17. *Chicago Daily Journal*, October 23, 1918.
18. Ibid., October 25, 1918.
19. Ibid., November 6, 1918.

20. Whitlock (1936), p. 501.
21. Darrow letter to Fremont Older, September 25, [1916].
22. Russell (1933), pp. 295–96.
23. Darrow letter to President Woodrow Wilson, July 29, 1919, in Wilson Papers, Library of Congress.
24. Darrow, *The Story of My Life* (1932), p. 24.
25. Attorney General A. Mitchell Palmer, "The Case against the 'Reds,'" *The Forum* 63 (February 1920): 173.
26. Gitlow (1940), p. 69.
27. Ibid., p. 70.
28. Darrow's plea appears in Gitlow [1919], pp. 9–12.
29. Darrow's plea in the Person trial was published as a pamphlet in 1920, probably by the defense committee of the Communist Labor party of Illinois.
30. *The New York Times,* June 13, 1920.
31. Darrow's plea in Lloyd et al. trial appears in Weinberg (1957), pp. 123–72.
32. Robert Morss Lovett, "The Trial of the Communists," *The Nation* 111 (August 12, 1920): 186.
33. *Letters from Russian Prisons* (1925), p. xiii.
34. Darrow letter to Mary Field, Thanksgiving 1920.
35. Darrow letter to Fremont Older, December 25, 1920.
36. Ibid., August 22, 1923.

Chapter XXII: "All Life Is Worth Saving" (pp. 297–316)

1. *The New York Times* (May 30, 1924).
2. Darrow, *The Story of My Life* (1932), p. 232.
3. "Alienist" was a term used at that time to describe forensic psychiatry. See also Freud letter to George Seldes, June 29, 1924, in Jones (1957), p. 103.
4. Ibid.
5. Leopold (1958), pp. 60–61.
6. Darrow statement to court changing the plea of Leopold and Loeb from "not guilty" to "guilty" appeared in the *Chicago Daily News,* July 21, 1924.
7. *Los Angeles Times,* July 21, 1924.
8. *Chicago Tribune,* July 22, 1924.
9. Darrow, *Crime: Its Causes and Treatment* (1922), p. vii.
10. Ibid., p. 145.
11. *Chicago Daily News,* July 23, 1924.
12. Ibid., August 2, 1924.
13. Ibid., August 8, 1924.

14. Leopold in conversation with LW; also Leopold (1958), p. 68.
15. *Los Angeles Times,* August 21, 1924.
16. Ibid.
17. Harrison (1931), p. 267.
18. *Los Angeles Times,* August 22, 1924.
19. Darrow's plea in the Leopold and Loeb trial is in Weinberg (1957), pp. 19–87.
20. *Los Angeles Times,* August 23, 1924.
21. Leopold (1958), p. 73.
22. Quoted in Darrow's plea in the Leopold and Loeb case (see Weinberg [1957], p. 84). Taken from A. S. Housman, *A Shropshire Lad.*
23. Ibid. (see Weinberg [1957], p. 36).
24. *Chicago Tribune,* March 17, 1957.
25. Darrow, *The Persian Pearl and Other Essays* (1899), p. 15.
26. Darrow quoted this stanza from Omar Khayyám's *Rubáiyát* in his plea for Leopold and Loeb (see Weinberg [1957], p. 87).
27. Darrow, *The Story of My Life* (1932), p. 242.
28. *Los Angeles Times,* August 25, 1924.
29. State's Attorney Crowe's summation is in McKernan (1957), pp. 290–92.
30. Judge Caverly's remarks at the conclusion of State's Attorney Crowe's argument is quoted in McKernan (1957), pp. 292–94.
31. For Judge Caverly's decision, see McKernan (1957), pp. 296–99.
32. Harrison (1931), p. 272.
33. Darrow letter to Leopold (October 3, 1928); letter is in possession of Elmer Gertz.
34. The Headline Club is the Chicago chapter of the professional journalism society, Sigma Delta Chi. Speakers on the program included Judge John Sbarbaro, an assistant prosecutor in the Leopold and Loeb trial; Dr. Preston Bradley; John Lapp; and Matilda Fenberg. Each had known Darrow. Arthur Weinberg was the moderator of the panel. It was in response to Weinberg's query that Judge Sbarbaro made his comment which is quoted in *Quill Magazine* (June 1957).
35. Hans Mattick letter to Illinois Parole Board, January 21, 1958; also in conversation with authors.
36. Darrow debate with Judge Alfred J. Talley, "Is Capital Punishment a Wise Policy?" New York, 1924; quoted in Weinberg (1957), pp. 89–103.
37. *Bloomington* (Ill.) *Daily Bulletin,* May 12, 1925.
38. *New Orleans Morning Tribune,* January 27, 1925.
39. *Washington* (D.C.) *Times,* February 1, 1926.
40. Speech delivered May 2, 1909.
41. Darrow debate with Dr. John Haynes Holmes, "Should the United States Continue the Policy of Prohibition as Defined in the Eighteenth Amendment?" New York, December 14, 1924; quoted in Weinberg (1963), pp. 107–23.

42. Paul Darrow in conversation with AW (see Weinberg, "I Remember Father," *Chicago Tribune Magazine*, May 9, 1956.

Chapter XXIII: Tennessee versus Scopes (pp. 317–329)

1. Scopes and Presley (1967), pp. 66–67.
2. Roger Baldwin quoted in Tompkins (1965), p. 57.
3. De Camp (1968), pp. 19–20.
4. Scopes and Presley (1967), pp. 80–81.
5. *New York Post*, June 11, 1925.
6. De Camp (1968), p. 141.
7. Ibid., p. 168.
8. H. L. Mencken quoted in Tompkins (1965), p. 38; reprinted from *Baltimore Sun*.
9. Attorneys' arguments, judge's comments and rulings, witnesses' testimony, and Darrow's examination of Bryan come from the transcript of the trial, published in *The World's Most Famous Court Trial: Tennessee Evolution Case* (1925).
10. Stone (1941), p. 442.
11. H. L. Mencken quoted in Tompkins (1965), p. 41; reprinted from *Baltimore Sun*.
12. Ibid., pp. 49–50.
13. Darrow, *The Story of My Life* (1932), pp. 276–77.
14. Quoted in Harrison (1931), pp. 326–27.
15. Ibid., p. 327.
16. Stone (1941), p. 464.
17. Darrow letter to H. L. Mencken, August 15, 1925, in Mencken Collection, New York Public Library.
18. Ernst (1968), p. 82.
19. Supreme Court of the U.S., No. 7, October term, 1968, Susan Epperson et al., Appellants vs. State of Arkansas, on appeal from the Supreme Court of Arkansas, November 12, 1968, pp. 10–12.

Chapter XXIV: "I Speak for a Million Blacks" (pp. 330–349)

1. Hays (1942), p. 40.
2. Darrow letter to H. L. Mencken, May 11, 1924, in mencken Collection, New York Public Library.
3. Darrow letter to Judge Frank Murphy, July 29, 1927, in Murphy Collection, Michigan Historical Collection, University of Michigan, Ann Arbor.
4. Darrow lecture, Congregational Church, Chicago, January 14, 1932.
5. *Chicago Evening American*, August 19, 1908.
6. White (1948), p. 76.

7. Ibid., pp. 76–77.
8. Quoted in Weinberg (1957), p. 540.
9. Hays (1928), p. 199.
10. Ibid., p. 199.
11. Haldeman-Julius (1927), p. 51.
12. Examination of witnesses, attorneys' and judge's statements are from the transcript. State of Michigan, in the Recorders' Court of the City of Detroit. The People vs. Ossian Sweet et al., No. 60317.
13. Testimony of Florence Ware, Sweet trial transcript, pp. 977–1016.
14. Testimony of William Goad, ibid., pp. 1153–54.
15. Haldeman-Julius (1927), p. 32.
16. Testimony of Eber A. Draper, Sweet trial transcript, pp. 424–72.
17. Testimony of George Suppus, ibid., pp. 698–728.
18. Testimony of Urlic Arthur, ibid., pp. 728–49.
19. Testimony of Dwight Hubbard, ibid., pp. 856–64.
20. Hays (1928), p. 214.
21. Ibid., p. 216.
22. *Detroit News,* November 17, 1925.
23. Ibid., November 19, 1925.
24. Weinberg (1957), p. 325.
25. Ibid., pp. 172, 86.
26. Darrow's closing argument in the first Sweet case is taken from the *Detroit Times,* November 25, 1925.
27. State's Attorney Toms's summation in the first Sweet case is taken from the *Detroit News,* November 26, 1925.
28. Hays (1942), p. 209.
29. Darrow letter to James Weldon Johnson, April 5, 1926, in NAACP Collection, Library of Congress.
30. Chawke (1958) in conversation with AW and William Friedkin, both of whom, with Francis Coughlin, were writing a play based on the Sweet case.
31. *Detroit Times,* April 22, 1926.
32. Ibid., February 26, 1926.
33. Weinberg (1971), pp. 77.
34. Ibid., p. 94.
35. Moll summation in the second Sweet trial is taken from the *Detroit Times,* May 11, 1926.
36. Chawke quote in ibid., May 11, 1926.
37. Darrow's summation in the second Sweet trial is in Weinberg (1957), pp. 233–63.
38. Toms's summation in the second Sweet trial is taken from the *Detroit News,* May 13, 1926.
39. Darrow letter to Judge Frank Murphy, October 9, 1935, in Murphy

Collection, Michigan Historical Collection, University of Michigan, Ann Arbor.
40. *Detroit News,* June 19, 1928.
41. Quoted in Weinberg (1957), p. 262.

Chapter XXV: Itinerant Debater (pp. 350–365)

1. Darrow letter to Fremont Older, January 2, [1914].
2. Ibid., February 14, [1927].
3. Darrow letter to Mary Field, July 15, 1927.
4. Darrow letter to Elmer Gertz, February 18, 1932,
5. *Chicago Daily News,* April 19, 1927.
6. Ibid., December 22, 1926.
7. The text of Darrow's response at his seventieth birthday party is in ms. in the Darrow Collection, Library of Congress.
8. Since then Durant has published widely, including the eleven-volume *History of Civilization.*
9. *Detroit News,* May 19, 1921.
10. Ibid.
11. Will Durant letter to authors, December 21, 1962; also quoted in Weinberg (1963), p. 46.
12. *Paris N.Y. Herald,* August 13, 1927.
13. Harrison (1931), pp. 353–54.
14. *Chicago Sun Times,* July 20, 1977; *Chicago Tribune,* July 20, 1977.
15. Wendt and Kogan (1953), p. 289.
16. *Chicago Daily News,* October 22, 1927.
17. *Chicago Journal,* October 24, 1927.
18. The incident in the hotel room is recounted in Harrison (1931), p. 357.
19. *The New York Times,* December 16, 1927.
20. Newspaper clipping [1928], in Darrow Collection, Library of Congress.
21. *The New York Times,* January 13, 1928.
22. Ibid.
23. Darrow letter to James Weldon Johnson, January 21, 1928, in NAACP Collection, Library of Congress.
24. *Crisis,* June 1928, p. 203.
25. Darrow letter to James Weldon Johnson, April 17, 1928, in NAACP Collection, Library of Congress.
26. *Proceedings* of the sixth annual meeting, American Society of Newspaper Editors, Washington, D.C., April 20–21, 1928.
27. *Belleville* (Ill.) *Daily News-Democrat,* November 3, 1928.
28. Darrow speech before Essex County Democratic Committee, Krueger Auditorium, Newark, N.J.; reported in the *Newark* (N.J.) *Star-Eagle,* October 13, 1928.

29. Hays (1942), p. 16.
30. *Newark* (N.J.) *Star-Eagle,* October 13, 1928.
31. *St. Louis Democrat,* November 1, 1928.
32. Ms. of Darrow speech at Armory, Gary, Indiana, November 5, 1928, is in Darrow Collection, Library of Congress.
33. Darrow, "At Seventy-Two," *The Saturday Evening Post* 202 (July 6, 1929): 23 ff.
34. Brand Whitlock letter to Albert Bigelow Paine, February 23, 1932, quoting Darrow (in Whitlock [1936], p. 512).
35. Darrow, *The Story of My Life* (1932), p. 320.
36. *The New Republic* 70 (February 17, 1932): 25.
37. Thurman Arnold, *Yale Law Review,* April 1932.
38. Darrow letter to grandchildren, July 7, 1929. Copy in possession of authors.
39. Ibid., n.d.
40. Symposium on religion, May 12, 1929, Columbus, Ohio.
41. Nashville, Tennessee, December 18, 1931.
42. *Houston Press,* March 13, 1931.
43. Darrow letter to Harry Elmer Barnes, March 6, [1931].
44. Radio debate between Darrow and James M. Beck, "The Trial of Benedict Arnold," 1931.
45. *The New York Times,* July 6, 1931.

Chapter XXVI: A Folk Hero in His Time (pp. 366–383)

1. *Crisis,* March 1932.
2. *Workers Defense Bulletin,* September 1932.
3. Darrow letter to Harry Elmer Barnes, March 5, [1932] in Barnes Collection, University of Wyoming.
4. Ibid., March 12, 1932.
5. Van Slingerland (1966), p. 218.
6. Early draft of a review by George S. Leisure of AW's *Attorney for the Damned* (1957) for the *University of Virginia Law Review.* Also letter to AW dated November 10, 1958.
7. *Honolulu Advertiser,* April 4, 1932.
8. *Honolulu Advertiser,* April 17, 1932.
9. Darrow's summation in Massie trial in Weinberg (1957), pp. 106–17.
10. Prosecution's summation, *Honolulu Advertiser,* April 28, 1932.
11. Darrow, *The Story of My Life* (1932), pp. 450–59.
12. *Honolulu Advertiser,* April 4, 1932.
13. Wright (1966), pp. 305–6.
14. Ibid., p. 306.
15. *Honolulu Advertiser,* May 3, 1932.

16. Weinberg (1957), p. 9.
17. *San Francisco Chronicle,* May 14, 1932.
18. *Saturday Press* (Oakland, Calif.), May 21, 1932.
19. Ibid.
20. *Newsweek,* February 17, 1933, p. 30.
21. *Chicago Evening American,* April 11, 1933.
22. Ibid.
23. Ibid., April 18, 1933.
24. Ibid.
25. *Chicago Daily News,* April 18, 1935.
26. Ibid.
27. *Atlanta* (Ga.) *Constitution,* March 29, 1936.
28. *Chicago Tribune,* March 31, 1936.
29. *Chicago Times,* December 22, 1936.
30. Darrow letter to Fremont Older, December 25, 1920.
31. *Chicago Daily News* clipping [1932], Darrow Collection, Library of Congress.
32. Darrow letter to General Hugh S. Johnson (n.d.), Darrow Collection, Library of Congress.
33. *The New York Times,* March 8, 1934.
34. Lowell Mason speaking at the University of Chicago Law School Convocation, Law Day, May 1, 1959; also in conversation with authors.
35. General Hugh S. Johnson's comment on the Darrow NRA Review Board Report was reported in *The New York Times,* May 21, 1934.
36. Congressional Committee, Investigation of National Recovery Administration, p. 297.
37. *The New York Times,* July 2, 1934.
38. Wells (1934), p. 673.
39. Entry, Mary Field's diary, January 18, 1934.
40. Ibid.
41. Darrow letter to Mrs. Porter, Kinsman Public Library, February 17, [1933].
42. George G. Whitehead, *Cleveland Plain Dealer,* April 18, 1937.
43. Darrow's answers to questions submitted by Victor Hackler, News Editor, Associated Press, Chicago, April 18, 1937.
44. *Chicago Tribune,* March 13, 1938.
45. Robert Black, one of the nurses who took care of Darrow during the last three weeks of his life, in conversation with LW, September 19, 1978.
46. Abe M. Weinberg in conversation with authors.
47. *Chicago American,* March 15, 1938.
48. Ibid.
49. Judge Holly's eulogy to Clarence appears in *In Memoriam,* special issue of *Unity,* May 16, 1938, pp. 86–96.

50. The American Federation of Labor's Weekly News Service, March 19, 1938. Green was Gompers's successor as AFL president.
51. *Unity,* May 16, 1938 (see n. 49).
52. Ibid.
53. Entry, Mary Field's diary, March 13, 1938.

Epilogue (pp. 384–385)

1. *Akron Times Press,* March 15, 1938.
2. Joseph N. Welch speaking at dinner which concluded the daylong Darrow Centennial Celebration in Chicago, May 1, 1957; *Chicago Times,* May 2, 1957.

Selected Bibliography

"The Ace Jury Picker." *Literary Digest* 121 (May 16, 1936): 35.

"The Acquittal of William D. Haywood." *Arena* 38, no. 214 (September 1907): 332–33.

Adamic, Louis. *Dynamite: The Story of Class Violence in America*. New York: Viking Press, 1931.

Adams, Graham, Jr. *Age of Industrial Violence 1910–15: The Activities and Findings of the U.S. Commission on Industrial Relations*. New York: Columbia University Press, 1966.

Addams, Jane. *Twenty Years at Hull-House*. New York: Macmillan Co., 1910.

Adelman, Abram E. "Clarence Darrow—'Take Him for All in All.'" *Age of Reason* 19, no. 10 (October 1955).

Allen, Frederick Lewis. *Only Yesterday: An Informal History of the Nineteen-Twenties*. New York: Harper & Bros., 1931.

Alschuler, Albert W. "Plea Bargaining and Its History." Mimeographed. September 1978.

Altgeld, John Peter. *Live Questions: Including Our Penal Machinery and Its Victims*. Chicago: Donohue & Henneberry, 1890.

American Federation of Labor. History, Encyclopedia, Reference Book. Prepared and published by Authority of the 1916 & 1917 Conventions. Washington, D.C.: A.F. of L. Building, 1919.

"An Evening with Clarence Darrow." *Etcetera,* September 1930.

Anderson, Paul Y. "Darrow Report." *The Nation,* May 30, 1934, p. 611.

Andrews, Wayne. *Battle for Chicago.* New York: Harcourt, Brace & Co., 1946.

Arnold, Thurman. "Review of Clarence Darrow's *Story of My Life.*" *Yale Law Review* 41 (April 1932): 932.

Ashley, W. J. *The Railroad Strike of 1894: The Statements of the Pullman Company and the Report of the Commission, Together with an Analysis of the Issues.* Issued semi-monthly, series B, no. 1. Cambridge, Mass.: Church Social Union, 1894.

Bailey, F. Lee, with Greenya, John. *For the Defense.* New York: Atheneum Publishers, 1975.

Baillie, Hugh. *High Tension: The Recollections of Hugh Baillie.* New York: Harper, 1959.

Bancroft, Edgar A. *The Chicago Strike of 1894.* Chicago: Privately printed by the Gunthrop-Warren Printing Co., 1895.

Barnard, Harry. *Eagle Forgotten: The Life of John Peter Altgeld.* Indianapolis and New York: Bobbs-Merrill Co., 1938; Charter ed., 1962.

—————. The Forging of an American Jew: The Life and Times of Judge Julian W. Mack. New York: Herzl Press, 1974.

Barrymore, Ethel. *Memories: An Autobiography.* New York: Harper & Bros., 1955.

Beer, Thomas. *Hanna.* New York: Alfred A. Knopf, 1929.

Belli, Melvin, with Kaiser, Robert Blair. *My Life on Trial.* New York: William Morrow & Co., 1976.

Bonelli, William G. *Billion Dollar Blackjack.* Beverly Hills, Calif.: Civic Research Press, 1954.

The Book of Chicagoans. Chicago: A. N. Marquis & Co., 1911.

Borah, W. E. *Haywood Trial: Closing Arguments of W. E. Borah.* Boise, Idaho: The Statesman Shop, n.d.

Bradley, Preston. *Along the Way.* New York: David McKay Co., 1962.

Bridges, Horace James. *The God of Fundamentalism and Other Studies.* Chicago: Pascal Covici, 1925.

Bright, John. *Hizzoner Big Bill Thompson: An Idyll of Chicago.* New York: Jonathan Cape & Harrison Smith, 1930.

Brissenden, Paul F. *The IWW: A Study of American Syndicalism. Studies in History, Economics and Public Law.* Vol. 83 (whole no. 193), 1919.

Brommel, Bernard. *Eugene V. Debs: A Spokesman for Labor and Socialism.* Chicago: Charles H. Kerr & Co., 1978.

Browne, Waldo Ralph. *Altgeld of Illinois: A Record of His Life and Work.* New York: B. W. Huebsch, Inc., 1924.

Bryan, William Jennings. *The Memoirs of William Jennings Bryan by Himself and His Wife Mary Baird Bryan.* Chicago, Philadelphia, and Toronto: John C. Winston Co., 1925.

Buder, Stanley. *Pullman: An Experiment in Industrial Order and Community Planning 1880–1930.* New York: Oxford University Press, 1967.

Burns, W. F. *The Pullman Boycott: A Complete History of the Great R.R. Strike.* St. Paul, Minn.: McGill Printing Co., 1894.

Burns, W. J. *The Masked War: The Story of a Peril That Threatened the U.S., by the Man Who Uncovered the Dynamite Conspirators and Sent Them to Jail.* New York: George H. Doran Co., 1913.

Busch, Francis X. *Casebook of the Curious and True.* Indianapolis and New York: Bobbs-Merrill Co., 1957; Charter ed., 1962.

————. *In and Out of Court.* Chicago: De Paul University Press, 1942.

————. *Prisoners at the Bar.* Indianapolis and New York: Bobbs-Merrill Co., 1952.

Butcher, Fanny. *Many Lives—One Love.* New York: Harper & Row, 1972.

Cargill, Oscar. *Intellectual America: Ideas on the March.* New York: Macmillan Co., 1941.

Carter, Dan T. *Scottsboro: A Tragedy of the American South.* Baton Rouge: Louisiana State University Press, 1969.

Carwardine, William H. *The Pullman Strike.* Chicago: Charles H. Kerr & Co., 1894.

Chaplin, Ralph. *Wobbly: The Rough-and-Tumble Story of an American Radical.* Chicago: University of Chicago Press, 1948.

"Clarence Darrow Birthday Party." *Industrial Engineer,* May 1927.

Clement, Trover, and Symes, Lillian. *Rebel America: The Story of Social Revolt in the United States.* New York: Harper & Bros., 1934.

Cleveland, Grover. *The Government in the Chicago Strike of 1894.* Princeton, N.J.: Princeton University Press, 1913.

Clough, Frank C. *William Allen White of Emporia.* New York: McGraw-Hill Book Co., 1941; London: Whittlesey House, 1941.

Cochran, Negley D. *E. W. Scripps.* New York: Harcourt, Brace & Co., 1933.

Cohn, Alfred, and Chisholm, Joe. *"Take the Witness!"* Garden City, N.Y.: Garden City Publishing Co., 1934; Paperback Library, 1964.

Coleman, McAlister. *Eugene V. Debs: A Man Unafraid.* New York: Greenberg Publishers, 1930.

Coletta, Paolo E. *William Jennings Bryan.* Vol. 1, *Political Evangelist 1860–1908;* vol. 2, *Progressive Politician and Moral Statesman 1909–1915;* vol. 3, *Political Puritan 1915–1925.* Lincoln: University of Nebraska Press, 1964, 1969, 1969.

Commons, John R., et al. *History of Labour in the United States.* New York, Macmillan Co., 1918.

"Communist Trial." *The New Republic* 23 (August 18, 1920): 323–24.

Conlin, Joseph R. "The Haywood Case: An Enduring Riddle." *Pacific Northwest Quarterly* 59, no. 1 (January 1968): 23–32.

Connolly, C. P. "Protest by Dynamite: Similarities and Contrast between the McNamara Affair in Los Angeles and the Moyer-Haywood-Pettibone Trial in Boise." *Collier's* 48 (January 13, 1912): 9–10, 23.

———. "The Saving of Clarence Darrow: Factors and Motives That Led to the Dramatic Close of the McNamara Case." *Collier's* 48 (December 23, 1911): 9–10, 22.

———. "The Trial at Los Angeles: Some Questions with Personalities in the McNamara Case." *Collier's* 48 (October 14, 1911): 17, 31–32.

Cornell, Robert J. *The Anthracite Coal Strike of 1902.* Submitted to the faculty of the graduate school of arts and sciences of the Catholic University of America in partial fulfillment of the requirements for the degree of Doctor of Philosophy. Washington, D.C.: Catholic University of America Press, 1957.

Cowart, B. T. "James McParland and the Haywood Case." *Idaho Yesterdays* 16 (Fall 1972): 24–29.

Coyle, William, ed. *Ohio Authors and Their Books.* Cleveland and New York: World Publishing Co., 1962.

Crandall, Allen. *The Man from Kinsman.* Sterling, Colo.: Published by the author, September 1933.

Crunden, Robert M. *A Hero in Spite of Himself: Brand Whitlock in Art, Politics, and War.* New York: Alfred A. Knopf, 1969.

Culin, Stewart. *A Trooper's Narrative of Service in the Anthracite Coal Strike, 1902.* Philadelphia: George W. Jacobs & Co., 1903.

Currey, J. Seymour. *Chicago: Its History and Its Builders.* 5 vols. Chicago: S. J. Clarke Publishing Co., 1913.

"The Darrow Acquittal." *Literary Digest,* August 31, 1912.

David, Henry. *The History of the Haymarket Affair: A Study in the American-Social Revolutionary and Labor Movements.* New York: Farrar & Rinehart, 1936.

Davidson, Jo. *Between Sittings: An Informal Autobiography.* New York: Dial Press, 1951.

Day, Donald. *Will Rogers: A Biography.* New York: David McKay Co., 1962.

Debs, Eugene V. *Writings and Speeches.* Introduction by Arthur M. Schlesinger. New York: Hermitage Press, 1948.

De Camp, L. Sprague. *The Great Monkey Trial.* Garden City, N.Y.: Doubleday & Co., 1968.

Decker, Mary Bell. "The Man Clarence Darrow." *University Review* 4, no. 4 (Summer 1938).

Deering, Mabel Craft. "The Women's Demonstration: How They Won and Used the Vote in California." *Collier's* 48, no. 16 (January 6, 1912): 17.

"The Defense of Haywood." *Current Literature* 43, no. 2 (August 1907): 134–36.

Dell, Floyd. "Chicago in Fiction." *The Bookman* 38, no. 3:270–77; 38, no. 4:375–79.

Derleth, A. W. *Still Small Voice: The Biography of Zona Gale.* New York: D. Appleton-Century Co., 1940.

Destler, Chester McArthur. *Henry Demarest Lloyd and the Empire of Reform.* Philadelphia: University of Pennsylvania Press, 1963.

Detzer, Karl W. *Carl Sandburg: A Study in Personality and Background.* New York: Harcourt, Brace & Co., 1941.

Doty, Duane (Mrs.). *The Town of Pullman: Its Growth with Brief Accounts of Its Industries.* Pullman, Ill.: T. P. Struhsacker, Publisher, 1893; reprint ed., Pullman Civic Organization, 1974.

Douglas, Melvyn. "Discovering Darrow." *The New Republic* 136 (May 27, 1957): 14–16.

Douglas, William O. *Go East, Young Man: The Early Years, the Autobiography of William O. Douglas.* New York: Random House, 1974.

Dowell, Eldridge Foster. *A History of Criminal Syndicalism Legislation in the United States.* Baltimore: The Johns Hopkins Press, 1939.

Drinnon, Richard. *Rebel in Paradise: A Biography of Emma Goldman.* Chicago: University of Chicago Press, 1961.

Dubofsky, Melvyn. "James H. Hawley and the Origins of the Haywood Case." *Pacific Northwest Quarterly* 58, no. 1 (January 1967): 23–32.

————. *We Shall Be All: A History of the Industrial Workers of the World.* Chicago: Quadrangle Books, 1969.

Du Bois, W. E. B. *The Autobiography of W. E. B. Du Bois.* New York: International Publishers Co., 1968.

————. "Postscript." *Crisis,* June 1928.

Duffus, Robert L. *The Tower of Jewels: Memories of San Francisco.* New York: W. W. Norton & Co., 1960.

Dunne, Edward F. *Constructive Contempt of Court: The Case of Hearst's Chicago American.* Chicago, December 7, 1901. Pamphlet.

Eastman, Max. *Enjoyment of Living.* New York: Harper & Bros., 1948.

Eaton, Walter. "C. D.: Crusader for Social Justice." *Current History* 35 (March 19, 1932): 786.

Echoes of the Sunset Club. Comprising a number of papers read and addresses delivered before the Sunset Club of Chicago. Chicago: Howard, Bartels & Co., July 1891.

Editorial on anthracite miners. *The Outlook* 72 (December 6, 1902): 763–64.

Editorial on Haywood-Moyer-Pettibone trial. *Current Literature* 42 (June 1907): 587–95.

Erbstein, Charles E. *The Show-Up: Stories before the Bar.* Chicago: Pascal Covici, 1926.

Ernst, Morris L. *A Love Affair with the Law: A Legal Sampler.* New York: Macmillan Co., 1968.

Ervin, Charles W. *Homegrown Liberal: The Autobiography of Charles W. Ervin.* Edited by Jean Gould. New York: Dodd, Mead, 1954.

Essell, Charles. "Clarence Darrow as He Is." *Psychology*, August 1932.

Fess, Simeon D., ed. *Ohio: A Four-Volume Reference Library on the History of a Great State.* Chicago and New York: Lewis Publishing Co., 1937.

Flowers, B. O. "Henry D. Lloyd: An Apostle of Progressive Democracy." *Arena* 30, no. 6 (December 1903): 649–56.

Foner, Philip S. *History of the Labor Movement in the United States.* Vol. 3, *The Policies and Practices of the American Federation of Labor 1900–1909;* vol. 4, *Industrial Workers of the World 1905–1917.* New York: International Publishers Co., 1964, 1965.

Ford, Patrick H., ed. *The Darrow Bribery Trial with Background Facts of McNamara Case and Including Darrow's Address to the Jury.* Whittier, Calif.: Western Printing Co., 1956.

Friedheim, Robert L. *The Seattle General Strike.* Seattle: University of Washington Press, 1964.

Friedman, Morris. *The Pinkerton Labor Spy.* New York: Wilshire Book Co., 1907.

Frost, Richard H. *The Mooney Case.* Stanford, Calif.: Stanford University Press, 1968.

Garland, Hamlin. *Companions on the Trail: A Literary Chronicle.* New York: Macmillan Co., 1931.

Garrison, W. E. "Darrow the Tolerant." *Christian Century* 49 (March 23, 1932): 386.

Gentry, Curt. *Frame-Up: The Incredible Case of Tom Mooney and Warren Billings.* New York: W. W. Norton & Co., 1967.

Gertz, Elmer. "Clarence Darrow: An American Legend." *The Progressive*, May 1957.

———. *A Handful of Clients.* Chicago: Follett Publishing Co., 1965.

Giesler, Jerry, as told to Pete Martin. *The Jerry Giesler Story.* New York: Simon & Schuster, 1960.

Ginger, Ray. *Altgeld's America: The Lincoln Ideal versus Changing Realities.* New York: Funk & Wagnalls Co., 1958.

———. *The Bending Cross: A Biography of Eugene Victor Debs.* New Brunswick, N.J.: Rutgers University Press, 1949.

———. "Clarence Darrow 1857–1938." *Antioch Review* 13, no. 1 (March 1953): 52–66.

———. *Six Days or Forever? Tennessee v. John Thomas Scopes.* Boston: Beacon Press, 1958.

Gitlow, Benjamin. *I Confess: The Truth about American Communism.* Introduction by Max Eastman. New York: E. P. Dutton & Co., 1940.

———. *The "Red Ruby."* Address to jury by Benjamin Gitlow; also Darrow plea and judge's remarks. Published by the Communist Labor party, U.S.A., [1919].

Glück, Elsie. *John Mitchell, Miner: Labor's Bargain with the Gilded Age.* New York: John Day Co., 1929.

Golden, Harry L. *Carl Sandburg.* Cleveland: World Publishing Co., 1961.

Goldman, Emma. *Anarchism and Other Essays.* New York: Mother Earth Publishing Association, 1911.

————. *Living My Life.* Garden City, N.Y.: Garden City Publishing Co., 1931.

Goldman, Eric F. *Rendezvous with Destiny: A History of Modern American Reform.* New York: Alfred A. Knopf, 1952.

Gompers, Samuel *The McNamara Case.* Washington, D.C.: American Federation of Labor, [1911]. Pamphlet.

————. *Seventy Years of Life and Labor: An Autobiography.* 2 vols. New York: E. P. Dutton & Co., 1925.

Grant, Luke. "The Haywood Trial: A Review." *The Outlook* 86, no. 17 (August 24, 1907): 855–62.

————. "The Idaho Murder Trial." *The Outlook,* April 6, 1907, pp. 805–6.

————. *The National Erectors' Association and the International Association of Bridge and Structural Iron Workers.* Washington, D.C.: U.S. Commission on Industrial Relations, 1915.

Griffes, James H. (alias Luke North). "A Man of the People." *Golden Elk,* May 1907.

Grover, David H. *Debaters and Dynamiters: The Story of the Haywood Trial.* Corvallis, Oreg.: Oregon State University Press, 1964.

Gunn, John W. *Wisdom of Clarence Darrow.* Girard, Kans.: Haldeman-Julius Publications, 1947.

Gurko, Miriam. *Clarence Darrow.* New York: Thomas Y. Crowell, 1965. A juvenile book.

Haldeman-Julius, Emmanuel. *The First Hundred Million.* New York: Simon & Schuster, 1928.

————. *My First 25 Years: An Autobiography Instead of a Footnote.* Girard, Kans.: Haldeman-Julius Publications, 1949.

Haldeman-Julius, Marcet. *Clarence Darrow's Two Great Trials: Reports of the Scopes Anti-Evolution Case and the Dr. Sweet Negro Trial.* Girard, Kans.: Haldeman-Julius Co., 1927.

————. *Famous and Interesting Guests of a Kansas Farm: Impressions of Upton Sinclair, Lawrence Tibbett, Mrs. Martin Johnson, Clarence Darrow, Will Durant, E. W. Howe, Alfred Kreymborg, and Anna Louise Strong.* Edited by E. Haldeman-Julius. Reviewers Library, no. 8. Girard, Kans.: Haldeman-Julius Publications, 1936.

Hamilton, Alice. *Exploring the Dangerous Trade: The Autobiography of Alice*

Hamilton. Boston: Little, Brown & Co., 1943.

"The Hangman Cheers Up." *The Independent* 114 (May 23, 1925): 571.

Hapgood, Hutchins. *The Spirit of Labor*. New York: Duffield & Co., 1907.

————. *A Victorian in the Modern World*. New York: Harcourt, Brace & Co., 1934.

Harris, Leon. *Upton Sinclair: American Rebel*. New York: Thomas Y. Crowell, 1975.

Harrison, Carter H. *Stormy Years: The Autobiography of Carter H. Harrison*. Indianapolis: Bobbs-Merrill Co., 1935.

Harrison, Charles Yale. *Clarence Darrow*. New York: Jonathan Cape & Harrison Smith, 1931.

Harvey, Rowland Hill. *Samuel Gompers: Champion of the Toiling Masses*. Stanford, Calif: Stanford University Press, 1935.

Hawley, James. "Steve Adams' Confession and the State's Case against Bill Haywood." *Idaho Yesterdays* 7 (Winter 1963–64): 16–27.

Hays, Arthur Garfield. *City Lawyer: The Autobiography of a Law Practice*. New York: Simon & Schuster, 1942.

————. *Let Freedom Ring*. New York: Boni & Liveright, 1928.

Haywood, William D. *Bill Haywood's Book: The Autobiography of William D. Haywood*. New York: International Publishers, 1929.

Hecht, Ben. *A Child of the Century*. New York: Simon & Schuster, 1954; New American Library, 1955.

Heumann, Milton. *Plea Bargaining: The Experience of Prosecutors, Judges and Defense Attorneys*. Chicago: University of Chicago Press, 1978.

Higdon, Hal. *The Crime of the Century: The Leopold and Loeb Case*. New York: G. P. Putnam's Sons, 1974.

Hinshaw, David. *A Man from Kansas: The Story of William Allen White*. New York: G. P. Putnam's Sons, 1945.

Hoffman, Frederick J. *The Twenties: American Writing in the Postwar Decade*. New York: Viking Press, 1955.

Holly, William H. *A Forgotten Governor*. Chicago: Public Ownership League, 1937.

House, Brant, ed. *Crimes That Shocked America*. New York: Ace Books, 1961.

"How Burns Caught the Dynamiters." *McClure's Magazine*, January 1912, pp. 325–29.

Howe, Frederic C. *The Confessions of a Reformer*. New York: Charles Scribner's Sons, 1926; Chicago: Quadrangle Paperback, 1967.

Hunter, Charles H. "Murder, Rape, and Carpetbaggers: An Essay-Review on Three Recent Books on the Massie Case." *Pacific Northwest Quarterly* 58, no. 3 (July 1967): 151–54.

Husband, Joseph. *The Story of the Pullman Car*. Chicago: A. C. McClurg & Co., 1917.

Jaffe, Carolyn. "The Press and the Oppressed—a Study of Prejudicial News Reporting in Criminal Cases. I. The Problem, Existing Solutions and Remaining Doubts." *Journal of Criminal Law, Criminology and Police Science*, March 1965.

Jessup, Philip C. *Elihu Root*. New York: Dodd, Mead & Co., 1938.

Johnson, Claudius O. *Carter Henry Harrison I, Political Leader*. Chicago: University of Chicago Press, 1928.

Jones, Ernest. *The Life and Work of Sigmund Freud*. Vol. 3, *The Last Phase 1919–1939*. New York: Basic Books, 1957.

Jones, Mother. *The Autobiography of Mother Jones*. Edited by Mary Field Parton. Foreword by Clarence Darrow. Chicago: Charles H. Kerr & Co., 1925.

Josephson, Matthew. *Sidney Hillman: Statesman of American Labor*. Garden City, N.Y.: Doubleday & Co., 1952.

Kahn, Karl M. "Clarence Darrow Looks at America." *Real America* 1, no. 2 (April 1933).

Kaplan, Justin. *Lincoln Steffens: A Biography*. New York: Simon & Schuster, 1974.

Kasner, David. *Debs: His Authorized Life and Letters from Woodstock Prison to Atlanta*. New York: Boni & Liveright, 1919.

Kaun, Alexander. *Maxim Gorky and His Russia*. New York: Jonathan Cape & Harrison Smith, 1931.

Kellogg, Charles Flint. *National Association for the Advancement of Colored People*. Vol. 1., 1909–1920. Baltimore: The Johns Hopkins Press, 1967.

Kinney, Charlotte. "Clarence Darrow as He Is, Not as the Newspapers Say He Is." *Psychology*, August 1932.

King, Ethel M. *Reflections of Reedy: A Biography of William Marion Reedy of Reedy's Mirror*. Brooklyn, N.Y.: Gerald J. Richard, 1961.

Kissane, Leedice. "The Haywood Trial: Steve Adams, the Speechless Witness." *Idaho Yesterdays* 4, no. 3 (Fall 1964): 18–21.

Knudten, Richard D., ed. *Criminological Controversies*. New York: Appleton-Century-Crofts, 1968.

Koenig, Louis W. *Bryan: A Political Biography of William Jennings Bryan*. New York: G. P. Putnam's Sons, 1971.

Kogan, Herman. *The First Century: The Chicago Bar Association 1874–1974*. Chicago: Rand McNally & Co., 1974.

———, and Wendt, Lloyd. *Chicago: A Pictorial History*. New York: E. P. Dutton & Co., 1958.

Konvitz, Milton R. *Civil Rights in Immigration*. Ithaca, N.Y.: Cornell University Press, 1953.

Kraus, Adolf. *Reminiscences and Comments: The Immigrant, the Citizen, a Public Office, the Jew*. Chicago: Toby Rubovits Inc., 1925.

Krutch, Joseph Wood. "Darrow vs. Bryan." *The Nation* 121 (July 1925): 136.

Kurland, Gerald. *Clarence Darrow, Attorney for the Damned.* Charlotteville, N.Y.: SamHar Press, 1972.

Lang, Lucy Robins. *Tomorrow Is Beautiful.* New York: Macmillan Co., 1948.

Langdon, Emma F. *Labor's Greatest Conflict.* Denver: Denver Press, 1908.

"Larger Bearings of the McNamara Case." *The Survey* 27 (December 30, 1911): 1411–29.

Larson, Orvin. *American Infidel: Robert G. Ingersoll.* Secaucus, N.J.: Citadel Press, 1962.

Leopold, Nathan F., Jr. *Life Plus 99 Years.* Garden City, N.Y.: Doubleday & Co., 1958.

Leopold, Nathan F., Jr., Plaintiff, vs. Meyer Levin, et al. Defendants. No. 59-C-14087. State of Illinois, County of Cook, in the Circuit Court of Cook County, Illinois. County Department—Law Division. Opinion filed March 29, 1968.

Lerner, Max, ed. *The Mind and Faith of Justice Holmes: His Speeches, Essays, Letters, and Judicial Opinions.* Boston: Little, Brown & Co., 1943.

Letters from Russian Prisons. Introduction by Roger Baldwin. Published for the International Committee for Political Prisoners. New York: Albert & Charles Boni, 1925.

Lewis, Lloyd, and Smith, Henry Justin. *Chicago: The History of Its Reputation.* New York: Harcourt, Brace & Co., 1929.

Lilienthal, David E. "Clarence Darrow." *The Nation* 124 (April 20, 1927): 416–19.

———. *Journals.* New York: Harper & Row, 1964–66.

Lindsey, Almont. *The Pullman Strike: The Story of a Unique Experiment and of a Great Labor Upheaval.* Chicago: University of Chicago Press, 1967 (originally publ. 1942).

Lindsey, Benjamin B., and O'Higgins, Harvey J. *The Beast.* New York: Doubleday, Page & Co., 1911.

Link, Arthur S. *Woodrow Wilson and the Progressive Era, 1910–1917.* New York: Harper & Bros., 1954.

Linn, James Weber. *Jane Addams: A Biography.* New York: D. Appleton-Century Co., 1935.

Lippmann, Walter. *American Inquisitors: A Commentary on Dayton and Chicago.* New York: Macmillan Co., 1928.

Lloyd, Caroline Augusta. *Henry Demarest Lloyd 1847–1903: A Biography.* 2 vols. New York: G. P. Putnam's Sons, 1912.

Lloyd, Henry Demarest. *Men, the Workers.* New York: Doubleday, Page & Co., 1909.

———. "The New Conscience." *North American Review* 147, no. 3 (September 1888): 325–39.

Long, John Cuthbert. *Bryan, the Great Commoner.* New York: D. Appleton & Co., 1928.

Lord, Walter. *The Good Years: From 1900 to the First World War.* New York: Harper & Bros., 1960.

Lorwin, Lewis Levitzki, with the assistance of Flexner, Jean Atherton. *The American Federation of Labor: History, Policies, and Prospects.* Washington, D.C.: The Brookings Institution, 1933.

Lovett, Robert Morss. *All Our Years: The Autobiography of Robert Morss Lovett.* New York: Viking Press, 1948.

————. "The Trial of the Communists." *The Nation* 111 (August 12, 1920): 185–86.

Lowe, David. *Lost Chicago.* Boston: Houghton Mifflin Co., 1975.

Luhan, Mabel Dodge. *Intimate Memories.* 4 vols. Vol. 3, *Movers and Shakers.* New York: Harcourt, Brace & Co., 1933–37.

Lundberg, Ferdinand. *Imperial Hearst: A Social Biography.* New York: Equinox Cooperative Press, 1936.

Lyon, Leverett, et al. *The National Recovery Administration: An Analysis and Appraisal.* Washington, D.C.: The Brookings Institution, 1935.

McKenna, Marian C. *Borah.* Ann Arbor: University of Michigan Press, 1961.

McKernan, Maureen. *The Amazing Criminal Trial of Leopold and Loeb.* New York: New American Library, 1957.

MacLane, John F. *A Sagebrush Lawyer.* New York: Privately printed, 1953.

Manning, Thomas G. *The Chicago Strike of 1894: Industrial Labor in the Nineteenth Century.* New York: Henry Holt & Co., 1960.

Mason, Alpheus T. *Brandeis: Lawyer and Judge in the Modern State.* Princeton, N.J.: Princeton University Press. 1933.

Mason, Lowell B. "Clarence Darrow's Unreported Case." Law Day address before the Law School Convocation, University of Chicago, May 1, 1959.

Masters, Edgar Lee. *Across Spoon River: An Autobiography.* New York: Farrar & Rinehart, 1936.

Miller, John Chester. *Crisis in Freedom: The Alien and Sedition Acts.* Boston: Atlantic Monthly Press, 1952.

Mitchell, John. *Organized Labor.* Philadelphia: American Book and Bible House, 1903.

Mitgang, Herbert, ed. *The Letters of Carl Sandburg.* New York: Harcourt, Brace & World, 1968.

Mordell, Albert. *Clarence Darrow, Eugene V. Debs and Haldeman-Julius: Incidents in the Careers of an Author, Editor and Publisher.* Girard, Kans.: Haldeman-Julius Publications, 1950.

Mowry, George E. *The Era of Theodore Roosevelt 1900–1912.* New York: Harper & Bros., 1958.

————. *Theodore Roosevelt and the Progressive Movement.* Madison: University of Wisconsin Press, 1946.

"Moyer-Haywood Trial." *The Outlook* 85 (April 6, 1907).

Murray, Robert K. *Red Scare: A Study in National Hysteria, 1919–1920.* Minneapolis: University of Minnesota Press, 1955.

Musmanno, Michael A. *Verdict!* New York: Doubleday & Co., 1958.

Nathan, George Jean. *The Intimate Notebooks of George Jean Nathan.* New York: Alfred A. Knopf, 1932.

"Nib of the Coal Controversy at Scranton." *Literary Digest* 25, no. 22 (November 29, 1902): 695–96.

Norris, Clarence, and Washington, Sybil O. *The Last of the Scottsboro Boys: An Autobiography.* New York: G. P. Putnam's Sons, 1979.

O'Hara, Barratt. *Congressional Record.* Proceedings and Debates of the 89th Congress, First Session. Remarks of Representative Barratt O'Hara of Illinois, April 13, 1965.

O'Higgins, Harvey J. "The Dynamiters: A Great Case of Detective William J. Burns." *McClure's Magazine* 37, no. 4 (August 1911): 347–64.

Older, Fremont. *My Own Story.* New York: Macmillan Co., 1926.

Orchard, Harry (Albert E. Horsley). *The Confession and Autobiography of Harry Orchard.* New York: McClure Co., 1907.

"Otistown of Open Shop." *Hampton's* 26 (January 1911): 31.

Palmer, A. Mitchell. "The Case against the 'Reds.'" *The Forum* 63 (February 1920): 173–85.

Parsons, Alice Beal. *The Trial of Helen McLeod.* New York: Funk & Wagnalls Co., 1938.

Parton, Margaret. *Journey through a Lighted Room.* New York: Viking Press, 1973.

Pasley, Fred D. *Al Capone: A Biography of a Self-Made Man.* New York: Ives Washburn, 1930.

Perlman, Selig, and Taft, Philip. *History of Labor in the United States, 1896–1932.* Vol. 4, *Labor Movements.* New York: Macmillan Co., 1935.

Perry, Louis B., and Perry, Richard S. *A History of the Los Angeles Labor Movement, 1911–1941.* Berkeley and Los Angeles: University of California Press, 1963.

Pickett, Calder M. *Ed Howe: Country Town Philosopher.* Lawrence: University Press of Kansas, 1968.

Pierce, Bessie Louise. *A History of Chicago.* Chicago: University of Chicago Press, 1933.

Pizer, Donald, ed. *Hamlin Garland's Diaries.* San Marino, Calif.: Huntington Library, 1968.

Poole, Ernest. *Giants Gone: Men Who Made Chicago.* New York: McGraw-Hill Book Co., 1943; London: Whittlesey House, 1943.

Pringle, Henry F. *The Life and Times of William Howard Taft.* New York: Farrar & Rinehart, 1939.

――――. *Theodore Roosevelt: A Biography*. New York: Harcourt, Brace & Co., 1931.

Pullman, George M., president, and Wickes, T. H., second vice-president, Pullman Company. Statements before the U.S. Strike Commission. Also *Published Statements of the Company Relating to the Strike*. N.d. Pamphlet.

Putzel, Max. *The Man in the Mirror: William Marion Reedy and His Magazine*. Cambridge, Mass.: Harvard University Press, 1963.

Ravitz, Abe C. *Clarence Darrow and the American Literary Tradition*. Cleveland: Press of Western Reserve University, 1962.

――――, and Primm, James N., eds. *The Haywood Case: Materials for Analysis*. San Francisco: Chandler Publishing Co., 1960.

Reynolds, Quentin. *Courtroom: The Story of Samuel S. Leibowitz*. New York: Farrar, Straus & Co., 1950.

Richberg, Donald R. *My Hero: The Indiscreet Memoirs of an Eventful but Unheroic Life*. New York: G. P. Putnam's Sons, 1954.

――――. "NRA and 'Fair Competition.'" *Rotarian*, November 1934.

――――. *The Rainbow*. Garden City, N.Y.: Doubleday, Doran & Co., 1936.

Robinson, W.W. *Bombs and Bribery*. Los Angeles: Dawson's Book Shop, 1969.

Rogers, James Grafton. *American Bar Leaders: Biographies of the Presidents of the American Bar Association 1878–1928*. Chicago: American Bar Association, 1932.

Rogers, Will. *Autobiography*. Selected and edited by Donald Day, with a Forward by Bill and Jim Rogers. Boston: Houghton Mifflin Co., 1949.

Roosevelt, Theodore. "Murder Is Murder." *The Outlook* 99 (December 16, 1911): 901–2.

Rosenthal, Louis A. "Darrow and the Archbishop." *Liberty,* January/February 1975.

Rovinsky, Alexander. "Russia and the Jews. I. The Kishinoff Massacre: Causes and Effect." *Arena* 30, no. 1 (July 1903): 123–37.

――――. "Russia and the Jews. II. The Kishinoff 'Pogrom.'" *Arena* 30, no. 1 (July 1903): 137–44.

Russell, Charles Edward. *Bare Hands and Stone Walls: Some Reflections of a Side-Line Reformer*. New York: Charles Scribner's Sons, 1933.

St. Johns, Adela Rogers. *Final Verdict*. Garden City, N.Y.: Doubleday & Co., 1962.

Sayer, James Edward. *Clarence Darrow: Public Advocate*. Monograph Series, no. 2. Dayton, Ohio: Wright State University, 1978.

Sandburg, Carl. *Always the Young Strangers*. New York: Harcourt, Brace & Co., 1953.

Sanger, Margaret. *An Autobiography*. New York: W. W. Norton & Co., [1938].

Schaaf, Barbara C. *Mr. Dooley's Chicago*. Garden City, N.Y.: Anchor Press/ Doubleday, 1977.

Scheinberg, Stephen. "The Haywood Trial: Theodore Roosevelt's 'Undesirable Citizens.'" *Idaho Yesterdays* 4, no. 3 (Fall 1960): 10–15.

Schlesinger Arthur M., Jr. *The Coming of the New Deal*. Boston: Houghton Mifflin Co., 1959.

————. *The Crisis of the Old Order 1919–1933*. Boston: Houghton Mifflin Co., 1957.

————. *The Politics of Upheaval*. Boston: Houghton Mifflin Co., 1960.

Schorer, Mark. *Sinclair Lewis: An American Life*. New York: McGraw-Hill Book Co., 1961.

Scopes, John T. "The Trial That Rocked the Nation." *Reader's Digest*, March 1961.

————, and Presley, James. *Center of the Storm: Memoirs of John T. Scopes*. New York: Holt, Rinehart & Winston, 1967.

Sellers, Alvin V. *Classics of the Bar: Stories of the World's Great Legal Trials and a Compilation of Forensic Masterpieces*. Washington, D.C.: Washington Law Book Co., 1942.

Shafer, Sara Andrew. "Through the Eyes of a Boy: Farmington." *Dial* 37 (October 16, 1904): 237.

Shapiro, Herbert. "Lincoln Steffens and the McNamara Case: A Progressive Response to Class Conflict." Unpublished manuscript.

————. "The McNamara Case: A Crisis of the Progressive Era." *Southern California Quarterly* 61, no. 3 (Fall 1977).

Sheean, Vincent. *Dorothy and Red*. Boston: Houghton Mifflin Co., 1963.

Silbert, Samuel H., with Eisenberg, Sidney A. *"Judge Sam."* Manhassat, N.Y.: Channel Press, 1963.

Smith, Henry Justin. *Chicago: The History of Its Reputation*. Part I by Lloyd Lewis. Introduction and Part II by Henry Justin Smith. New York: Harcourt, Brace & Co., 1927.

————. *Deadlines 1923*. Chicago: Covici-McGee, 1923.

Smith, T.V. *Live without Fear*. New York: New American Library, 1956.

Spaulding, William A. *History and Reminiscences: Los Angeles City and County, California*. Vol. 3. Los Angeles: J. R. Finnell & Sons Publishing Co., [1931].

Starrett, Vincent. *Born in a Bookshop: Chapters from the Chicago Renaissance*. Norman: University of Oklahoma Press, 1965.

Steffens, Lincoln. "Attorney for the Damned." *Saturday Review of Literature*, February 27, 1932.

————. *The Autobiography of Lincoln Steffens*. New York: Harcourt, Brace & Co., 1931.

————. *The Letters of Lincoln Steffens*. Edited with introductory notes by Ella Winter and Granville Hicks. New York: Harcourt, Brace & Co., 1938.

Stimson, Grace Heilman. *Rise of the Labor Movement in Los Angeles.* Berkeley and Los Angeles: University of California Press, 1955.

Stolberg, Benjamin. "Clarence Darrow." *The Nation* 134 (March 2, 1932): 261.

Stone, Irving. *Clarence Darrow for the Defense.* Garden City: N.Y.: Garden City Publishing Co., 1941.

Stone, Melville E. *Fifty Years a Journalist.* Garden City, N.Y.: Doubleday, Page & Co., 1921.

"Stories of the Miners." *Literary Digest* 25 (December 27, 1902): 861–63.

"The Story of Harry Orchard." *Current Literature* 43, no. 1 (July 1907): 1–5.

Stuart, William H. *The 20 Incredible Years: As "Heard and Seen" by William H. Stuart.* Chicago and New York: M. A. Donahue & Co., 1925.

Sunset Club, Chicago, Yearbooks. Minutes of meetings from 1891 to 1901.

Sutton, William A. *The Road to Winesburg.* Metuchen, N.J.: Scarecrow Press, 1972.

Swanberg, W. A. *Citizen Hearst: A Biography of William Randolph Hearst.* New York: Charles Scribner's Sons, 1961.

———. *Dreiser.* New York: Charles Scribner's Sons, 1965.

Swing, Raymond G. *Forerunners of American Fascism.* New York: J. Messner, Inc., 1935.

Taft, Philip. *The A. F. of L. in the Time of Gompers.* New York: Harper & Bros., 1957.

Taylor, Graham. *Pioneering on Social Frontiers.* Chicago: University of Chicago Press, 1930.

Tebbel, John. *The Life and Good Times of William Randolph Hearst.* New York: E. P. Dutton & Co., 1952.

Tierney, Kevin. *Darrow: A Biography.* New York: Thomas Y. Crowell, 1979.

Tompkins, Jerry R., ed. *D-Days at Dayton: Reflections on the Scopes Trial.* Baton Rouge: Louisiana State University Press, 1965.

Turner, John. "The Protest of an Anarchist." *The Independent* 55 (December 24, 1903): 3052–54.

Urofsky, Melvin I. *A Mind of One Piece: Brandeis and American Reform.* New York: Charles Scribner's Sons, 1971.

———, and Levy, David W., eds. *Letters of Louis D. Brandeis.* Vol. 1, *1870–1907: Urban Reformer.* Albany, N.Y.: State University of New York Press, 1971.

Van Slingerland, Peter. *Something Terrible Has Happened.* New York: Harper & Row, 1966.

Wade, Louise C. *Graham Taylor: Pioneer for Social Justice 1851–1938.* Chicago: University of Chicago Press, 1964.

Wagenknecht, Edward Charles. *Chicago.* Norman: University of Oklahoma Press, 1964.

Warne, Coleston E., ed. *The Pullman Boycott of 1894: The Problem of Federal Intervention*. Boston: D.C. Heath & Co., 1955.

Weil, "Yellow Kid." As told to W. T. Brannon. *Autobiography*. Chicago: Ziff-Davis Publishing Co., 1948.

Weinberg, Arthur, edited and with notes by. Foreword by Justice William O. Douglas. *Attorney for the Damned*. New York: Simon & Schuster, 1957.

———. "Clarence Darrow and the Negro." *Ebony*, August 1959.

———. "Darrow: Friend of Man." *Chicago Sun-Times*, April 28, 1957.

———. "I Remember Father." Darrow's son remembers. *Chicago Tribune Magazine*, May 6, 1956.

———, and Weinberg, Lila. "Masters and Darrow, Attorneys at Odds." *Chicago Sunday Sun-Times*, July 3, 1973.

———, and Weinberg, Lila, edited with an introduction by. *Verdicts Out of Court*. Chicago: Quadrangle Books, 1963.

———, and Weinberg, Lila. *Some Dissenting Voices*. Cleveland and New York: World Publishing Co. A young adult book.

Weinberg, Kenneth G. *A Man's Home, a Man's Castle*. Introduction by Haywood Burns. New York: McCall Publishing Co., 1971.

Wells, Evelyn. *Fremont Older*. New York: D. Appleton-Century Co., 1936.

Wells, H. G. *Experiment in Autobiography: Discoveries and Conclusions of a Very Ordinary Brain (Since 1866)*. New York: Macmillan Co., 1934.

Wendt, Lloyd, and Kogan, Herman. *Big Bill of Chicago*. Indianapolis: Bobbs-Merrill Co., 1953.

———. *Lords of the Levee: The Story of Bathhouse John and Hinky Dink*. Indianapolis: Bobbs-Merrill Co., 1943.

White, Horace. *The Life of Lyman Trumbull*. Boston: Houghton Mifflin Co., 1913.

White, Walter Francis. *A Man Called White: The Autobiography of Walter White*. New York: Viking Press, 1948.

White, William Allen. *The Autobiography of William Allen White*. New York: Macmillan Co., 1946.

Whitehead, George G. "Back Home with Clarence Darrow." *Cleveland Plain Dealer*, April 18, 1937.

———. *Clarence Darrow—the Big Minority Man*. Girard, Kans.: Haldeman-Julius Publications, n.d.

———. *Clarence Darrow: "Evangelist" of Sane Thinking*. Girard, Kans.: Haldeman-Julius Publications, 1931.

———. "Environment vs. Heredity." *Debunker*, November 1930.

Whitlock, Brand. *Forty Years of It*. New York: D. Appleton & Co., 1914.

———. *The Letters and Journal of Brand Whitlock*. 2 vols. Biographical Introduction by Allan Nevins; Introduction by Newton D. Baker. New York: D. Appleton-Century Co., 1936.

"Who Is This Man Darrow?" *Current Literature* 43, no. 2 (August 1907): 157–59.

Williams, Wayne C. *William Jennings Bryan.* New York: G. P. Putnam's Sons, 1936.

Wilson, Clarence. "Darrow, Friendly Enemy." *The Forum* 100 (July 1938): 14.

Winkler, John Kennedy. *W. R. Hearst: An American Phenomenon.* New York: Simon & Schuster, 1928.

Winter, Ella. *And Not to Yield: An Autobiography.* New York: Harcourt, Brace & World, 1963.

————, and Hicks, Granville, edited with introductory notes by. Memorandum by Carl Sandburg. *The Letters of Joseph Lincoln Steffens.* 2 vols. New York: Harcourt, Brace & Co., 1938.

"With the Death of Clarence Darrow." *The Nation* 416 (March 19, 1938): 316.

Woehlke, Walter V. "The End of the Dynamite Case—Guilty." *Outlook* 99 (December 16, 1911): 903–8.

Wood, Fremont. *The Introductory Chapter to the History of the Trials of Moyer, Haywood, and Pettibone, and Harry Orchard.* Caldwell, Idaho: Caxton Printers, Ltd., 1931.

Woodford, Howard J. *Mr. Justice Murphy: A Political Biography.* Princeton, N.J.: Princeton University Press, 1968.

The World's Most Famous Court Trial: Tennessee Evolution Case. Cincinnati: National Book Co., 1925.

Wright, Frank Lloyd. *An Autobiography.* New York: Duell, Sloan & Pierce, 1943.

Wright, Theon. *Rape in Paradise.* New York: Hawthorn Books, 1966.

Yaffe, James. *Nothing But the Night.* New York: Bantam Books, 1959.

Yarros, Victor S. *My 11 Years with Clarence Darrow.* Girard, Kans.: Haldeman-Julius Publications, 1950.

Yates, Stirling. *Sea Duty: The Memoirs of a Fighting Admiral.* New York: G. P. Putnam's Sons, 1939.

Young, Art. *His Life and Times.* New York: Sheridan House, 1939.

Books by Clarence Darrow

A Persian Pearl: and Other Essays. Chicago: C. L. Ricketts, 1899.

Resist Not Evil (original publication in 1902). Girard, Kans.: Haldeman-Julius Company, 1925.

Farmington (original publication 1904). New York: Charles Scribner's Sons, 1932.

An Eye for an Eye. Girard, Kans.: Haldeman-Julius Company, [1905].

Crime: Its Causes and Treatment. New York: Thomas Y. Crowell Company, 1922.

The Prohibition Mania (with Victor Yarros). New York: Boni and Liveright, Inc., 1927.

Infidels and Heretics: An Agnostic's Anthology (with Walter Rice). Boston, Mass.: Stratford Company, 1929.

The Story of My Life. New York: Charles Scribner's Sons, 1932; rev. ed., 1934.

Lectures, Debates, Magazine Articles, Pamphlets.*

"Free Trade or Protection? A Plea for the Wilson Bill." *Current Topics*, April 1894.

Rights and Wrongs of Ireland. Address delivered in Chicago, 1895. Pamphlet. Reprinted in *Everyman*, August–September 1914.

"The Problem of the Negro." Lecture before black audience, Chicago, 1901. *International Socialist Review*, November 1901.

"Conduct and Profession." *The Rubric*, 1901.

"Tolstoy." *The Rubric*, 1902.

John Peter Altgeld, Memorial Address, March 14, 1902. Reproduced in Darrow's *Story of My Life*, 1932.

"Easy Lessons in Law." Series of short stories. *Chicago American*, July 1902.

Crime and Criminals. Address delivered to the prisoners in the Chicago County jail, 1902. Pamphlet.

"Little Louis Epstine." *The Pilgrim*, December 1903.

"Literary Style." *Tomorrow*, 1905.

"The Holdup Man." *International Socialist Review*, February 1909.

Dry vs. Wet. Speech delivered May 2, 1909. Pamphlet.

*Many of these appear either in Weinberg 1957, or Weinberg 1963. The opponents in the debates are indicated.

The Open Shop. 1909. Pamphlet.
Liberty vs. Prohibition. Address at New Bedford, Mass. December 1909. Pamphlet.
The Theory of Non-Resistance. Debate with Arthur M. Lewis, 1910. Pamphlet.
"Why Men Fight for the Closed Shop." *American Magazine,* September 1911.
"John Brown." Address before Radical Club, San Francisco. *Everyman,* March 1913.
"On Land and Labor." Address at Single Tax League mass meeting, Los Angeles. *Everyman,* June 1913.
"Henry George." Address to the Single Tax Club. *Everyman,* September–October 1913.
"On Single Tax." Address at the L.A. Single Tax banquet. *Everyman,* August–September 1914.
The War in Europe. Lecture before the Chicago Society of Rationalism, Fall 1914. Pamphlet.
"The Cost of War." *International Socialist Review,* December 1914.
"If Man Had Opportunity." *Everyman,* January–February 1915.
"An Appeal for the Despoiled." *Everyman,* January 1916.
"Straight Talk to the Rails." *International Socialist Review,* June 1916.
"Nietzsche." *Athena,* June–July 1916.
"Crime and Economic Conditions." *International Socialist Review,* October 1916.
Will Democracy Cure the Social Ills of the World? Debate with Scott Nearing, January 1917. Pamphlet.
"Schopenhauer." *Liberal Review,* March 1917.
"Brief for the War." *Liberal Review,* July 1917.
The War. Address, under the auspices if the National Security League, Chicago, November 1917. Pamphlet.
Response to Birthday Greetings. 1918. Pamphlet.
Are Internationalism and the League of Nations Practical and Desirable Schemes for Ending War? Debate with Professor John C. Kennedy, 1918. Pamphlet.
George Burman Foster. Memorial Address, 1919. Pamphlet.
Will Socialism Save the World? Debate with Professor John C. Kennedy, 1919. Pamphlet.
The Consolations of Pessimism. Lecture before the Rationalist Educational Society, Chicago, 1920. Pamphlet.
Is Civilization a Failure? Debate with Dr. Frederick Starr, 1920. Pamphlet.
"How Liberty Is Lost." Speech before the third annual meeting of the American Liberty League, 1921.
Speech at Illinois State Bar Association. 46th annual meeting, 1922.
"Society Held Responsible for the Crime." *Current Opinion,* 1923.
"Against Capital Punishment." *Success Magazine,* 1924.

Capital Punishment. Debate with Judge Alfred J. Talley, 1924. Pamphlet.

"Ordeal of Prohibition." *American Mercury,* August 1924.

Should the United States Continue the Policy of Prohibition as Defined in the 18th Amendment? Debate with Reverend John Haynes Holmes, New York, 1924. Pamphlet.

"Crime and Punishment. The Responsibility of Criminals and the Purpose of Punishment" (with Horace J. Bridges). *Century Magazine,* March 1925.

"Human Love Is Best Remedy for Crime." *The Daily Bloomington* (Ill.), 1925.

"How to Be a Salesman." *American Mercury,* August 1925.

"The Edwardses and the Jukeses." *American Mercury,* October 1925.

"Where are the Pre-War Radicals?" *Survey Graphic,* February 1926.

"Crime and the Alarmists." *Harper's,* October 1926.

"The Eugenics Cult." *American Mercury,* June 1926.

"Liberty, Equality, Fraternity." *Vanity Fair,* December 1926.

"What to Do About Crime." Address before Nebraska Bar Association meeting, December 1926.

"The Foreign Debt and America." *Vanity Fair,* February 1927.

"The Divorce Problem." *Vanity Fair,* August 1927.

"Is Zionism a Progressive Policy for Israel and America?" Debate with Dr. Stephen S. Wise at Sinai Temple, Chicago, October 24, 1927.

"Birthday Speech at 61." *Kessinger's Mid-West Review,* n.d.

"Is Man Fundamentally Dishonest?" *The Forum,* December 1927.

Dry-Law. Debate with Wayne B. Wheeler, 1927. Pamphlet.

Concerning a General Purpose in the Universe. Debate with Alfred W. Wishart, 1928. Pamphlet.

"What Life Has Meant to Me." *The World,* February 19, 1928.

"The Lord's Day Alliance." *Plain Talk,* March 1928.

"This is What I Don't Like about the Newspapers." Address before the sixth annual meeting of the American Society of Newspaper Editors, Washington, D.C., 1928.

"Frank Lowden, the Farmer's Friend." *Scribner's,* April 1928.

"The Futility of the Death Penalty." *The Forum,* September 1928.

"Why Was God So Hard on Women and Snakes?" *Haldeman-Julius Monthly,* September 1928.

"The Myth of the Soul." *The Forum,* October 1928.

Facing Life Fearlessly. Lecture at the University of Chicago, 1928. *American Parade,* October–November–December 1928.

"Personal Liberty." In *Freedom and the Modern World,* edited by Horace M. Kallen, pp. 115–137. New York: Coward-McCann, Inc., 1928.

"Why I Am an Agnostic." Symposium with Bishop Holt Hughes, Protestant; Judge John P. McGoority, Catholic; Rabbi Jacob Tarshish, Columbus, Ohio, 1929. Mimeographed.

Letter to the editor. *The Nation,* June 1929.

"At Seventy-Two." *The Saturday Evening Post,* July 6, 1929.

"Combating Crime." *The Forum,* November 1929.

Is the U.S. Immigration Law Beneficial? Debate with Lothrop Stoddard, 1929. Pamphlet.

"Let No Man Therefore Judge You in Meat or Drink." *Collier's,* October 11, 1930.

Is Religion Necessary? Debate with Reverend Robert MacGowan, Carnegie Music Hall, Pittsburgh, 1931. Pamphlet.

Should the 18th Amendment Be Repealed? Debate with Clarence True Wilson, 1931. Pamphlet.

"The Trial of Benedict Arnold" (with James M. Beck). A radio presentation, 1931.

Lecture to Congressional Church, Chicago, January 14, 1932. Mimeographed.

"Who Knows Justice?" *Scribner's,* February 1932.

"Scottsboro." *Crisis,* March 1932.

Address to members of Mahoning County Bar Association, 1932.

"Civilization at the Crossroads. Whither Are We Going?" Symposium with Scott Nearing (economics); Dr. Preston Bradley (religion); Dr. Louis Mann (the planned society); Darrow (law and government). Sinai Temple, Chicago, 1932. Mimeographed.

Does Man Live Again? Debate with Judge M. A. Musmanno, Carnegie Music Hall, Pittsburgh, 1932. Pamphlet.

Why I Am an Agnostic. Symposium with Dr. John A. Lapp (Catholic); Dr. Charles W. Gilkey (Protestant); Rabbi Solomon Goldman (Jewish); at Orchestra Hall, Chicago, 1932. Pamphlet.

"Capital Punishment—No." *Rotarian Magazine,* November 1933.

"What I Think of Nazi Germany." Symposium with Dr. Preston Bradley and Dr. Louis L. Mann. Washington Boulevard Temple, Chicago, December 7, 1933. Mimeographed.

"NRA and Fair Competition." *Rotarian Magazine,* November 1934.

"Many Faults in NRA." *Commercial Bulletin and Apparel Merchant,* February 1935.

"Attorney for the Defense." *Esquire,* May 1936.

"It's a Humbug!" *Chicago Daily Times,* Christmas Battle Page, December 22, 1936.

Absurdities of the Bible. N.d. Pamphlet.

Are We Machines? Debate with Will Durant, n.d. Pamphlet.

"Can the Church Meet the Needs of Our New Age?" Debate. Dr. Louis L. Mann and Dr. Preston Bradley, affirmative; Darrow and Harry Elmer Barnes, negative, n.d. Mimeographed.

Do Human Beings Have Free Will? Debate with George Burman Foster, n.d. Pamphlet.

Insects and Men: Instinct and Reason. Address before the Rationalist Society of Chicago, n.d. Pamphlet.

Is Life Worth Living? Debate with Frederick Starr, n.d. Pamphlet.

Is the Human Race Getting Anywhere? Debate with Frederick Starr, n.d. Pamphlet.

Some Paragraphs Addressed to Socialists. N.d. Pamphlet.

Darrow Court Pleas, Public Documents, Transcripts

In re Debs. U.S. Supreme Court, October term, 1894. Argued March 25, 26, 1895. Decided May 27, 1895.

U.S. Strike Commission. *Report on the Chicago Strike of June–July 1894,* with appendices containing testimony, proceedings, and recommendations. Washington, D.C.: Government Printing Office, 1895.

Argument in the Woodworkers Conspiracy—the Kidd case. Oshkosh, Wis., 1898. Pamphlet. Appears in Weinberg, 1957.

Documents Relating to the Anthracite Strike of 1902. Scranton and Philadelphia. Anthracite Coal Strike Commission. *Report to the President on the Anthracite Coal Strike of May–October, 1902.* Washington, D.C.: Government Printing Office, 1903.

Brief and Argument of Appellant in the Supreme Court of the United States. October term, A.D. 1903. United States ex rel. John Turner vs. William Williams, Commissioner, etc.

In the Supreme Court of the United States. October term, A.D. 1905. City of Chicago, appellant vs. John C. Fetzer, et al., receivers, etc., appellees. Appeals from the Circuit Court of the U.S. for the Northern District of Illinois. Statement, brief, and argument, James Hamilton Lewis, corporation counsel, Clarence Darrow, Edgar Bronson Tolmen, Glenn E. Plumb, of Council. 1905.

Argument in the Case of the State of Idaho against Steve Adams. Wallace, Idaho, 1907. Pamphlet. Appears in Weinberg, 1957.

Plea in Defense of William D. Haywood. Boise, Idaho, 1907. Pamphlet. Appears in Weinberg, 1957.

Before the Department of State in the Matter of the demand of the Imperial Russian Government for the extradition of Christian Rudovitz. Clarence Darrow, Peter Sissman, Peter Hide, Charles Cheney, counsel for the accused. 1909.

People of the State of California, plaintiff, vs. Clarence Darrow, 1912. Transcript.

Argument in Own Defense. Lockwood charge. Los Angeles, 1912. Pamphlet. Appears in Weinberg, 1957.

Argument in Own Defense. Bain charge. Los Angeles. *Everyman,* May 1913.

Darrow Address to the Jury in the Benjamin Gitlow case. New York, 1920 Pamphlet.

Argument in Defense of Chicago Communists. 1920. Pamphlet. Appears in Weinberg, 1957.

Argument in the trial of Arthur Person. Rockford, Ill., 1920. Pamphlet.

Argument in defense of Loeb and Leopold. Chicago, 1924. Pamphlet. Appears in Weinberg, 1957.

Argument People of the State of Illinois vs. Faherty and Detwiler. Chicago, 1924. Transcript.

Tennessee Evolution case: A Word-for-Word Report—State of Tennessee vs. John Thomas Scopes. Dayton, Tenn., 1925. Cincinnati, Ohio: National Book Co., 1925.

Argument before the Supreme Court of Tennessee at Nashville, Tenn., in John Thomas Scopes vs. State of Tennessee. 1926.

People of the State of Michigan vs. Ossian Sweet, et al. 1925. Transcript.

Argument in the case of Henry Sweet. Detroit, Mich., 1926. Pamphlet. Appears in Weinberg, 1957.

Report to the President by Clarence Darrow, National Recovery Board. Special and Supplementary Report to the President by Clarence Darrow and William O. Thompson, members. 1934.

Collections

Addams, Jane. Correspondence, Swarthmore College, Library, Swarthmore, Pa.

————. Hull-House, Chicago.

Barnes, Henry Elmer. Correspondence, William Robertson Coe Library, Division of Rare Books and Special Collections, University of Wyoming, Laramie.

Cash, Asher. Correspondence, Michigan Historical Collection, University of Michigan, Ann Arbor.

Darrow, Clarence Seward. Collection, Library of Congress. Contains much of the material used by Irving Stone in *Clarence Darrow for the Defense*; also includes Ruby Darrow letters to Stone.

————. Collection, Michigan Historical Collection, University of Michigan, Ann Arbor.

————. Special Collections, University of Chicago, Chicago, Ill.

————. Collection, Newberry Library, Chicago, Ill.

Davis, LeCompte. Special Collections, University of California, Los Angeles.

Debs, Eugene Victor. Papers, Debs House, Terre Haute, Ind.

————. Papers, Cunningham Library, Indiana State University, Terre Haute.

Ely, Richard T. Correspondence, Archives of the State Historical Society of Wisconsin, Madison.

Field, Mary. Letters and diary, personal collection of Margaret Field Parton.

Germer, Adolph. Correspondence, Archives of the State Historical Society of Wisconsin, Madison.

Gertz, Elmer. Darrow Collection, Northwestern University, Evanston, Ill.

Harrison, Carter H. Papers, Newberry Library, Chicago.

————. 1825–1914. Scrapbooks of newspaper clippings illustrating the political careers of Carter Harrison and Carter Harrison, Jr., Newberry Library, Chicago, Ill.

Ickes, Harold. Papers, Library of Congress.

Kidd, Thomas I. Scrapbook, 1895–1953. Archives of the State Historical Society of Wisconsin, Madison.

Labadie, Joe. Collection, University of Michigan, Ann Arbor.

Lindsey, Benjamin B. Letters, Library of Congress, Washington, D.C.

Lloyd, Henry Demarest. Letters, Library of the State Historical Society of Wisconsin, Madison.

Mencken, H. L. Letters, New York Public Library, New York.

Murphy, Frank. Letters, University of Michigan, Ann Arbor.

National Association for the Advancement of Colored People. Library of Congress.

Richberg, Donald R. Library of Congress.

Older, Fremont. Bancroft Library, University of California, Berkeley.

Pullman Co. Scrapbooks, Newberry Library.

Whitlock, Brand. Library of Congress.

Wilson, Woodrow. Library of Congress.

Index

Non-Fiction